W9-ABY-860

JAPAN

BELL AT KYŌTO.

Frontispiece.

The Story of the Nations

JAPAN

BY

DAVID MURRAY, Ph.D., LL.D.

SUPERINTENDENT OF EDUCATION IN THE EMPIRE OF JAPAN, AND ADVISER TO THE
IMPERIAL MINISTER OF EDUCATION, FROM 1873 TO 1879

REVISED EDITION, CONTINUING THE HISTORY TO THE
CLOSE OF 1905, WITH THE PROVISIONS OF THE
TREATY OF PORTSMOUTH BETWEEN
RUSSIA AND JAPAN, AND

SUPPLEMENTARY CHAPTERS

BY

BARON KENTÁRO KANEKO, LL.D.

NEW YORK
G. P. PUTNAM'S SONS
LONDON: T. FISHER UNWIN
1906

The Knickerbocker Press, New York

PUBLISHER'S NOTE.

THE death in March, 1905, of David Murray, the author of this volume, prevented him from carrying out his intention of bringing the narrative down to include the important events of the last fifteen years in the "Story of Japan."

The chapters presenting the record of these fifteen years, including an account of the more important and epoch-making of the events in the Russo-Japanese War of 1904–05, have been prepared by Albert White Vorse.

The Baron Kentaro Kaneko, LL.D., who has himself been charged with important responsibilities by the Imperial Government of his country, has most generously contributed two very interesting and important chapters to this new edition, this contribution being made in recognition of the valuable work done by David Murray, LL.D., who served during the years from 1873 to 1879 as special adviser to the Imperial Janpanese Minister of Education, who was able to render most valuable co-operation in the foundation of the present Japanese system of Education, and, to quote Baron

Kaneko's own words, "through whose earnest and untiring efforts the Japan of to-day and the ideal of the Japan of the future have been brought to the knowledge of a wondering and admiring world."

April 2, 1906.

PREFACE.

It is the object of this book to trace the story of Japan from its beginnings to the establishment of constitutional government. Concerned as this story is with the period of vague and legendary antiquity as well as with the disorders of mediæval time and with centuries of seclusion, it is plain that it is not an easy task to present a trustworthy and connected account of the momentous changes through which the empire has been called to pass. It would be impossible to state in detail the sources from which I have derived the material for this work. I place first and as most important a residence of several years in Japan, during which I became familiar with the character of the Japanese people and with the traditions and events of their history. Most of the works treating of Japan during and prior to the period of her seclusion, as well as the more recent works, I have had occasion to consult. They will be found referred to in the following pages. Beyond all others, however, I desire to acknowledge my obligations to the *Transactions of the Asiatic Society of Japan*. A list of the contributors to these trans-actions would include such names as Satow, Aston, Chamberlain, McClatchie, Gubbins, Geerts, Milne, Whitney, Wigmore and others, whose investigations have made possible a reasonably complete knowledge of Japan. The *Transactions of the German Asiatic Society* are scarcely less noteworthy than those of her sister society. To these invaluable sources of information are to be added Chamberlain's *Things Japanese*, Rein's *Japan* and the *Industries of Japan*, Griffis' *Mikado's Empire*, Mounsey's *Satsuma Rebellion*, Dening's *Life of Hideyoshi*, the published papers of Professor E. S. Morse, and the two handbooks prepared successively by Mr. Satow and Mr. Chamberlain.

To friends who have taken an interest in this publication I owe many thanks for valuable and timely help: to Dr. J. C. Hepburn, who for so many years was a resident in Yokohama; to Mr. Benjamin Smith Lyman of Philadelphia who still retains his interest in and knowledge of things Japanese; to Mr. Tateno, the Japanese Minister at Washington, and to the departments of the Japanese government which have furnished me material assistance.

In the spelling of Japanese words I have followed, with a few exceptions, the system of the Roman Alphabet Association (Rōmaji Kai) as given in its published statement. I have also had constantly at hand Hepburn's *Dictionary*, the *Dictionary of Towns and Roads*, by Dr. W. N. Whitney, and *Murray's Handbook of Japan*, by B. H. Chamberlain. In accordance with these authorities, in the pronunciation of Japanese words the consonants are to be taken at their usual English values and the vowels at their values in Italian or German.

DAVID MURRAY.

CONTENTS.

ILLUSTRATIONS.

* From Régamey's " *Japan in Art and Industry.*"
† From Chamberlain's " *Translation of Kojiki.*"
‡ From Henry von Siebold's " *Japanese Archæology.*"
§ From Charlevoix's " *Histoire et Description de Japon.*"

xi

* From Régamey's " *Japan in Art and Industry.*"

PREACHER.

DANCER.

ASSISTANT.

THE MIRROR-DANCE.

SHINTOISTS.

THE STORY OF JAPAN.

CHAPTER I.

THE JAPANESE ARCHIPELAGO.

THE first knowledge of the Japanese empire was brought to Europe by Marco Polo after his return from his travels in China in A.D. 1295. He had been told in China of "Chipangu,[1] an island towards the east in the high seas, 1500 miles from the continent ; and a very great island it is. The people are white, civilized, and well favored. They are idolaters, and are dependent on nobody. And I can tell you the quantity of gold they have is endless ; for they find it in their own islands." The name Chipangu is the transliteration of the Chinese name which modern scholars write Chi-pen-kue, by which Japan was then known in China. From it the Japanese derived the name Nippon, and then prefixed the term Dai (great), making it Dai Nippon, the name which is now used by them to designate

[1] *The Book of Ser Marco Polo, the Venetian ;* translated by Colonel Henry Yule, C.B. Second edition, London, 1875, vol. ii., p. 235.

their empire. Europeans transformed the Chinese name into Japan, or Japon, by which the country is known among them at present.

Marco Polo's mention of this island produced a great impression on the discoverers of the fifteenth century. In Toscanelli's map, used by Columbus as the basis of his voyages, "Cipango" occupies a prominent place to the east of Asia, with no American continent between it and Europe. It was the aim of Columbus, and of many subsequent explorers, to find a route to this reputedly rich island and to the eastern shores of Asia.

The islands composing the empire of Japan are situated in the northwestern part of the Pacific ocean. They are part of the long line of volcanic islands stretching from the peninsula of Kamtschatka on the north to Formosa on the south. The direction in which they lie is northeast and southwest, and in a general way they are parallel to the continent.

The latitude of the most northern point of Yezo is 45° 35', and the latitude of the most southern point of Kyūshū is 31°. The longitude of the most eastern point of Yezo is 146° 17', and the longitude of the most western point of Kyūshū is 130° 31'. The four principal islands therefore extend through 14° 35' of latitude and 15° 46' of longitude.

The Kurile islands [1] extending from Yezo northeast to the straits separating Kamtschatka from the island of Shumushu belong also to Japan. This last

[1] These islands belonged to Russia until 1875, when by a treaty they were ceded to Japan in exchange for the rights of possession which she held in the island of Saghalien.

island has a latitude of 51° 5′ and a longitude of 157° 10′. In like manner the Ryūkyū islands, lying in a southwest direction from Kyūshū belong to Japan. The most distant island has a latitude of 24° and a longitude of 123° 45′. The whole Japanese possessions therefore extend through a latitude of 27° 5′ and a longitude of 33° 25′.

The empire consists of four large islands and not less than three thousand small ones. Some of these small islands are large enough to constitute distinct provinces, but the greater part are too small to have a separate political existence, and are attached for administrative purposes to the parts of the large islands opposite to which they lie. The principal island is situated between Yezo on the north and Kyūshū on the south.

From Omasaki, the northern extremity at the Tsugaru straits, to Tōkyō, the capital, the island runs nearly north and south a distance of about 590 miles, and from Tōkyō to the Shimonoseki straits the greatest extension of the island is nearly east and west, a distance of about 540 miles. That is, measuring in the direction of the greatest extension, the island is about 1130 miles long. The width of the island is nowhere greater than two hundred miles and for much of its length not more than one hundred miles.

Among the Japanese this island has no separate name.[1] It is often called by them Hondo[2] which

---

[1] E. M. Satow, *Transactions of the Asiatic Society*, vol. i., p. 30.

[2] This word is not a *proper name* but a descriptive designation, and must be understood in this way when used by Dr. Griffis in his

may be translated Main island. By this translated name the principal island will be designated in these pages. The term Nippon or more frequently Dai Nippon (Great Nippon) is used by them to designate the entire empire, and it is not to be understood as restricted to the principal island.

The second largest island is Yezo, lying northeast from the Main island and separated from it by the Tsugaru straits. Its longest line is from Cape Shiretoko at its northeast extremity to Cape Shira- kami on Tsugaru straits, about 350 miles ; and from its northern point, Cape Soya on the La Per- ouse straits to Yerimosaki, it measures about 270 miles. The centre of the island is an elevated peak, from which rivers flow in all directions to the ocean. Hakodate the principal port is situated on Tsugaru straits and possesses one of the most commodious harbors of the empire.

The third in size of the great islands of Japan is Kyūshū, a name meaning nine provinces, referring to the manner in which it was divided in early times. It lies south from the western extremity of the Main island. Its greatest extension is from north to south, being about 200 miles. Its width from east to west varies from sixty to ninety miles. Its

Mikado's Empire and by Dr. Rein in his two works on Japan. In the successive issues of the *Résumé Statistique*, published by the Statistical Bureau, the term Nippon is used to designate the principal island. This name has the advantage of having been used exten- sively in foreign books, but its restricted use is contrary to the cus- tom of Japan. After much consideration we have determined to designate the principal island by the term "Main island," which is the translation of the word *Hondo*.

temperature and products partake of a tropical character.

To the east of Kyūshū lies Shikoku (meaning four provinces) which is the fourth of the great islands of Japan. It is about one half as large as Kyūshū, which in climate and productions it much resembles. It is south of the western extension of the Main island and is nearly parallel to it. Its length is about 170 miles.

In the early history of Japan one of its names among the natives was Ōyashima, meaning the Great Eight Islands. The islands included in this name were : the Main island, Kyūshū, Shikoku, Awaji, Sado, Tsushima, Oki, and Iki. The large island of Yezo had not then been conquered and added to the empire.

Awaji is situated in the Inland sea between the Main island and Shikoku. It is about fifty miles long and has an area of 218 square miles. Sado is situated in the Japan sea, off the northwest coast of the Main island. It is about forty-eight miles long and has an area of about 335 square miles. Tsushima lies half-way between Japan and Korea, and has a length of about forty-six miles, and an area of about 262 square miles. Oki lies off the coast of Izumo and has an area of about 130 square miles. Finally Iki, the smallest of the original great eight islands, lies west of the northern extremity of Kyūshū and has an area of fifty square miles.

The Japanese islands are invested on the east by the Pacific ocean. They are separated from the continent by the Okhotsk sea, the Japan sea, and the Yellow sea. The Kuro Shiwo (black current) flows from the tropical waters in a northeast direction, skirting the islands of Japan on their east coasts, and deflecting its course to the eastward carries its ameliorating influences to the west coast of America. It is divided by the projecting southern extremity of the island of Kyūshū, and a perceptible portion of it flows on the west coast of the Japanese islands through the Japan sea and out again into the Pacific ocean through the Tsugaru and the La Perouse straits. The effect of the Kuro Shiwo upon the climate and productions of the lands along which it flows is not greatly different from that of the Gulf Stream in the Atlantic ocean, which in situation, direction, and volume it resembles.

The body of water known among foreigners as the Inland sea, but which the Japanese call Seto-no-Uchi-Umi (the sea within the straits), is a picturesque sheet of water situated between the Linschoten straits on the east and the Shimonoseki straits on the west. The latter is seven miles long and at its narrowest part not more than two thousand feet wide. It separates Kyūshū on the south from the Main island on the north. The Inland sea is occupied by an almost countless number of islands, which bear evidence of volcanic origin, and are covered with luxuriant vegetation. The lines of steamers from Shanghai and Nagasaki to the various ports on the Main island, and numberless smaller craft in every direction, run through the Inland sea.

The principal islands of Japan are interspersed

with mountains, hills and valleys. Yeżo the most northern of these islands is traversed by two ranges of mountains; the one being the extension of the island of Saghalien, the other the extension of the Kurile islands. These two ranges cross each other at the centre of the island, and here the greatest elevation is to be found. The shape given to the island by these intersecting ranges is that of a four-pointed star. The rivers in nearly all cases flow from the centre outward to the sea. There are few large rivers. The most important is the Ishikari which empties into Ishikari bay. The valley of this river is the most rich and fertile part of the island.

The mountain ranges on the Main island extend usually in the greatest direction of the island. In the northern and central portions the ranges chiefly run north and south. In the western extension of this island the mountain ranges run in nearly an east and west direction. The ordinary height attained by these ranges is not great, but there are many volcanic peaks which rise out of the surrounding mass to a great elevation. The highest mountain in Japan is Fuji-san (sometimes called Fuji-yama). It is almost conical in shape; although one side has been de-formed by a volcanic eruption which occurred in 1707. It stands not far from the coast, and is di-rectly in view from the steamers entering the bay of Tōkyō on their way to Yokohama. It is about sixty miles from Tōkyō in a direct line, and there are many places in the city from which it can be seen. Its top is covered with snow during ten months of the year, which the heat of August and September melts away. The height of Fuji-san according to the measurement of English naval officers is 12,365 feet.[1]

Next to Fuji-san the mountains most worthy of notice are Gas-san in Uzen, Mitake in Shinano, the Nikkō mountains in Shimotsuke, Haku-san in Kaga, Kirishima-yama in Hyūga, and Asama-yama in Shinano. Asama-yama is about 8,000 feet high, and is an active volcano.

From time immemorial the Japanese islands have been affected with earthquakes. Occasionally they have been severe and destructive, but usually slight and ineffective. It is said that not less than five hundred shocks[2] occur in Japan each year. The last severe earthquake was in the autumn of 1891, when the central part of the Main island, especially in the neighborhood of Gifu, was destructively disturbed. During the long history of the empire many notable cases[3] have occurred. Mr. Hattori-Ichijo in a paper read before the Asiatic Society of Japan, March, 1878, has compiled a list of destructive earthquakes, and has deduced from it some important generalizations.

[1] See Satow and Hawes' *Handbook*, p. 108.

[2] See Chamberlain's *Things Japanese*, second edition, p. 122.

[3] One of the most notable of these is that which occurred in 1596 when Hideyoshi was at Fushimi. In 1854 a series of shocks followed by tidal waves occurred on the east coast of the Main island. The town of Shimoda, which had been opened as a port for foreign trade was almost destroyed, and the Russian frigate *Diana* which was lying there was so injured that she had to be abandoned. In 1855 a severe earthquake occurred at Yedo, which was accompanied by a great fire. About 16,000 dwelling-houses and other buildings are said to have been destroyed, and a large number of lives were lost. *Transactions of Asiatic Society of Japan*, vol. vi., p. 249.

Closely associated with earthquakes in Japan as elsewhere are the phenomena of volcanoes. The whole archipelago bears evidence of volcanic formation. The long line of islands stretching from Kamtschatka to Borneo is plainly the product of continued volcanic action. Dr. Rein [1] enumerates eighteen active volcanoes now in existence within the empire. Fuji-san in all its beauty was no doubt thrown up as a volcano. The last time it was in action was in 1707, when in connection with a series of severe earthquake shocks, an eruption took place on the south side of the mountain, and its symmetrical form was destroyed by the production of the new crater, Hōye-san.

Among the mountainous districts many small lakes are found, a few of which are large enough to be navigated. In Yezo there are six considerable lakes. In the Main island the largest lake is Biwa, in the beautiful mountain region north of Kyōto. It received its name from its fancied resemblance to the shape of a musical instrument called a *biwa*. There is a legend that this lake came into existence in a single night, when the volcanic mountain Fuji-san 300 miles distant was raised to its present height. It is about fifty miles long and about twenty miles broad at its greatest width. It is said to be not less than 330 feet at its greatest depth. It is navigated by steamboats and smaller craft. It is situated about 350 feet above the ocean. Lake Suwa in Shinano is 2,635 feet above the ocean. Lake Chū-

[1] Rein's *Japan*, p. 44. In *Things Japanese* second edition, p. 122, Japan is credited with no less than fifty-one active volcanoes.

zenji in the Nikkō mountains is 4,400 feet ; and
Hakoné lake near Yokohama is 2,400 feet.

Owing to the narrowness of the Main island, there
are no rivers of a large size. Most of them take
their rise in the mountainous regions of the middle
of the islands, and by a more or less circuitous route
find their way to the ocean. The Tone-gawa (*gawa*
means river) is the longest and broadest of the
rivers of Japan. It rises in Kōtsuke and flows in an
eastern direction, receiving many tributaries, attains
a breadth of more than a mile, and with a current
much narrowed, empties into the Pacific ocean at
Chōshi point. It is about 170 miles long and is
navigated by boats for a great distance. The
Shinano-gawa, which may be named as second in
size, rises in the province of Shinano, flows in a
northern direction, and empties into the Japan sea
at Ni-igata. The Kiso-gawa also rises in the high
lands of Shinano, and, flowing southward, empties
into Owari bay. The Fuji-kawa[1] takes its rise in
the northern part of the province of Kai, and in its
course skirting the base of Fuji-san on the west,
empties into Suruga bay. It is chiefly notable for
being one of the swiftest streams in Japan and liable
to sudden and great floods.

To these rivers may be added the Yodo-gawa,
which is the outlet of Lake Biwa, in the province of
Ōmi, and which flows through Kyōto, and empties
into the Inland sea at Ōsaka. This river is navigable
for flat-bottomed steamboats as far as Kyōto. In

[1] The word *gawa* (river) takes the form *kawa* when euphony so
requires.

the islands of Kyūshū and Shikoku there are no large rivers; but there are many streams which give to these islands their richness and fertility.

The climate of Japan, as might be expected from its great stretch from north to south, and the varied circumstances of ocean currents, winds, and mountains, is very different in the different parts. The latitude of Tōkyō is 35°, which is not very different from that of Cyprus in the Mediterranean, or the city of Raleigh in North Carolina. Besides the latitude of the islands of Japan, the most noticeable cause of their climatic condition is the Kuro Shiwo (black current). This current flows from the tropical regions near the Philippine islands, impinges on the southern islands, and is divided by them into two unequal parts. The greater part skirts the Japanese islands on their east coast, imparting to them that warm and moist atmosphere, which is one source of the fertility of their soil and beauty of their vegetation. To this important cause must be added another, which is closely related to it in its effects. The Japanese islands are in the region of the northeast monsoon,[1] which affects in a marked degree the climate of all parts over which the winds extend. The same monsoon blows over the eastern countries of the continent, but the insular character of Japan and the proximity of the warm current on both sides of the islands give to the winds which prevail a character which they do not possess on the con-

---

[1] Dr. Rein was the first clearly to apprehend and state the influence of the northeast monsoon on the climate of Japan. See Rein's *Japan*, p. 104.

tinent. During the greater part of September the northern wind blows, which brings a colder temperature, condensing the moisture contained in the atmosphere. This month is therefore generally a rainy month. Gradually the atmosphere becomes more dry, and the beautiful autumn and early winter follow in course.

The winter is very different in the different parts. On the east coast the temperature is very moderate. Even as far north as Tōkyō the snow rarely falls to a depth of more than a few inches, and then rapidly melts away. Ice seldom forms to a thickness, even on protected waters, to permit skating. In all this region, however, snow covers the high mountains.

On the west coast of the Main island the conditions are very different. The winds of the continent take up the moisture of the Japan sea, and carry it to the west coast, and then, coming in contact with high ranges of mountains which run down the middle of the island, impart their moisture in the form of rain in summer, and snow in winter. These circumstances produce extraordinary falls of snow on the west coast. This is particularly true of the provinces of Kaga, Noto, Etchū, Echigo, and even farther north, especially in the mountainous regions. In the northern part of these districts the snow is often as much as twenty feet deep during the winter months. The inhabitants are obliged to live in the second stories of their houses and often find it necessary to make steps from their houses out to the top of the snow. One effect of these deep snows is to cover up with a safe protection the shrubs and tender plants which would otherwise be exposed to the chilling winds of winter. By this means the tea-shrub and the camellia, which could not withstand the open winter winds, are protected so as to grow luxuriantly.

The southern islands are materially warmer than the Main island. The tropical current together with the warm sunshine due to their low latitude, immerses them in a moist and warm atmosphere. Their productions are of a sub-tropical character. Cotton, rice, tobacco, sugar, sweet potatoes, oranges, yams, and other plants of a warm latitude, flourish in Kyūshū and Shikoku. The high mountains and the well watered valleys, the abundance of forest trees, and wild and luxuriant vegetation,[1] give to these islands an aspect of perennial verdure.

The productions of the Main island are, as might be expected, far more various. In the southern part, especially that part bordering on the Inland sea, the productions are to a large extent similar to those in the southern islands. Rice and cotton are raised in great abundance. Tea flourishes particularly in the provinces near Kyōto and also in the rich valleys of the east coast. Silk-raising is a principal occupation. Nearly one half in value of all the exports from Japan is raw and manufactured silk, and a large part of the remainder is tea. The principal food raised in nearly all the islands is rice. The streams of water which abound everywhere make the irrigation which rice cultivation requires easy and effective. Besides the rice which is raised

[1] Camellia trees are frequently found from twenty to twenty-five feet high.

in paddy land there is also a variety called upland rice. This grows without irrigation but is inferior to the principal variety in productiveness. In the early rituals of the Shintō temples prayers were always offered for the five cereals. These were understood to be rice, millet, barley, beans, and sorghum. All these have been cultivated from early times, and can be successfully raised in almost all parts of the islands. Rice cannot, however, be raised north of the Main island. Millet, barley, and beans are cultivated everywhere, and are the principal articles of food among the country population. Buckwheat is also cultivated in all northern parts. It is believed to have been introduced from Manchuria where it is found growing wild.

The domestic animals of Japan are by no means so abundant as in the corresponding parts of the continent. The horse has existed here from antiquity but was only used for riding or as a pack-horse, but never until recently was used for driving. The cow, owing perhaps to the restrictive influence of the Buddhist doctrines, was never used for food. Even milk, butter, and cheese, which from time immemorial formed such important articles of food throughout Europe and among the nomadic peoples of Asia, were never used. Sheep are almost unknown even to this day, and where they have been introduced it is only in very recent times and by foreign enterprise. Goats are sometimes but not commonly found. On the island of Ōshima,[1] off the province of Izu, they had multiplied to so great an extent

---

[1] Chamberlain, *Asiatic Society Transactions*, vol. xi., p. 162.

and were so destructive to vegetation that about 1850 the inhabitants combined to extirpate them. Swine are found in the Ryūkyū islands, where they had been brought from China and they are found only incidentally in other places when introduced by foreigners. Dogs and cats and barnyard fowl are found in all the islands.

Wild animals are only moderately abundant, as is natural in a country so thickly inhabited. The black bear is found frequently in the well-wooded mountains of Yezo and the northern part of the Main island. The great bear, called also by the Japanese the red bear, and which is the same as the grizzly bear of North America, is also common in the Kurile islands and in Yezo. The wolf is sometimes found and the fox is common. The superstitions concerning the fox are as remarkable as those in the north of Europe, and have doubtless prevented its destruction. Deer are found in abundance in almost all parts of the islands. They are, however, most common in Yezo where immense herds feed upon the plentiful herbage.

The waters around Japan abound in fish. The coast is indented by bays and inlets which give opportunity for fishing. The warm currents flowing past the islands bring a great variety of fish which otherwise would not reach these islands. By far the most common article of food, other than vegetable, is the fish of various kinds and the shell-fish which are caught on the coasts and carried inland to almost all parts.

The division of the empire into provinces (*kuni*)

was an important step in practical administration, and it is often referred to in these pages. This division was first made by the Emperor Seimu A.D. 131–190, when thirty-two provinces were constituted. The northern boundary of the empire was indicated by a line across the Main island from Sendai bay to a place on the west coast nearly corresponding to the present situation of Ni-igata. North of this line was the acknowledged territory of the Ainos, and even south of it were many tracts which were the disputed border.

The Empress Jingō, after her return from the expedition against Korea in A.D. 303, introduced the Korean system of division, by constituting the home provinces and circuits. After some changes and subdivisions in subsequent times the apportionment was settled as follows: *Gokinai* or the five home provinces, viz. Yamashiro, Yamato, Kawachi, Izumi, and Settsu ; *Tōkaidō*, or eastern sea circuit, 15 provinces ; *Tōzandō*, or eastern mountain circuit, eight provinces ; *Sanindō*, or mountain back circuit, eight provinces ; *Sanyōdō*, or mountain front circuit, eight provinces ; and *Saikaidō*, or western sea circuit, nine provinces ; in all sixty-eight provinces. After the close of the war of restoration in 1868, the large territories in the north of the Main island represented by the provinces of Mutsu and Dewa, which had been conquered from the Ainos, were subdivided into seven provinces, thus making seventy-three. Still later the island of Yezo, with which were associated the Kurile islands, was created a circuit under the name of *Hok-kaidō*, or north sea circuit, having eleven provinces, The number of existing provinces therefore is eighty-four. In recent times these eighty-four provinces have for administrative purposes been consolidated into three imperial cities *(fu)*, forty-seven prefectures *(ken)*, and one territory *(chō)*. The imperial cities *(fu)* are Tōkyō, Ōsaka, and Kyōto; the one territory *(chō)* comprises the island of Yezo and the adjacent small islands including the Kuriles; and the prefectures *(ken)* have been formed from the provinces by combining and consolidating them in accordance with their convenience and proximity.

There are only a few large cities in Japan, but very many of a small size.[1] Tōkyō,[2] the capital, contains 1,803,584 inhabitants. Ōsaka, the second largest city, contains 1,026,767; Kyōto, the old capital, 379,409; Nagoya, 284,829; Kōbé, 283,839; and Yokohama, 324,775. There are eight cities containing as many as 100,000 inhabitants. Besides these there are seven cities which have between 100,000 and 60,000; nine which have between 60,000 and 40,000, and twenty-five which have between 40,000 and 30,000. The number of smaller towns is very great. The division of the country into *daimiatcs*, and the maintenance of a *daimyō* town in each led to the establishment of many cities and large villages.

---

[1] These details of the population, area, etc., are taken from various government publications, and refer to the years 1903 and 1904 unless otherwise stated.

[2] In the population of the imperial cities is included that of the suburban districts politically attached to them.

2

The population of the empire of Japan is to a large extent massed in cities and villages. Even in the country, among the farmers, the people are gathered in settlements with wide spaces of cultivated and uncultivated land between. This is due in a great measure to the character of the crops and to the primitive nature of the cultivation. Rice, which is the most common crop, requires irrigation for its successful tillage. This limits the area occupied to the valleys and to those hillsides where the streams can be diverted to the rice fields. The area of land under actual cultivation is about 12,000,000 acres. It has been estimated that the average amount of land under cultivation is only three quarters of an acre for each of those engaged in farming. This amount seems to us very little and can only be explained by the character of the cultivation. The land almost always is made to bear two crops each year. As soon as one crop is cleared away, and often even before that, another is planted.

According to official estimates in 1903, the population of the Japanese empire is as follows:

Kwazoku (nobles).   4,551
Shizoku (*samurai*).   2,105,698
Heimin (common people),   . . . 41,648,868

Total 43,759,117

The population of the several large islands and their dependencies is given below from the statistics of 1903:

Main island and dependencies 35,459,993
Shikoku and dependencies 3,167,696
Kyūshū and dependencies 7,260,834
Hokkaido 843,615
                                     ─────────
Total 46,732,138

The population for 1906 is estimated at 48,610,000 or including Formosa, at 51,742,000.

CHAPTER II.

THE ORIGINAL AND SURVIVING RACES.

IN the present population of Japan there are two distinct races, the Ainos and the Japanese. Of the former there is only a small number now remaining in the island of Yezo. There was also a remnant in the island of Saghalien, but in 1875, when a treaty was made with Russia ceding the Japanese claim to the southern half of Saghalien in exchange for the Kurile islands, permission was granted for all Japanese subjects who wished, to remove to the Japanese island of Yezo. Accordingly among other Japanese subjects seven hundred and fifty Ainos removed to the valley of the Ishikari, where they have continued to reside.

The Ainos are probably the original race, who in early times inhabited the Main island down to the Hakoné pass and possibly farther to the south. From Japanese history we learn that the military forces of the empire were constantly employed to suppress the disturbances caused by the barbarous people of the north. The necessity of this forcible repression, which frequently recurred, was a chief reason for the formation of a military class in the

AINO FAMILY.

early history of Japan. One of the duties imposed on Yamato-dake by his imperial father (A.D. 71–130) was to chastise and subdue the Yemishi. This is the name by which the barbarous peoples of the north and east were known among the Japanese. According to Chamberlain[1] in his translation of *Kojiki*, the Chinese characters with which the Yemishi is written mean Prawn Barbarians, in allusion to the long beards which make their faces resemble a prawn's head. The hairy people now known as Ainos are almost certainly referred to. The origin of the term Aino is unknown. By the Japanese it is believed to be derived from *inu*, meaning a dog, and to have been bestowed on them in contempt. The name is not used by the Ainos themselves. In common with the inhabitants of the Kurile islands and the Japanese portion of Saghalien they call themselves Yezo.

The present characteristics of the Ainos have led many to doubt whether they are really the descendants of the hardy barbarians who so long withstood the military power of the Japanese. But the effect of centuries of repression and conquest must be taken into account. The Ainos have become the peaceable and inoffensive people which we now find them, by many generations of cruel and imperious restraint. That they should have become in this sequence of events a quiet and submissive people is not wonderful. The number of Ainos in the island of Yezo is given in 1880, which is the last census made of them, as 16,637[2]; and this number is be-

---

[1] *Asiatic Society Transactions*, supplement to vol. x., p. 213.
[2] Batchelor, *Asiatic Society Transactions*, vol. x., p. 211.

lieved to be gradually decreasing. Travellers who have visited them unite in testifying to their great amiability and docility. Physically they are a sturdy and well developed race. The characteristic which has been noticed in them more than any other is the abundant growth of hair. The men have a heavy and bushy head of hair and a full beard which is allowed to grow down to their chests. Other parts of the body are also covered with a growth which far surpasses that of the ordinary races. In the matter of food, clothing, houses and implements, they remain in the most primitive condition. In personal habits they are far less cleanly than their Japanese neighbors. Travellers[1] who have remained with them for many weeks assert that in all that time they never saw them wash either their persons or their clothes.

They practise few arts. The making of pottery even in its rudest forms is unknown. All vessels in use are obtained by barter from the Japanese. Occasionally an old-fashioned Japanese matchlock gun is found among them, but mainly their hunting is carried on with bows and arrows. Their fishing is conducted with the rude apparatus which their ancestors used. They have no written language, and even the pictorial writing, which has often been found among rude people, seems to be utterly unknown among them. Their religious ideas[2] are of the most vague and incoherent description. The objects of worship are chiefly inanimate objects such as rivers, rocks and mountains. They seem to have a

[1] Batchelor, *Asiatic Society Transactions*, vol. x., p. 216.
[2] Miss Bird's *Unbeaten Tracks in Japan*, vol. ii., p. 96.

certain fear of the spirit land. They do not readily talk about their deceased ancestors. Their places of burial are concealed, and foreigners rarely obtain access to them.

In their rude superstitions the bear seems to have a singular part. Whether their traditions concerning this animal had their origin in some earlier fear of the bear as a ferocious neighbor it is impossible to determine. In every community the men capture each spring a young cub which they bring home. They entrust it to a woman who feeds it on the milk from her breast. When it is too old to be further nursed in this way, it is confined in a bear cage provided for the purpose. Then in the autumn of the following year the grand bear festival is held. At an appointed signal the door of the cage is opened and the bear, which has been infuriated by hunger and teasing attacks, rushes out. The assembled hunters rush upon him with bows and arrows, clubs and knives, and after an exciting struggle despatch him. The carcass is cut in pieces and distributed among the families of the community, who feast upon it with great delight. Mingled with this rough and exciting scene is much *saké* drinking. This is one accomplishment which they have learned from the Japanese. The men are all confirmed *saké* drinkers, and both men and women persistent smokers. Of the meaning and object of this bear feast the Ainos themselves are ignorant. It goes back to a period beyond their present traditions. Whether it has in it an element of bear worship it is impossible to learn.

The remains of the Stone age which are found in the northern part of the Main island are usually attributed to the Ainos. These remains have been collected and studied both by native scholars and by foreigners. Among the most important of them have been the articles found in shell heaps uncovered in different parts of the empire. The first [1] to which foreign attention was drawn was that at Ōmori, near Tōkyō. Since then many others have been opened and many valuable finds have been reported. The shell heaps have evidently been used like kitchen-middens in Europe and elsewhere, as places for dumping the refuse of shell-fish used for food. These became places for the throwing of useless and broken articles used in the household, and thus have been the means of preserving many of the implements used in prehistoric times. The most significant discovery made in these shell heaps was that at Ōmori, of the bones of human beings artificially broken in such a way as to indicate that cannibalism had been prevalent at the time. Whether this can be assumed as sufficient proof of so grave a charge has been disputed. It is claimed [2] that in at least seven similar shell heaps no human bones and no evidences of cannibalism were found. If however the case is considered as sufficiently proved, it is clear from this as well as from many other circumstances that the Ainos of that early day were by no means the mild and gentle race which we now find

[1] Professor E. S. Morse, *Memoirs of the University of Tokio,* vol. i., part i.

[2] Henry von Siebold, *Notes on Japanese Archæology,* p. 14.

them. It is interesting to note that Marco Polo[1] mentions cannibalism as one of the customs which were believed to exist in Japan in his day.

Besides the Ainos there is evidence of the existence of another savage tribe, which at an early date seems to have been found in many parts of the Main island, and at a later date in the island of Yezo and the Kurile islands on the north. They are the so-called pit-dwellers. In the very earliest writings of the Japanese we find references to them. They dug pits in the earth and built over them a roof, and used these pits or cellars as rooms in which to sleep. The Japanese conquerors in the central parts of the Main island had many conflicts with these pit-dwellers. And in the north and east they as well as the Ainos were encountered by the military forces of the empire. They were probably driven north by the more powerful Ainos and have almost disappeared. Abundant evidence[2] however is found in the island of Yezo of their previous existence. The Ainos in their traditions call them Koro-pok-guru,[3] or hole-men. Among the Japanese they are spoken of as Ko-bito, or dwarfs. There are said to be still

[1] " But I must tell you one thing still concerning that island (Japan) (and 'tis the same with the other Indian Islands), that if the natives take prisoner an enemy who cannot pay a ransom, he who hath the prisoner summons all his friends and relations, and they put the prisoner to death, and then they cook him and eat him, and they say there is no meat in the world so good ! "—*The Book of Ser Marco Polo,* London, 1875, vol. ii., p. 245.

[2] Professor Milne, *Transactions of the Asiatic Society of Japan,* vol. viii., p. 82.

[3] Rev. John Batchelor, *Transactions of the Asiatic Society of Japan,* vol. x., p. 209.

in Yezo the remains of villages where these men lived in earlier times. In the Kurile islands, in the peninsula of Kamtschatka, and in the southern part of Saghalien remnants of this primitive people are met with.

Turning now to the Japanese race which extends from the Kurile islands on the north to the Ryūkyū islands on the south, we see at once that it is a mixed race containing widely different elements. Even after the many centuries during which the amalgamation has been going on, we recognize still the varying types to which the individuals tend. In the south more than in the north, and more among the ruling classes than in the laboring classes there are specimens of a delicate, refined appearance, face oval, eyes oblique, nose slightly Roman, and frame delicate but well proportioned. Then there is another type which has been recognized by all observers. It is found more in the north than the south and is much more common among the laboring population than among the higher classes. The face is broad and the cheek bones prominent. The nose is flat and the eyes are horizontal. The frame is robust and muscular, but not so well proportioned and regular as in the former type. These two types with many intervening links are found everywhere. The characteristics are perhaps more marked among the women than the men. Especially among the aristocracy the women have been less affected by weather and exposure and physical exertion than the men. In the regions about Kyōto and in the western portions of the Main island the prevalence of what may be called the aristocratic type is most marked. Even in the time of the Dutch trade with Japan, Kaempfer [1] refers to the women of Saga, on the south coast of the Inland sea, as " handsomer than in any other Asiatic country." The northern regions, including the old provinces of Mutsu and Dewa, show a much larger element of the more robust type. The men are more muscular and of a darker complexion. Their faces are broader and flatter and their hair and beard more abundant. They show probably the influence of the admixture with the Aino race, which within historic times inhabited these provinces.

Dr. Baelz, a German scholar who has spent many years in Japan, has devoted much study to the races of Japan, and has made elaborate measurements both of living specimens and skeletons. His conclusions may be safely followed, as having been reached by adequate study and by personal investigation. [2] Mainly following him therefore we give briefly the results of the best thought in regard to the ethnography of the races now inhabiting the Japanese islands.

The Ainos of the present day are the descendants of the original occupants of northern and central portions of the Main island. Their share in the ancestry of the present Japanese people is not great, but still sensible, and has contributed to the personal peculiarities which are found in the inhabitants

---

[1] Hildreth's *Japan*, etc., p. 337.

[2] *Mittheilungen der Deutschen Gesellschaft*, etc., as reviewed in *The Chrisanthemum*, May, 1883

of these regions. They probably came originally from the continent by way of the Kurile islands, or by the island of Saghalien. They belong to the northern group of the Mongolians who inhabit the regions about Kamtschatka and adjacent parts of Siberia. They have left marks of their occupancy on the Main island as far south as the Hakoné pass, in the shell heaps, flint arrow-heads, and remains of primitive pottery which are still found. These marks indicate a low degree of civilization, and the persistence with which they withstood the Japanese conquerors, and the harshness and contempt with which they were always treated, have prevented them from mingling to any great extent with their conquerors or accepting their culture.

The twofold character of the Japanese race as it is seen at present can best be explained by two extensive migrations from the continent. The first of these migrations probably took place from Korea, whence they landed on the Main island in the province of Izumo. This will account for the mythological legends which in the early Japanese accounts cluster to so great an extent around Izumo. It will also explain why it was that when Jimmu Tennō came on his expedition from the island of Kyūshū, he found on the Main island inhabitants who in all essential particulars resembled his own forces, and with whom he formed alliances. This first migration seems to have belonged to a rougher and more barbarous tribe of the Mongolian race, and has given rise to the more robust and muscular element now found among the people.

The second migration may have come across by the same route and landed on the island of Kyūshū. They may have marched across the island or skirted around its southern cape and spread themselves out in the province of Hyūga, where in the Japanese accounts we first find them. This migration probably occurred long after the first, and came evidently from a more cultured tribe of the great Mongolian race. That they came from the same race is evident from their understanding the same language, and having habits and methods of government which were not a surprise to the new-comers, and in which they readily co-operated. On the contrary, the ruder tribes at the north of the Main island were spoken of as Yemishi,—that is, barbarians, and recognized from the first as different and inferior.

While the natural and easiest route to Japan would be by way of the peninsula of Korea, and by the narrow straits about 125 miles in width,—divided into two shorter parts by the island Tsushima lying about half-way between,—it is possible that this second migration may have taken place through Formosa and the Ryūkyū islands. This would perhaps account better for the Malay element which is claimed by many to be found in the population of the southern islands. This is attempted to be accounted for by the drifting of Malay castaways along the equatorial current upon the Ryūkyū islands, whence they spread to the southern islands of Japan. But the existence of this Malay element is denied by many observers who have visited the Ryūkyū islands and aver that among the islanders there is no evidence of the existence at any time of a Malay immigration, that the language is only slightly different from the Japanese, and in personal appearance they are as like to the Koreans and Chinese as the Japanese themselves.

Some of the most important measurements which Dr. Baelz has made of the Japanese races are here given, converted into English measures for more ready comprehension.

The average height of the males among the Japanese, as obtained by the measurements of skeletons verified by measurements of living specimens, is 5.02 feet, ranging from 4.76 feet to 5.44 feet. The average height of the females measured was 4.66 feet, ranging from 4.46 feet to 4.92 feet. Referring to the skulls measured by him he says that relatively they are large, as is always the case among people of small size.

The measurements of the Ainos by Dr. Scheube as given by Dr. Rein [1] are: average height of males 4.9 feet to 5.2 feet, and of females 4.8 feet to 5.0 feet, which do not differ very greatly from the measurements of the Japanese as given by Dr. Baelz.

[1] Rein's *Japan*, p. 383.

CHAPTER III.

MYTHS AND LEGENDS.

THE art of writing and printing was not introduced into Japan until A.D. 284, when it was brought from China. Up to that time therefore no written accounts existed or could exist of the early history of the country. Oral tradition was the only agency by which a knowledge of the events of that epoch could be preserved and transmitted. That such a method of preserving history[1] is uncertain and questionable no one can doubt. We may expect to find therefore in the accounts which have come down to us of those centuries which transpired before written records were introduced, much that is contradictory and unintelligible, and much out of which the truth can be gleaned only by the most painstaking research.

The oldest book of Japanese history which has come down to us is called *Kojiki*,[2] or *Records of An-*

[1] "We know that for all points of detail and for keeping a correct account of time, tradition is worthless."—*The History of Rome*, by Rev. Thomas Arnold, D.D., 1864, p. 10.

[2] For easy access to this valuable Japanese work we are indebted to the translation by Basil Hall Chamberlain, *Transactions of the Asiatic Society of Japan*, vol. x., Supplement.

cient Matters. This work was undertaken by the direction of the Emperor Temmu (A.D. 673–686), who became impressed with the necessity of collecting the ancient traditions which were still extant, and preserving them in a permanent record. Before the work was ended the emperor died, and for twenty-five years the collected traditions were preserved in the memory of Hiyeda-no-are. At the end of that time the Empress Gemmyō superintended its completion, and it was finally presented to the Court in A.D. 711. By a comparison of this work with *Nihongi*, or *Chronicles of Japan*, which was completed A.D. 720, only nine years after the other, we are convinced that the era of Chinese classicism had not yet fallen upon the country. The style of the older book is a purer Japanese, and imparts to us the traditions of Japanese history uncolored by Chinese philosophical ideas and classic pedantry which shortly after overwhelmed Japanese literature. But in many particulars these two works, almost equally ancient, supplement and explain each other. The events given in the two are in most respects the same, the principal difference being that the *Chronicles* is much more tinctured with Chinese philosophy, and the myths concerning the creation especially show the influence of that dual system which had been introduced to give a philosophical aspect to the Japanese cosmogony.

The *Kojiki*[1] has been translated into English, to

[1] See Chamberlain's translation of *Kojiki*, or *Records of Ancient Matters*, *Transactions of the Asiatic Society of Japan*, vol. x., Supplement.

which have been added a valuable introduction and notes. The *Nihongi (Chronicles of Japan)* has never been translated entire into English, but has been used by scholars in connection with the *Kojiki*. Among the Japanese it has always been more highly esteemed than the *Kojiki*, perhaps because of its more learned and classical style.

Besides these two historical works the student of early times finds his chief assistance in the Shintō rituals [1] contained in a work called *Yengishiki (Code of Ceremonial Law)*. They have been in part translated by Mr. Satow, who for many years was the learned Japanese secretary of the British legation, and who read two papers on them before the Asiatic Society of Japan, and afterward prepared an article on the same subject for the *Westminster Review*. [2]

It will be apparent from these circumstances that the knowledge of the earlier events, indeed of all preceding the ninth century, must be derived from tradition and cannot claim the same certainty as when based on contemporaneous documents. Not only the whole of the so-called divine age, but the reigns of the emperors from Jimmu to Richū, must be reckoned as belonging to the traditional period of Japanese history, and must be sifted and weighed by the processes of reason.

Relying on the narratives of the *Kojiki* and the *Nihongi*, Japanese scholars have constructed a table of the emperors which has been accepted by the great

[1] Satow, " Ancient Japanese Rituals," *Transactions of the Asiatic Society of Japan*, vols. vii. and ix.

[2] Satow, *Westminster Review*, July, 1878.

mass of the readers, both foreign and native. It will be found in the Appendix.[1] It must be remembered that the names of these early emperors, their ages at the time of accession and at the time of death, and the length of reign, must have all been handed down by tradition during almost a thousand years. That errors and uncertainties should have crept in seems inevitable. Either the names and order of the successive emperors, or the length of time during which they reigned would be liable to be misstated. If we examine the list of emperors[2] we find that the ages at death of the first seventeen, beginning with Jimmu and ending with Nintoku, sum up 1853 years, with an average of 109 years[3] for each. The age of Jimmu is given as 127 years, of Kōan 137 years, of Kōrei 128 years, of Keikō 143 years, of Nintoku, the last, 110 years, etc. Then suddenly the ages of the emperors from Richū onward drop to 67, 60, 80, 56, etc., so that the ages of the seventeen emperors, beginning with Richū, have an average of only 61½ years. This reasonable average extends down through the long series to the present time. It is plain that up to this time there must have existed a different system of reckoning the ages than that which pertained afterwards. Either the original epoch of the Emperor Jimmu has been rendered more remote and

[1] See Appendix I.

[2] Bramsen, *Japanese Chronological Tables*, p. 30.

[3] I remember presenting this point to a Japanese scholar in this way, and he answered me that he thought this great age of the Japanese emperors no more wonderful or unreasonable than the ages of the patriarchs in the Bible.

the lives of the emperors have been prolonged to fill up the space, or, if we assume the epoch of Jimmu to be correct, we must suppose that a number of the emperors have been dropped from the count.

The sudden depression in the ages occurs about the time of the introduction of writing from China, which occurred in A.D. 284. Wani, who came from Korea to Japan bringing continental culture with him, was appointed tutor to the heir-apparent who became the Emperor Nintoku. During his and subsequent reigns a knowledge of Chinese writing gradually spread, so that the annals of the Imperial court were kept in regular and stated order. This will account without difficulty for the sudden change and for the irregularity of the early chronology.

Notwithstanding the almost absolute certainty of error which exists in the received Japanese chronology, it is by far more convenient to accept it in the form it is presented to us, and use it as if it were true. The early history must be treated as traditional and only the later period from the beginning of the fourth century can be accepted as in any sense historical. Yet the events of the earlier period which have been preserved for us by oral tradition are capable with due care and inspection of furnishing important lessons and disclosing many facts in regard to the lives and characteristics of the primitive Japanese.

In writing the history of Rome, Dr. Thomas Arnold [1] said that the only way to treat its early history

---

[1] "I wished to give these legends at once with the best effect, and at the same time with a perpetual mark, not to be mistaken by the

was to give the early legends in as nearly the form in which they had been handed down as possible ; that in this way the spirit of the people would be preserved and the residuum of truth in them would become the heritage of the present generation. We have tried to treat the myths and legends of Japanese history in this manner, and have given the principal stories as they are preserved among the Japanese.

The Origin of the Celestial Deities.

The scene opens in the plain of high heaven. When heaven and earth began there were three deities [1] in existence, that is :

    Master-of-the-August-Centre-of-Heaven,
    High-August-Producing-Wondrous-Deity,
    Divine-Producing-Wondrous-Deity.

These three came into existence without creation and afterwards died.

Then two other deities were born from a thing that sprouted up like unto a reed shoot when the earth, young and like unto floating oil, drifted about medusa-like, viz. :

    Pleasant-Reed-Shoot-Prince-Elder-Deity,
    Heavenly-Externally-Standing-Deity.

These two deities likewise came into existence without creation and afterward died.

---

most careless reader,—they are legends and not history."—*The History of Rome* by Thomas Arnold, D.D., 1864, Preface, p. vii.

[1] For the translation of these names, and for the principal events of these myths, we rely upon Mr. Chamberlain's translation of the *Kojiki*, and his admirable notes and introduction. *Transactions of the Asiatic Society of Japan*, vol. x., Supplement.

The five deities above named are called the Heavenly Deities.

Next were born,

Earthly-Eternally-Standing-Deity,

Luxuriant-Integrating-Master-Deity.

These two deities likewise came into existence without creation and afterwards died.

Next were born,

Mud-Earth-Lord and Mud-Earth-Lady,

Germ-Integrating-Deity and Life-Integrating-Deity,

Elder-of-the-Great-Place and Elder-Lady-of-the-Great-Place,

Perfect-Exterior and Oh-Awful-Lady,

The-Male-who-invites and The-Female-who-invites ; or Izanagi and Izanami.

The two deities named above together with these five pairs are called the seven divine generations.

The Creation of the Japanese Islands.

Then the heavenly deities gave commandment to Izanagi and Izanami to make, consolidate, and give birth to this drifting land. For their divine mission they received a heavenly jewelled spear. With this, standing on the floating bridge of heaven, they reached down and stirred the brine and then drew up the spear. The brine that dripped from the end of the spear was piled up and became the island of Onogoro [1] or Self-Coagulated Island. Then the pair descended upon

---

[1] This is supposed to have been one of the small islands off the coast of Awaji in the Inland sea.

this island and erected thereon a palace eight
fathoms long. Here they lived and begat successive islands. The first was the island of Hirugo,
which, as it was a miscarriage, they put in a boat of
bulrushes and let it float away. The second was the
island of Awa, which also is not reckoned among their
offspring. The next was the island of Awaji,[1] and
the next the land of Iyo by which is understood the
present island of Shikoku.

So in succession they produced the islands of Mi-
tsugo, near the island of Oki, the island of Tsukushi,
which is now called Kyūshū, the island of Iki, the
island of Tsu, and the island of Sado, and lastly the
Great-Yamato-the-Luxuriant-Island-of-the-Dragon-
Fly, which is supposed to mean the principal island,
named in these pages the Main island. Afterward
they produced Kojima in Kibi, Ōshima, the island
of Adzuki, the island of Hime, the island of Chika,
and the islands of Futago.

Thus were finished the labors of this industrious pair
in producing the islands of Japan. Then they turned
to the duty of begetting additional deities, and thirty-
five are named as their descendants. But as their
names do not appear in the record of subsequent
events, we omit them here. Finally the Deity of
Fire was born, and the mother in giving birth to
this child died and departed into hades. Izanagi
was overwhelmed with grief at his wife's death. The
tears which he shed turned into the Crying-Weeping-
Female-Deity. In his madness he drew the ten-

---

[1] An island about fifty miles long in the Inland sea.

grasp [1] sabre with which he was augustly girded, and
cut off the head of the Deity of Fire.   Three deities
were born from the blood that stuck to the blade ;
three were born from the blood that besprinkled the
sword guard; two were born from the blood which
oozed out through his fingers as they grasped the
hilt ; and eight were born from the head and trunk
of the slaughtered deity.

Descent into Hades.

Then Izanagi resolved to follow his spouse into
the land of hades. At the gate of the palace of
hades she came out to meet him. After an interview with him she went back to seek the advice of
the deities of hades. To her impatient husband
she seemed to tarry too long. So he broke off the
end-tooth of the comb stuck in his hair, and kindling
it as a torch he went in. He was appalled by the
dreadful pollution of the place, and by the loath-
some condition of his spouse. He fled from the
scene followed by the furious guards. By guile and
by force, however, he escaped and came again to
the upper regions.

Purification of Izanagi.

Then Izanagi, in order to purify himself from the
pollution of hades, came to a small stream on the
island of Tsukushi. So he threw down the august
staff which he carried and it became a deity. He

---

[1] This probably means that the sword was ten breadths of the hand
in length.

took off his girdle and it became a deity. He threw down his skirt and it became a deity. And he took off his upper garment and it became a deity. And from his trousers which he threw down there was born a deity. Three deities were born from the bracelet which he took from his left arm, and three from the bracelet which he took from his right arm. Thus twelve deities were born from the things which he took off.

Then he found that the waters in the upper reach were too rapid, and the waters in the lower reach were two sluggish. So he plunged into the waters of the middle reach. And as he washed, there were born successive deities, whose names it is not needful to mention. But when he washed his left august eye there was born from it the Heaven-Shining-Great-August-Deity,[1] or as she is often called the Sun Goddess.

When he washed his right august eye there was born His-Augustness-Moon-Night-Possessor. Then when he washed his august nose there was born His-Brave- Swift- Impetuous- Male- Augustness. Thus fourteen deities were born from his bathing. All these deities, as well as those before produced, seem to have come into being in full maturity, and did not need years of growth to develop their final powers.

Izanagi was greatly delighted with the beauty and brilliancy of these last three children. He took from his neck his august necklace and gave it to the

---

[1] The Japanese name of this most venerated goddess is Ama-terasu-ō-mi-kami.

Sun Goddess, saying, Rule thou in the plains of high heaven. Then he gave command to the Moon-Night-Possessor, Rule thou the dominion of the night.

And to His - Impetuous - Male - Augustness he commanded, Rule thou the plain of the sea. But His-Impetuous-Male-Augustness did not assume command of his domain, but cried and wept till his beard reached the pit of his stomach. Then Izanagi said to him, How is it that thou dost not take possession of thy domain, but dost wail and weep? He replied, I weep because I wish to go to my mother in hades. Then Izanagi said, If that be so thou shalt not dwell in this land. So he expelled him with a divine expulsion (whatever that may mean).

Visit of His - Impetuous - Male - Augustness to the Heavenly Plains.

Then His-Impetuous-Male-Augustness said, I will first take leave of my sister who rules in the plains of heaven. When the Sun Goddess saw her brother coming she put jewels in her hair and on her arms, slung two quivers of arrows on her back, put an elbow pad upon her left arm, and, brandishing her bow, she went out to meet him. She demanded of him why he ascended hither. Then he replied that he had no malicious intentions; that his august father had expelled him with a divine expulsion, and that he had come to take leave of her before departing to the land of hades.

Thereupon she proposed to him a test of his sincerity. They stood on opposite sides of the tranquil river of heaven. She begged him to reach her his mighty sabre. She broke it into three pieces and crunched the pieces in her mouth, and blew the fragments away. Her breath and the fragments which she blew away were turned into three female deities. Then His-Impetuous-Male-Augustness took the jewels which she wore in her hair, and the jewels which she wore in her head-dress, and the jewels she wore on her left arm, and the jewels she wore on her right arm, and crunched them and blew them out, and they were turned into five male deities. Then the Sun Goddess declared that the three female deities which were produced from her brother's sword belonged to him, and the five male deities which were produced from her own jewels belonged to her. But His-Impetuous-Male-Augustness was angry at this decision, and broke down the fences of her rice fields, and filled up the water sluices, and defiled her garden. And as she sat with her maidens in the weaving hall, he broke a hole in the roof and dropped upon them a piebald horse which he had flayed with a backward flaying.[1]

Retirement of the Sun Goddess.

Then the Sun Goddess closed the door of the cave in which the weaving hall was, and the whole plain of heaven and the Central-Land-of-Reed-Plains were darkened, and night prevailed, and portents of

[1] There seemed to have been an old superstition about flaying from the tail toward the head.

woe were seen on every hand. Myriads of deities assembled in the bed of the tranquil river of heaven and besought the deity Thought-Includer, child of the High-August-Producing-Wondrous-Deity, the second of the original trio of deities, to propose a plan for inducing the Sun Goddess to reappear. They gathered the cocks of the barn-door fowl and made them crow; they wrought a metal mirror; they constructed a string of beautiful jewels; they performed divination with the shoulder-blade of a stag; they took a plant of Sakaki and hung on its branches the strings of jewels, the mirror, and offerings of peace. Then they caused the rituals to be recited, and a dance to be danced, and all the assembled deities laughed aloud. The Sun Goddess heard these sounds of merriment and was amazed. She softly opened the door and looked out, and asked the meaning of all this tumult. They told her it was because they had found another goddess more illustrious than she. At the same time they held before her luminous face the mirror which they had made. Astonished, she stepped out, and they shut and fastened the door behind her. And the plain of heaven and the Central-Land-of-Reed-Plains became light again.

Then the assembled deities took council together, and caused His-Impetuous-Male-Augustness to be punished and expelled with a divine expulsion.

His-Impetuous-Male-Augustness in Izumo.

So His-Impetuous-Male-Augustness came to the river Hi in Izumo. And he found there an old man and an old woman and a young girl, and they were weeping. And he asked them why they wept. And the old man answered. I once had eight daughters; but every year an eight-forked serpent comes and devours one of them; and now it is the time for it to come again. Then the deity said, Wilt thou give me thy daughter if I save her from the serpent? And he eagerly promised her. Then the deity said, Do you brew eight tubs of strong *saké*, and set each on a platform within an enclosure. So they brewed and set the *saké* according to his bidding. Then the eight-forked serpent came and putting a head in each tub drank up all the *saké*, and being intoxicated therewith went to sleep. The deity then with his sabre hacked the serpent in pieces, and the blood flowed out and reddened the river. But when he came to the middle tail his sabre was broken, and when he searched he found that within the tail was a great sword which he took out. And this is the herb-quelling-great-sword.

Then His-Impetuous-Male-Augustness built for himself a palace and dwelt there with his wife, and made the old man the master of his palace.

Here follows a line of legends relating to the deities of the land of Izumo, which do not concern particularly our story, except that they show that Izumo was closely connected with the early migrations from the continent. It must be remembered that Izumo lies almost directly opposite to Korea, and that this would be a natural point to which the nomadic tribes of Asia would turn in seeking for new fields in which to settle.

Plans for Pacifying the Land.

Then the heavenly deities consulted together how they might pacify the lands of Japan. They sent down one of their number to report on its condition. But he went no farther than the floating bridge of heaven, and seeing the violence which prevailed he returned. Then they sent another; but he made friends with the insurgent deities and brought back no report. Again they sent an envoy, who married the daughter of the insurgent deity, and for eight years sent back no report. After this they sent a pheasant down to inquire why a report was not sent. This bird perched on a cassia tree at the palace gate of the delinquent envoy, and he hearing its mournful croaking shot it with an arrow, which flew up through the ether and landed in the plains of heaven. The arrow was shot down again and killed the envoy. Finally two other envoys were sent down, who landed in Izumo, and after some parley with the refractory deities of the land received their adhesion and settled and pacified the land. Then they returned to the heavenly plains and reported that peace was established.

Descent of the August Grandchild.

The Central-Land-of-Reed-Plains[1] being now reported as peaceful, the heavenly deities sent His-Augustness - Heaven - Plenty-Earth-Plenty-Heaven's-Sun-Height-Prince-Rice-Ear-Ruddy-Plenty,[2] who was

[1] This is one of the ancient names of the Main island of Japan.

[2] The name of th .s prince of which the translation is here given is usually shortened to Ninigi-no-Mikoto.

a grandson of Her-Augustness-the-Sun-Goddess, to dwell in and rule over it. There were joined to him in this mission [1] the Deity-Prince-of-Saruta as his vanguard and five chiefs of companies. They gave him also the string of jewels and the mirror with which the Sun Goddess had been allured from the cave, and also the herb-quelling-great-sword which His - Augustness - the - Impetuous - Male - Deity had taken from the tail of the serpent. And they charged him saying, Regard this mirror precisely as if it were our august spirit, and reverence it as if reverencing us.

Then His-Augustness-Heaven's-Prince-Rice-Ear-Ruddy-Plenty, taking leave of the plains of heaven, and pushing asunder the heavenly spreading clouds, descended upon the peak of Takachiho [2] in Tsukushi, a mountain which is still pointed out in the present island of Kyūshū. And noting that the place was an exceedingly good country, he built for himself a palace and dwelt there. And he married a wife who was the daughter of a deity of the place, who bore him three sons whom he named Prince Fire-Shine, Prince Fire-Climax, and Prince Fire-Subside.

Princes Fire-Shine and Fire-Subside.

Now Prince Fire-Shine was a notable fisherman and Prince Fire-Subside was a hunter. And Prince

---

[1] Nakatomi-no-Muraji is also among these, who was the ancestor of the Fujiwara family that from the reign of the Emperor Tenji attained great political distinction.

[2] Dr. Rein in 1875 was shown an old sword on the top of this mountain which is claimed to have been carried on this occasion.— Rein's *Japan*, p. 214, note.

Fire-Subside said unto his elder brother, Let us exchange our occupations and try our luck. And after some hesitation on the part of the elder brother the exchange was made. But Prince Fire-Subside was not successful and lost the fish-hook in the sea. Then Prince Fire-Shine proposed to his younger brother to exchange back the implements which they had used. But the younger brother said he had had no luck and had lost the hook in the sea. But Prince Fire-Shine was angry and demanded his hook. Then Prince Fire-Subside broke his sword into many fragments and made them into fish-hooks, which he gave to his brother in place of the one he had lost. But he would not receive them. Then he made a thousand fish-hooks and offered these. But he said, I want my original hook.

And as Prince Fire-Subside was weeping by the sea shore the Deity Salt-Possessor came to him and asked him why he wept. He replied, I have exchanged a fish-hook with my elder brother, and have lost it, and he will not be satisfied with any compensation I can make, but demands the original hook. Then the Deity Salt-Possessor built a boat and set him in it, and said to him, Sail on in this boat along this way, and you will come to a palace built of fishes' scales. It is the palace of the Deity Ocean-Possessor. There will be a cassia tree by the well near the palace. Go and sit in the top of that tree, and the daughter of the Ocean-Possessor will come to thee and tell thee what to do.

So he sailed away in the boat and came to the

palace of the Ocean-Possessor, and he climbed the cassia tree and sat there. And the maidens of the daughter of the Sea Deity came out to draw water, and saw the beautiful young man sitting in the tree. Then he asked them for some water. And they drew water and gave it to him in a jewelled cup. Without drinking from it he took the jewel from his neck and put it in his mouth and spat it into the vessel, and it clung to the vessel. So the maidens took the vessel and the jewel clinging to it into the palace to their mistress. And they told her that a beautiful young man was sitting in the cassia tree by the well.

The Sea Deity then went out himself and recognized the young man as Prince Fire-Subside. He brought him into the palace, spread rugs for him to sit on, and made a banquet for him. He gave him his daughter in marriage, and he abode there three years.

At last one morning his daughter reported to the Sea Deity that Prince Fire-Subside, although he had passed three years without a sigh, yet last night he had heaved one deep sigh. The Sea Deity asked him why he sighed. Then Prince Fire-Subside told him about his difficulty with his brother, and how he would accept no compensation for his lost fish-hook, but demanded the return of the original. Thereupon the Sea Deity summoned together all the fishes of the sea and asked them if any one of them had swallowed this hook. And all the fishes said that the *tai* had complained of something sticking in its throat, and doubtless that was the lost

4

hook. The throat of the *tai* therefore being examined, the hook was found and given to Prince Fire-Subside.

Then the Sea Deity dismissed him to his own country, and gave him two jewels, a flow-tide jewel and an ebb-tide jewel. And he set him on the head of an immense crocodile and bade the crocodile convey him carefully and come back and make a report. And Prince Fire-Subside gave the recovered hook to his brother. But a spirit of animosity still dwelt in his heart, and he tried to kill his brother. Then Prince Fire-Subside threw out the flow-tide jewel, and the tide came in upon the Prince Fire-Shine and was about to drown him. And he cried out to his brother and expressed his repentance. Then Prince Fire-Subside threw out the ebb-tide jewel and the tide flowed back and left him safe.

Then Prince Fire-Shine bowed his head before his younger brother, and said, Henceforth I will be thy guard by day and night, and will faithfully serve thee.

And His-Augustness-Prince-Fire-Subside succeeded his father and dwelt in the palace of Takachiho five hundred and eighty years. The place of his tomb is still shown on Mount Takachiho in the province of Hyūga of the island of Kyūshū. And he left as his successor his son, whom the daughter of the Sea Deity had borne him. And this son was the father of His-Augustness-Divine-Yamato-Iware-Prince, who is known to posterity by his canonical name of Jimmu, the first emperor of Japan.

CHAPTER IV.

FOUNDING THE EMPIRE.

WE have now come to the time when the movements which resulted in the establishment of the
empire of Japan took place. The events are still
overlaid with myth and legend, which could only
have been transmitted by oral tradition. But they
have to do with characters and places which are tied
to the present by stronger cords than those of the
divine age. What the events really were which are
involved in the myths of the preceding chapter it is
impossible to predicate. That the celestial invasion
of the island of Kyūshū means the coming thither
of a chief and his followers from the continent by
way of Korea seems most reasonable. The inter-
mixture of Izumo with these legends may mean
that another migration of a kindred race took place
to that part of the Main island. The easy access to
both Izumo and Kyūshū from Korea makes these
migrations the natural explanation of the landing
of the Japanese upon these fertile and tempting
islands.

Without settling the difficult ethnographical questions which are involved in this problem, we propose

to follow the Kyūshū invaders into the Main island.
We will note the slow and laborious steps by which
they proceeded to establish a government, which
through many changes and emergencies continues
to this day.

The Prince, whom we will continue to call Jimmu,[1]
had an elder brother, Prince Itsu-se, who seems, however, to have been less active and energetic than the
younger. At least, even from the first it is Prince
Jimmu who is represented as taking the initiative in
the movements which were now begun. The two
brothers consulted together and resolved to conduct
an expedition towards the east. It will be remembered that their grandfather had established his
palace on Mount Takachiho, which is one of the two
highest peaks in Kyūshū, situated in the province of Hyūga, nearly in the middle of the southern
extension of the island of Kyūshū. It was from
this place that the two brothers started on their expedition. It was no doubt such an expedition as
the Norse Vikings of a later day often led into the
islands of their neighbors. They had with them a
force composed of the descendants of the invaders
who had come with their grandfather from the continent. They marched first through the country
called Toyo, which was a luxuriant and fertile region on the northeast part of the island. Thence
they marched to the palace of Wokada, situated in

[1] This canonical name was given to him in the reign of the
Emperor Kwammu, who commanded Mifune-no-Mikoto to select
suitable canonical names for all past emperors, and these have since
been used.

a district of the island of Tsukushi, lying on the
northwest coast facing Tsushima and the peninsula
of Korea, and bordering on the straits of the Inland
sea. Here they remained a year and probably
built the boats by which they crossed the Inland sea.

From Tsukushi they crossed to the province of
Aki in the Main island on the coast of the Inland sea, where it is said they remained seven years.
The progress seems like that of the hordes of the
Goths in the early ages of European history. It
was not merely a military expedition, but a migration of a tribe with all its belongings, women and
children, old men and old women, and household
and agricultural effects. The military band under
Prince Jimmu and his brother formed the vanguard
and protection of the tribe. During their seven
years' sojourn in Aki they were compelled to resort
to agriculture as well as fishing for their support.

Then they skirted along the north coast of the
Inland sea to Takashima in the province of Kibi.
Thence they crept with their awkward boats eastward among the luxuriant islands. They met a
native of the coast out in his boat fishing and engaged his services as a guide. He conducted them
to Naniwa, which now bears the name of Ōsaka,
where they encountered the swift tides and rough
sea which navigators still meet in this place. Finally
they landed at a point which we cannot recognize,
but which must have been in the neighborhood of
Ōsaka at the mouth of the Yodo river.

Here their conflicts with the natives began. The
whole region seems to have been occupied by tribes

not unlike their own, who had probably come thither from the settlements in Izumo. The first to dispute their progress was Prince Nagasuné (Long Legs), of Tomi, who raised an army and resisted the landing of the invaders. It was in the battle that ensued at this place that Prince Itsu-se, the elder brother, received a wound in his hand from an arrow shot by Prince Nagasuné. The reason given reveals a curious superstition which seems to have prevailed from this early time. The Japanese prince on receiving the wound exclaims, "It is not right for me, an august child of the Sun Goddess, to fight facing the sun. It is for this reason that I am stricken by the wretched villain's hurtful hand." Prince Itsu-se, after a few days, died from the effects of the wound. He is buried on mount Kama in the province of Kii.

It is needless to recount all the legends which cluster around this invasion of the central provinces of Japan; about the wild boar which came out of the mountains near Kumano, before which Prince Jimmu and all his warriors fell down in a faint; about the miraculous sword which was sent down from the heavenly plains to aid him in subduing the Central-Land-of-Reed-Plains; about a crow eight feet long which was sent to guide him in his expedition, and about the deities with tails who in several places were encountered. To our conception they seem meaningless, and do not in any measure contribute to the progress of the story. They bear evidence of a later invention, and do not belong legitimately to the narrative.

At Uda, on the east coast of the Yamato peninsula, there lived two brothers named Ukashi. The elder brother undertook to deceive Prince Jimmu, and set a trap in which to capture and slay him. But the younger brother revealed the plot, whereupon the followers of Prince Jimmu compelled the traitor to retreat into his own trap, where they killed him. The younger brother was honored and rewarded by Jimmu, and appears afterward among the hereditary princes of the country.

Again, as he was making his progress through the country Prince Jimmu came upon a company of the savages known as pit-dwellers,[1] whom the *Kojiki* calls earth-spiders, and describes them as having tails. There appear to have existed at this period remnants of these tribes as far south as the 35th parallel. At a later period they were driven out by the Ainos, and nothing but some of their relics now exists, even in Yezo. The peculiarity by which they were known was, that they lived in a sort of pit dug out of the earth in the sides of the mountains, over which they built a roof of limbs and grass. In the present case there were eighty of the warriors of this tribe. Prince Jimmu made a banquet for them in one of their pits and assigned an equal number of his own men to act as attendants. Each of these attendants was girded with a sword. Then from a post outside he sang a song,[2] and at a given signal

[1] See Milne's paper on "Pit-Dwellers of Yezo and Kurile Islands," *Transactions of the Asiatic Society of Japan*, vol. x., p. 187.

[2] A large number of songs are handed down in the traditions of this period. They are in the most ancient form of the language and are not easy to translate. We give as a specimen Jimmu's song from

in this song the eighty attendants fell upon the
eighty earth-spiders and slew them all.

Thus having subdued all opposing forces and
brought the country into subjection, Prince Jimmu
established himself in a palace built for him at Kashi-
wara in the province of Yamato. This is usually
regarded by Japanese historians as the beginning of
the empire, and the present era[1] is reckoned from
this establishment of a capital in Yamato. From
the record of the length of the reigns of the several
emperors contained in the *Kojiki*, and the *Nihongi*,
and later books, the date of the accession of the
Emperor Jimmu is fixed at 660 B.C. We have given
elsewhere[2] our reason for believing the record of
the early reigns of doubtful authenticity. Nevertheless, as it is impossible to propose a definite
change, it is better to use the accepted scheme with
its admitted defects.

Chamberlain's translation of *Kojiki*, *Asiatic Society Transactions*,
vol. x., Supplement, p. 142.

> Into the great cave of Ōsaka people have
> entered in abundance and are there.
> Though people have entered in abundance
> and are there, the children of the augustly
> powerful warriors will smite and finish them
> with their mallet-headed swords, their
> stone-mallet swords : the children of the
> augustly powerful warriors, with their
> mallet-headed swords, their stone-
> mallet swords, would now do well to
> smite.

[1] For example, the organization of a parliament took place in 1890
which in the Japanese reckoning would be 2550 from Jimmu's setting
up his capital in Yamato.

[2] See p. 32.

The Emperor Jimmu after his accession continued to reign seventy-five years and, according to the *Kojiki*, died at the age of one hundred and thirty-seven. The *Nihongi*, however, gives his age at death as one hundred and twenty-seven, and this has been adopted by the government in its published chronology.[1] His burial place is said to be on the northern side of mount Unebi in the province of Yamato. It is just to assign to the Emperor Jimmu the exalted place which the Japanese claim for him in their history. That he was a prince of high enterprise is evident from his adventurous expedition from the home of his family into the barbarous and unknown regions of the Main island. He accomplished its conquest with less slaughter and cruelty than the customs of the times seemed to justify. He made it his policy to effect terms with the native princes and seek their co-operation in his government. He extended his sway so that it covered Anato, now known as Nagato, and Izumo on the west, and reached probably to Owari on the east. All this time he had held a firm hand on the island from which he had come, so that few if any outbreaks occurred among its restless Turanian or native inhabitants.

The Emperor Jimmu was succeeded by his third son, known by his canonical name as the Emperor Suizei. The reigning emperor, it seems, exercised the right to select the son who should succeed him. This was not always the oldest son, but from the time he was chosen he was known as *taishi*, which is

[1] See list of emperors, Appendix I.

nearly equivalent to the English term crown prince. The Emperor Suizei, it is said, occupied a palace at Takaoka, in Kazuraki, in the province of Yamato. This palace was not far from that occupied by his father, yet it was not the same. And in the reigns of the successive sovereigns down to A.D. 709, when the capital was for a time established at Nara, we observe it as a most singular circumstance that each new emperor resided in a new palace. In the first place, the palace spoken of in these early times was probably a very simple structure. Mr. Satow, in his paper[1] on the temples at Isé, gives an account of the form and construction of the prehistoric Japanese house. The Shintō temple in its pure form is probably a survival of the original palace. Before the introduction of edge-tools of iron and boring implements or nails, the building must have been constructed in a very primitive fashion. It will be understood that stone or brick were never used. Wood was the only material for the frame. The roof was thatched with rushes or rice straw. The pure Shintō temples of modern times are built with the utmost simplicity and plainness. Although the occasion for adhering to primitive methods has long since passed away, yet the buildings are conformed to the styles of structure necessary before the introduction of modern tools and appliances. To build a new palace therefore for a new emperor involved by no means such an outlay of time and work as might be imagined.

[1] Satow, *Transactions of the Asiatic Society of Japan*, vol. ii., p. 113.

It is not improbable that when a young man was chosen crown prince he had an establishment of his own assigned to him, and this became his palace which he occupied when he became emperor. When a man died, and especially when an emperor died, it

SHINTŌ TEMPLE.

was an ancient custom to abandon his abode. It became unclean by the presence in it of a dead body, and therefore was no longer used.

Nothing is narrated of the immediate successors of the Emperor Jimmu of importance to this story.

The accounts contained in either of the oldest histories relate merely to the genealogies of the several
sovereigns.

The Emperor Suizei was, as we have seen, the
third son of Jimmu and reigned thirty-two years,
dying at the age of eighty-four.[1]

The third emperor was Annei, the only son of the
Emperor Suizei. He reigned thirty-seven years and
died at the age of fifty-seven.

The fourth emperor was Itoku, the oldest son of
the Emperor Annei. He reigned thirty-three years
and died at the age of seventy-seven.

The fifth emperor was Kōshō, the oldest son of
the Emperor Itoku. He reigned eighty-two years
and died at the age of one hundred and fourteen
years.

The sixth emperor was Kōan, the oldest son of
the Emperor Kōshō. He reigned one hundred and
one years and died at the age of one hundred and
thirty-seven.

The seventh emperor was Kōrei, the second son
of the Emperor Kōan. He reigned seventy-five
years and died at the age of one hundred and twenty-
eight.

The eighth emperor was Kōgen, the oldest son of
the Emperor Kōrei. He reigned fifty-six years and
died at the age of one hundred and sixteen.

The ninth emperor was Kaikwa, a younger son
of the Emperor Kōgen. He reigned fifty-nine years
and died at the age of one hundred and eleven.

[1] We follow in these figures the chronology which has been authorized by the government.   Appendix I.

The tenth emperor was Sūjin, a younger son of the Emperor Kaikwa. He reigned sixty-seven years and died at the age of one hundred and nineteen. It is narrated that during his reign a pestilence broke out which was so severe that the country was almost depopulated. The emperor was greatly disturbed by this calamity, and there appeared to him in the night a divine vision. The Great Deity, the Great Master of Things, appeared and revealed to him, that if he would cause him to be appropriately worshipped the pestilence would cease. The worship was accordingly ordained and executed, and the pestilence forthwith abated.

In this reign expeditions were also sent into the northwestern and northeastern districts of the Main island to repress the disturbances which had arisen. The reports from these expeditions were in each case favorable, and the whole empire was in a condition of quiet and prosperity, such as had not before existed. Taxes were for the first time levied on the proceeds of the chase and on the handiwork of the women. Reservoirs for the collection of water, used in the irrigation of the rice crops, were constructed in the imperial provinces, and encouragement was everywhere given to the growing industries of the country.

The Emperor Sūjin was succeeded by his younger son who is known as the eleventh emperor under the name of Suinin. He is said to have reigned ninety-nine years, and to have died at the age of one hundred and forty-one.

A conspiracy came near ending the life of this

emperor. A brother of the empress was ambitious to attain supreme authority. He approached his sister with the subtle question, Which is dearer to thee, thine elder brother or thy husband? She replied, My elder brother is dearer. Then he said, If I be truly the dearer to thee, let me and thee rule the empire. And he gave her a finely tempered dagger and said to her, Slay the emperor with this in his sleep. So the emperor, unconscious of danger, was sleeping one day with his head on the lap of the empress. And she, thinking the time had come, was about to strike him with the dagger. But her courage failed her, and tears fell from her eyes on the face of the sleeping emperor. He started up, awakened by the falling tears, and said to her, I have had a strange dream. A violent shower came up from the direction of Saho and suddenly wet my face. And a small damask-colored snake coiled itself around my neck. What can such a dream betoken? Then the empress, conscience-stricken, confessed the conspiracy with her brother.

The emperor, knowing that no time was to be lost, immediately collected a force of troops and marched against his brother-in-law. He had entrenched himself behind palisades of timber and awaited the emperor's attack. The empress, hesitating between her brother and her husband, had made her escape to her brother's palace. At this terrible juncture she was delivered of a child. She brought the child to the palisades in sight of the emperor, and cried out to him to take it under his care. He was deeply moved by her appeal to him and forthwith planned to rescue both the child and its mother. He chose from among his warriors a band of the bravest and most cunning, and commanded them, saying, When ye go to take the child, be sure that ye seize also the mother.

But she, fearing that the soldiers would try to snatch her when they came for the child, shaved off her hair and covered her head with the loose hair as if it were still adhering. And she made the jewel-strings around her neck and arms rotten, and she rendered her garments, by which they might catch hold of her, tender by soaking them in *saké*. When the soldiers came to her she gave them the child and fled. Then they seized her by the hair and it came away in their hands; and they clutched at the jewel-strings and they broke; and then they grasped her garments, but they had been rendered tender and gave way in their hands. So she escaped from them and fled. Then they went back to the emperor and reported that they had been unable to capture the mother, but they had brought the babe. The emperor was angry at what the soldiers told him. He was angry at the jewellers who had made the rotten jewel-strings and deprived them of their lands. He called to the empress through the burning palisades around the palace—for the soldiers had set fire to the palace—saying, A child's name must be given by its mother; what shall be the name of this child? And she answered, Let it be called Prince Homu-chiwake. And again he called: How shall he be reared? She replied, Take for him a foster-mother and bathing woman who

shall care for him. Then he asked again, saying:
Who shall loosen the small, fresh pendant which you
have tied upon him? And she gave directions concerning this also. Then the emperor paused no
longer, but slew the rebellious prince in his burning
palace, and the empress perished with her wicked
brother.

Following this is a long legend concerning this
child which was dumb from its birth, and how he
was sent to worship at the temple of the deities of
Izumo, and how he miraculously attained the power
of speech and was brought back to his father.

It was during the reign of this emperor also that
Tajima-mori was sent to China to fetch specimens
of the orange-tree for introduction into Japan. He
returned with them, but when he reached the capital
the emperor was dead. The messenger was shocked
and brought the specimens of the orange-tree to the
burial place of the emperor, where he died from grief.

Up to this time it seems to have been the cruel
custom to bury with the deceased members of the
imperial family, and perhaps with others of high
rank, the living retainers and horses who had been
in their service. It is said that when the emperor's
younger brother died (B.C. 2) they buried along with
him his living retainers, placing them upright in a
circle around him and leaving their heads uncovered.
Night and day were heard the agonizing cries of
these thus left to die of starvation. The emperor
was greatly moved and resolved that this terrible
custom should be abolished. Four years later the
empress herself died, and the emperor called together

his counsellors to propose some plan by which this practice of living sacrifices could be avoided. Thereupon one of his counsellors, Nomi-no-Sukuné, advanced and begged the emperor to listen to a scheme which he had to present. He suggested that, instead of burying the living retainers with their master or mistress, clay images of men and women and horses be set up in a circle around the burial place. The plan pleased the emperor vastly, and images were at once made and buried around the dead empress. As a mark of his high appreciation Nomi-no-Sukuné was appointed chief of the clay-workers guild.

It appears probable that this cruel usage of burying living retainers with their dead master was not entirely ended by this substitution of clay images. As late as A.D. 646 the emperor found it necessary to prescribe regulations for funerals and to forbid the burial of living retainers. Mr. Satow[1] has given a most interesting account of this edict which pertains not only to the practice of burial of retainers, but also to the size of vaults and mounds and the number of laborers who might be employed in preparing the structure.

The images used as a substitute for living retainers were called *Tsuchio Ningio* (clay images). They have been found in many parts of the country, especially in the home provinces where the burial of the imperial families and the connected nobility took place. This burying of images seems to have died out about A.D. 700. Its discontinuance probably

[1] E. M. Satow, "Ancient Sepulchral Mounds in Kaudzuke," *Transactions of the Asiatic Society of Japan*, vol. viii., pp. 11, 330.

was owing to the growing prevalence of Buddhism which discountenanced a custom founded on a religion anterior to it.

The Emperor Suinin was succeeded by his younger son Keikō who became the twelfth emperor. He reigned fifty-nine years, and died at the age of one hundred and forty-three. His son, Prince O-usu, who afterward was known as Yamato-dake, is represented as pursuing a most daring and romantic career. The myths concerning him are among the most picturesque in Japanese history.

The first adventure narrated of him was regarding his elder brother. His father asked him, Why does not thy elder brother make his appearance at the imperial banquets? Do thou see after this and teach him his duty.

A few days after his father said again to him, Why dost not thy brother attend to his duty? Hast thou not warned him as I bade thee?

The young prince replied that he had taken that trouble. Then his father said, How didst thou take the trouble to warn him? And the prince coolly told him that he had slain him and thrown his carcass away.

The emperor was alarmed at the coolness and ferocity of his son, and bethought how he might employ him advantageously. Now there were at Kumaso in Kyūshū two brothers, fierce and rebellious bandits, who paid small respect to the imperial wishes. The emperor conceived that it would be a fitting achievement for his fearless son to put an end to these reckless outlaws. So Yamato-dake bor-

BURIED IMAGES.

From *Japanese Archæology*, by Henry von Siebold.

rowed from his aunt her female apparel, and hiding a sword in the bosom of his dress, he sought out the two outlaws in their hiding-place. They were about to celebrate the occupancy of a new cave which they had fitted up for themselves. They had invited a goodly number of their neighbors, and especially of the female sex. Prince Yamato-dake, who was young and fresh-looking, put on his female disguise and let down his hair which was still long. He sauntered about the cave and went in where the two outlaws were amusing themselves with their female visitors. They were surprised and delighted to see this new and beautiful face. They seated her between them and did their best to entertain her.

Suddenly, when the outlaws were off their guard, he drew his sword from his bosom and slew the elder brother. The younger rushed out of the door of the cave, the prince close at his heels. With one hand he clutched him by the back and with the other thrust him through with his sword. As he fell he begged the prince to pause a moment and not to withdraw his sword from his fatal wound.

Then the outlaw said, Who art thou? And he told him and for what purpose he had come.

The outlaw said, There were in the west none so brave as we two brothers. From this time forward it shall be right to praise thee as the August Child Yamato-dake (the bravest in Yamato).

As soon as he had said this, the prince " ripped him up like a ripe melon." [1]

[1] Chamberlain's translation of *Kojiki,—Transactions of the Asiatic Society of Japan*, vol. x., Supplement, p. 208.

Then after he had subdued and pacified the rebellious princes of the districts about the straits of Shimonoseki he returned to the emperor and made his report.

Following this account of Yamato-dake's adventures in the West, there are given the interesting traditions concerning his expedition to the East, and his encounters with the Ainos, who inhabited the northern part of the island. That there was a basis of fact to these traditions there cannot be a doubt. Yet the events have such an air of fable and poetry that it is impossible to separate the fact from the legend. As we have done in previous instances, we give the stories in their essential entirety, leaving to scholars hereafter the task of winnowing the grains of fact out of the chaff which the imagination of the race has left for us.

Prince Yamato-dake took on his expedition to the East the Prince Mi-suki-tomo-mimi-take. The emperor gave him these instructions: "Subdue and pacify the savage deities, and likewise the unsubmissive people of the twelve roads[1] of the East."

Prince Yamato-dake first visited the temple of the Sun Goddess in Isé, where he worshipped at the shrine of his great ancestress. He must have had a presentiment that he never would return alive from this expedition. His aunt Yamato-hime,[2] who was

[1] The roads or circuits here spoken of refer to the roads constructed by the government along contiguous provinces and used for the passage of troops and other government purposes. These circuits have continued in use down to the present time.

[2] Yamato-hime or Yamato-princess had been appointed high priest.

the priestess of this temple, gave him on his departure the sword[1] which the Impetuous-Male-Deity discovered in the tail of the snake which he slew in Izumo. She also gave him a bag which he was not to open until he found himself in pressing difficulty.

He came to the land of Owari, and appears there to have been smitten by the charms of the Princess Miyazu. And, planning to wed her on his way back, he plighted to her his troth and went on. Then he came to the province of Sagami, where he met the chief of the land. But he deceived him and said that in the midst of a vast moor there is a lagoon where lives a deity. Yamato-dake went over the moor to find the deity. Whereupon the chief set fire to the grass, expecting to see him consumed. But Yamato-dake seeing his danger, and being assured that the time of pressing difficulty had come, opened the bag which his aunt, Yamato-hime, had given him. There he found a fire drill,[2] with which a fire could be struck. He cut away the grass around him with the sword which had been given him, and then set fire to the moor. When he was safe from the fire he sought out and slew the traitorous chief and all the chiefs who were associated with him.

ess of the temples in Isé, and in that capacity had charge of the imperial regalia which were deposited there. She is a very celebrated person in Japanese legendary story and is said to have lived several hundred years.

See Chamberlain's translation of *Kojiki*, p. 183, note 7 ; *Asiatic Society Transactions*, vol. x., Supplement.

[1] See p. 45.

[2] See Satow's paper on the use of the fire drill in Japan, *Transactions of Asiatic Society of Japan*, vol. vii., p. 223.

From Sagami he undertook to cross in a boat the waters of Yedo bay to Kazusa opposite. But the sea was rough and they were on the point of being overwhelmed and drowned. Then his wife, the Princess Oto-Tachibana, who accompanied him on this expedition, threw out mats from the boat, and saying, "I will enter the sea instead of the prince; you must finish the task on which you are sent," she sprang from the boat and sat down on the mats[1] she had thrown out. Immediately the waves were quiet and the boat sailed on in safety. And the comb of the princess was washed ashore, and the people built for it a sacred mausoleum in which it was kept.

Then Prince Yamato-dake penetrated the regions occupied by the Ainos[2] and subdued them. Having accomplished this principal object of his undertaking, he returned by way of the Usui pass opposite to mount Fuji. As he stood in this lofty position and looked out on the sea where his wife had sacrificed herself for his safety, he cried out: "Azuma ha ya!" (O my wife!) Azuma is a name often used in poetry for the part of Japan north of this pass. But whether this myth was invented to explain the name, or the name was derived from the incident, it is impossible to determine.

[1] It is one of the favorite subjects of Japanese art to represent the Princess Oto-Tachibana sitting upon a pile of mats and the boat with her husband sailing off in the quieted waters.

[2] The name by which these savage tribes were designated was Yemishi; the name however is written in Chinese characters which signify Prawn-Barbarians; in allusion to their heavy beards which gave them the appearance of prawns. See p. 22.

Then Prince Yomato-dake went into the high lands of Shinano and after he had settled the disturbances which existed there, he came back to Owari where he had left the Princess Miyazu. In one of his excursions into the rebellious regions he was stricken with a fatal illness. In his enfeebled condition he struggled on, almost unable to walk. He made his way towards Isé. At Ōtsu, a village on the coast of Owari bay, he recovered the sword which he had left on his way to the East. In his painful journey he sat down under a pine tree. The spirit of poesy even in his pain came upon him and he sang this little poem [1] in praise of the pine tree:

> O mine elder brother, the single pine tree
> That art on cape Ōtsu, which directly faces Owari!
> If thou single pine tree! wert a person,
> I would gird my sword upon thee,
> I would clothe thee with my garments,—
> O mine elder brother, the single pine tree!

He went on a little farther to Nobono and his sickness became more serious. And there in the open fields he felt that his end had come. He sent the spoils of his expedition to the temple of his great ancestress, the Sun Goddess. He sent his faithful companion Prince Kibi-no-Takehito to the emperor to carry his last message. It was: " I have chastised the eastern barbarians according to your imperial order with the help of the gods and with your imperial influence. I hoped to return in triumph

[1] See Chamberlain's translation of *Kojiki,—Asiatic Society Transactions*, vol. x., Supplement, p. 218.

with my weapons wrapped in white. But I have been seized with a mortal disease, and I cannot recover. I am lying in the sweet open fields. I do not care for my life. I only regret that I cannot live to appear before thee and make my report of my expedition."

And he died in the thirty-second year of his age. And they buried him there and built a mausoleum over his remains. The emperor lamented the death of his gallant and immortal son, and made an imperial progress into the regions which he had conquered and pacified.

The successor to the Emperor Keikō was known by the canonical name of Seimu. He was the thirteenth emperor, and was the grandson of his predecessor, having been a son of the hero Yamato-dake who was the crown prince until his death. The Emperor Seimu reigned fifty-nine years and died at the age of one hundred and eight. Nothing note-worthy is narrated of his reign.

His successor, the fourteenth emperor, was Chūai, his eldest son. He reigned only eight years and died at the age of fifty-two. It is remarkable that his capital was in the island of Kyūshū and not in the Main island, like his predecessors from the time of the Emperor Jimmu. This removal was probably due to the preparations which had already begun for the invasion of Korea. The island of Kyūshū is most favorably situated for the preparation and sailing of such an expedition. The wife of this emperor was Jingō-Kōgō, who was a much more forcible and energetic character than her husband.

She is one of the heroines around whom much tradition has gathered, and her successful invasion of
Korea is an event which the Japanese writers and
artists are never tired of representing. The legend
—for undoubtedly much of the story is legendary—
is essentially as follows:

The emperor was busy in Kyūshū in reducing to
subjection the tribes of the Kumaso who inhabited
the southern portion of the island. Up to this time
these restless tribes had given much trouble to the
empire and expeditions were constantly needed to
keep them in order. They were unquestionably of
a kindred race with the Japanese who accompanied
the Emperor Jimmu into the Main island. The
empress, afterward known as Jingō-Kōgō and the
faithful prime-minister Take-no-uchi [1] were at their
temporary palace at Kashihi. The empress in an interview on the campaign became divinely possessed.
And she spoke to the emperor in the name of the
deity that possessed her saying, " There is a land at
the westward, and in that land there is abundance of
various treasures dazzling to the eye, from gold and
silver downwards. I will now bestow this land upon
thee."

Then the emperor replied, " If you ascend to a
high place and look westward, no country is to be
seen; there is only the great sea." And he pushed
away the lute upon which he was playing and said,
" They are lying deities which have spoken to you."

---

[1] He is chiefly notable to foreigners because he is said to have
lived through the reigns of three emperors and to have reached the
age of three hundred years.

Then the deity was very angry and spoke again through the empress. "This empire is not a land over which thou art fit to rule. Go thou the one road."

The prime-minister Take-no-uchi then said to the emperor, " I am filled with awe, my heavenly sovereign, at this fearful message. I pray thee continue playing thy august lute." Then he played softly ; and gradually the sound died away and all was still. And they took a light and looking in his face, behold he was dead.

The empress and the prime-minister Take-no-uchi concealed for the time the death of the emperor, and she herself proceeded to carry out the plan for the invasion of Korea. With indefatigable energy she gathered her forces and equipped a fleet for the descent upon Korea. She set out from Wani in Kyūshū in the tenth month of the year A.D. 202. Even the fish of the sea were her allies, for with one accord they bore the ship in which she sailed across the intervening straits on their backs.

The coming of the Japanese was a complete surprise to the people of Korea. At this time the peninsula now known to us as Korea and to the Japanese as Chōsen, was divided into three kingdoms, Kōrai, Shiraki, and Kudara. The fleet of Jingō-Kōgō landed in the kingdom of Shiraki. The king was so completely unprepared for this incursion that he at once offered his subjection and proposed to become a tributary kingdom. The proposition was accepted. The kings of Kōrai and Kudara made similar proposals which also were accepted.

Each was to make an immediate contribution to the empress, and annually thereafter to send tribute to the capital of Japan. Thus they became the three tributary countries (*sankan*) dependent on Japan. Although this invasion of a foreign country without cause or provocation must be pronounced indefensible, yet it is not unlikely that the subject kingdoms were quite as safe and free under the distant and little intermeddlesome dominion of the Japanese empire, as they had been in the past or were likely to be in the future from their troublesome neighbors, China and the restless Mongolian tribes. To Japan the connection with the continent was of momentous value. It opened up a natural and easy way for the influx of those continental influences which were to be of so great service in their future history.

The empress, having within three years completely accomplished the object of her expedition, returned with her fleet to Kyūshū. She brought back with her hostages from the conquered kingdoms, to ensure their fulfilment of the promises they had made. She had learned many lessons of government which she was not slow to introduce into her administration at home. Soon after reaching Kyūshū she was delivered of the son of whom she was pregnant at the time of the death of the emperor, and who afterwards became the Emperor Ōjin.

The object which she and her faithful prime-minister had in concealing the death of the emperor was accomplished. They now made the fact public, and proclaimed her own son as her successor. Two older sons of Chūai by another empress were unwilling to submit to the rule of a younger brother. But the Empress Jingō, who had now become a national idol by her Korean expedition, soon put down the conspiracy of these princes and reigned till the end of her life and left a quiet succession to her son.

She is said to have reigned as empress-regent[1] sixty-eight years, and to have died at the age of one hundred.

Her son became the fifteenth emperor and is known by the canonical name of Ōjin. He commenced his reign in the year A.D. 270, and reigned forty years and died at the age of one hundred and ten. But the beginning of his reign is reckoned in the government list from the death of his father. The Emperor Ōjin is widely worshipped as Hachiman the god of war, although he is by no means noted as a warrior. The explanation of this curious circumstance is found in the fact that his mother was pregnant with him during her famous invasion of Korea, and her heroism and success are attributed to the martial character of her unborn son.

The good fruits of the Korean conquest particularly showed themselves in A.D. 284, when the king of Kudara sent his usual tribute to the emperor of Japan. The ambassador for that year was Ajiki, a learned man who was familiar with Chinese literature. At the request of the emperor he gave the young prince, who afterwards became the Emperor Nintoku, lessons in the Chinese language and litera-

---

[1] She is not included in the government list of emperors, and is given in Appendix I. as empress-regent.

ture. The year following the king of Kudara seeing how much his efforts to furnish Chinese learning
were appreciated, sent an eminent Chinese scholar,
Wani, who took with him the *Confucian Analects* and
the *Thousand Character Essay*, two noted Chinese
classics and presented them to the emperor. The
prince continued his studies under Wani and became
a very learned man.

The emperor had three sons between whom he
wished to divide his authority, wishing however to
establish his youngest son as the crown prince and
his successor. He summoned them before him and
put this question to the elder, "Which should be
preferred, a younger son or an older?" Then the
elder son replied that he thought the older son
should be preferred. But the emperor turned to the
second son and asked him the same question. He
replied that as the older son was more grown and
less of a care, he thought the younger son would be
more of a favorite. The emperor was pleased with
this reply because it coincided with his own sentiment. He created his youngest son, Prince Waka-
iratsu, the crown prince and ordered his second son,
Prince Osasagi, to assist him. He gave the charge
of the mountains, rivers, forests, fields, etc. to his
eldest son.

So when the Emperor Ōjin died A.D. 310, the
younger son urged his brother to accept the imperial
power; but he declined, saying: "How can I disobey
the commands of my father?" The oldest of the
three brothers, learning of the controversy, undertook to secure the authority for himself by a plot.
The conspiracy was, however, soon put down and

the elder brother slain. The friendly dispute between the two other brothers lasted three years
and was finally ended by the younger committing
suicide, and thus devolving the imperial office on
his remaining brother. This brother was the noted
Emperor Nintoku. He began his reign in the year
A.D. 313, and died A.D. 399 in the one hundred and
tenth year of his age. He was a most careful and
considerate ruler. By observing his subjects he
was convinced that they were overburdened and
impoverished with the taxes which the government
collected from them. So he announced by an imperial decree that for three years all taxes should
be remitted. Even the sums which were necessary
to keep the palace in repair and to provide his court
with suitable clothing were not collected. And the
palace grew shabby, and its roof leaked, and he himself went about in coarse and cheap garments. And
the farmers came to him and begged that they might
contribute to his wants. But he refused, and suffered three years to pass. In the meantime the
country revived, and the farmers being relieved from
the burdens which they had so long borne entered
on a long period of encouraging prosperity. He
surveyed the land from a high outlook, and saw the
curling smoke and the fertile fields and rejoiced.
Then he gave commands, and the taxes were renewed, and the people paid them willingly, and they
in their gratitude called Nintoku the Sage Emperor.

It was in the reign of the Emperor Nintoku that
the noted prime-minister Prince Take-no-uchi is said
to have died. He had served six emperors, viz.:
Keikō, Seimu, Chūai, Jingō-Kōgō, Ōjin, and Nintoku.

His age[1] is given variously from two hundred and eighty-two to three hundred and eighty, in different books, one of which is a Chinese work and one a Korean. It will be remembered that he was the chief adviser of the warlike Empress Jingō in her invasion of Korea, and took an active part in the events which followed that expedition. That there was such a figure in Japanese history there can be little doubt, but that much of his life and the great age to which he lived are like many of the stories of the characters in the midst of which he lived, legendary and mythical, no one can question.

It was in this reign also that we have it stated that historiographers were sent out to the provinces and directed to make record of all important events and forward them to the court.

We have now reached a point in Japanese history where the accounts compiled by the historians of the times have written records on which to rely. The legendary and marvellous stories which have been the bulk of the preceding history may now be replaced by the soberer narrations which writing has preserved for us. It will be seen that the lives[2] of the emperors now drop from the astonishing age which in previous years they attained to a very moderate and reasonable length. In the subsequent chapters will be found the sober and chastened story to which Japanese history is henceforth reduced.

[1] See *Kokushian*, compiled under the Department of Education. *Ad Locum.*

[2] See Appendix I.

CHAPTER V.

NATIVE CULTURE AND CONTINENTAL INFLUENCES.

BEFORE going on to the meagre story which is supplied to us by the early years of Japanese history, it will be well to glean from the myths and legends which tradition has preserved the lessons which they contain. Although we may be unable to concede the truth of these traditions in their entirety, and believe in the celestial origin of the race and the wonders of the divine age, we may be able to obtain from them many important facts regarding the habits and manner of life of the early Japanese.

We have often referred to the admirable work Mr. Chamberlain has done in his translation of the *Kojiki*, and in the scholarly notes he has added. But in our present enquiries we must give him still greater credit for the important lessons which he has drawn from the myths and legends of the *Kojiki* in his learned introduction. No writer at the present day can afford to dispense with the deductions which he has been able to draw from the oldest writings of the Japanese, and from the traditions of an older date which these writings have preserved.

Relying therefore chiefly on this learned intoduc-
tion,[1] we propose to enumerate in a summary manner
the particulars concerning the early Japanese life.

In the first place the government of the early
Japanese was of the tribal order. The emperor was
the chieftain of an expedition which came from the
island of Kyūshū and established a government by
conquest. The chiefs of the various localities were
reduced to subjection and became tributary to the
emperor, or were replaced by new chiefs appointed
by the emperor. The government was therefore
essentially feudal in its characteristics. The emperor depended for the consideration of his plans
and for their execution upon officers who were attached to his court. There were guilds composed
of those who manufactured various articles, or who
were employed to execute special plans. Thus we
have guilds of clay image makers, guilds of ladies
attendant on the emperor, guilds of butlers, guilds
of cooks, guilds of guards, etc. To each of these
there was a captain who became by appointment
hereditary chief. We have no mention of money for
the payment of services rendered. The taxes were
probably paid in kind. And all transactions as far
as they are mentioned at all seem to have been of
the nature of barter.

The religious notions of the prehistoric Japanese
were founded on the myths relating to their ancestor. Notwithstanding the vast number of deities
who came into existence according to tradition,
most of them vanish as soon as they are named and

[1] *Transactions of the Asiatic Society of Japan*, vol. x., Supplement.

are no more heard of. Even deities like Izanagi and
Izanami, who are represented as taking so important
a part in events, are not perpetuated as objects of
worship in Japanese history, and have no temples
erected to their memory and no service prescribed
or maintained in their honor. The most important
deity in the Pantheon of the Japanese was Amaterasu-ō-mi-kami, who is also called in Chinese characters Tensho Daijin or the Sun Goddess. She appears
not only in the myths concerning the origin of the
Japanese race, but as the grandmother of the divine
prince Hiko-ho-no-ni-nigi, who first came down to
rule the Japanese empire. In the Shintō temples at
Isé the principal deity worshipped at Gekū is Uké-
moche-no-Kami, and the secondary deities Ninigi-
no-Mikoto, who came down to found the Japanese
empire and was the grandmother of the Emperor
Jimmu, and two others. At the Naikū the principal
deity is Amaterasu-ō-mi-kami (from heaven shining
great deity), also called the Sun Goddess, and two
secondary deities. The temples at Isé, especially
those that are dedicated to the Sun Goddess, are the
most highly regarded of any in Japan. Other
temples of considerable popularity are situated in
other parts of the empire. Thus there are Shintō
temples in Kyūshū and in Izumo, which are old
parts of Japan settled long before Buddhism was
introduced.

The Shintō religion must be regarded as the primitive religion of the Japanese people. It prevailed
among them long before Buddhism was propagated
by priests from Korea. It differs from all known

systems of religion, in having no body of dogma by which its adherents are held together. The greatest advocate of Shintoism, Moto-ori, a writer of the 18th century, admits that it has no moral code. He asserts that "morals [1] were invented by the Chinese because they were an immoral people, but in Japan there was no necessity for any system of morals, as every Japanese acted rightly if he only consulted his own heart."

Reference is frequently made in the early stories to divination, or the process of obtaining the will of the gods by indirection. The oldest method of divination was by using the shoulder-blade of a deer. It was scraped entirely free from flesh, and then placed over a fire made from cherry wood. The divine will was determined by the cracks caused by the fire in the bone. A later method of divination was by using the shell of a tortoise in the same way as the shoulder-blade of the deer was used. They had superstitions about fighting with the back to the sun; about using only one light in the house at once; about breaking off the teeth of a comb in the night-time; about the destination of the first arrow shot in battle, etc.

The superstition of impurity being attached to the mother at the birth of a child, and to the house and those associated with it in which a death occurred, is often mentioned. A mother, when about to be delivered, was required to retire alone into a separate dwelling or hut without windows. This cruel cus-

[1] E. M. Satow, *Transactions of the Asiatic Society of Japan,* vol. ii., p. 135.

tom has prevailed in the island of Hachijō [1] down almost to the present time. A custom prevailed, also, of abandoning the dwelling in which a death had occurred. The dead body was removed to a mourning hut, where amid sobs and weeping the mourners continued to hold a carousal, feasting upon the food provided for the dead. This abandonment of the house occupied by the living may explain the custom, so often referred to, of each new emperor occupying a different palace from that of his predecessor. We have already referred to the dreadful custom which prevailed until the reign of the Emperor Suinin, of burying living retainers around the sepulchre of their dead master. The custom was replaced by burying clay images of servants and animals around the tomb, and this continued till about A.D. 700.

There is no evidence that children received any kind of education other than a training in the use of arms and implements. The art of writing was brought over from Korea in A.D. 284. Up to this time there is nothing to show that the Japanese possessed any means of recording the events which occurred. No books existed, and reading and writing were unknown. The language spoken by the people was an ancient form of that which now prevails. The earliest examples of this language are found in the songs preserved in the *Kojiki* and *Nihongi*. As in every language, the earliest preserved specimens are poetry, so in Japanese the fragments which have

[1] E. M. Satow, *Transactions of the Asiatic Society of Japan,* vol. vi., p. 435.

been remembered and brought down to us, are scraps of songs. The origin of this language is, like the origin of the race, impossible at present to verify. It seems plain that the race came from the continent by way of Korea. If this is to be taken as the origin of the race, then the language which developed into the Japanese came from the northern tribes of China and of Siberia.

There is no indication of the method by which the early Japanese reckoned time. The sun in the day-time and the cocks by night, must have given them their division of hours. The year made itself apparent by the changes of temperature. It was not, however, till the introduction of calendars from China that anything like an accurate system of estimating and recording time was introduced.

The food of the primitive Japanese was much more largely animal than it became in later times. To the early Japanese there was no restriction in the use of animal food, such as the Buddhists introduced. Fish and shell-fish have always been, and doubtless from the first were, principal articles of food. The five grains, so called, are often referred to, and are specially mentioned in the Shintō rituals, whose origin goes back to prehistoric times. These grains[1] are rice, millet, barley, and two kinds of beans. Silk-worms and their food plant, the mulberry, are likewise spoken of. The only kind of drink referrrd to is *saké*. It will be remembered that in the myth concerning the Impetuous Male Deity in Izumo,

[1] Satow, "Ancient Japanese Rituals," *Asiatic Society Transactions*, vol. vii., p. 423.

the old man and old woman were directed to prepare eight tubs of *saké*, by drinking which the eight-headed serpent was intoxicated. In the traditional history of the emperors, they are represented as drinking *saké*, sometimes even to intoxication. And in the rituals recited when offerings are made to their deities, the jars of *saké* are enumerated among the things offered. The Japanese writers claim that *saké* was a native discovery, but there is a well supported belief that in very early times they borrowed the art of manufacturing it from the Chinese. There is at least a difficulty in believing that this liquor should have been invented independently in the two countries. Chopsticks are mentioned in early Japanese times, and clay vessels for food, and cups for drinking made of oak leaves. On the whole, the conclusions to be drawn from the earliest traditions concerning the Japanese lead us to regard them as having attained a material degree of civilization in all matters pertaining to food and drink. Yet it cannot be regarded as other than strange that milk, cheese and butter are nowhere mentioned, and had never been used.

In the matter of clothing we have little except hints to guide us in forming inferences. The rituals enumerate[1] "bright cloth, soft cloth, and coarse cloth." Mr. Satow remarks[2] on this enumeration that "in the earliest ages the materials used were the bark of the paper-mulberry (*broussonetia papyrifera*), wistaria tendrils and hemp, but when the

[1] E. M. Satow, *Asiatic Society Transactions*, vol. vii., p. 109.
[2] Ditto, p. 119.

silkworm was introduced the finer fabric naturally
took the place of the humbler in the offerings to the
gods." The paper-mulberry which is now used for
making paper, was in early times twisted into a
thread and woven into a very serviceable cloth.
Cotton[1] which now furnishes so large a part of the
clothing of the people is nowhere mentioned. The
skins of animals were doubtless used as clothing before the introduction of Buddhism made the killing
of animals uncommon. In the legend of the purifi-
cation of Izanagi[2] we read of a girdle, of a skirt, of
an upper garment, of trousers, and of a hat. What
the shapes of these garments were we cannot tell,
but the number of different garments indicates a considerable development in the ideas of clothing. In
the same myth, and in many other places, mention
is made of the bracelets which Izanagi wore on the
left and right arm. And when he wished to show
his pleasure in the daughter who had been produced
in washing his left eye, he invested her with his necklace taken from his own neck. Jewelry seems in
these prehistoric times to have been more commonly worn than in modern historical times. The
jewels[3] used were the *magatama* and *kudatama*
which have been found in the ancient burial places.

---

[1] Cotton is said to have been brought to Japan from India in the
reign of the Emperor Kwammu, A.D. 800. T.B. Poate, *Transactions
of the Asiatic Society of Japan*, vol. iv., p. 146.

[2] *Transactions of the Asiatic Society of Japan*, vol. x., Supplement, pp. 39 and 40.

[3] Henry von Siebold, *Japanese Archæology*, Yokohama, 1879,
p. 16. The diagram in the text is from this work on Archæology,
and shows the variety of jewels in use in prehistoric times.

MAGATAMA AND KUDATAMA.

Rings have also been found which are believed to date back to prehistoric times. From the clay images which have come down to us it is now ascertained that the rings were worn as ornaments to the ears and never as rings to the fingers. These rings are of copper or bronze, plated with gold or silver. Combs and mirrors are spoken of, but how the metal mirrors are made we do not know.

The only indications of the character of the houses[1] used by the early Japanese are found in the traditions respecting the primitive Shintō temples. The early methods of building were perpetuated in these temples, and in the eighteenth century a very persistent effort was made for the revival of pure Shintō. Under the influence of this movement the temples at Isé and elsewhere were purified from the contaminations which had been introduced by Buddhism. After the close of the war which resulted in the restoration of the emperor to his proper authority in 1868 a small temple in the most severe Shintō style was built at Kudan, one of the picturesque heights of Yedo, in memory of the soldiers who perished in the conflict. From a careful examination of all that can illustrate the houses of the early Japanese, we infer that they were of extreme simplicity. Stone was never used. The structures were entirely of wood. Even the palaces of the emperors were what we would call merely huts. Four upright posts sunk in the ground formed the corners. At the half-way intervals between these posts, were planted four other posts; those at

[1] For the so called cave dwellings see p. 68.

the gable ends were high enough to sustain the ridge pole. On the other sides on the top of the posts were laid two plates. Abutting on these plates and crossing each other at the ridge pole stood the rafters, which sustained the thatched roof. In the absence of nails and pins, the timbers were fastened together by the tough tendrils of climbing plants. A hole in the gable end permitted the escape of the smoke from the fire built on the ground floor. Around the sides of the interior stood a raised couch on which the occupants sat by day and slept at night. The other parts of the floor were uncovered and consisted only of earth. They used mats made from the skins of animals or from rushes, on which they sat and slept. The doors of their dwellings were fastened by means of iron hooks, and swung on hinges unlike the modern Japanese door which always is made to slide.

The agricultural plants spoken of are numerous but leave unmentioned many of the plants of first importance. Tea, now so extensively cultivated, is nowhere spoken of. Tobacco was a late importation and came in with the Portuguese in the sixteenth century. Cotton was not introduced, as we have already said, until the beginning of the ninth century. Potatoes, including both the sweet potato and the white potato, are unmentioned. The orange came to Japan according to the received tradition at the close of the reign of the Emperor Suinin (A.D. 29–70).

Very little is said of the implements used by the primitive Japanese. Metal of any kind was almost unknown. We read of swords and fish-hooks, but these are the only implements referred to which seem to have been made of metal. Pots and cups of earthenware were used. The axes which they must have used to cut down the trees for building and for fuel must have been of stone, or sometimes of deer's horn. Archæologists both native and foreign have brought to light many ancient implements of the Stone age. An interesting and detailed account of these discoveries will be found in the work on *Japanese Archæology* by Henry Von Siebold, Yokohoma, 1879.

The arms used by the warriors were spears, bows and arrows, and swords. Numerous arrow heads have been found which bear a striking likeness to those found in Europe and America. Spear heads of flint have also been found. That the people were emerging from the Stone age is shown by the swords made of metal which they are represented as habitually using. They also seem to have had a small sword or dagger, as in the myth of the traitorous plot entered into by the empress and her brother against the Emperor Suinin. Castles in the modern sense are not referred to, although the same word *shiro* is used to represent the stockades with which they protected themselves. The castles of modern times, such as those at Kumamoto, Owari, and Yedo, are without doubt the outgrowth of the primitive stockade, and the same name has continued to be applied in all the successive changes.

Few domestic animals are mentioned. The horse is spoken of as an animal for riding, but not for driving. The same thing may be said of the use of horses in Japan even until modern times. The domestic fowl is referred to in the myth of the disappearance of the Sun Goddess. Dogs are mentioned in the later parts of the traditional period, but not cats. The cow and the products of the cow are not referred to. To these domestic animals may be added the cormorant,[1] which was used for fishing, in the same way that it is used in the eastern parts of China and to a small extent in the waters of Owari and Mino at the present time. The wild animals of that day were the deer, the bear, the boar, the hare, etc. These animals were hunted for their flesh and for their skins.

The islands of Japan being largely interspersed with water much of the travel even from the earliest time was performed in boats. The expedition of Jimmu from the island of Kyūshū was in part conducted in the boats which the colony had constructed for the purpose. Whether these boats were of the form now used in Japan it is impossible to determine. It is probable however that the present form of boat is an evolution of the primitive boat, which was used by the prehistoric Japanese and which was a part of the equipment with which their ancestors came over from Korea to the islands of Japan. Travel on land was principally on foot, although as we have said the horse was used at this early day for riding. No wheeled vehicle is mentioned. The bullock cart used in later times was restricted to the use of the imperial household, and probably was introduced by the

[1] *Asiatic Society Transactions*, vol. v., p. 110.

Buddhists. There were government roads constructed from the home provinces in different directions to those more distant. It is said that this scheme was more fully carried out after the return of the Empress Jingō from her conquest of Korea.

Let us now turn from these evidences of native culture to the events of Japanese history which have to do with the introduction of the civilization from the continent. For three thousand years before the Christian era China has been looked upon as one of the cultured nations of the earth. No written language has ever been or is now understood by so many people as the Chinese. The Chinese were a civilized people centuries before the Japanese had, even according to their own uncertain legends, emerged into the light as an empire. If we accept the opinion which seems most reasonable, that the Japanese came over to the Japanese islands from the continent by way of Korea, and belong to the Mongol tribes of central Asia, then we must assume that the Japanese were closely related to a large section of the Chinese. They have been from the beginning of their history a receptive people. They have stood ready to welcome the good things which were offered to them, coming from whatever direction. They accepted eagerly the Chinese written language and the philosophy with which it came charged. They accepted Buddhism with its priesthood and dogma and ritual, and permitted it to crowd their native religion until it became a pitiful minority. They have in recent times accepted with a hearty impetuosity the civilization of western nations, and are absorbing it as rapidly as the habits and thoughts of a people can take in so important a change.

We have already referred to the first introduction [1] of Chinese literature into Japan. It took place in the reign of the Emperor Ōjin A.D. 284. The ambassador who brought the tribute from Korea that year was Ajiki who was familiar with the Chinese literature. He gave lessons in Chinese to the crown prince. The next year the king of Korea sent out an eminent scholar named Wani,[2] who continued to give instruction to the crown prince. From this time a knowledge of Chinese gradually spread and scholars were attached to the government to make a written record of the events which took place. Historiographers were sent out during the reign of the Emperor Hanzei, A.D. 404, who were directed to make a record of all important events and forward them to the court. These steps soon began to show themselves in the absence of the wonderful and legendary from the narrative of events. Beginning with the reign of the Emperor Richū the ages of the emperors which before his time had been of such a marvellous length now drop to a reasonable and moderate period.

The nineteenth emperor was Inkyō, the fourth son of the Emperor Nintoku. He was of an amiable

[1] See p. 32.

[2] In the *Kojiki* it is said that the king of Kudara sent with Wani the *Confucian Analects* in ten volumes and the *Thousand Character Essay* in one volume. It conflicts seriously with the chronology of this period to learn, as both Mr. Satow and Mr. Chamberlain have pointed out, that the *Thousand Character Essay* was not written until two centuries after the date assigned to the advent of Wani.

and philanthropic temperament, and accepted the position of emperor with great reluctance. His health was delicate, and he feared to take upon himself such a responsibility. In the meantime there was an interregnum, and the court officials were anxious to have him enter upon the duties of emperor. At last he consented and became emperor A.D. 412. It was during his reign that confusion arose concerning the family names, or rather, that the confusion which had been long growing now had its settlement. Family names had been a matter of growth, and many persons claimed the right to use a certain name who were in no wise entitled to it. The emperor took a singular and effectual method to settle the troublesome and personal questions that arose. He summoned all those who claimed to belong to any family whose claim was disputed to appear at Amakashi and show that they were entitled to the names they claimed. He placed jars of boiling water and required each one to plunge his hand in the water. He who was injured by the hot water was pronounced a deceiver, and he who came off unhurt was pronounced as entitled to the name. The emperor took occasion to settle the questions concerning names, and put the matter on a more stable basis. And as the art of writing now began to be more common among the people mistakes in regard to names did not again seriously recur.

The emperor's ill-health was the occasion for the introduction of another of the civilizing arts of the continent. When the annual tribute from Korea was sent it so chanced that the ambassador who came with it was a person versed in the medical art. If we estimate this man's science or skill by that of the Chinese practitioner of a later day, we should certainly not place a very high value on it. It is narrated, however, that he cured the imperial invalid, and by this means gained great credit for his profession, and added another to the obligations which Japan owed to the continent.

After the death of the Emperor Inkyō there was a quarrel about the succession between his two sons, Prince Kinashi-no-Karu and Prince Anaho-no-Ōji. The courtiers all favored the latter, who was the younger brother, and he surrounded his elder brother in the house of Monobe-no-Omai. Seeing no way of escape he committed suicide.[1] The younger brother then became the twentieth emperor, who is known under the canonical name of Ankō. He had another difficulty growing out of social complications. He wanted to make the younger sister of Okusaka-no-Ōji, who was the brother of the preceding Emperor Inkyō, the wife of Ōhatsuse-no-Ōji, his own younger brother, who afterwards became the Emperor Yuriyaku. He sent as a messenger the court official, Ne-no-Ōmi, to ask the consent of her elder brother, who gladly gave it, and as a token of his gratitude for this high honor he sent a rich necklace. Ne-no-Ōmi, overcome with covetousness, kept the necklace for himself, and reported to the emperor that Okusaka-no-Ōji refused his consent. The emperor was very angry, and sent

[1] The *Kojiki's* statement is that the elder brother was banished to Iyo.

7

a detachment of troops against the supposed offender. They surrounded the house and put him to death. His chief attendants, knowing his innocence, committed suicide by the side of their dead master. The emperor then completed his design of taking the sister of Okusaka-no-Ōji as the wife of the Prince Ōhatsuse-no-Ōji, and he also took his widow and promoted her to be his empress.

Out of these circumstances arose serious troubles. His new empress had a young son by her first husband named Mayuwa-no-Ō, said to have been only seven years old. With his mother he was an inmate of the palace, and was probably a spoiled and wayward boy. The emperor was afraid lest this boy, when he came to understand who had been the cause of the death of his father, would undertake to revenge himself. He talked with the empress about his fears and explained his apprehensions. The boy accidentally heard the conversation, and was probably stimulated thereby to do the very thing which the emperor feared. Creeping stealthily into the room where the emperor lay asleep he stabbed him and then fled, taking refuge in the house of the Grandee Tsubura. The emperor was fifty-six years of age at the time of his death. This tragical event produced a great excitement. The younger brother of the emperor, Ōhatsuse, amazed and angry because his two older brothers were not, as he thought, sufficiently enraged by the murder of the emperor, killed them both. Then he attacked the Grandee Tsubura and the boy Mayuwa in their refuge. Seeing no way of escape Tsubura, at the request of the boy, first slew him and then killed himself.

Subsequently Ōhatsuse, who seemed to have been of a violent disposition, murdered Ichinobe-no-Oshiha, son of the seventeenth emperor, Richū. His two sons, then merely boys, Ōke and Woke (literally big basket and little basket), hearing of this catastrophe escaped into the province of Harima where they worked as cow-herds. Ōhatsuse was crowned as the twenty-first emperor and is known by the canonical name of Yūriyaku Tennō.

In the year A.D. 470 an ambassador came from Go in China and by order of the emperor was entertained by the Grandee Ne-no-Ōmi. A court official, Toneri, was directed to see that this duty was suitably performed. Now Ne-no-Ōmi, it will be remembered, was the grandee who, on a former occasion, was sent by the Emperor Ankō to solicit the hand of the Princess Hatahi-no-Ōji for the present emperor, who was then the crown prince. In order to entertain the Chinese ambassador with becoming magnificence, Ne-no-Ōmi robed himself in a gorgeous manner and among other things put on the rich necklace which he had stolen. Toneri reported to the emperor the superb entertainment which Ne-no-Ōmi had accorded to the Chinese ambassador, and especially the necklace which he wore. The emperor innocently asked that Ne-no-Ōmi should appear before him in order that he might see his superb dress. The empress, who was with her husband when Ne-no-Ōmi came in, recognized the necklace which had been sent by her brother to the late emperor. The theft was charged and Ne-no-Ōmi compelled to confess. The emperor proclaimed the innocence of Okusaka-no-Ōji and his great regret at the mistaken punishments.

There are many traditions current in Japanese early history concerning this emperor. In one he is represented in his imperial journeys to have seen a house belonging to Lord Shiki built with a raised roof like that of the imperial palace. He was greatly enraged that any subject should dare to take such a liberty, and sent his attendants to burn the house down. The poor frightened lord hastened to the emperor and humbly apologized for his stupidity. And he presented to the emperor in token of his humble submission a white dog clothed with cloth and led by a string. So he was forgiven and his house was spared.

In another legend he is said to have come upon a beautiful girl by the river side washing clothes. He stopped and conferred with her, and said to her, " Do not thou marry a husband, I will send for thee." With this he returned to the palace and forgot about his promise. But the poor girl did not forget. Year after year passed, till at last after eighty years of waiting she was a very old woman. Then she thought, " My face and form are lean and withered, there is no longer any hope. Nevertheless, if I do not show the Heavenly Sovereign how truly I have waited, my disappointment will be unbearable." And so with such gifts as she could afford she presented herself before the emperor. He wondering at her and her gifts asked her, " What old woman art thou, and why art thou come hither ? " She replied, " Having in such and such a month and such and such a year received the Heavenly Sovereign's commands, I have been reverently awaiting the great command until this day, and eighty years have passed by. Now, my appearance is decrepit and there is no longer any hope. Nevertheless, I have come forth in order to show and declare my faithfulness." Thereupon the Heavenly Sovereign, greatly agitated, exclaimed, " I had quite forgotten my command ; and thou mean-while, ever faithfully awaiting my commands, hast vainly let pass by the years of thy prime. It is too pitiful." He sent her back to her home with such consolation as rich gifts could impart.

We give one more of the legends which cling to the name of this emperor.

He was making an imperial progress to the moor of Akizu for the purpose of hunting. And as he sat down to rest a horse-fly bit his august arm. But immediately a dragon-fly came and seized the horse-fly and flew away. Thereupon he composed an august song as follows :

> Who is it tells in the great presence that game is lying on the peak of Womuro, at Mi-Yeshinu ? Our Great Lord who tran-quilly carries on the government, being seated on the throne to await the game, a horse-fly alights on and stings the fleshy part of his arm fully clad in a sleeve of white stuff, and a dragon-fly quickly eats up the horse-fly. That it might properly bear its name, the land of Yamato was called the Island of the Dragon-Fly.[1]

After a long reign Yūriyaku is said in *Kojiki* to have died at the age of one hundred and twenty-four.

[1] The name, " Island of the Dragon-Fly " had already been given to the Main island by Jimmu Tenno.

The son of the Emperor Yūriyaku, Prince Shiraka, succeeded him. He is known in history as the Emperor Seinei. He lived only five years after his accession and left no descendant to fill the throne. Search was accordingly made for some one of imperial blood who might become emperor.   It will be remembered that the Emperor Yūriyaku, before his accession, had murdered Prince Ichinobe-no-Oshiwa, son of the eighteenth emperor, and that his two sons, then young boys, Princes Ōke and Woke, made their escape into the province of Harima.   A new governor of this province had just arrived and was in attendance at the festivities in honor of the opening of a new cave[1] by a citizen of the place.   As usual there was feasting, and drinking, and dancing. The two young men Ōke and Woke, who occupied menial positions in this household, were called upon to dance.   After some hesitation they each in succession danced and sang some of the songs which they had learned in their boyhood.[2]   The new governor recognized these songs to be such as were taught at the court, and on enquiring found the young men to be grandsons of the Emperor Richū. He brought them to the palace and presented them to their aunt Queen Ii-Toyo.   After a friendly contest between the two brothers, the younger one, Prince Woke, became the twenty-third emperor

[1] In these early days a *muro* or excavation of the earth, roofed with timber, was often used as a residence. See p. 68.

[2] In this story the princes are represented as boys, but as they fled on the murder of their father by the Emperor Yūriyaku before his accession, this must have been at least twenty-eight years before ; so that they could nor have been less than forty years of age.

under the canonical name of Kenzō. His reign was
a very short one, only eight years according to the
Kojiki and three years according to the *Nihongi*. The
only incident of consequence recorded of him is that
he sought out the burial place of his father, who had
been murdered by the Emperor Yūriyaku, and transferred his remains to a fitting mausoleum. He also
contemplated the desecration of the mausoleum of
the murderer as a mark of his vengeance, but was
dissuaded by his brother from the undertaking.

He died without children and was succeeded by
his elder brother Prince Ōke who became A.D. 488
the twenty-fourth emperor under the canonical name
of Ninken.

Concerning the emperor and several of his successors there is little of interest to record. The
twenty-fifth emperor, Muretsu (A.D. 499), who was a
son of the emperor Ninken, was chiefly notable for
his cruelty. Some of the acts recorded of him can
only be equalled by those of the degenerate occupants of the imperial throne of Rome in its worst
days. He reigned eleven years and died without
children. The twenty-sixth emperor was Keitai
Tennō, who was the fifth descendant from Ōjin
Tennō. The only noticeable events in his reign
were an expedition to Korea to settle difficulties
which had then intervened, and an expedition to
Chikushi, the northern part of Kyūshū, to repress
tumults which had arisen. The next emperors were
Ankan Tennō and Senkuwa Tennō, whose reigns
were uneventful.

The twenty-ninth emperor was Kimmei Tennō,

(A.D. 540–571), who was the son of Keitai Tennō. He reigned thirty-two years and died at the age of sixty-three. It was during his reign, in A.D. 552, that an ambassador from Kudara, one of the three provinces of Korea, presented to the emperor an image of Shaka, and also Buddhist books explaining the doctrine. He commended highly the new religion, and the emperor was deeply impressed with its novelties. This seems the more probable because up to this time Japan looked upon China and Korea as leaders in civilization, and therefore was disposed to regard what had obtained a footing there as worthy of acceptance.

The prime-minister Soga-no-Iname favored the new religion, and urged that the image of Shaka which had been brought over should be duly set up and worshipped. But the ministers Monobe-no-Okoshi and Kumako opposed the proposition, saying, "Our country has its own gods; and they perhaps will be angry with us if we pay our devotions to a foreign god."

But the emperor settled the matter by saying, "Let Iname try it." He gave the idol to Iname with the directions that he should set it up and pray to it. Accordingly Iname took the image of Shaka and established it in a house of his own, which he created a temple, and worshipped it.

But shortly after this an epidemic broke out in the country, and Okoshi and Kumako declared that it was due to the strange god which had been received from the western barbarians, and besought the emperor to have it thrown away. The image therefore by the emperor's command was thrown into the sea near Naniwa,[1] and the temple in which it had been erected was destroyed. This was the first movement towards the introduction of Buddhism.

In the reign of the thirtieth emperor, Bitatsu Tennō, A.D. 572, who was the son of Kimmei Tennō, Kudara again made a contribution of Buddhist emblems, viz.: books of Buddhist doctrine ; a priest of Ritsu sect ; a priest ; a nun ; a diviner ; an image maker ; and a Buddhist temple carpenter. These were all housed in the temple of Owake-no-O at Naniwa. Seven years after this two Japanese ambassadors who had been sent to Kudara brought back with them several Buddhist images of stone, which the Daijin Umako obtained as his possession. He built several Buddhist temples in which he placed the images and other precious relics which he had secured. He also built a pagoda and houses in which the priests and nuns resided. When Umako was sick he asked from the emperor that he might avail himself of the Buddhist ritual. The emperor gave him this privilege, but commanded him to restrict it to himself.

The Emperor Bitatsu died A.D. 585 at the age of forty-eight. His successor was Emperor Yōmei the thirty-first in order from the Emperor Jimmu. He was by his mother a descendant of the Soga family and his first wife was also a daughter of the prime-

---

[1] After the triumph of Buddhism a temple called Tennoji was erected near this place in honor of this image, which was miraculously rescued from the sea and is still preserved at this temple.

minister, the Noble Iname who was also of the Soga
family. The bitter hostility between the members
of the court who favored Buddhism and those who
opposed it continued. The leader of the former
party was Umako now the prime-minister, while the
opponents of Buddhism were led by Moriya. One
of the occasions when their hostility broke out was
when the emperor was taken sick and he wished to
try the effect of the Buddhist Sampō, that is, the
three precious elements of Buddhism, Buddha, the
rites of Buddhism, and the Buddhist priests. Moriya
and his party advised against this conformity to
Buddhism, but Umako supported him in his wishes
and introduced a Buddhist priest into the palace to
attend upon the emperor. In spite of all this effort,
however, the emperor died, having reigned only
three years.

The death of the emperor was the signal for the
breaking out of serious disturbances. Moriya the
champion of the old religion was killed and his
party overpowered. From this time Buddhism may
be said to have triumphed in Japan. The thirty-
second emperor, Sujun, was crowned A.D. 588. He
was the son of the Emperor Kimmei, and at the
time of his accession was sixty-nine years of age.
The communication with Korea continued, and more
and more of the Buddhist culture was introduced.
Umako, who now had undisputed sway in the
government, sent out to Korea persons to study the
Buddhist faith, and consecrated many priests and
nuns and erected temples for the new worship.

But everything did not move smoothly. Umako,

with all his zeal and enthusiasm for Buddhism, was suspected of personal ambition, and was looked upon with distrust. A plot to assassinate the emperor was planned by Umako, which terminated his life, after a reign of only four years, in the seventy-third year of his age.

The thirty-third sovereign was the Empress Suiko, who was the sister of the Emperor Yōmei. Her coronation took place A.D. 593. Her reign was chiefly remarkable for the active influence of Umaydo-no-Ōji (A.D. 572–622), who was the second son of the Emperor Yōmei, and who was made crown prince under the empress, and aided her in the administration of the political affairs of the government. This prince is better known by his posthumous title of Shōtoku Taishi (great teacher of the divine virtue), and is held in great reverence as the principal founder and promoter of Buddhism in Japan. His name has been linked with many legends, which are still current after the lapse of fourteen hundred years. It is said that as soon as he was born he was able to speak, and was in all respects a very clever boy. His memory was wonderfully acute. He had Napoleon the Great's talent of attending to several things at the same time. He could hear the appeals of eight persons at once, and give to each a proper answer. From this circumstance he sometimes went by the name of Yatsumimi-no-Ōji, that is, Prince of Eight Ears.

The prince threw the whole influence of the government in favor of Buddhism. Many temples were built in different central districts for the convenience of the new religion. Under his influence the officers of the government rivalled each other in founding temples and maintaining them at their own expense. He took as his teacher a priest who had recently come from Korea, and from him for the first time learned the five Buddhist commandments:

1. Against stealing.
2. Against lying.
3. Against intemperance.
4. Against murder.
5. Against adultery.

He gave command to an artificer in copper to make large images of Buddha for each of the officers in the government. The king of Koma in Korea hearing of this great undertaking sent a contribution of three hundred *ryō* of gold. The images were finished in due time and an imposing religious ceremonial was held in honor of the event. Many of the principal temples of Buddhism in different parts of Japan take their origin from the time of Shōtoku Taishi, and no single character in history is so intimately connected with the development of Buddhism.

It was not only as a religious reformer, however, that he deserves to be remembered. He was a a most painstaking and enlightened ruler. He studiously gathered from the Chinese the elements and methods of government and adapted them to his own country.[1] From his time the study of

[1] See the laws which he compiled and published as found in the 12th volume of *Dai Nihon Shi*, Appendix IV.

Chinese literature became the essential culture of the active minds of Japan.

Shōtoku Taishi died A.D. 622, having been the principal officer of the government for twenty-nine years.

The impulse which Shōtoku had given to Buddhism did not subside. In the year following his death officers were appointed to govern the growing religious communities, called Sosho and Sozu, which in dignity and power corresponded to archbishops and bishops in Christian nomenclature. The first archbishop was Kwankin, a priest from Kudara, and the first bishop was Tokuseki of Kurabe. These officials examined every priest and nun and made a register of them. A census of Buddhism is also given which belongs to this same period. According to this there were forty-six Buddhist temples and 1385 priests and nuns.

In the year A.D. 626, Soga-no-Umako the *daijin* and a life-long friend and promoter of Buddhism died, and two years later the Empress Suiko died. So nearly all the prominent participants in the events which had taken place since the first entrance of Buddhism into Japan, had disappeared. In the meantime a religion had taken possession of a field in which it was destined to exert a wide influence and undergo a national development.

Along with this religion had come a literature and a culture, which when absorbed into the life of this people gave them the permanent characteristics which we now recognize as the Japanese civilization. The freer and more frequent intercourse with China and

Korea brought with it not only a knowledge of books and writing, but many improvements in arts and many new arts and agricultural industries. When the forces of the Empress Jingō returned from Korea they brought with them persons skilled in many industrial occupations. It is a tradition that a descendant of the Kan dynasty in China had fled to Korea on the fall of that dynasty, and in the twentieth year of the Emperor Ōjin (A.D. 290) had migrated to Japan with a colony who were familiar with weaving and sewing. In the thirty-seventh year of the same emperor an officer was sent to China to obtain more weavers and sewers. The cultivation of the mulberry tree and the breeding of silk-worms[1] was introduced from China in A.D. 457, and in order to encourage this industry the empress herself engaged in it. At this early period this important industry was begun, or at least received an impulse which has been continued down to the present time.

With these industrial arts came in rapid succession the elements of a higher civilization. Books on almanac-making, astronomy, geography and divination were brought to Japan from Korea and China. The Chinese calendar[2] was first used in the reign of the Empress Suiko under the regency of Shōtoku Taishi. This almanac was based on the lunar periods and the civil year began with the new moon

[1] This must mean that improved methods of silk culture were introduced, for we have seen that this art was already known to the Japanese.

[2] Bramsen's *Japanese Chronological Tables*, Tokio, 1880, p. 18.

occurring about the beginning of February. But as the length of the civil year is not an exact multiple of the number of days contained in a lunation, the twelve lunar months used by the Chinese and Japanese will be about eleven days shorter than the solar year. Hence to prevent the discrepancy from increasing and throwing the seasons entirely out of their place in the calendar, an intercalary month was inserted nearly every third year. It was inserted not at the end of the year but whenever the discrepancy had reached the number of days in a lunation. The month thus inserted was called by the same name as the preceding with an explanatory prefix. From this period therefore the dates of Japanese events may be relied upon with some degree of certainty. For events occurring before this period, a knowledge of which must have been transmitted by oral tradition, the dates assigned to them in the *Nihongi* must have been computed by counting back to the supposed time according to the calendar in use at the time of the writing.

The astronomy and geography introduced into Japan along with almanac-making in the fifth century were without question very primitive sciences. At this time even in Europe the knowledge of these sciences was not advanced beyond the imperfect notions of the Greeks. It was not until the sixteenth century, when the discoveries of the Portuguese and the Spaniards and the English had revealed the shape and the divisions of the earth, and the Jesuits had carried this knowledge to China and Japan, that anything like a correct astronomy or geography was possible. By divination, which is mentioned as one of the sciences brought over from Korea, was meant the determination of future events or of lucky or unlucky conditions.

The most important civilizing force introduced from China at this period was the formal institutions of education. Although the first establishment of a school dates from the reign of the Emperor Tenji (A.D. 668–671), yet it was not till the reign of the Emperor Mommu (A.D. 697–707) that the university was regularly organized. Branch schools were also established in the several provinces. In the university there were departments for Chinese literature, for medicine, for astronomy and almanac-making, and for astrology. Under the first head were included the art of writing the Chinese characters, the practice of composition, the study of the Chinese classics, and the reading of books of Chinese history. In like manner the training of the students in medicine chiefly consisted in making them familiar with the methods which prevailed in China. The properties of medicinal plants, the variations of the pulse in health and disease and in the changing seasons, and the anatomy of the human body were the chief subjects of study. The human cadaver was never dissected, but a knowledge of anatomy was obtained from diagrams which were wholly hypothetical. In early times medical officers were appointed to experiment with medicines upon monkeys, and also to dissect the bodies of monkeys. From these dissections, as well as from the printed diagrams of Chinese books the imperfect knowledge which they had reached was derived. It was not till 1771 that

Sugita Genpaku [1] and several other Japanese scholars had an opportunity to dissect the body of a criminal, and by personal observation found the utter falsity of the Chinese diagrams on which they had hitherto relied, and the correctness of the Dutch books, which they had, contrary to the laws of the country, learned to read.

The great reverence felt for Chinese culture led to the introduction at an early date of the Chinese system of official rank. The system remained in force down to the restoration in 1868. The officers were *Daijō-daijin* (Prime-Minister), *Sa-daijin* (Minister of the Left), *U-daijin* (Minister of the Right), together with eight boards,[2] charged with the various duties of administration. These boards were divided into sections, and the various departments of the government were respectively performed by them. In this way the administration became thoroughly bureaucratic, in imitation of the Chinese empire, to which the Japanese at this time looked up with the most complete reverence.

In addition to these official boards, six official ranks were also introduced from China. These ranks were designated, first, virtue ; second, humanity ; third, propriety ; fourth, truth ; fifth, righteousness, and sixth, wisdom. Each of these ranks[3] was divided

---

[1] The author is indebted to the valuable paper read before the Asiatic Society of Japan by Willis Norton Whitney, M.D., for much of the information concerning medicine in Japan.—*Asiatic Society Transactions*, vol. xii., part iv., p. 329.

[2] For an enumeration of these boards and the officers and duties of each, see Walter Dickson's *Japan*, p. 72.

[3] See a note by Mr. Satow in Adams' *History of Japan*, London, vol. i., p. 24.

into two orders termed respectively the Greater and the Lesser. Thus there were twelve distinctions in this system. It was introduced in the reign of the Empress Suiko, A.D. 604, and is generally attributed to the Regent Shōtoku, who was a great admirer of the continental civilization. It existed in this form until the time of the Emperor Kōtoku, when, A.D. 649, it was extended to nineteen distinctions. These were not given to the individual in recognition of talent, but to families to be by them transmitted to their posterity as hereditary rank.

For many years during this period of active intercourse with China and Korea, Dazaifu, situated on the west coast of Kyūshū, north of the present situation of Nagasaki, was the recognized port where strangers were received. This city was the seat of a vice-royalty, having control over the nine provinces of Kyūshū. The office of vice-governor was considered a place of honorable banishment to which distinguished men who were distasteful at court could be sent.

These continental influences continued for many years and indeed have never ceased. There has always existed a class of scholars who looked upon Chinese learning as the supreme pinnacle to which the human mind could attain. This was especially true of the admirers of Confucius and Confucianism. Although it was not until a much later period that the culture of a Chinese philosophy attained its highest mark, yet even in the early arrangement of the studies in the university we see the wide influence which the writings of the Chinese classics exerted.

We close this chapter with an event which evinced the advance which Japanese civilization had made, and aided greatly in promoting this advance in the subsequent centuries. This event was the publication of the *Kojiki* (Record of Ancient Things) and the *Nihongi* (Chronicles of Japan). A book still older than these is said to have been composed in A.D. 620, but it perished in a fire in A.D. 645, although a fragment is said to have been rescued. The circumstances attending the preparation of the *Kojiki* are given by Mr. Satow in his paper [1] on the " Revival of Pure Shintō," and also by Mr. Chamberlain [2] in his introduction to the translation. The Emperor Temmu had resolved to take measures to preserve the true traditions from oblivion. He had the records carefully examined and compiled. Then these collated traditions were one by one committed to one of the household officers, Hiyeda-no-Are, who had a marvellously retentive memory. Before the work of compilation was finished the emperor died ; but the Empress Gemmyō, who after an interval succeeded him, carried it on to its completion in A.D. 712. By her direction the traditions were taken down from Are's dictation in the form in which we now have them. It is by no means a pleasing or attractive work, even in the opinion of the Japanese. It is bald and archaic in its form and composition. It is, however, notable as being freer from the admixture of Chinese learning, and therefore a better index of the native culture of the race than the

---

[1] *Asiatic Society Transactions*, vol. iii., part i.
[2] *Asiatic Society Transactions*, vol. x., Supplement.

works which followed it.[1] Much of it consists of
mere genealogies of the emperors and naked state-
.nents of leading events, but there are besides this
many legends and poems which bear evidence of
having been handed down in essentially their present
form. As an authority for the chronology of the early
events it is, of course, of small value. It is evident
that where a narrative of events has been carried
through many centuries by tradition alone, without
written records to check or assist it, no dependence
can be placed on the chronology of the events, further than, perhaps, on the order of sequence.

Only eight years after the publication of the
Kojiki, a second work termed *Nihongi* or Chronicles
of Japan was issued. It was prepared by imperial
command and appeared in A.D. 720 in the reign of
the Empress Genshō. It differs from the older book
in being composed in the Chinese idiom, and in
being much more tinctured with the ideas of Chinese
philosophy. These two works, so nearly contemporaneous, both of them composed in so great a
degree of the legendary elements of Japanese history, must be looked upon as marking a distinct
epoch in the story of Japan.

[1] The *Kojiki* has been translated into English by Professor B. H
Chamberlain, *Asiatic Society Transactions*, vol. x., Supplement.

CHAPTER VI.

THE MIDDLE AGES OF JAPAN.

THE theory of the Japanese government during the greater part of its long career has been that of an absolute monarchy. The emperor was supposed to hold in his hands the supreme authority, and to dispose, as he saw fit, of honors and emoluments, offices and administrative duties. There was no fundamental law of succession, by which the order of accession to the throne was regulated. The reigning emperor usually selected during his lifetime some one of his sons, or, if he had no sons, some other prince of the imperial family, who became the crown prince during the life of the emperor, and on his death succeeded to the throne.[1] The selection was usually made with the concurrence of the officers of the court, and very often must be credited entirely to the preference of these officers. Sometimes the emperor died before the appointment of a crown prince had taken place. In this case the selection lay in the hands of the court officers, and many cases are recorded in the history of the em-

[1] See Mori Arinori's introduction to *Education in Japan*, New York, 1873, p. 17.

pire where serious disturbances arose between the partisans of different aspirants to the throne. These disturbances usually account for the *interregna* which are so often found between the reigns of successive sovereigns.

To the freedom which has prevailed, not only in the imperial house but also in all the families of the empire, in regard to the rights of succession, must be attributed the long and unbroken line which the imperial house of Japan is able to show. That a line of sovereigns should continue from the time of Jimmu down to the present without break by reason of the failure of children, is of course impossible. But the difficulty disappears when it is remembered, that in case of the failure of a son to succeed, the father provided for the want by adopting as his son some prince of the imperial family, and appointing him as his heir. With this principle of adoption must be mentioned the practice of abdication [1] which produced a marked and constantly recurring influence in the history of Japan. Especially was this the case in the middle ages of Japanese history. The practice spread from the imperial house downwards into all departments of Japanese life. Although the principle of abdication and adoption was probably brought from China and was adopted by the Japanese as a mark of superior culture, yet these practices were carried to a much greater extent in Japan than was ever thought of in their original

[1] See a paper on "Abdication and Adoption," by Mr. Shigeno An-Eki, translated by Mr. Walter Dening, in *Asiatic Society Transactions*, vol. xv., p. 72.

home. We shall see in the story of Japanese times the amazing and ludicrous extent to which the abdication of reigning sovereigns was carried. We shall witness even the great and sagacious Ieyasu himself, after holding the office of shōgun for only two years, retiring in favor of his son Hidetada, and yet from his retirement practically exercising the authority of the office for many years.

In A.D. 668 the Emperor Tenji[1] began a brief reign of three years. As he had been regent during the two preceding reigns, and chiefly managed the administration, very little change occurred after his accession to power. His reign is mainly remarkable for the first appearance in a prominent position of the Fujiwara family. The emperor appointed his counsellor Nakatomi-no-Kamatari as *nai-daijin* (private minister), an office next in rank after *sa-daijin*, and which was created at this time. Naka-tomi, was authorized to assume the family name of Fujiwara, meaning wistaria-field. The ancestor of this family, Nakatomi-no-Muraji,[2] was fabled to have come down from the celestial plains to the island of Kyūshū. The family therefore ranks with that of the emperor as the oldest and most honored in the empire. From the time of its establishment down to the present it has enjoyed many honors and privileges, and has played a very distinguished part in the history of the country. This family first be-

---

[1] His predecessor died A.D. 661, and there was an *interregnum* during which Tenji was regent till A.D. 668, when he was made emperor.

[2] See p. 47, note.

came prominent during the reign of the Emperor Kōtoku. The Soga family from the times of the first introduction of Buddhism had grown to be the most powerful and influential in the empire. Umako had held the position of *daijin* and his son Yemishi became *daijin* after his father's death. Yemishi presumed upon his promotion to this high office and put on the airs of hereditary rank. He built castles for himself and son and organized guards for their defence. His son Iruka became *daijin* after his father's death and conducted himself with even greater arrogance. At last his conduct became intolerable and he was assassinated A.D. 645. The chief actor in this plot was Nakatomi-no-Kamatari, who was at this time on intimate terms with the prince who afterwards became the Emperor Tenji.

Further experiences, this time disastrous, with Korea were encountered during this reign. A Japanese garrison had been maintained in Kudara, the western division of Korea. But at this time the people of Shiraki with help from China attacked this garrison and compelled it to retreat to Japan. Along with the Japanese came many of the Koreans who had been friendly with them, and who carried with them, like the Huguenots when driven from France, a knowledge of many arts and a culture which were eagerly welcomed by the rising Japanese empire. They were colonized in convenient quarters in different provinces, and as an encouragement freed from taxation for a time. Their influence upon the opening civilization of Japan cannot be overlooked or neglected in our estimate of the forces which con-

spired to produce the final result. In the book of
Japanese annals called *Nihon Shoki* there is a statement [1] that in the fifth month of the second year of
Reiki (A.D. 717) 1799 Koreans were collected together in the province of Musashi and formed the
district of "Koma-gōri" or Korean district. Again
in the third year of *Tempyō Hōji* (A.D. 760) forty inhabitants of Shinra (a kingdom of Korea) and thirty-
four priests and priestesses came to Japan and
founded the "Shinra-gōri," or Korean district.
These events occurred not long after the time we
are now considering and show that the Korean
colonization still continued and that the influence of
the arts and culture which the colonists introduced
was marked and important.

Few events are noted during the reigns which succeeded. The following are the most worthy of mention. The Emperor Temmu (A.D. 673–686) added several new degrees of rank to those already established.
He also favored the Buddhist religion by making its
services obligatory, and by forbidding the eating of
flesh. Silver was first discovered in Tsushima A.D.
674, which was followed twenty years later by the
manufacture of the first silver money. Copper was
discovered in Musashi in the reign of the Empress
Gemmyō (A.D. 708–715) and the making of copper
money came into vogue. Before that time the
copper money in use was obtained from Korea and
China. Gold coin is said to have been first issued
under the Emperor Junnin (A.D. 759–765). An

---

[1] Quoted in Henry von Siebold's *Japanese Archæology*, Yokohama
1879, p. 8.

observatory was established for the inspection of the
stars in connection with the new department of
astrology. The cultivation of the lacquer tree and
the mulberry and the raising of silk-worms were still
further encouraged and extended. Cremation was
first practised about A.D. 700 in the case of a Buddhist
priest who left directions that his body should be
burned. Since that time cremation has been employed for the disposal of the dead by the Shin (or
Monto) sect, and is now authorized but not made
obligatory by the government. The progress made
by Buddhism is shown by the census of temples
which was made in the reign of the Empress Jito
(A.D. 690–702) and which gave the number as 545.
The publication of the *Kojiki* in A.D. 712, and of the
Nihongi eight years later, has already been referred
to at the close of the preceding chapter. These
works are still looked upon as the foundations of
Japanese literature and the highest authorities of
Japanese history.

In the reign of the Empress Gemmyō (A.D. 710)
the imperial residence was fixed at Nara. Up to
this time the custom[1] derived from antiquity had
prevailed of changing the residence on the accession
of each new emperor. But the court continued at
Nara for a period of seventy-five years running
through seven reigns ; and in consequence Nara has
always been looked upon with peculiar reverence,
and is the seat of several of the most notable
Buddhist and Shintō temples[2] and structures. It is

[1] See p. 58.
[2] Satow and Hawes' *Handbook of Japan*, London, 1884.

here that Kasuga-no-miya was founded in A.D. 767 and dedicated to the honor of the ancestor of the Fujiwara family. Here also is Tō-dai-ji a Buddhist temple famed for containing the bronze statue of Great Buddha. This colossal idol was constructed in A.D. 736 under the Emperor Shōmu, during the time that the imperial court resided at Nara. The height of the image is fifty-three feet, being seven feet higher than the Daibutsu at Kamakura. The temple was built over the image and A.D. 1180 was destroyed by a fire which melted the head of the image. This was replaced. The temple was burned again A.D. 1567, from which time the image has remained as the Japanese say "a wet god."

In A.D. 794[1] during the reign of the Emperor Kwammu (A.D. 782–806) the capital was removed to Kyōto on the banks of the Kamogawa. The situation and the environs are lovely, and justify the affectionate reverence with which it has ever been regarded. Here were built the palaces and offices for the emperor and his court. It was officially called Miyako, that is, residence of the sovereign. It continued to be occupied as the capital until A.D. 1868, when the court was moved to Tōkyō. At this time the name of the city was changed to Saikyō, which means western capital, in distinction from Tōkyō, which means eastern capital.

The Emishi in the northern part of the Main island continued to give much trouble to the government. During the reign of the Emperor Shōmu (A.D. 724–756) Fujiwara-no-Umakai was sent against these restless neighbors and succeeded in reducing

[1] For ten years preceding 794 the capital was a wanderer.

them to subjection, which lasted longer than usual.
A fort was built to keep them in subjection, called
the castle of Taga.   There is still standing a stone
monument at Taga, between Sendai and Matsushima, on which is an inscription which has been
translated by Mr. Aston,[1] of the British legation.
The inscription gives the date of its first construction, which corresponds to A.D. 724, and of its
restoration, A.D. 762.   Mr. Aston points out that the
ri here mentioned is not the present Japanese *ri*
equivalent to miles 2.44, but the ancient *ri* which
is somewhat less than half a mile.   This makes it
evident that the part of the Main island north of a
point near Sendai was at this time denominated
Yezo, and was occupied by the barbarous tribes who
then as now called themselves Yezo.

The employment of a Fujiwara in this expedition
was probably purely perfunctory.   So far as we
know, this family, which had by this time risen to a
position of great influence, was in no respect military, and the appointment of Umakai as chief of the
forces sent against the Ainos was due to the political
prominence of his family.   For many centuries the
relations of the Fujiwara family to the imperial
house was most intimate.   Indeed the late Viscount
Mori,[2] in his introduction to *Education in Japan,*

---

[1] See the *Transactions of the Asiatic Society of Japan*, vol. viii.,
p. 88.   The inscription is in part as follows

Castle of Taga,

Distant from the capital	.	.	.	Ri	1500
Distant from the frontier of Yezo	.	.	"	120
Distant from Hitachi	.	.	.	.	"	412
Distant from Shimotsuke	.	.	.	"	274
Distant from Makkatsu	.	.	.	"	3000

[2] *Education in Japan*, New York, 1873, p. 17.

speaks of this relation as a "proprietorship." "The throne for a time became virtually the property of one family, who exclusively controlled it." This family was that of Fujiwara,[1] to which reference has already been made. The founder of this house, Kamatari, was a man of great talent and administrative ability, and his immediate successors were worthy of their ancestor's fame, and in succession filled the office of *daijin*. In this way the office came to be regarded as hereditary in the Fujiwara family. The office of *kuambaku*, also from about A.D. 880, became hereditary in the Fujiwara house. Owing to the great age and prominence of the family, it became customary to marry the emperors and princes of the imperial house to ladies taken from it, so that after a time the mothers and wives of the princes of the imperial house were without exception descendants of the Fujiwara, and the offices of the court were in the hands of this family. In this condition of things the abdication of emperors, before they had reigned long enough to learn the duties of their position, became the common practice. This vicious custom was encouraged by the Fujiwara, because it placed greater authority in their hands, and left them to conduct the administration without troublesome interference. The Emperor Seiwa (A.D. 859–880) commenced to reign when he was nine years of age, and abdicated when he was twenty-six.[2] Shujaku (A.D. 931–952) became

[1] See p. 47.

[2] These instances are taken from the paper on abdication and adoption, by Shigeno An-eki, as translated by Mr. Walter Dening, *Asiatic Society Transactions*, vol. xv., p. 74.

emperor when he was eight years of age and abdicated at the age of twenty-three. Toba became
emperor (A.D. 1108) at five years of age, and resigned
at the age of twenty. Rokujō was made emperor
(A.D. 1166) at the age of two and resigned at the
age of four. Takakura, who succeeded Rokujō
(A.D. 1169), was eight years of age and abdicated at
the age of nineteen. It often happened that there
were living at the same time several retired emperors,
besides the actual emperor.[1] Thus, in the period
when Ichijō began his reign at the age of seven
(A.D. 987), there were three retired emperors still
living, viz.: Reizei, who began to reign (A.D. 968) at
eighteen, and retired at twenty; Enyū, who began
to reign (A.D. 970) at eleven, and retired at twenty-
six; Kwazan, who began to reign (A.D. 985) at
seventeen, and retired at nineteen. At a period
somewhat later than the one now under consideration, during the reign of Go-Nijō, who had just been
made emperor (A.D. 1301) at seventeen, and who
retired at nineteen, there were four retired emperors
living. When the emperors retired they often went
into a Buddhist monastery, taking the title of *hō-ō*
or *cloistered emperor*. From this sacred seclusion
they continued many times to wield the powers of
government.

The object of this abdication was twofold. The
sovereigns themselves often became restless and dissatisfied in the constrained attitude which they were
compelled to maintain. If they were in the least

[1] See Chamberlain's *Things Japanese*, under the article on abdication. Yokohama, 1892.

ambitious to meet the requirements of their elevated position and realized in any degree the legitimate claims which their country had upon them, their natural efforts to take part in the administration were promptly checked, and they were reminded that it was unbecoming and unfitting for the descendants of the gods to mingle in ordinary earthly affairs. In this way it often fell out that the ablest of the emperors retired from the actual position of reigning emperor in order to free themselves from the restraints of etiquette and from the burden of *ennui* which held them captive. They assumed the dignity of retired emperors, and often from their retirement wielded a greater influence and exerted a far more active part in the administration of affairs than they ever had been able to do when upon the imperial throne.

Besides this motive which affected the occupants of the throne, there was a corresponding one which led the officers of the court to encourage and perhaps sometimes to compel the emperors to abdicate. These administrative officers, into whose hands the management of the government had fallen, were desirous to retain their authority, and therefore whenever an emperor exhibited signs of independence, or any disposition to think or act for himself, they contrived means to have him retire and leave in his place some inexperienced boy who could be more easily controlled.

In this kind of supervising statesmanship the Fujiwara family became, and for centuries remained, supreme experts. For a period of four hundred years, from A.D. 645 to 1050, they monopolized nearly all the important offices in the government. The wives and concubines of the feeble emperors were all taken from its inexhaustible *repertoire*. The men of the family, among whom were always some of administrative ability, found it a task of no great difficulty to rule the emperor who was supposed to be divinely inspired to rule the empire, especially when he was usually a boy whose mother, wife, and court favorites were all supplied from the Fujiwara family. This kind of life and environment could not fail to produce on the successive emperors a sadly demoralizing effect. They were brought up in an enervating atmosphere and their whole life was spent in arts and employments which, instead of developing in them a spirit of independence and a high ambition and ability to govern well the empire committed to them, led them to devote themselves to pleasures, and to leave to others less fortunate the duty of administering the affairs of government.

The same circumstances which demoralized the occupants of the imperial throne served in a certain though less degree to enervate and enfeeble the Fujiwara family. Although they sometimes appointed one of their number the commander of an expedition against the Emishi, or to put down fresh revolts in the island of Kyūshū, yet his duties were purely honorary. He usually remained at home and sent one or more of the active military chieftains to lead the forces against the enemy in the field. If the expedition was successful, however, the honorary commander did not forget to have himself duly promoted, and rewarded with additional lands and income.

Other families besides the Fujiwara, rose in these long and weary centuries to prominence, and seemed on the point of disputing the security of their position. Thus the Tachibana in the eighth century attained high honors and distinction. It was an old family, and even as far back as the legend of Yamato-dake [1] we find that a princess of the Tachibana family was his wife, who sacrificed herself in the bay of Yedo to appease the turbulent waters. It was Maroyé, a member of the Tachibana family and a favorite of the Emperor Shōmu (A.D. 724–756), who compiled the collection of ancient Japanese poetry called Man-yōshū or collection of Myriad Leaves.

Another family which attained prominence was the Sugawara. It originated in the province of Kawachi. The most noted representative of this family was Sugawara Michizané, who was first conspicuous as the teacher of the young prince who afterward became the Emperor Uda (A.D. 888–898). He was a brilliant scholar in Chinese, which was then the learned language of the East. Even down to modern times his family has been devoted to learning. The Sugawara [2] and Ōye families both had adopted literature as their hereditary profession, and the government made them an allowance for

[1] See p. 66 *et seq*.

[2] At the time that Dickson collected his statistics of the families of the court, two of the Sugawara family were teachers of the young emperor. Six families of *kuges* count their descent from the Sugawara. Dickson's *Japan*, London, 1869, p. 59.

9

the expenses[1] of those who might be pursuing their studies in the national university. The influence of Michizané over the emperor was marked and salutary. Under his wise tutelage Uda showed so much independence that the Fujiwara *Kwambaku* found means to lead him to abdicate in favor of his son, who became the sixtieth emperor, and is known under the historic name of Daigo. Michizané became the counsellor and was created *nai-daijin* under the new emperor, who at the time of his accession was only fourteen years old. But the *Kwambaku* Tokihira determined to free himself from the adverse influence of this wise and honest counsellor. So he had him sent in a kind of honorable banishment to Dazaifu, the seat of the vice-royalty of the island of Kyūshū. It is said that he died here in A.D. 903. There was a great re-action in regard to him after his death, and he was canonized under the name of Tenjin[2] (Heavenly god), and is held sacred as the patron saint of men of letters and of students. The twenty-fifth day of each month is kept as a holiday in schools, sacred to Tenjin-Sama, and the twenty-fifth of June as an annual *matsuri*.

But the families which finally displaced the Fujiwara from their position of supremacy were what were technically called the military families. The separation of officers into civil and military was

[1] See chapter on "Education in the Early Ages," by Otsuki Sinji, in *Japanese Education*, New York, 1876, p. 64.

[2] While I write these lines there is hanging before me a *kakemono* representing Sugawara Michizané, which it has been proposed to hang in every public school under the care of the Department of Education, as an emblem of the true scholarly temperament.

MICHIZANÉ.

131

made under the reforms introduced from China. The Fujiwara in the main restricted themselves to civil duties. Wherever it was necessary to send military expeditions against the barbarians of the north, or rebels in Kyūshū, or into the disaffected districts of Korea, commanders were selected from families devoted to military service. The Taira family was of this class. Hei is the Chinese equivalent of the Japanese name Taira, and is more often used in the literature of the times. The Taira family sprang from the Emperor Kwammu (A.D. 782–806) through one of his concubines. The great-grandson of Kwammu, Takamochi, received permission to adopt the name of Taira, and thus became the founder of the family. They were the military vassals of the crown for many generations.

A little later than the Taira arose another family, the Minamoto, whose equivalent Chinese name was Gen. It sprang from the Emperor Seiwa (A.D. 859–880). His son Tadazumi became minister of war. Tadazumi had two sons, who were granted the family name of Minamoto; the descendants of one of them, Tsunemoto, being created military vassals.

The almost constant wars in which the empire was engaged led to the extension of the military class. From the time now under discussion the military class came to be looked upon as a distinct and separate part of the population. It was composed of those who in the time of war showed an aptitude for arms, and who were most serviceable in the campaigns which they undertook. Gradually they became distinct from the agricultural peasantry, and by education and training came to look upon arms as their legitimate profession. They naturally attached themselves to the military commanders who led them in their various expeditions, and thus were in time regarded as the standing troops of the empire. This growth of a military class, whose commanders were restless and ambitious, gradually undermined the authority which the Fujiwara up to the tenth century had almost unrestrictedly exercised. The employment of commanders from the military families raised in them an ambition to share in the powers of government. The struggles which ensued, first between the Fujiwara and Taira, and then between the Taira and Minamoto, continued to keep the country embroiled for more than a century. The suffering and desolation resulting from these weary internecine wars can only be paralleled by such conflicts as that between the White and Red Roses in England, or the Thirty Years' War in Germany. Of these struggles it will be possible to give only an outline.

It has already been mentioned that the Taira family sprang from the Emperor Kwammu,[1] whose great-grandson, Takamochi received permission to take Taira as his family name. The Emperor Shirakawa tired of the arrogance of the Fujiwara in A.D. 1087 retired into a cloister, and from this seclusion continued to exercise a controlling influence in the conduct of affairs. Tadamori a descendant of Taira-no-Takamochi was a favorite in his court, and even had a *liaison* with one of his concubines.

[1] See p. 132.

The ex-emperor complaisantly informed the courtier that if the child to be born proved to be a daughter he himself would adopt it, but if a son then it should belong to Tadamori. Accordingly the child being a son was a Taira, and rose to great eminence as Taira-no-Kiyomori. Tadamori acquired for himself great credit by his successful expedition against Korean pirates who had cruised along the eastern coasts of Japan. In the troubles which subsequently arose in reference to the succession the Taira took an important part. The Emperor Toba, who succeeded to the throne in A.D. 1108 at the age of six, abdicated in A.D. 1123 at the age of twenty-six. Both his father, the ex-Emperor Horikawa, and his grandfather, the ex-Emperor Shirakawa, were still living in retirement. He was succeeded by his son the Emperor Shutoku in A.D. 1124, then six years old, who after reigning seventeen years abdicated. He had a son but was succeeded A.D. 1142 by his brother Konoye who was four years of age. This mature youth reigned thirteen years and died without abdicating. On his death-bed he adopted as the crown prince his brother Go-Shirakawa, thus displacing the lineal heir. The succession was now bitterly disputed. The Minamoto chiefly espoused the cause of the displaced heir, while Kiyomori and the Taira together with Minamoto-no-Yoshitomo supported Go-Shirakawa. In a battle fought A.D. 1156 Kyomori won the victory. This victory raised him to a pinnacle of power. He began a career of nepotism and patronage which was not inferior to that of the Fujiwara. The ex-Emperor Shutoku and his son were banished to the province of Sanuki where it is said that Shutoku died of starvation. Tametomo a member of the Minamoto clan who was famed for his great strength and for his skill in archery was sent as an exile to the island of Hachijō, southeast of the promontory of Izu. From this island he escaped, and it is a tradition that he made his way to the Ryūkyū islands where he rose to prominence and became the ancestor of the kings of these islands.

Yoshitomo of the Minamoto clan, who had sided with Kiyomori in the recent dynastic conflict was a brother of the Tametomo just mentioned. He was greatly offended by the violent use which Kiyomori made of the power which had come into his hands. With all the Minamoto and Fujiwara he conspired to overthrow the victorious and arrogant Taira. But Kiyomori suspecting the plans of his enemies took measures to counteract them and suddenly fell upon them in the city of Kyōto. Yoshitomo was obliged to save himself by fleeing to Owari, where he was assassinated by the agents of Kiyomori. The death of the head of the Minamoto only made the tyrant more determined to crush all opposition. Even the ex-Emperor Go-Shirakawa, who was a son-in-law of Kiyomori, but who showed some signs of disapproval, was sent into exile. Several of the sons of Yoshitomo were put to death; but Yoritomo then a boy of thirteen was saved by the interference of the mother-in-law of Kiyomori, and was sent into exile in the province of Izu, and put into the safe-keeping of two faithful Taira men, one of whom Hōjō Tokimasa will be heard of hereafter.

Besides the four sons of Yoshitomo by his wife, he had also three sons by a concubine named Toki-wa. She was a woman of great beauty, and for that reason as well as because she was the mother of the romantic hero Yoshitsuné, she has often been chosen by Japanese artists as the subject of their pictures. Tokiwa and her three children, of whom Yoshitsuné was then an infant at the breast, fled at the breaking out of the storm upon Yoshitomo and the Minamoto clan. They are often represented as wandering through a storm of snow, Yoshitsune being carried as an infant on the back of his mother, and the other two little ones pattering along with unequal steps at her side. In this forlorn condition they were met by one of the Taira soldiers, who took pity on them and gave them shelter. From him they learned that Kiyomori had taken the mother of To-kiwa prisoner, and held her in confinement, knowing that this would surely bring back to him the fair fugitive and her children. In the Chinese teachings of that day, in which Tokiwa had been educated, the duty of a child to its mother was paramount to that of a mother to her child. So Tokiwa felt that it was unquestionably her duty to go back at once to the capital and surrender herself in order to pro-cure the release of her mother. But her maternal heart rebelled when she remembered that her babes would surely be sacrificed by this devotion. Her woman's wit devised a scheme which might possibly furnish a way between these terrible alternatives. She determined to surrender herself and her children to Kiyomori, and depend upon her beauty to save them from the fate which had been pronounced upon all the Minamoto. So with her little flock she went back and gave herself up to the implacable tyrant. Softened by her beauty and urged by a number of his courtiers, he set her mother at liberty in exchange for her becoming his concubine, and distributed her children in separate monasteries. The chief interest follows the youngest boy, Yoshi-tsuné, who was sent to the monastery at Kurama Yama [1] near Kyōto. Here he grew up a vigorous and active youth, more devoted to woodcraft, archery, and fencing than to the studies and devo-tions of the monastery. At sixteen years of age he was urged by the priests to become a monk and to spend the rest of his days in praying for the soul of his father. But he refused, and shortly after he escaped from the monastery in company with a merchant who was about to visit the northern prov-inces. Yoshitsuné reached Mutsu, where he entered the service of Fujiwara-no-Hidehira, then governor of the province. Here he spent several years devot-ing himself to the military duties which chiefly pertained to the government of that rough and bar-barous province. He developed into the gallant and accomplished soldier who played a principal part in the wars which followed, and became the national hero around whose name have clustered the choicest traditions of his country.

Meanwhile, as we have seen, Yoritomo,[2] the oldest

[1] See Satow and Hawes' *Handbook*, p. 383.
[2] He was born in A.D. 1146 and therefore was twelve years older than Yoshitsuné.

son of Yoshitomo, and by inheritance the head of
the Minamoto clan, had been banished to Izu and
committed to the care of two faithful Taira adherents. Yoritomo married Masago, the daughter of
Hōjō Tokimasa, one of these, and found means to
induce Tokimasa to join him in his plans to overthrow the tyrant Kiyomori, who now ruled the
empire with relentless severity. Even the retired
emperor joined in this conspiracy and wrote letters
to Yoritomo urging him to lead in the attempt to
put down the Taira. Yoritomo summoned the
scattered members of the Minamoto clan and all the
disaffected elements of every kind to his assistance.
It does not seem that this summons was responded
to with the alacrity which was hoped for. The in-
experience of Yoritomo and the power and resources
of him against whom they were called upon to array
themselves, led the scattered enemies of Kiyomori
to hesitate to join so hopeless a cause. The rendezvous of the Minamoto was at Ishibashi Yama, and it
is said that only three hundred men gathered at the
call. They were followed and attacked by a greatly
superior force, and utterly routed. It is a tradition
that Yoritomo and six friends, who had escaped
from the slaughter of this battle, hid themselves in
the hollow of an immense tree. Their pursuers, in
searching for them, sent one of their number to
examine this tree. He was secretly a friend of the
Minamoto, and when he discovered the fugitives he
told them to remain, and announced to those who
sent him that the tree was empty. He even inserted
his spear into the hollow and turned it about to

show that there was nothing there. When he did this two doves [1] flew out, and the artful soldier reported that spiders' webs were in the mouth of the opening.

Yoritomo now fled to the promontory of Awa, east of what became known afterward as Yedo bay. He sent messages in every direction summoning the enemies of Kiyomori to join him. His brother Yoshitsuné gathered what forces he could from the north and marched to the region which was to become famous as the site of Kamakura. He was joined by others of his clan and soon felt himself in such a position as to assume the aggressive. He fixed upon Kamakura as his headquarters about A.D. 1180, and as his power increased it grew to be a great city. It was difficult of access from Kyōto and by fortifying the pass of Hakoné,[2] where the mountainous regions of Shinano come down to the eastern coast not far from Fujisan, it was rendered safe from attacks coming from the south.

While these notes of preparation were being sounded Kiyomori, who as *daijō-daijin* had ruled the empire for many years, died A.D. 1181, at the age of sixty-four. He was fully aware of the portentous clouds which were gathering around his family. On his death-bed he is said to have warned them of the danger arising from the plans of Yori-

---

[1] Doves are not eaten by the Minamoto to this day, owing, it is said, to this miraculous interposition in behalf of Yoritomo.

[2] About A.D. 1618 Hakoné was created a barrier to separate the eastern from the central provinces. Persons were not allowed to go through this barrier without a passport.

tomo. According to the *Nihon-Gwaishi*, he said, " My regret is only that I am dying, and have not yet seen the head of Yoritomo of the Minamoto. After my decease do not make offerings to Buddha on my behalf nor read sacred books. Only cut off the head of Yoritomo of the Minamoto and hang it on my tomb."

The death of Kiyomori [1] hastened the triumph of Yoritomo. Munemori the son of Kiyomori became the head of the Taira clan, and continued the contest. But Yoritomo's combinations speedily reduced the country to his power. Yoshitsuné with his army from the north was at Kamakura ; Yoshinaka, a cousin of Yoritomo, was in command of an army gathered in the highlands of Shinano ; while Yoritomo himself led the forces collected in Awa, Kazusa and Musashi. The point to which all the armies were directed was the capital where the Taira were still in full control. Yoshinaka was the first to come in collision with the forces of the capital. Munemori had sent out an army to oppose Yoshinaka who was swiftly approaching along the Nakasendō. The Taira army was completely defeated and Yoshinaka marched victoriously into the capital. Munemori with the reigning emperor Antoku, then only a child six years of age, and all the imperial court crossed the Inland sea to Sanuki, the northern province of the island of Shikoku. The two retired emperors Go-Shirakawa, and Takakura who sympathized with

---

[1] In A.D. 1286, more than a century after his death, a monument was erected to Kiyomori in Hyōgo which still exists. Satow and Hawes' *Handbook*, p. 338.

the revolutionary movements of Yoritomo, remained behind and welcomed Yoshinaka to the capital. The retirement of the emperor from the palace was taken as his abdication, and his younger brother, Go-Toba, then seven years old, was proclaimed em- . peror.

Yoshinaka, puffed up by his rapid success, and disregarding the paramount position of Yoritomo, assumed the superintendence of the government and had himself appointed *sei-i-shōgun*,[1] which was the highest military title then bestowed upon a subject. He even went so far as to antagonize Yoritomo and undertook to pluck the fruits of the military move- ments which had brought about this revolution of the government.

Yoritomo at once despatched Yoshitsuné at the head of his army to Kyōto to put down this most unexpected and unnatural defection. He met Yoshinaka's army near lake Biwa and inflicted upon it a severe defeat. Overwhelmed with shame and knowing that he deserved no consideration at the hands of his outraged relatives, Yoshinaka committed suicide. Yoshitsuné then followed the fugitive court. He destroyed the Taira palace at Hyōgo,

---

[1] The title of shōgun is said to have been created ·by the Emperor Sujin, who divided the empire into four military divisions, each commanded by a shōgun or general. When Yoshinaka assumed control in Kyōto at the time of his victory he was appointed *sei-i-shōgun* (barbarian compelling general). Subsequently Yoritomo secured the supreme military authority and having resigned the civil offices held by him he was appointed by imperial edict *sei-i-tai-shōgun* or great barbarian compelling general.

See G. Appert's *Ancien Japon*, vol. iii., p. 84 ; also Satow's note to Adams' *History of Japan*, vol. i., p. 42.

and then crossed over to Sanuki, whither the court had fled. Alarmed by the swift vengeance which was pursuing them, Munemori together with the emperor and his mother and all the court hastily embarked for what they hoped might be an asylum in the island of Kyūshū. They were pursued by the Minamoto army in the junks which had brought them to Sanuki. They were overtaken at Dan-no-ura not far from the village of Shimonoseki, in the narrow straits at the western extremity of the Inland sea. The naval battle which here took place is the most famous in the annals of the Japanese empire. According to the *Nihon-Gwaishi* the Taira fleet consisted of five hundred junks, and the Minamoto of seven hundred. The vessels of the Taira were encumbered by many women and children of the escaping families, which put them at a great disadvantage. The young emperor, with his mother and grandmother, were also the precious freight of this fugitive fleet. Of course, at this early date the vessels which contended were unlike the monstrous men-of-war which now make naval warfare so stupendous a game. They were not even to be compared with the vessels which made up the Spanish Armada in A.D. 1588, or the ships in which the gallant British sailors repulsed them. Cannon were no part of their armament. The men fought with bows and arrows, and with spears and swords. It was, however, a terrible hand-to-hand fight between men who felt that their all was at stake. Story-tellers draw from this battle some of their most lurid narratives, and artists have depicted it with realistic horrors. The grandmother of the emperor, the widow of Kiyomori, seeing that escape was impossible, took the boy emperor in her arms, and in spite of the remonstrances of her daughter, who was the boy's mother, she plunged into the sea, and both were drowned.

The great mass of the Taira perished in this battle, but a remnant escaped to the island of Kyūshū and hid themselves in the inaccessible valleys of the province of Higo. Here they have been recognized in recent times, and it is claimed that they still show the surly aversion to strangers which is an inheritance derived from the necessity under which they long rested to hide themselves from the vengeance which pursued them.[1]

This battle was decisive in the question of supremacy between the Taira and Minamoto clans. The same policy of extermination which Kiyomori had pursued against the Minamoto was now remorselessly enforced by the Minamoto against the Taira. The prisoners who were taken in the battle were executed to the last man. Munemori was taken prisoner and decapitated. Whenever a Taira man, woman, or child was found, death was the inevitable penalty inflicted. Yoritomo stationed his father-in-law Hōjō Tokimasa at Kyōto to search out and eradicate his enemies as well as to supervise the affairs of the government.

[1] Adams, in his *History of Japan*, vol. i., p. 37, gives a quaint quotation from *Nihon-Gwaishi* as follows: "The crimes of the Heishi against the imperial family were atoned for by their services, and heaven therefore would not cut off their posterity. And this probably was right."

It will be remembered that Go-Toba, a mere
child (A.D. 1186) only seven years of age, had been
put on the throne, in the place of the fugitive Antoku.   Now that the latter had perished at Dan-no-
ura, there could be no question about the legitimacy
and regularity of Go-Toba's accession.   The retired
Emperor Go-Shirakawa, who had been a friend and
promoter of the schemes of Yoritomo, was still alive,
and rendered important aid in the re-organization of
the government.

The darkest blot upon the character of Yoritomo
is his treatment of his youngest brother Yoshitsuné.
It was he who had by his generalship and gallantry
brought these terrible wars to a triumphant conclusion.   He had crushed in the decisive battle of
Dan-no-ura the last of the enemies of Yoritomo.
With his victorious troops he marched northward,
and with prisoners and captured standards was on
his way to lay them at the feet of his now triumphant brother at Kamakura.   But the demon of jealousy had taken possession of Yoritomo.   He resented
the success and fame of his more winning and heroic
brother.   He sent orders to him not to enter Kamakura, and to give up his trophies of battle at Koshi-
goye near to Enoshima.   Here at the monastery of
Mampukuji is still kept the draft of the touching
letter [1] which he sent to his brother, protesting his
loyalty and denying the charges of ambition and
self-seeking which had been made against him.   But
all this availed nothing.   Yoshitsuné returned to
Kyōto and, in fear of bodily harm from the machina-

[1] See Satow and Hawes' *Handbook*, p. 57.

tions of his brother, made his escape with his faithful
servant Benkei,[1] into his old asylum with his friend
Fujiwara Hidehira the governor of Mutsu. Shortly
after his arrival, however, Hidehira died, and his son
Yasuhira abjectly connived at his assassination [2]
A.D. 1189, with a view to secure Yoritomo's favor.

[1] There are almost as many legends current concerning Benkei as
his master. Their first encounter was upon the Gojō bridge in Kyōto,
where Benkei prowled for the purpose of robbing passengers. Yoshitsuné, then only a youth of sixteen years, displayed so much agility
and swordsmanship that the veteran robber yielded to him, and ever
after followed him as his faithful body servant. The *Japanese Fairy
World*, by W. E. Griffis, contains the legend of Benkei stealing a
huge bell five feet high from the monastery at Miidera, and carrying
it on his shoulders to Hiyēsan (see p. 93). When Yoshitsuné was
compelled to flee from the vengeance of his brother, he came with
Benkei, both disguised as begging priests, to a guarded barrier.
The custodians refused them passage, but Benkei, who was cunning
as well as strong, pulled out from his bosom a roll of blank paper
and pretended to read a commission from the abbot of Hōkōji, in
Kyōto, authorizing the two travellers to collect funds throughout the
country for casting a great bell for their temple. The custodians
were deeply impressed with this holy message and allowed the
travellers to pass without further question.

[2] There are many legends, existing among the Ainos, of Yoshitsuné
having lived among them and taught them improved arts of hunting
and fishing. There is a wooden image of him at the village of Upper
Piratori, which is saluted (not worshipped) in token of honor to his
memory. Rev. John Batchelor, who has lived as a missionary among
the Ainos many years, is of the opinion that this reverence is largely
due to a desire on the part of the Ainos to conciliate their Japanese
masters. It has seemed not unreasonable to suppose that the traditions concerning Yoshitsuné among the Ainos have been carried from
the Main island by the retreating tribes, and that Yoshitsuné never
lived with them in Yezo, but was only familiar with them in the wild
regions of Mutsu and Dewa.
    See paper by Rev. J. Batchelor, *Asiatic Society Transactions*, vol.
xvi., part 1, p. 20.
    10

He was at the time of his death only thirty years of age. He has lived down to the present time in the admiring affection of a warlike and heroic people. Although Yoritomo is looked upon as perhaps their greatest hero, yet their admiration is always coupled with a *proviso* concerning his cruel treatment of his brother.

In order not to rest under the imputation of having encouraged this assassination, Yoritomo marched at the head of a strong force and inflicted punishment upon Yasuhira for having done what he himself desired but dared not directly authorize.

The way was now clear for Yoritomo to establish a system of government which should secure to him and his family the fruits of his long contest. In A.D. 1190, he went up to the capital to pay his respects to the Emperor Go-Toba as well as to the veteran retired Emperor Go-Shirakawa. The latter was now in his sixty-sixth year, and had held his place through five successive reigns, and was now the friend and patron of the new government. He died, however, only two years later. Yoritomo knew the effect produced by a magnificent display, and therefore made his progress to the capital with all the pomp and circumstance which he could command. The festivities were kept up for a month, and the court and its surroundings were deeply impressed with a sense of the power and irresistible authority of the head of the Minamoto clan.

Yoritomo did not, however, choose to establish himself at Kyōto amid the atmosphere of effeminacy which surrounded the court. After his official visit, during which every honor and rank which could be bestowed by the emperor were showered upon his head and all his family and friends, he returned to his own chosen seat at Kamakura. Here he busied himself in perfecting a system which, while it would perpetuate his own power, would also build up a firm national government.

His first step, A.D. 1184, was to establish a council at which affairs of state were discussed, and which furnished a medium through which the administration might be conducted. The president of this council was Ōye-no-Hiromoto.[1] Its jurisdiction pertained at first to the Kwantō—that is, to the part of the country east of the Hakoné barrier. This region was more completely under the control of the Minamoto, and therefore could be more easily and surely submitted to administrative methods. He also established a criminal tribunal to take cognizance of robberies and other crimes which, during the lawless and violent disturbances in the country, had largely prevailed.

But the step, which was destined to produce the most far-reaching results, consisted in his obtaining from the emperor the appointment of five of his own family as governors of provinces, promising on his part to supervise their actions and to be responsible for the due performance of their duty. Up to this time the governors and vice-governors of provinces

[1] Ōye-no-Hiromoto was a powerful adherent of Yoritomo, and was a member of his administrative council. He was the ancestor of the Mōri family, who afterward became famous as the daimyōs of Chōshū.

had always been appointed from civil life and were taken from the families surrounding the imperial court. He also was authorized to send into each province a military man, who was to reside there, to aid the governor in military affairs. Naturally, the military man, being the more active, gradually absorbed much of the power formerly exercised by the governor. These military men were under the authority of Yoritomo and formed the beginning of that feudal system which was destined to prevail so long in Japan. He also received from the court, shortly after his visit to Kyōto, the title of *sei-i-tai-shōgun*, which was the highest military title which had ever been bestowed on a subject. This is the title which, down to A.D. 1868, was borne by the real rulers of Japan. The possession of the power implied by this title enabled Yoritomo to introduce responsible government into the almost ungoverned districts of the empire, and to give to Japan for the first time in many centuries a semblance of peace.

There were also many minor matters of administration which Yoritomo, in the few remaining years of his life, put in order. He obtained from the emperor permission to levy a tax on the agricultural products of the country, from which he defrayed the expenses of the military government. He established tribunals for the hearing and determining of causes, and thus secured justice in the ordinary affairs of life. He forbade the priests and monks in the great Buddhist monasteries, who had become powerful and arrogant, to bear arms, or to harbor those bearing arms.

[1] See note, p. 141.

In all these administrative reforms Yoritomo was careful always to secure the assent and authority of the imperial court.[1] In no case did he assume or

YORITOMO.

[1] We owe to Kaempfer, perhaps, the erroneous notion which has been repeated by subsequent writers that there was both an ecclesiastical and a temporal emperor. This was never true. There has been only one emperor, who, in the Japanese theory, was the direct descendant of divine ancestors and who has always been the supreme authority. From the time of Yoritomo, however, the administration was in the hand of an hereditary shōgun who always received the commission of the emperor for the performance of his duties. See Kaempfer's *Histoire de l'Empire du Japon*, vol. i., p. 182.

exercise independent authority. In this way was introduced at this time that system of dual government which continued until the resignation of the Tokugawa Shōgun in 1868. After his first visit to Kyōto, in A.D. 1190, Yoritomo devoted the remaining years of his life to the confirmation of his power and the encouragement of the arts of peace. In A.D. 1195 he made a second magnificent visit to Kyōto and remained four months. It is because of these peaceful results, which followed the long internecine struggles, that the Japanese regard Yoritomo as one of their most eminent and notable men. Under the influence of his court Kamakura grew to be a great city and far outranked even Kyōto in power and activity, though not in size.

In the autumn of the year A.D. 1198, when returning from the inspection of a new bridge over the Sagami river, he had a fall from his horse which seriously injured him. He died from the effects of this fall in the early part of the following year, in the fifty-third year of his age. He had wielded the unlimited military power for the last fifteen years. His death was almost as much of an epoch in the history of Japan as his life had been. We shall see in the chapters which follow the deplorable results of that system of effeminacy and nepotism, of abdication and regency, which Yoritomo had to resist, and which, had he lived twenty years more, his country might have escaped.

CHAPTER VII.

EMPEROR AND SHŌGUN.

THE death of Yoritomo brought into prominence the very same system which had been the bane of the imperial house during many centuries. His son and the hereditary successor to his position and power was Yoriiye, then eighteen years of age. He was the son of Masago, and therefore the grandson of Hōjō Tokimasa, who had been Yoritomo's chief friend and adviser. He was an idle, vicious boy, and evinced no aptitude to carry on the work of his father. In this wayward career he was not checked by his grandfather, and is even said to have been encouraged to pursue a life of pleasure and gayety, while the earnest work of the government was transacted by others. Tokimasa assumed the duties of president of the Council as well as guardian of Yoriiye, and in these capacities conducted the administration entirely according to his own will. The appointments of position and rank which the father had received from the emperor were in like manner bestowed upon the son. He was made head of the military administrators stationed in the several provinces, and he also received the military title of *sei-i-tai-shōgun*, to which Yoritomo had been appointed. But these appointments were only honorary, and the duties pertaining to them were all performed by the guardian of the young man.

In the year A.D. 1203, that is in the fourth year succeeding Yoritomo's death, Yoriiye was taken sick, and was unable to fulfil his duties even in the feeble manner which was customary. His mother consulted with Tokimasa, and they agreed that Yoriiye should abdicate and surrender the headship of the military administration to his brother Semman, who was twelve years of age, and his son Ichiman. Yoriiye seems to have resisted these suggestions, and even resorted to force to free himself from the influence of the Hōjō. But Tokimasa was too powerful to be so easily dispensed with. Yoriiye was compelled to yield, and he retired to a monastery and gave up his offices. Not content with this living retirement, Tokimasa contrived to have him assassinated. Semman, his brother, was appointed *sei-i-tai-shōgun*, and his name changed to Sanetomo. But Sanetomo did not long enjoy his promotion, because his nephew, the son of his murdered predecessor, deemed him responsible for his father's murder, and took occasion to assassinate him. Then in turn the nephew was put to death for this crime, and thus by the year A.D. 1219 the last of the descendants of the great Yoritomo had perished. In the meantime Tokimasa had, A.D. 1205, retired to a Buddhist monastery in his sixty-eighth year, and in A.D. 1216, when he was seventy-eight, he died. The court at Kamakura was now prepared to go on in its career of effeminacy after the pattern of that at Kyōto.

Mesago, the widow of Yoritomo and daughter of Tokimasa, although she too had taken refuge in a Buddhist nunnery, continued to exercise a ruling control in the affairs of the government. She solicited from the court at Kyōto the appointment of Yoritsuné, a boy of the Fujiwara family, only two years old, as *sei-i-tai-shōgun* in the place of the murdered Sanetomo. The petition was granted, and this child was entrusted to the care of the Hōjō, who, as regents[1] of the shōgun, exercised with unlimited sway the authority of this great office. The situation of affairs in Japan at this time was deplorable. Go-Toba and Tsuchi-mikado were both living in retirement as ex-emperors. Juntoku was the reigning emperor, who was under the influence and tutelage of the ex-Emperor Go-Toba. Fretting under the arrogance of the Hōjō, Go-Toba undertook to resist their claims. But Yoshitoku, the Hōjō regent at this time, quickly brought the Kyōto court to terms by the use of his military power. The ex-Emperor Go-Toba was compelled to become a monk, and was exiled to the island of Oki. The Emperor Juntoku was forced to abdicate, and was banished to Sado, and a grandson of the former Emperor Takakura placed on the throne. Even the ex-Emperor Tsuchi-mikado, who had not taken any part in the conspiracy, was sent off to the island of Shikoku. The lands that had belonged to the implicated nobles were confiscated and distributed

[1] The Japanese term is *Shikken*, which is usually translated *regent.*

by Yoshitoku among his own adherents. The power of the Hōjō family was thus raised to its supreme point. They ruled both at Kyōto and Kamakura with resistless authority. They exercised at both places this authority without demanding or receiving the appointment to any of the high positions which they might have claimed. They were only the regents of young and immature shōguns, who were the appointees of a court which had at its head an emperor without power or influence, and which was controlled by the creatures of their own designation. This lamentable state of things lasted for many years. The shōguns during all this time were children sent from Kyōto, sons of emperors or connections of the royal family. The Hōjō ruled them as well as the country. Whenever it seemed best, they relentlessly deposed them, and set up others in their places. In A.D. 1289 the Regent Sadatoki, it is said, became irritated with one of these semi-royal shōguns, named Koreyasu, and in order to show his contempt for him, had him put in a *nori-mono*[1] with his heels upward, and sent him under guard to Kyōto. Some of the Hōjō regents, however, were men of character and efficiency. Yasutoki, for instance, who became regent in A.D. 1225, was a man of notable executive ability, taking Yoritomo as his model. Besides being a soldier of tried capacity, he was a true friend of the farmer in his seasons of famine and trial, and a promoter of legal reforms and of the arts, which found a congenial home among the Japanese.

[1] A travelling palanquin.

But this condition of affairs could not last always. The very same influences which put the real power into the hands of the regents were at work to render them unfit to continue to wield it. Abdication and effeminacy were gradually dragging down the Hōjō family to the same level as that of the shōguns and emperors. In A.D. 1256 Tokiyori, then only thirty years old, resigned the regency in favor of his son Tokimune, who was only six years. He himself retired to a monastery, from which he travelled as a visiting monk throughout the country. In the meantime his son was under the care of a tutor, Nagatoki, who, of course, was one of the Hōjō family. Thus it had come about that a tutor now controlled the regent ; who was supposed to control the shōgun ; who was supposed to be the vassal of the emperor ; who in turn was generally a child under the control of a corrupt and venal court. Truly government in Japan had sunk to its lowest point, and it was time for heroic remedies !

Occasionally, in the midst of this corruption and inefficiency, an event occurs which stirs up the national enthusiasm and makes us feel that there is still left an element of heroism which will ultimately redeem the nation from impending ruin. Such was the Mongolian invasion of Japan in A.D. 1281. According to accounts given by Marco Polo, who evidently narrates the exaggerated gossip of the Chinese court,[1] Kublai Khan had at this time conquered the Sung dynasty in China and reigned with unexampled

[1] See *Travels of Marco Polo*, second edition, London, 1875, vol. ii., p. 240.

magnificence. He had heard of the wealth of Japan
and deemed it an easy matter to add this island empire to his immense dominions. His first step was
to despatch an embassy to the Japanese court to demand the subjection of the country to his authority.
This embassy was referred to Kamakura, whence it
was indignantly dismissed. Finally he sent an invading force in a large number of Chinese and
Korean vessels who took possession of Tsushima, an
island belonging to Japan and lying midway between
Korea and Japan. Trusting to the effects of this
success a new embassy was sent, which was brought
before the Hōjō regent at Kamakura. The spot on
the seashore is still pointed out where these imperious ambassadors were put to death, and thus a de-
nial which could not be misunderstood was given to
the demands of the Grand Khan. A great invading
force, which the Japanese put at a hundred thousand
men, was immediately sent in more than three hundred vessels, who landed upon the island of Kyūshū.
This army was met and defeated [1] by Tokimune, and,
a timely typhoon coming to their aid, the fleet of vessels was completely destroyed. Thus the only seri-

[1] In the year A.D. 1890 two pictures were brought to light which
represent the events of this memorable battle. They are believed to
have been painted about A.D. 1294 by Naganori and Nagatoki,
painters of the Tosa school. They have been in the family of one of
the captains in the Japanese army of that day, and while the figures
of the men and horses are not well drawn the pictures in other respects have great historical value. Alongside of the scenes represented, legends are written in explanation. It is said that these
valuable historical pictures are likely to come into the Household
Department and thus be more carefully preserved than they are likely
to be in a private house.—*Japan Weekly Mail*, 1890, p. 581.

ous attempt at the invasion of Japan which has ever been made was completely frustrated.

But notwithstanding this heroic episode the affairs of Japan remained in the same deplorable condition. As a rule children continued to occupy the imperial throne and to abdicate whenever their Hōjō masters deemed it best. Children of the imperial house or of the family of Fujiwara were sent to Kamakura to become shōguns. And now at last the Hōjō regency had by successive steps come down to the same level, and children were made regents, whose actions and conduct were controlled by their inferiors.

In the midst of this state of things, which continued till A.D. 1318, Go-Daigo became emperor. Contrary to the ordinary usage, he was a man thirty-one years old, in the full maturity of his powers. He was by no means free from the vices to which his surroundings inevitably tended. He was fond of the gayety and pomp which the court had always cultivated. But he realized the depth of the degradation to which the present condition of affairs had dragged his country. A famine brought great suffering upon the people, and the efforts which the emperor made to assist them added to his popularity, and revealed to him the reverence in which the imperial throne was held. His son Moriyoshi, as early as A.D. 1307, was implicated in plans against the Hōjō, which they discovered, and in consequence compelled Go-Daigo to order his retirement into a monastery. Later Go-Daigo undertook to make a stand against the arrogance and intolerance of the Hōjō and induced the Buddhist monks to join him

in fortifying Kasagi in the province of Yamato. But
this effort of the emperor was fruitless. Kasagi was
attacked and destroyed and the emperor taken prisoner. As a punishment for his attempt he was sent
as an exile to the island of Oki. The Hōjō Regent
Takatoki put Go-Kōgen on the throne as emperor.
But Go-Daigo from his exile continued his exertions
against the Hōjō, and assistance came to him from
unexpected quarters. He effected his escape from
the island and, having raised an army, marched upon
Kyōto. Kusunoki Masashigé, who had given his aid
to the emperor on former occasions, now exerted
himself to good purpose. He is held in admiring
remembrance to this day by his grateful country as
the model of patriotic devotion, to whom his emperor was dearer than his life. Another character
who stands out prominently in this trying time was
Nitta Yoshisada. He was a descendant of Yoshiiye,
who, for his achievements against the Emishi, had
received the popular title of Hachiman-tarō. Nitta
was a commander in the army of the Hōjō, which
had been sent against Kusunoki Masashigé. But at
the last moment he refused to fight against the army
of the emperor and retired with his troops and went
over to the side of Masashigé. He returned to his
own province of Kōtsuke and raised an army to fight
against the Hōjō. With this force he marched at
once against Kamakura through the province of
Sagami. His route lay along the beach. But at
Inamura-ga-saki the high ground, which is impassable
for troops, juts out so far into the water that Nitta
was unable to lead them past the promontory.

Alone he clambered up the mountain path and looked out upon the sea that lay in his way. He was bitterly disappointed that he could not bring his force in time to share in the attack upon the hateful Hōjō capital. He prayed to the Sea-god to withdraw the sea and allow him to pass with his troops. Then he flung his sword into the waves in token of his earnestness and of the dire necessity in which he found himself. Thereupon the tide retreated and left a space of a mile and a half, along which Nitta[1] marched upon Kamakura.

The attack was spirited and was made from three directions simultaneously. It was resisted with determined valor on the part of the Hōjō. The city was finally set on fire by Nitta, and in a few hours was reduced to ashes. Thus the power and the arrogant tyranny of the Hōjō family were sealed. It had lasted from the death of Yoritomo, A.D. 1199, to the destruction of Kamakura, A.D. 1333, in all one hundred and thirty-four years. It was a rough and tempestuous time and the Hōjō have left a name in their country of unexampled cruelty and rapacity. The most unpardonable crime of which they were guilty was that of raising their sacrilegious hands against the emperor and making war against the imperial standard. For this they must rest under the charge of treason, and no merits however great or commanding can ever excuse them in the eyes of their patriotic countrymen.

The restoration of Go-Daigo to the imperial throne,

---

[1] For a description of this locality, which is justly famed in Japanese annals, see Satow and Hawes' *Handbook*, p. 56.

under so popular an uprising, seemed to betoken a
return to the old and simple system of Japanese government. The intervention of a shōgun between
the emperor and his people, which had lasted from
the time of Yoritomo, was contrary to the precedents
which had prevailed from the Emperor Jimmu down
to that time. It was the hope and wish of the best
friends of the government at this time to go back
to the original precedents and govern the country
directly from Kyōto with the power and authority
derived from the emperor. But the emperor was
not equal to so radical a change from the methods
which had prevailed for more than a century. He
gave great offence by the manner in which he distributed the forfeited fiefs among those who had
aided his restoration. To Ashikaga Taka-uji he
awarded by far the greatest prize, while to Kusunoki and Nitta, who had in the popular estimation
done much more for him, he allotted comparatively
small rewards. Among the soldiers, who in the long
civil wars had lost the ability to devote themselves
to peaceful industries, this disappointment was most
conspicuous. They had expected to be rewarded
with lands and subordinate places, which would enable them to live in that feudal comfort to which
they deemed their exertions had entitled them.

At this time a feud broke out between Ashikaga
Taka-uji and Nitta. The former had accused Nitta
of unfaithfulness to his emperor and Nitta was able
to disprove the charge. He received the imperial
commission to punish Ashikaga and marched with
his army upon him in the province of Tōtōmi. In

the battles (A.D. 1336) which ensued, the forces of
Ashikaga were completely victorious. The emperor
and his court were obliged to flee from Kyōto and
took up their residence in a Buddhist temple at
Yoshino in the mountainous district south of Kyōto.
This was the same monastery where Yoshitsuné and
Benkei had taken refuge previous to their escape
into Mutsu. Almost every tree and every rock in
the picturesque grounds of this romantic spot [1]
bear some evidence of the one or other of these
memorable refugees. The southern dynasty lasted
in all fifty-seven years, down to A.D. 1374, and
although it was compelled to starve out a miserable
existence in exile from the capital, it is yet looked
upon by historians as the legitimate branch; while
the northern dynasty, which enjoyed the luxury of a
palace and of the capital, is condemned as illegitimate.

This period of exile witnessed many notable events
in the bloody history of the country. Ashikaga
Taka-uji was of course the ruling spirit while he lived.
He proclaimed that Go-Daigo had forfeited the
throne and put Kōmyō Tennō, a brother of Kōgen
Tennō upon it in his stead. The insignia of the imperial power were in the possession of Go-Daigo, but
Kōmyō, being supported by the battalions of Ashikaga, cared little for these empty baubles. The
bloody sequence of affairs brought with it the death of
the heroic Kusunoki Masashige. He with Nitta and
other patriots had undertaken to support Go-Daigo.
It is said that contrary to his military judgment he
attacked the forces of Ashikaga, which were vastly

---

[1] See Chamberlain's *Handbook*, 1891, p. 337.

superior in number.   The battle took place A.D. 1336
on the Minato-gawa, near the present site of Hyōgo
The Ashikaga forces had cut off Kusunoki with a
small band of devoted followers from the main army.
Seeing that his situation was hopeless and that his
brave troops must be destroyed, with one hundred
and fifty men—all that were left of his little army—
he retired to a farmer's house near by and there
they all committed *hara-kiri*.[1]   Kusunoki Masashige,
when about to commit suicide, said to his son Ma-
satsura : " For the sake of keeping yourself out of
danger's way or of reaping some temporal advantage, on no account are you to submit to Taka-uji.
By so doing you would bring reproach on our name.
While there is a man left who belongs to us let our
flag be hoisted over the battlements of Mount Konzo,
as a sign that we are still ready to fight in the emperor's cause."

A little later than this, in A.D. 1338, the great
companion and friend of Kusunoki, Nitta Yoshisada, came to his end.   He had undertaken to
promote the cause of the Emperor Go-Daigo in the
northwestern provinces by co-operating with Fuji-
wara-no-Yoritomo.   Nitta with about fifty followers
was unexpectedly attacked by Ashikaga Tadatsune,
with three thousand men near Fukui in the province
of Echizen.   There was no way of escape with his

---

[1] Quite an animated and interesting controversy took place a few
years ago with reference to this suicide of Kusunoki.   Popular
opinion strongly justifies the act and rewards with its highest approval
the memory of the patriot.   But Mr. Fukuzawa, one of the most
radical of the public men of to-day and an active and trenchant
writer, condemned the act as indefensible and cowardly.

little troop. In this condition he was urged to
secure his personal safety. But he refused to survive his comrades. Then he rode with his brave
company upon the enemy until his horse was disabled and he himself was pierced in the eye with an
arrow. He drew out the arrow with his own hand,
and then, in order that his body might not be
identified, with his sword cut off his own head, at
least so it is said ! Each member of his troop
followed this grewsome example, and it was only
after examining the bodies of these headless corpses
and the finding upon one a commission from the
Emperor Go-Daigo, that the remains of the heroic
Nitta were recognized. The head was sent to
Kyōto and there exposed by the Ashikaga commander, and the body was buried near the place
where the tragic death occurred.[1]

The Ashikaga family had now the uninterrupted
control of affairs. They resided at Kyōto and inherited in succession the office of shōgun. Taka-uji
the founder of the Ashikaga shōgunate, and who had
held the office from A.D. 1334, died in A.D. 1358,
when about fifty-three years old. He was succeeded
by his son Yoshinori who was shōgun from A.D. 1359
to A.D. 1367. Having retired he was succeeded by
his grandson Yoshimitsu who in turn retired in favor
of his son Yoshimotsu. By this time the precedents
of abdication and effeminacy began to tell upon the

[1] Mr. Griffis says that when he resided in Fukui in A.D. 1871—
more than five hundred years after the event,—he saw the grave of the
heroic Nitta almost daily strewed with flowers.— *The Mikado's Empire*, 1876, p. 190.

Ashikaga successors, and like all the preceding ruling families it gradually sank into the usual insignificance. Some of the Ashikaga shōguns, however, were men of uncommon ability and their services to their country deserve to be gratefully remembered. A number of them were men of culture and evinced their love of elegance and refinement by the palaces which they built in Kyōto. Ashikaga Yoshimitsu was shōgun from A.D. 1368 to 1393, and at the latter date retired in favor of his young son Yoshimotsu, but lived in official retirement in Kyōto till A.D. 1409. He built the palace now known as the Buddhist monastery Kinkakuji.[1] Its name is derived from *kinkaku* (golden pavilion) which Yoshimitsu erected. The whole palace was bequeathed by him to the Zen sect of Buddhists and is still one of the sights best worth seeing in Kyōto.

Yoshimitsu has been visited by much obloquy because he accepted from the Chinese government the title of King of Japan, and pledged himself to the payment of one thousand ounces of gold as a yearly tribute. It is said in explanation of this tribute that it was to compensate for damages done by Japanese pirates to Chinese shipping. But it was probably negotiated for the purpose of securing an ambitious title on the one hand and on the other making a troublesome neighbor a tributary kingdom.

Another building which takes its origin from the Ashikaga is the Tō-ji-in. It was founded by Ashikaga Taka-uji and contains carved and lacquered wooden figures of the Ashikaga shōguns which

---

[1] Satow and Hawes' *Handbook*, p. 356.

are believed in most cases to be contemporary portraits.[1]

Another of the notable Ashikaga shōguns was Yoshimasa, who held the office from A.D. 1443-1473. He retired at the latter date, and lived as retired shōgun until A.D. 1490. In this interval of seclusion he cultivated the arts, and posed as the patron of literature and painting. That curious custom called *cha-no-yu*, or tea ceremonies,[2] is usually adjudged to him as its originator, but it is most probable that he only adopted and refined it until it became the fashionable craze which has come down to modern times. These ceremonies and his other modes of amusement were conducted in a palace which he had built called *gin-kaku* (silver pavilion). Yoshimasa left this palace to the monks of Shō-koku-ji, with directions that it should be converted into a monastery, and in that capacity it still serves at the present time.

The period of the two imperial dynasties lasted until A.D. 1392, when a proposition was made by the Shōgun Yoshimitsu to the then reigning emperor of the south, that the rivalry should be healed. It was agreed that Go-Kameyama of the southern dy-

[1] It is an evidence of the feeling which still exists towards the Ashikaga shōguns that in 1863 these figures were taken from the Tō-ji-in and beheaded and the heads pilloried in the dry bed of the Kamogawa, at the spot where it is customary to expose the heads of the worst criminals. Several of the men who were guilty of this outrage were captured and were put into the hands of various daimyōs by whom they were kept as prisoners.—Satow and Hawes' *Handbook*, p. 357.

[2] See the full account of tea ceremonies in Chamberlain's *Things Japanese*, 1892, p. 404.

nasty should come to Kyōto and surrender the insignia to Go-Komatsu, the ruling emperor of the northern dynasty. This was duly accomplished, and Go-Kameyama, having handed over the insignia to Go-Komatsu, took the position of retired emperor. Thus the long rivalry between the northern and southern dynasties was ended, and Go-Komatsu stands as the ninety-ninth in the official list of emperors. In that list, however, none of the other emperors [1] of the northern dynasty appear, they being regarded as pretenders, and in no case entitled to the dignity of divine rulers of Japan.

This settlement of dynastic difficulties and the unrestricted ascendancy of the Ashikaga shōguns gave the country a little interval of peace. The condition of the peasantry at this time was most deplorable. The continual wars between neighboring lords and with the shōguns had kept in the field armies of military men, who were forced to subsist on contributions exacted from the tillers of the soil. The farmers everywhere were kept in a state of uncertainty, and had little encouragement to cultivate

[1] The official list of emperors will be found in Appendix I. The names of the northern which are not included in this list are as follows:

DATE OF ACCESSION.

	From Jimmu.	A.D.
Kōmiō	1996	1336
Shukō	2009	1349
Go-Kōgen	2012	1352
Go-Enyū	2032	1372
Go-Komatsu	2043	1383

crops which were almost sure to fall into the hands of others.

On the coasts of Kyūshū and other islands facing towards the continent piracy also sprang up and flourished apace. It was indeed an era of piracy all over the world. The Portuguese, Spanish, and Dutch traders of this period were almost always ready to turn an honest penny by seizing an unfortunate vessel under the pretence that it was a pirate. The whole coast of China, according to the accounts of Pinto, swarmed with both European and Asiatic craft, which were either traders or pirates, according to circumstances. Under this state of things, and with the pressure of lawlessness and want behind them, it was not surprising that the inhabitants of the western coasts of Japan should turn to a piratical life.

Knowing the Japanese only since centuries of enforced isolation had made them unaccustomed to creep beyond their own shores, we can scarcely conceive of their hardihood and venturesomeness during and subsequent to this active period. Mr. Satow [1] has gathered a most interesting series of facts pertaining to the intercourse between Japan and Siam, beginning at a period as early as that now under review. Not only did this intercourse consist in sending vessels laden with chattels for traffic, but a colony of Japanese and a contingent of Japanese troops formed part of the assistance which Japan furnished to her southern neighbor.

While these signs of activity were apparent on the

[1] See *Asiatic Society Transactions*, vol. xiii., p. 139.

coast, the provinces in the interior were alive with
political unrest.   Particularly the principal daimyōs,
who had never since the days of Yoritomo felt a
master's power over them, took the present occasion
to extend their dominions over their neighbors.
For centuries the conflicts among them were almost
unending.   It is needless to undertake to disentangle
the story of their wars.   These daimyōs were a far
more distinct and pressing reality than the harmless
emperor, or even than the far-removed shōgun.
While their ceaseless civil wars rendered the condition of the country so uncertain and so unsettled,
yet the authority of the local rulers tended to preserve peace and dispense a rude kind of justice
among their own subjects.   Thus while in many
parts of Japan poverty and desolation had eaten up
everything, and lawlessness and robbery had put an
end to industry, yet there were some favored parts
of the islands where the strong hand of the daimyōs
preserved for their people the opportunities of life,
and kept alive the chances of industry.[1]

[1] It is said that in this disastrous time the poverty of the country
was so great that when, in A.D. 1500, Go-Tsuchimikado died at his
palace in Kyōto, the corpse was kept for forty days because the means
for the usual funeral expenses could not be had.   M. von Brandt as
quoted in Rein's *Japan*, p. 261.

CHAPTER VIII.

FROM THE ASHIKAGA SHŌGUNS TO THE DEATH OF NOBUNAGA.

IN almost the worst period of the Ashikaga anarchy, A.D. 1542, the Portuguese made their first appearance in Japan. Galvano, who had been governor of the Moluccas, gives an account of this first visit, when three fugitives from a Portuguese vessel in a Chinese junk were driven upon the islands of southern Japan. Concerning the doings[1] of these fugitives we have no account in any foreign narratives.

[1] Mr. W. A. Woolley, in a paper read before the Asiatic Society of Japan, gives an account derived from Japanese sources as follows: "Amongst those who landed on this occasion was one of the *Literati* of China, who acted as interpreter between the foreigners and the chief of the island Hyōbu-no-jō Tokitada. [Since both the Chinese and Japanese used the same ideographic characters, they could understand each other's writing but not speech.] In reply to questions the interpreter is represented as having described his friends the foreigners as being ignorant of etiquette and characters, of the use of wine cups and chop sticks, and as being, in fact, little better than the beasts of the field. The chief of the foreigners taught Tokitada the use of firearms, and upon leaving presented him with three guns and ammunition, which were forwarded to Shimazu Yoshihisa, and through him to the shōgun."—*Asiatic Society Transactions*, vol. ix., p. 128.

But Fernam Mendez Pinto,[1] in his travels, etc., gives
a detailed narrative of the visit which he and his
companions made a few years later in a ship with a
Chinese captain and merchandise. The exact year
cannot be ascertained from Pinto's narrative, but
Hildreth[2] assumes that it could not have been earlier than A.D. 1545. Pinto landed on Tane-ga-shima,
an island south of the extreme southern point of the
island of Kyūshū. They were received with great
cordiality by the prince, who evinced the utmost
curiosity concerning the Portuguese who were on
this ship. Pinto naïvely confesses that " we rendered him answers as might rather fit his humor
than agree with the truth, . . . that so we might
not derogate from the great opinion he had conceived of our country."[3]

As a return for some of the kindnesses which the
prince showed them, the Portuguese gave him a
harquebuse, and explained to him the method of
making powder. The present seems to have been
most acceptable, and Pinto declares the armorers
commenced at once to make imitations of it, "so
that before their departure (which was five months
and a half after) there were six hundred of them
made in the country." And a few years later he
was assured that there were above thirty thousand
in the city of Fucheo,[4] the capital of Bungo, and

[1] See *Adventures of Mendez Pinto*, done into English by Henry
Cogan, London, 1891, pp. 259 etc.

[2] Hildreth's *Japan*, etc., 1855, p. 27, note.

[3] *Adventures of Mendez Pinto*, p. 281.

[4] This is the name by which Pinto calls this city (see *Adventures of
Mendez Pinto*, London, 1891, p. 265); the real name, however, at
this time was Fumai, and is now Ōita.

above three hundred thousand in the whole province. And so they have increased from this one *harquebuse* which they gave to the prince of Tane-ga-shima, until every hamlet and city in the empire in a short time were supplied with them.[1]

A short time after their reception at Tane-ga-shima the Prince of Bungo, who was a relative of the Prince of Tane-ga-shima, sent for one of the Portuguese, and Pinto, by his own consent, was selected as being of a "more lively humor." He was received with great consideration, and proved himself of vast service in curing the prince of gout, with which he was affected. His success in this cure gave him immense repute, and he was initiated into all the gayeties and sports of the prince's court. In particular he amused and interested them all by firing the matchlock which he had brought with him. A son of the prince of about sixteen or seventeen years of age was infatuated with this sport, and one day, unknown to Pinto, he undertook to load and fire the matchlock, as he had seen the foreigner do. An explosion occurred, by which the young prince was much injured, and owing to this Pinto came near being put to death for having wrought this disaster. But the young prince had more sense than the attendants, and at his request Pinto was given a chance to bind up the wounds and take care

---

[1] The author himself saw in Japan in 1874 the native hunters using an old-fashioned matchlock, in which the powder was fired by a slow burning match, which was brought down to the powder by a trigger. This kind of firearm, which was in use in Europe in the fifteenth century, was taken to Japan by the Portuguese, and continued to be used there until the re-organization of the army introduced the modern form of gun.

of him. The result was that the young prince
quickly recovered, and the fame of this cure was
spread everywhere. "So that," says Pinto, "after
this sort I received in recompense of this my cure
above fifteen hundred ducats that I carried with me
from this place."

Pinto made a second visit to Japan in the interests
of trade in 1547, which was attended by a circumstance which had far-reaching results. In critical
circumstances they were called upon to take off two
fugitives who appealed to them from the shore. A
company of men on horseback demanded the return
of the fugitives, but without answer they pulled off
to the ship and took them aboard. The principal of
these two fugitives [1] was Anjiro, whom the Jesuits
usually name Anger, and his companion was his servant. They were taken in the Portuguese vessel to
Malacca, where Pinto met Father Francis Xavier,
who had just arrived upon his mission to the East.
Xavier became intensely interested in these Japanese
fugitives, and took them to Goa, then the principal
seat of Jesuit learning and the seat of an arch-
bishopric in the East Indies. Here both the Japanese became converts and were baptized, Anjiro
receiving the name of Paulo de Santa Fé [2] (Paul of
the Holy Faith), and his companion the name of
John. They learned to speak and write the Portuguese language, and were instructed in the elements

[1] In the accounts given by the biographers of Xavier, it is said that
there were two companions of Anjiro who in the subsequent baptism
received the names of John and Anthony.

[2] This was the name of the seminary in Goa where Anjiro had
been educated.

of the Christian religion. With these efficient helps
Xavier was ready to enter Japan and commence the
evangelization on which his heart had long been set.

At last arrangements were made with a Chinese
vessel, which according to Pinto's account was a
piratical craft, to convey Xavier and his companions
to Japan. They arrived at Kagoshima, the capital
of the province of Satsuma, August 15, A.D. 1549.
Besides Xavier and his Japanese companions there
were Cosme de Torres, a priest, and Jean Ferdinand,
a brother of the Society of Jesus. They were cordially received by the Prince of Satsuma, and after
a little, permission was given them to preach the
Christian religion in the city of Kagoshima. The
family and relatives of Anjiro, who lived in Kagoshima, were converted and became the first fruits of
the mission. In the letters which Xavier wrote
home about this time we have his early impressions
concerning the Japanese. The princess took great
interest in the subjects discussed by Anjiro, and was
especially struck with a picture of the Madonna and
child which he showed her. She asked to have the
heads of the Christian faith put in writing in order
that she might study them. For this reason a creed
and a catechism were prepared and translated into
the Japanese language, for the use of the princess
and other enquirers. In one of his early letters he
says : " I really think that among barbarous nations
there can be none that has more natural goodness
than Japan." [1] In the same letter he says : " They

[1] See Coleridge's *Life and Letters of St. Francis Xavier*, London,
1872, p. 237.

are wonderfully inclined to see all that is good and honest and have an eagerness to learn." Xavier, in letter 79, narrates his meeting with the Buddhist priest whom he calls Ningh-Sit, which name he says means Heart of Truth. This priest was eighty years old, and in the conversation expressed great surprise that Xavier should have come all the way from Portugal to preach to the Japanese.

The biographers of Xavier have given us the fullest details of his life and works. That he was a man of the most fervent piety as well as the most conspicuous ability, is apparent from the energy and success with which he conducted his short but brilliant mission. Both in their accounts of him, as well as in the papal bull announcing his canonization, the claim is distinctly set forth of his possession of miraculous power. He is represented as having raised a Japanese girl from the dead ; as possessing the gift of tongues, that is, as being able to speak in fluent Japanese, although he had not learned the language ; as having given an answer which when heard was a satisfactory reply to the most various and different questions,[1] such as, " the immortality of the soul, the motions of the heavens, the eclipses of the sun and moon, the colors of the rainbow, sin and grace, heaven and hell."

Yet it must be stated that Xavier himself does not claim these miraculous powers. Indeed among the letters published by Father Horace Tursellini is one in which he thus speaks of himself : " God grant that as soon as possible we may learn the

[1] Bouhour's *Life of Xavier*, p. 274.

ST. FRANCIS XAVIER.

The portrait here given of St. Francis Xavier is from a photograph furnished by the College of St. Francis Xavier of New York and is vouched for as his traditional likeness.

language of Japan in order to make known the divine mysteries ; then we shall zealously prosecute our Christian work. For they speak and discourse much about us, but we are silent, ignorant of the language of the country. At present we are become a child again to learn the elements of the language."

The desire for trade with the Portuguese seems to have been a principal reason for the ready reception of the missionaries. And when the Portuguese merchant ships resorted to Hirado, an island off the west coast of Kyūshū, instead of the less accessible Kagoshima, the Prince of Kagoshima turned against the missionaries and forbade them from preaching and proselyting. From Kagoshima Xavier went to Hirado, where he was received with a salvo of artillery from a Portuguese vessel then at anchor there. Here he made a short stay, preaching the gospel as usual and with the approval of the prince establishing a church. Leaving Kosmé de Torres at Hirado and taking with him Fernandez and the two Japanese assistants he touched at Hakata, famous as the place where the Mongol invaders were repulsed. Then he crossed over to the Main island and travelling by land along the Sanyōdō he entered Yamaguchi in the province of Nagato. His humble and forlorn appearance did not produce a favorable impression on the people of this city and he was driven out with obloquy. He set out for Kyōto with a party of Japanese merchants, and as it was winter and Xavier had to carry on his back a box containing the vestments and vessels for the celebration of mass, the journey

was trying and difficult. He arrived at Kyōto A.D.
1550 in the midst of great political troubles. A fire
had destroyed a great part of what had been once a
beautiful and luxurious city. Many of the principal
citizens had abandoned it and taken up their residence with local princes in the provinces. Xavier
could obtain a hearing neither from the emperor
nor from the Ashikaga shōguns, who maintained a
representative in the capital at this time. He
preached in the street as he could obtain opportunity. But the atmosphere was everywhere unfavorable, and he resolved to abandon the field for
the present. Accordingly he went back to Bungo,
whence he sailed for China November 20, A.D. 1551,
with the purpose of establishing a mission. He had
spent two years and three months in Japan and
left an impression which has never been effaced.
He died on his way, at the little island of Sancian,
December 2, A.D. 1552, aged forty-six. His body
was carried to Malacca and afterward to Goa, where
it was buried in the archiepiscopal cathedral.[1]

The departure and death of Xavier did not interrupt the work of the mission in Japan. Kosmé de
Torres was left in charge and additional helpers,

---

[1] In the *Life of St. Francis Xavier* by Bartholi and Maffei the
following circumstance is given : "It seems that a rat had invaded
the sanctuary and gnawed the ornaments of the altar. The sacristan
appealed to the saint thus : 'Father Francis ! people say that you
passed from this life in the vicinity of China ; that you were a saint,
that your body still remains entire and incorrupt at Goa. Now here
am I your sacristan ; and I ask is it consistent with your honor that a
rat should have the audacity to gnaw the ornaments of your altar ? I
demand his death at your hand.' On opening the door of the sanctuary the next morning the sacristan found the culprit quite dead."

both priests and lay brothers, were sent to prosecute what had been so conspicuously begun. The political disturbances in Yamaguchi for a time interfered with the labors of the missionaries there. Bungo was the principal province where their encouragement had made their success most conspicuous. The prince had not indeed been baptized but he had permitted the fathers to preach and he had allowed converts to adopt the new religion, so that the work had assumed a promising appearance. The Prince of Ōmura became a convert and by his zeal in the destruction of idols and other extreme measures aroused the hostility of the Buddhist priesthood. In Kyōto the progress of the work encountered many vicissitudes. The political troubles arising out of the contests between Mōri of Chōshū and the rival house interfered with the propagation of Christianity both in Yamaguchi and Kyōto. Mōri himself, the most powerful prince of his time and who once held the control in ten provinces, was hostile to the Christians. By his influence the work in Kyōto was temporarily abandoned and the fathers resorted to Sakai, a seaport town not far from Ōsaka, where a branch mission was established.

It was in A.D. 1573 that Nagasaki became distinctively a Christian city. At that time the Portuguese were seeking various ports in which they could conduct a profitable trade, and they found that Nagasaki possessed a harbor in which their largest ships could ride at anchor. The merchants and Portuguese fathers therefore proposed to the Prince of Ōmura, in whose territory the port of

Nagasaki was situated, to grant to them the town with jurisdiction over it. .The prince at first refused, but finally by the intervention of the Prince of Arima the arrangement was made.[1] The transference to Nagasaki of the foreign trade at this early day made it a very prosperous place. The Prince of Ōmura had the town laid out in appropriate streets, and Christian churches were built often on the sites of Buddhist temples which were torn down to give place for them. It is said that in A.D. 1567 "there was hardly a person who was not a Christian."

We shall have occasion often in the subsequent narrative to refer to the progress of Christianity in the empire. In the meantime we must trace the career of Nobunaga, who exerted a powerful effect on the affairs of his country and particularly upon the condition of both Buddhism and Christianity. He must be regarded always as one of the great men of Japan who at an opportune moment intervened to rescue its affairs from anarchy. He prepared the way for Hideyoshi and he, in turn, made it possible for Ieyasu to establish a peace which lasted without serious interruption for two hundred and fifty years.

Ota Nobunaga was descended from the Taira family through Ota Chikazane a great-grandson of Taira Kiyomori. The father of Chikazane had perished in the wars between the Taira and Minamoto families, and his mother had married as her second husband the chief man in the village of Tsuda in the province of Ōmi. The step-child was adopted by

[1] See Woolley, " Historical Notes on Nagasaki, *Asiatic Society Transactions*, vol. ix., p. 129.

a Shintō priest of the village of Ota in the province of Echizen, and received the name of Ota Chikazane. When he grew up, he became a Shintō priest and married and became the father of a line of priests. One of this succession was Ota Nobuhide, who seems to have reverted from the priestly character back to the warlike habits of his ancestors. In the general scramble for land, which characterized that period, Nobuhide acquired by force of arms considerable possessions in the province of Owari, which at his death in A.D. 1549 he left to his son Ota Nobunaga. This son grew up to be a man of large stature, but slender and delicate in frame. He was brave beyond the usual reckless bravery of his countrymen. He was by character and training fitted for command, and in the multifarious career of his busy life, in expeditions, battles, and sieges, he showed himself the consummate general. Like many other men of genius he was not equally as skilful in civil as military affairs. He was ambitious to reduce the disorders of his country, and he was able to see in a great measure the success of his schemes. But he failed in leaving when he died any security for the preservation and continuance of that peace and unity which he had conquered.

At the time Nobunaga became prominent, the Emperor Go-Nara had died and Ōgimachi in A.D. 1560 had just succeeded to the throne as the one hundred and fifth emperor. Ashikaga Yoshifusa had become shōgun in A.D. 1547 as a boy eleven years old, and was at this time a young man, who as usual devoted himself to pleasure while the affairs of government were conducted by others. Both emperor

and shōgun were almost powerless in the empire, the
real power being held by the local princes.   In many
cases they had largely increased their holdings by
conquest, and were almost entirely independent of
the central authority.   For more than a century this
independence had been growing, and at the time of
Nobunaga there was little pretence of deferring to
the shōgun in any matter growing out of the relations of one prince to the other, and none at all in
reference to the internal government of the territories within their jurisdiction.   The principal local
rulers at this time were the following : Imagaya
Yoshimoto controlled the three provinces of Suruga,
Tōtōmi, and Mikawa ; Hōjō Ujiyasu from the town
of Odowara ruled the Kwanto, including the provinces of Sagami, Musashi, Awa, Kazusa, Shimosa,
Hitachi, Kōtsuke, and Shimotsuke ; Takeda Shingen
ruled the province of Kai and the greater part of
the mountainous province of Shinano ; Uesugi
Kenshin held under his control the northwestern
provinces of Echizen, Echigo, Etchū, and Noto ;
Mōri Motonari after a severe contest had obtained control of almost all the sixteen provinces which composed the Chūgoku or central
country ; the island of Kyūshū had been the
scene of frequent civil wars and was now divided between the houses of Shimazu of Satsuma, Ōtomo
of Bungo, and Ryōzoji of Hizen ; and finally the
island of Shikoku was under the control of Chōsokabe Motochika.[1]   Besides these principal rulers,

[1] For these facts concerning Nobunaga and Hideyoshi, and the
condition of the country during their times, the author is largely
indebted to the *Life of Toyotomi Hideyoshi*, by Walter Dening,
Tokio, 1890.

there were many smaller holders who occupied fiefs subordinate to the great lords, and paid for their protection and their suzerainty in tribute and military service. In the letters of the Jesuit missionaries of this period the great lords are denominated *kings*, but neither according to the theory of the Japanese government, nor the actual condition of these rulers can the name be considered appropriate. The term daimyō [1] came into its full and modern use only when Ieyasu reorganized and consolidated the feudal system of the empire. But even at the period of Nobunaga the name was employed to indicate the owners of land. We prefer to continue down to the time of the Tokugawa shōguns the use of the terms *prince* and *principality* for the semi-independent rulers and their territories.

The holdings which Ota Nobunaga inherited from his father consisted only of four small properties in the province of Owari. Acting according to the fashion of the times he gradually extended his authority, until by A.D. 1559 we find him supreme in Owari with his chief castle at Kiyosu near to the city of Nagoya. His leading retainers and generals were Shibata Genroku and Sakuma Yemon, to whom must be added Hideyoshi, [2] who gradually and

---

[1] The word *daimyō* means *great name*, and was used in reference to the ownership of land; *shomyō* means *small name*, and was at first employed to indicate the small land-owner. But the word never obtained currency, the small land-owner always preferring to call himself a daimyō. See Chamberlain's *Things Japanese*, p. 84.

[2] The element of comedy shows itself from the beginning in Hideyoshi's character when he adopted the calabash, in which he had carried water, as his symbol of victory. He added a new one for

rapidly rose from obscurity to be the main reliance of his prince. Nobunaga was a skilful general, and whenever an interval occurred in his expeditions against his hostile neighbors he employed the time in carefully drilling his troops, and preparing them for their next movements. He found in Hideyoshi an incomparable strategist, whose plans, artifices, and intrigues were original and effective, and were worth more to his master than thousands of troops.

It was not difficult in those days to find excuses to invade neighboring domains, and hence we find Nobunaga, as soon as he had made himself master of Owari, on one pretext or another making himself also master of the provinces of Mino, Ōmi, and Isé. Before this was accomplished, however, we see plain indications both on the part of Nobunaga and his retainers that the ultimate aim in view was the subjugation of the whole country, and the establishment of a government like that of Yoritomo.

At this time (A.D. 1567) the affairs of the Ashikaga shōguns, who ruled in the name of the emperor, were in a state of great confusion. Yoshiteru, the shōgun, had been assassinated by one of his retainers, Miyoshi Yoshitsugu. The younger brother of Yoshiteru was Yoshiaki, who desired to succeed, but this did not comport with the designs of the assassins. Accordingly after making several unsuccessful applications for military aid he finally applied to Nobunaga. This was exactly the kind of alliance that

each victory, and at last adopted a bunch of calabashes for his coat-of-arms. Afterwards he had this constructed of gold, which was carried as the emblem of his triumphant career.

Nobunaga wanted to justify his schemes of national conquest. With his own candidate in the office of shōgun, he could proceed without impediment to reduce all the princes of the empire to his supreme authority. He therefore undertook to see Yoshiaki established as shōgun, and for this purpose marched a large army into Kyōto. Yoshiaki was installed as shōgun in A.D. 1568, and at his suggestion the emperor conferred on Nobunaga the title of Fuku-shōgun [1] or vice-shōgun. This was Nobunaga's first dealings with the imperial capital, and the presence of his large army created a panic among the inactive and peaceful citizens.

He appointed Hideyoshi as commander-in-chief of the army at the capital, who with a sagacity and energy that belonged to his character set himself to inspire confidence and to overcome the prejudice which everywhere prevailed against the new order of things. Kyōto had suffered so much from fires and warlike attacks, and still more by poverty and neglect, that it was now in a lamentable condition. To have somebody, therefore, with the power and spirit to accomplish his ends, undertake to repair some of the wastes, and put in order what had long run to ruin, was an unexpected and agreeable surprise. The palaces of the emperor and the shōgun were repaired and made suitable as habitations for the heads of the nation. Streets and bridges, temples and grounds were everywhere put in order. Kyōto for the first time in many centuries had the benefit of a good and strong government.

[1] See Dening's *Life of Hideyoshi*, p. 207.

It was the custom to celebrate the establishment of a new year-period with popular rejoicings. The period called Genki was begun in December A.D. 1570 by the Emperor Ōgimachi. Nobunaga brought to Kyōto on this occasion a very large army in order to impress on the minds of the nation his overwhelming military power. He intended, moreover, to march his forces, as soon as this celebration was over, against Prince Asakura Yoshikage of the province of Echizen, who had not yet submitted himself to Nobunaga's authority, and who had not given in his adhesion to the new shōgun. Taking with him Hideyoshi and all the troops that could be spared from Kyōto, Nobunaga marched north into the domains of Yoshikage. He was aided in his resistance by Asai Nagamasa, the governor of the castle of Itami in the province of Ōmi. An attempt had been made by Nobunaga to conciliate Nagamasa by giving him his sister in marriage. But Nagamasa was still cool, and now at this critical time he turned to help Nobunaga's enemy. The unexpected combination came very near causing Nobunaga a disastrous defeat. At an important battle which was fought in this short campaign, we see together the three most noted men of their time, Nobunaga, Hideyoshi, and Ieyasu. The last of the three was only a few years younger than Hideyoshi, and had already shown indications of the clear and steady character of which he afterward gave such indubitable proof. The result was the defeat of Nobunaga's enemies and his victorious return to the castle of Gifu in the province of Mino.

But his way was not yet quite free from obstacles. Asakura Yoshikage and Asai Nagamasa although defeated were not crushed, and made various efforts to regain the advantage over Nobunaga. The most noted of these was when Nobunaga was absent from Kyōto with troops quelling a disturbance in Ōsaka, Asakura and Asai took advantage of the opportunity and marched a strong force upon the city. They had proceeded as far as Hiei-zan on the borders of Lake Biwa. This mountain was then occupied by an immense Buddhist monastery called Enriaku-ji from the year-period when it was established. It was said, that at this time there were as many as three thousand buildings belonging to the monastery. The monks of this establishment were exceedingly independent, and were so numerous and powerful that they were able to exact whatever concessions they desired from the government at Kyōto, from which they were only a few miles distant. They disliked Nobunaga and his powerful government with which they dared not take their usual liberties. Accordingly they made common cause with Asakura and Asai and furnished them with shelter and supplies on their march to Kyōto. But Nobunaga met them before they reached Kyōto, and so hemmed them in that they were glad to sue for peace and get back to their own provinces as well as they could. But on the ill-fated monastery Nobunaga in A.D. 1571 visited a terrible revenge. He burned their buildings, and what monks survived the slaughter he drove into banishment. The monastery was partially restored subsequently by Ieyasu, but it

was restricted to one hundred and twenty-five buildings and never afterwards was a political power in
the country.

During these years of Nobunaga's supremacy, the
Jesuit fathers had been pushing forward their work
of proselyting and had met with marvellous success.
The action of the Buddhist priests in siding with his
enemies and the consequent aversion with which he
regarded them, led Nobunaga to favor the establishment of Christian churches. In the letters of the
fathers at this period frequent references are made
to Nobunaga and of his favorable attitude toward
Christianity and their hope that he would finally become a convert. But it is plain that the fathers did
not comprehend fully the cause for the enmity of
Nobunaga to the Buddhist monks, and his political
reasons for showing favor to the Christian fathers.
He remained as long as he lived friendly to the
Christian church, but made no progress towards an
avowal of his faith. Under his patronage a church
was built in Kyōto, and another at Azuchi on Lake
Biwa, where he built for himself a beautiful castle
and residence. By this patronage and the zeal of
the fathers the Christian church rose to its greatest
prosperity [1] during the closing years of Nobunaga's
life. In the year A.D. 1582 a mission was sent to the
pope, consisting of representatives from the Christian princes of Bungo, Arima, and Ōmura. This
mission consisted of two young Christian princes
about sixteen years of age, accompanied by two

[1] In Chamberlain's *Things Japanese* the estimate is given that at
this most prosperous time the number of Japanese professing Christianity was not less than six hundred thousand, p. 297.

counsellors who were of more mature years, and by Father Valignani, a Portuguese Jesuit, and by Father Diego de Mesquita as their preceptor and interpreter. They visited the capitals of Portugal and Spain, which at this time were combined under the crown of Philip II. of Spain, and were received at both with the most impressive magnificence. They afterward visited Rome and were met by the bodyguard of the pope and escorted into the city by a long cavalcade of Roman nobles. They were lodged in the house of the Jesuits, whence they were conducted by an immense procession to the Vatican. The Japanese ambassadors rode in this procession on horseback dressed in their richest native costume. They each presented to the pope the letter[1] which they had brought from their prince, to which the reply of the pope was read. The presents which they had brought were also delivered, and after a series of most magnificent entertainments, and after they had been decorated as Knights of the Gilded Spears, they took their departure. In the meantime Pope Gregory XIII., who had received them, a few days later suddenly died A.D. 1585. His successor was Pope Sixtus V., who was equally attentive to the ambassadors, and who dismissed them with briefs addressed to their several princes.

Shōgun Ashikaga Yoshiaki, whom Nobunaga had been instrumental in installing, became restive in the subordinate part which he was permitted to play. He sought out the princes who still resisted Nobu-

[1] See the letter which the ambassador from the Prince of Bungo presented on this occasion. Hildredth's *Japan*, etc., p. 89.

naga's supremacy and communicated with them in reference to combining against him. He even went so far as to fortify some of the castles near Kyōto. Nobunaga took strenuous measures against Yoshiaki, and in A.D. 1573 deposed him. He was the last of the Ashikaga shōguns, and with him came to an end a dynasty which had continued from Taka-uji in A.D. 1335 for two hundred and thirty-eight years.

Nobunaga assumed the duties which had hitherto been performed by the shōgun, that is he issued orders and made war and formed alliances in the name of the emperor. But he never took the name of shōgun [1] or presumed to act in a capacity which from the time of Yoritomo had always been filled by a member of the Minamoto family, while he was a member of the Taira family. Whether this was the cause of his unwillingness to call himself by this title to which he might legitimately have aspired we can only conjecture. Of one thing we may be sure, that he was disinclined to arouse the enmity of the ambitious princes of the empire, whose co-operation he still needed to establish his power on an enduring basis, by assuming a position which centuries of usage had appropriated to another family. The emperor bestowed upon him the title of *nai-daijin*, which at this time however was a purely honorary designation and carried no power with it.

[1] In the First Part (1873) of *Mittheilungen der Deutschen Gesellschaft für Natur und Völkerkunde Ostasiens*, p. 15, the times of Nobunaga, Hideyoshi, etc., are termed "die zeit der usurpatoren," the time of the usurpers. But Nobunaga and Hideyoshi were no more usurpers than the Tokugawas, who succeeded them by force of arms.

The Prince of Chōsū was one of the most powerful of those who had not yet submitted to the supremacy of Nobunaga. The present prince was
Mōri Terumoto, the grandson of the Mōri Motonari
who by conquest had made himself master of a
large part of the central provinces. Nobunaga despatched Hideyoshi with the best equipped army
that at that time had ever been fitted out in Japan,
to subdue the provinces lying to the west of Kyōto.
He did not overrate the ability of the general to
whom he entrusted this task. They set out in the
early part of the year A.D. 1578. Their first movement was against the strongholds of the province of
Harima, which he reduced. We for the first time
find mention in this campaign of Kuroda [1] Yoshitaka, who in the invasion of Korea was a notable figure. His services to Hideyoshi at this time were
most signal. The campaign lasted about five years
and added five provinces to Nobunaga's dominions.
Then after a visit to Kyōto he continued his conquests, never meeting with a defeat. The most
remarkable achievement was the capture of the
castle of Takamatsu, in the province of Sanuki.
This castle was built with one side protected by the
Kōbe-gawa and two lakes lying on the other sides, so
that it was impossible to approach it by land with a
large force. Hideyoshi, with the genius for strategy
which marked his character, saw that the only way
to capture the fort was to drown it out with water.

---

[1] Mr. Satow with rare literary insight has identified this Kuroda
with the Condera Combiendono of the Jesuit fathers. *Asiatic Society
Transactions*, vol. vii., p. 151.

He then set his troops to dam up the river below the fortress. Gradually this was accomplished and as the water rose the occupants of the castle became more uncomfortable. Hideyoshi understanding his master's character feared to accomplish this important and critical exploit without Nobunaga's knowledge. He therefore wrote asking him to come without delay to his assistance. Nobunaga set out with a group of generals, among whom was Akechi Mitsuhide, with the troops under their command. They started from Azuchi on Lake Biwa, which was occupied as Nobunaga's headquarters. They were to proceed to the besieged fort by the shortest route. Nobunaga with a small escort went by way of Kyōto, expecting soon to follow them. He took up his temporary abode in the temple of Honnōji. It was observed that Akechi with his troops took a different route from the others and marched towards Kyōto. When spoken to about his purpose he exclaimed, "My enemy is in the Honnōji." He explained to his captains his purpose and promised them unlimited plunder if they assisted him. He led his troops to Kyōto and directly to the Honnōji. Nobunaga hearing the noise looked out and at once saw who were the traitors. He defended himself for a time, but soon saw that he was hopelessly surrounded and cut off from help. He retired to an inner room of the temple, set it on fire, and then calmly committed *hara-kiri*. His body was buried in the burning and falling ruins. His death occurred in A.D. 1582.

Thus ended the career of one of Japan's great men. He had shown the possibility of uniting the provinces of Japan under one strong government. He had given to Kyōto and the provinces lying east and north of it a period of peace and quiet under which great progress had been made in agriculture, the arts and in literature. He was a warrior and not a statesman, and for this reason less was done than might have been in confirming and solidifying the reforms which his conquest had made possible. Personally he was quick-tempered and overbearing, and often gave offence to those who were not able to see through his rough exterior to the true and generous heart which lay beneath. The cause of the plot against him was probably the consequence of a familiarity with which he sometimes treated his military subordinates. It is said that on one occasion in his palace when he had grown somewhat over-festive he took the head of his general Akechi [1] under his arm and with his fan played a tune upon it, using it like a drum. Akechi was mortally offended and never forgave the humiliating joke. His treason, which resulted in Nobunaga's death, was the final outcome of this bit of thoughtless horse-play.

[1] See Shiga's *History of Nations*, Tōkyō, 1888, p. 128.

CHAPTER IX.

TOYOTOMI HIDEYOSHI.

THE death of Nobunaga in the forty-ninth year of his age left the country in a critical condition. Sakuma and Shibata had been his active retainers and generals for many years, and they had the most bitter and envious hatred toward Hideyoshi, whom they had seen advance steadily up to and past them in the march of military preferment. It was to Hideyoshi that the country looked to take up the work which Nobunaga's death had interrupted. Akechi began to realize when too late that he must reckon with him for his terrible crime. He appointed two of his lieutenants to assassinate Hideyoshi on his way back to the capital. He sent word to Mōri Terumoto, who was trying to raise the siege of the castle of Takamatsu, concerning Nobunaga's death, hoping that this tragedy would encourage Terumoto to complete his designs.

In the meantime the news had reached Hideyoshi. Terumoto had heard of the starting of Nobunaga with additional troops, and had determined to make peace with Hideyoshi. He had sent messengers with a proposition for peace. The measures for taking the castle had succeeded and it was surrendered. In this state of things Hideyoshi[1] pursued a course which was characteristic of him. He sent word to Terumoto that Nobunaga was now dead and that therefore his proposition for peace might, if he wished, be withdrawn. You must decide, he said, whether you will make peace or not; it is immaterial whether I fight or conclude a treaty of peace. To such a message there could be only one answer. Peace was at once concluded and Hideyoshi started for Kyōto to deal with the traitors.

The attempt to assassinate Hideyoshi on his journey came very near being successful. He was in such eagerness to reach his destination that he hurried on without regard to his army which accompanied him. A small body-guard kept up as well as they could with their impatient chief. At Nishinomiya in this journey Hideyoshi, when in advance of his body-guard, was attacked by a band of the assassins. His only way of escape was by a narrow road between rice fields, leading to a small temple. When he had traversed part of this lane he dismounted, turning his horse around along the way he had come, and stabbed him in the hind leg. Mad with pain, he galloped back with disastrous effect upon the band which was following him. Meanwhile Hideyoshi hurried to the temple. Here the priests were all in a big common bath-tub, taking their bath. Hastily telling them who he was, and begging their protection, he stripped off his clothes and plunged in among the naked priests.

[1] Dening's *Life of Toyotomi Hideyoshi*, p. 274.

When the assassins arrived, they could find nothing but a bath-tub full of priests, whom they soon left in search of the fugitive. As they disappeared, the anxious body-guard arrived, and were astonished and amused to find their chief clad in the garb of a priest and refreshed after his hurried journey with a luxurious bath.[1]

Hideyoshi, as soon as he arrived at Kyōto, issued an invitation to all the princes to join him in punishing those who had brought about the death of Nobunaga. A battle was fought at Yodo, not far from Kyōto, which resulted in the complete defeat of Akechi. He escaped, however, from this battle, but on his way to his own castle he was recognized by a peasant and wounded with a bamboo spear. Seeing now that all hope was gone, he committed *hara-kiri*, and thus ended his inglorious career. His head was exposed in front of Honnōji, the temple where Nobunaga perished.

As might have been expected, this premature death of Nobunaga—for he was only forty-nine years old—created an intense excitement. The idea of heredity had so fixed a place in men's minds, that the only thought of Nobunaga's friends and retainers was to put forward in his place some one who should be his heir. There were living two sons, both by concubines, viz. Nobuo and Nobutaka, and a grandson, Sambōshi, still a child, who was a son of his son Nobutada, now deceased. Each of these representatives had supporters among the powerful retainers of the dead prince. It may be assumed

[1] See Dening's *Life of Toyotomi Hideyoshi*, p. 278.

that each was supported not because of the rightful claim which he had to the estates and the power which the dead prince had left behind him, but solely because the supporters of the successful heir would be entrusted with special authority, and endowed with conquered provinces. It is sufficient to explain here that Hideyoshi supported the candidacy of the grandson, Sambōshi, probably with no higher motive nor more disinterested purpose than the others. After a noisy and hot debate it was finally agreed that the grandson should be installed as successor, and Hideyoshi undertook to be his guardian. He had a large army at Kyōto, and with this he felt strong enough to carry things with a high hand. He appointed a funeral ceremony to be held in honor of Nobunaga, to which all the princes were invited, and he posted his troops in such a way as to command every avenue of approach. He claimed for himself, as guardian of the child Sambōshi, precedence of all the princes and generals. So at the funeral service, with the child Sambōshi in his arms, he proceeded in advance of all others to pay memorial honors to the dead. He supported this action with such an overwhelming display of military force that his enemies were afraid to show any resistance.

The disappointed princes retired to their provinces and hoped that by some fortuitous circumstances they might still be able to circumvent the plans of Hideyoshi. He saw well that he must meet the opposition which would be concentrated on him by activity and force. As a general not one of his enemies could compare with him in fertility of resources, in decisiveness of action, and in command of military strength. His first contest was with his old comrade in arms Shibata Katsuie, who had served with him under Nobunaga, and who was intensely jealous of Hideyoshi's rapid rise in military rank and territorial authority. Shibata had championed the cause of Nobutaka in the contest as to the successor of Nobunaga. He had command of troops in Echizen, and Nobutaka was governor of the castle of Gifu in the province of Mino. The campaign was a short and decisive one. The battle was fought at Shigutake and resulted in the complete defeat of Shibata and his allies. It is notable that in this battle artillery were used and played a conspicuous part. Shibata after his overthrow committed *hara-kiri.* Nobutaka having escaped also put an end to himself. Thus the active enemies of Hideyoshi in the north and west were overcome and the forfeited territory made use of to reward his friends.

His next contest was with the adherents of Nobuo, the other son of Nobunaga. This was made memorable by the assistance which Ieyasu rendered to Nobuo. Hideyoshi's army, himself not being present, was defeated. Ieyasu being satisfied with this victory and knowing that he could not ultimately triumph now made peace with Hideyoshi. The island of Shikoku, which was under the control of Chōsokabe Motochika was reduced to subjection in a brief campaign and the chiefs compelled to do duty to Hideyoshi as their head.

It seems that at this time Hideyoshi was ambi

tious to attain official appointment which would
legitimately descend to his children and make him
the founder of a new line of shōguns. He applied
to the ex-shōgun Yoshiaki, whom Nobunaga had deposed[1] and who was now living in retirement, inti-
mating that it would be to his interest to adopt
him as his son so that he could be appointed by the
emperor as shōgun. But Yoshiaki declined to com-
ply with this suggestion on account of Hideyoshi's
humble origin. In place of this appointment, however, he was installed A.D. 1585 by the Emperor
Ōgimachi as *Kuambaku*, which is higher in rank
than any other office in the gift of the imperial
court. Hitherto this title had been borne exclusively by members of the Fujiwara family, and it
must have been a severe blow to their aristocratic
pride to have a humble plebeian who had risen
solely by his own talents thus elevated by imperial
appointment to this dignified position. He also
received at this time the name of Toyotomi[2] by
which he was afterward called, and in recognition of
his successful conquest of much territory he received
A.D. 1575 the honorary title of Chikuzen-no-kami.

There were a few years from about A.D. 1583—
with an important exception which will be given

[1] See p.189.

[2] His original name was Nakamura Hyoshi, the family taking its
name from the village where he was born. Then at his induction to
manhood A.D. 1553 his name was changed to Tokichi Takayoshi. At
another turn in his career he became Kinoshita Tokichi Takayoshi,
In the year A.D. 1562 he received permission to use the name Hideyoshi instead of Tokichi, and A.D. 1575 his name was again changed
to Hashiba, which the Jesuit fathers wrote Faxiba.

below—when peace reigned in all the territories of Japan, and when Hideyoshi devoted himself wisely and patiently to the settlement of the feudal condition of the country. It was at this time he began building his great castle at Ōsaka which occupied about two years. Workmen were drawn from almost all parts of Japan, and a portion of it is said to have been finer and more massive than had ever been seen in Japan. This magnificent work[1] survived its capture by Ieyasu in 1614 and remained undisturbed down to the wars of the restoration in 1868, when it was burned by the Tokugawa troops at the time they were about to evacuate it.

The exception to which reference is made above was the important campaign which Hideyoshi was called upon to conduct in the island of Kyūshū against the Satsuma clan.[2] The distance at which Kyūshū lay from the centre of imperial operations, the mountainous and inaccessible character of a great part of the territory, made it no easy matter to deal with the refractory inhabitants of this island. The Satsuma clan even at that early day had a reputation for bravery and dash which made them feared by all their neighbors. The prince of Satsuma at this time was Shimazu Yoshihisa, a member of the same family who held the daimiate until the abolition of the feudal system. It is a tradition that the first of this family was a son of Yoritomo, who in

---

[1] See Satow and Hawes' *Handbook*, p. 341.

[2] The facts here related concerning this most interesting episode in the life of Hideyoshi are chiefly taken from a paper furnished by Mr. J. H. Gubbins to the *Asiatic Society Transactions*, vol. viii., p. 92.

the year A.D. 1193 was appointed governor of Satsuma. Like all the feudal princes of the period, the
prince of Satsuma was ambitious to extend his do
minion as far as possible. Hyūga, Bungo, Higo,
and Hizen were either wholly or in part subject to
his authority, so that by the year A.D. 1585 it was
the boast of the prince that eight provinces acknowledged him as lord.[1]

It was in this critical period that Hideyoshi was
appealed to for help by the threatened provinces.
He first sent a special envoy to Kagoshima, who was
directed to summon the prince to Kyōto to submit
himself to the emperor and seek investiture from
him for the territories which he held. Shimazu
received this message with scorn, tore up the letter
and trampled it under his feet, and declared that to
a man of mean extraction like Hideyoshi he would
never yield allegiance. Both parties recognized the
necessity of deciding this question by the arbitra-
ment of war.

Hideyoshi called upon thirty-seven provinces to
furnish troops for this expedition. It is said that
150,000 men were assembled at Ōsaka ready to be
transported into Kyūshū. The vanguard, consisting of 60,000 men under Hidenaga, the brother of
Hideyoshi, set sail January 7, A.D. 1587. Troops
from the western provinces joined these, so that this
advanced army numbered not less than 90,000 men.

---

[1] The Emperor Ōgimachi retired from the throne A.D. 1586, and
was succeeded by Go-Yojō, then sixteen years old. It shows of how
small account the emperors had become, that this change in the head
of the nation is scarcely mentioned in the histories of the time.

In due time, January 22d, Hideyoshi himself, with his main army, consisting of 130,000 men, left Ōsaka, marching by land to Shimonoseki, and from this point crossing over to Kyūshū. The Satsuma armies were in all cases far outnumbered, and step by step were compelled to retreat upon Kagoshima. Hideyoshi had by means of spies [1] acquired a complete knowledge of the difficult country through which his armies must march before reaching Kagoshima. After much fighting the Satsuma troops were at last driven into the castle of Kagoshima, and it only remained for Hideyoshi to capture this stronghold in order to end in the most brilliant manner his undertaking.

It was at this juncture that Hideyoshi made one of these surprising and clever movements which stamp him as a man of consummate genius. Instead of capturing the fortress and dividing up the territory among his deserving generals, as was expected, he restored to the Shimazu family its original buildings, viz., the provinces of Satsuma and Ōsumi and half the province of Hyūga, only imposing as a condition that the present reigning prince should retire in favor of his son, and that he should hold his fief as a grant from the emperor. Thus ended one of the most memorable of the

[1] The spies and guides employed by Hideyoshi were priests of the Shin sect of Buddhists, who after the fall of Kagoshima were discovered and crucified. A decree was also issued that every inhabitant of Satsuma who was connected with this sect must renounce his creed. To this day there exists among the people of Satsuma a general hostility to the Buddhists which can be traced to this trying episode. See *Asiatic Society Transactions*, vol. viii., p. 143.

campaigns which Hideyoshi had up to this time
undertaken, and with this also closed a series of
events which exerted a permanent influence on the
history of Japan.

It will be desirable at this point to trace the in-
cidents which had transpired in connection with the
Jesuit fathers. It will be remembered that the work
of the fathers [1] was much interfered with by the
political troubles which preceded the advent of Nobunaga. Owing to their taking sides with his
enemies he was very much incensed against the
Buddhist priests and visited his indignation upon
them in a drastic measure. [2] His desire to humiliate the Buddhist priests probably led him to assume
a favorable attitude towards the Christian fathers.
As long therefore as Nobunaga lived, churches were
protected and the work of proselyting went on.
Even after the death of Nobunaga in A.D. 1582 nothing occurred for some time to interfere with the
spread of Christianity. Hideyoshi was too much
occupied with political and military affairs to give
much attention to the circumstances concerning
religion. Indeed the opinion of Mr. Dening [3] in his
Life of Hideyoshi is no doubt true, that he was in no
respect of a religious temperament. Even the superstitions of his own country were treated with scant
courtesy by this great master of men.

Gregory XIII. seeing what progress the Jesuits
were making, and realizing how fatal to success any
conflict between rival brotherhoods would be, issued

[1] See p. 178.   [2] See p. 186.
[3] See Dening's *Life of Toyotomi Hideyoshi*, pp. 148, 344.

a brief in A.D. 1585, that no religious teachers except Jesuits should be allowed in Japan. This regulation was exceedingly distasteful to both the Dominicans and the Franciscans, especially after the visit of the Japanese embassy to Lisbon, Madrid, and Rome had directed the attention of the whole religious world to the triumphs which the Jesuits were making in Japan. Envy against the Portuguese merchants for their monopoly of the Japanese trade had also its place in stirring up the Spaniards at Manila to seek an entrance to the island empire. The opposition with which Christianity had met was represented as due to the character and behavior of the missioners. In view of these circumstances the Spanish governor of Manila sent a letter to Hideyoshi, asking for permission to open trade with some of the ports of Japan. Four Franciscans attached themselves to the bearer of this letter and in this way were introduced into the interior of Japan. Among the valuable presents sent to Hideyoshi by the governor of Manila was a fine Spanish horse [1] with all its equipments. These Franciscans who came in this indirect way were permitted to establish themselves in Kyōto and Nagasaki. They were at once met by the protest of the Jesuits who urged that the brief of the pope excluded them. But these wily Franciscans replied that they had entered Japan as ambassadors and not as religious fathers,

[1] When Father Valignani came to Japan in A.D. 1577 it is said that he brought as one of his presents a beautiful Arabian horse. It is not improbable that some of the improved breeds, now seen in the southern provinces, owe their origin to these valuable horses sent over as presents.

and that now when they were in Japan the brief of
the pope did not require them to leave.

A very bitter state of feeling from the first therefore manifested itself between the Jesuits and Franciscans. The latter claimed that the opposition they
met with was due to the plots and intrigues of the
Jesuits, and they openly avowed that the Jesuit
fathers through cowardice failed to exert themselves
in the fulfilment of their religious duties, and in a
craven spirit submitted to restrictions on their
liberty to preach. Hideyoshi's suspicion was aroused
against the foreigners about this time, A.D. 1587, by
the gossip of a Portuguese sea-captain which had
been reported to him. This report represented the
captain as saying: " The king, my master, begins
by sending priests who win over the people;
and when this is done he despatches his troops
to join the native Christians, and the conquest is easy and complete." [1] This plan seemed
so exactly to agree with experiences in China,
India, and the East Indies, that Hideyoshi resolved
to make it impossible in Japan. He therefore
issued an edict in the year A.D. 1587 commanding
all foreign religious teachers on pain of death to
depart from Japan in twenty days. This edict,
however, gave leave to Portuguese merchants " to
traffic and reside in our ports till further order; but
withal we do hereby strictly forbid them, on pain of

---

[1] See Chamberlain's *Things Japanese*, 1892, p. 298, note. According to Charlevoix this indiscreet speech was made by a Spanish
captain. See Gubbin's paper, *Asiatic Society Transactions*, **vol.
vi.**, part ii., p. 16.

having both their ships and merchandises confiscated, to bring over with them any foreign
religious." [1]

In consequence of this edict, in A.D. 1593 six
Franciscans and three Jesuits were arrested in
Ōsaka and Kyōto and taken to Nagasaki, and there
burnt. This was the first case of the execution of
Christians by the order of the government. To
explain the transportation of these missionaries to
Nagasaki and their execution there, it should be
stated that in A.D. 1586, at the close of the Satsuma
campaign, Nagasaki had been taken from the prince
of Ōmura and made a government city, to be controlled by a governor appointed immediately from
Kyōto. Shortly after this, in A.D. 1590, on account
of its superior harbor, it was fixed upon as the only
port at which foreign vessels would be admitted.

There was still one refractory element in his
dominions which it was necessary to deal with.
Hōjō Ujimasa maintained a hostile attitude at
Odawara. He was determined once for all to
reduce this rebellious chief and the others who
might be influenced by his example. It is unnecessary to give the details of this short but decisive
undertaking. Only one incident deserves to be
given as illustrative of the character of Hideyoshi.
In sending troops to the field of action it was necessary that a large number of horses should cross the
sea of Enshū,[2] which was usually very rough at that
time of year. The boatmen, as is usual, were very

---

[1] For the text of this edict see Dickson's *Japan*, p. 172.
[2] See Satow and Hawes' *Handbook*, 2d ed., p. 72.

superstitious, and had a decided aversion to transporting the horses in their boats ; averring that the god of the sea Ryūgū had a special dislike for horses. Hideyoshi sent for the boatmen and told them that he had undertaken this expedition at the command of the emperor, and that the god of the sea was too polite to interfere in anything pertaining to the transportation of troops for such a purpose. He said however that he would make it all right by writing a letter to Ryūgū, instructing him to insure the safe passage of the ships. This was done, and a letter addressed " Mr. Ryūgū " was thrown into the sea. The boatmen were satisfied, and the horses were taken over without difficulty.[1]

With the fall of Odawara the whole of the Kwantō, comprising the provinces of Sagami, Musashi, Kōtsuke, Shimotsuke, Hitachi, Shimōsa, Kazusa, and Awa came into the possession of Hideyoshi. During the progress of the siege, it is said that he and Ieyasu were standing in a watch tower which they had built on the heights above the castle of Odawara. Hideyoshi pointed to the great plain before them and said[2] : " Before many days I will have conquered all this, and I propose to give it into your keeping."

Ieyasu thanked him warmly and said : " That were indeed great luck."

Hideyoshi added : " Wilt thou reside here at Odawara as the Hōjō have done up to this time ? "

Ieyasu answered : " Aye, my lord, that I will."

[1] See Dening's *Life of Toyotomi Hideyoshi*, p. 405.
[2] See Adams' *History of Japan*, vol. i., p. 66.

"That will not do," said Hideyoshi. "I see on the map that there is a place called Yedo about twenty *ri* eastward from us. It is a position far better than this, and that will be the place for thee to live."

Ieyasu bowed low and replied: "I will with reverence obey your lordship's directions."

In accordance with this conversation after the fall of Odawara, Ieyasu was endowed with the provinces of the Kwantō and took up his residence at Yedo. This is the first important appearance of Yedo in the general history of Japan. It had however an earlier history, when in the fifteenth century it appears as a fishing village called *Ye-do*, that is *door of the bay*. Near this fishing village Ōta Dōkwan, a feudal baron, built himself in A.D. 1456 a castle. With the advent of Ieyasu, Yedo became a place of first importance, a rank which it still holds. The object of Hideyoshi in thus entrusting this great heritage to Ieyasu seems to have been to secure him by the chains of gratitude to himself and his family. Already Ieyasu was connected by marriage with Hideyoshi, his wife being Hideyoshi's sister. By making him lord of an immense and powerful country he hoped to secure him in perpetual loyalty to himself and his heirs.

In order that he might be free from the cares and responsibilities of the government at home, Hideyoshi retired from the position of *kwambaku* A.D. 1591 and took the title of *Taikō*. By this title he came to be generally known in Japanese history, Taikō Sama, or my lord Taikō, being the form by which he was commonly spoken of. His nephew and heir Hidetsugu was at this time promoted to the title of *kwambaku*, and was ostensibly at the head of the government. The Jesuit fathers speak of him as mild and amiable, and as at one time a hopeful student of the Christian religion. They note however a strange characteristic in him, that he was fond of cruelty and that when criminals were to be put to death he sought the privilege of cutting them into pieces and trying cruel experiments upon their suffering bodies.

In A.D. 1592 Taikō Sama had by one of his wives a son, whom he named Hideyori. Over this new-born heir, whom, however, many suspect of not being Taikō Sama's son, he made great rejoicing throughout the empire. He required his nephew to adopt this new-born son as his heir, although he had several sons of his own. The result of this action was a feeling of hostility between the uncle and nephew. Hidetsugu applied to Mōri, the chief of Chōsū, to aid him in the conflict with his uncle. But Mōri was too wary to enter upon such a contest with the veteran general. Instead of helping Hidetsugu, he revealed to Taikō Sama the traitorous proposition of his nephew. Hidetsugu was thereupon stripped of his office and sent as an exile to the monastery of Kōya-san in the province of Kii. A year later he was commanded with his attendants to commit *hara-kiri;* and with an unusual exhibition of cruelty, his counsellors, wives, and children were likewise put to death.

Hideyoshi had for a long time contemplated the

invasion of Korea and ultimately of China. In a conversation with Nobunaga when he was about to set out on his conquest of the western provinces he is represented as saying[1]: "I hope to bring the whole of Chūgoku into subjection to us. When that is accomplished I will go on to Kyūshū and take the whole of it. When Kyūshū is ours, if you will grant me the revenue of that island for one year, I will prepare ships of war, and purchase provisions, and go over and take Korea. Korea I shall ask you to bestow on me as a reward for my services, and to enable me to make still further conquests; for with Korean troops, aided by your illustrious influence, I intend to bring the whole of China under my sway. When that is effected, the three countries [China, Korea, and Japan] will be one. I shall do it all as easily as a man rolls up a piece of matting and carries it under his arm." He had already carried out part of this plan; he had brought the whole of Chūgoku and of the island of Kyūshū under his rule. It remained for him to effect the conquest of Korea and China in order to complete his ambitious project.

For this purpose he needed ships on a large scale, for the transportation of troops and for keeping them supplied with necessary provisions. From the foreign merchants, who traded at his ports, he hoped to obtain ships larger and stronger than were built in his own dominions. It was a great disappointment to him when he found this impossible, and that the merchants, whom he had favored, were un-.

[1] See Dening's *Life of Toyotomi Hideyoshi*, p. 263.

14

willing to put their ships at his disposal. It is claimed by the Jesuit fathers that this disappointment was the chief reason for the want of favor with which Hideyoshi regarded them during the last years of his life. It is also advanced as one reason for his entering on the invasion of Korea, that he might thus employ in distant and dangerous expeditions some of the Christian princes whose fidelity to himself and loyalty to the emperor he thought he had reason to doubt. He was ambitious, so they said, to rival in his own person the reputation of the Emperor Ōjin, who rose in popular estimation to the rank of Hachiman, the god of war, and who is worshipped in many temples, because, while he was still unborn, his mother led a hostile and successful expedition into this same Korea.

The immediate pretext [1] for a war was the fact that for many years the embassies which it had been the custom to send from Korea to Japan with gifts and acknowledgments had been discontinued. In A.D. 1582 he sent an envoy to remonstrate, who was unsuccessful. Subsequently he sent the prince of Tsushima, who had maintained at Fusan, a port of Korea, a station for trade, to continue negotiations. After some delay and the concession of important conditions the prince had the satisfaction, in A.D. 1590, of accompanying an embassy which the government of Korea sent to Hideyoshi. They arrived

[1] We are indebted to Mr. W. G. Aston for a full and clear account of Hideyoshi's invasion of Korea, which he had derived not only from Japanese books and documents, but from Korean sources which, until his researches, were inaccessible. See *Asiatic Society Transactions*, vol. vi., p. 227; ix., pp. 87, 213.

at Kyōto at the time when Hideyoshi was absent on his campaign against Hōjō Ujimasa at Odawara. He allowed them to await his return, and even when he had resumed his residence at the capital he showed no eagerness to give them an audience. On the pretence that the hall of audience needed repairs, he kept them waiting many months before he gave orders for their reception. It seemed that he was trying to humiliate them in revenge for their dilatoriness in coming to him. It is not impossible that he had already made up his mind to conduct an expedition in any event into Korea and China, and the disrespect with which he treated the embassy was with the deliberate intention of widening the breach already existing.

Mr. Aston has given us an account of the reception which was finally accorded to the ambassadors, drawn from Korean sources, and which shows that they were entertained in a very unceremonious fashion. They were surprised to find that in Japan this man whom they had been led to look upon as a sovereign was only a subject. They presented a letter from the king of Korea conveying his congratulations and enumerating the gifts [1] he had sent. These enumerated gifts consisted of horses, falcons, saddles, harness, cloth of various kinds, skins, ginseng, etc. These were articles which the Japanese of an earlier age had prized very highly and for the more artistic production of some of which the Ko-

[1] The peculiarly Eastern form of expression is noticeable in announcing these presents : " You will find enclosed a list of some of the poor productions of our country, which we beg you will refrain from laughing at immoderately."

reans had rendered material assistance. Hideyoshi suggested that the embassy should return to their own country at once without waiting for an answer to their letter. This they were unwilling to do. So they waited at Sakai whence they were to sail, till the *kwambaku* was pleased to send them a message for their king. It was so arrogant in tone that they had to beg for its modification several times before they dared to carry it home. The letter plainly announced his intention to invade China and called upon the Koreans to aid him in this purpose.

The ambassadors went home with the conviction that it was Hideyoshi's intention to invade their country. At their instigation the government made what preparations it could, by repairing fortresses, and collecting troops, arms, and provisions. The country was a poor country, and had had the good fortune or the misfortune to remain at peace for two hundred years. The arts of war had been forgotten. They had no generals who could cope with the practised soldiers of Japan. Firearms which had been introduced into the military equipments of Japanese armies were almost unknown in Korea. It is true that they had been taken under the protection of China and could call upon her for aid. But China was distant and slow, and Korea might be destroyed before her slumbering energies could be aroused.

The preparations which Hideyoshi made, as was his custom, were thorough and extensive. Each prince in Kyūshū, as being nearest to the seat of war, was required to furnish a quota of troops in proportion to his revenues. Each prince in Shikoku and in the Main island, in like manner, was to provide troops proportionate to his revenue and his proximity to the seat of war. Princes whose territories bordered on the sea were to furnish junks and boats, and men to handle them. The force which was thus assembled at Nagoya, now called Karatsu, in Hizen was estimated at 300,000 men, of whom 130,000 were to be immediately despatched. Hideyoshi did not personally lead this force. It was under the command of two generals who were independent of each other, but were ordered to co-operate. One of these generals was Konishi Yukinaga Settsu-no-kami, whom the Jesuit fathers refer to under the name of Don Austin. From an humble position in life he had risen to high and responsible rank in the army. Under the influence of Takeyama, a Christian prince, whom the Jesuit fathers call Justo Ucondono, he had been converted to Christianity. Hideyoshi, as has been pointed out, was desirous of securing the help of the Christian princes in Kyūshū, and therefore appointed a Christian as one of the generals-in-chief. Under him were sent the contingents from Bungo, Ōmura, Arima, and other provinces where the Christian element was predominant. This division of the invading army may therefore be looked upon as representing the Christian population of the empire. The other general-in-chief was Katō Kiyomasa,[1] who had been

---

[1] He became one of the most famous heroes of Japan, and is worshipped under the name of Seishōkō, at a shrine connected with the temple of Hommonji at Ikegami. Satow and Hawes' *Handbook*, p. 30.

associated with Hideyoshi ever since the times of
Nobunaga. He was the son of a blacksmith and in
A.D. 1563 he became one of Hideyoshi's retainers.
He was a man of unusual size and of great personal
bravery. He commanded an army collected mainly
from the northern and eastern provinces, which comprised the experienced veterans of Hideyoshi's earlier
campaigns. He is usually spoken of as inimical to
the Christians, but this enmity probably grew up
along with the ill-feeling between the two armies in
Korea.

Konishi's division arrived in Korea April 13, A.D.
1592, and captured the small town of Fusan,
which had been the port at which the Japanese had
for generations maintained a trading post. After
the arrival of Katō the two divisions marched towards the capital, reducing without difficulty the
castles that lay in their way. The greatest terror
prevailed among the inhabitants, and the court, with
King Riyen at its head, resolved to flee into the
province bordering on China. The armies reached
the capital and then set out northward. The dissensions between the commanders had by this time
reached such a point that they determined to separate. Katō traversed the northeastern provinces
and in his course captured many Koreans of rank.

Konishi marched to the north and found the king
at Pingshang on the borders of the river Taitong-
Kiang. Here he was joined by Kuroda Noritaka,
whom the Jesuit fathers named Condera [1] Combien-

---

[1] See Mr. Satow's identification of this name. *Asiatic Society
Transactions*, vol. vii., p. 151.

dono, and by Yoshitoshi the prince of Tsushima, who had marched with their forces by a different route. An effort at negotiations at this point met with no success. The king continued his flight northward to Ichiu, a fortified town on the borders of China. After he left a sharp contest took place between the besiegers and defenders, which resulted in the abandonment of the town and its capture by the Japanese. The stores of grain which had been collected by the Koreans were captured with the town.

Konishi was anxious to conduct further military operations in connection with the Japanese vessels which had been lying all this time at Fusan. Directions were accordingly sent to have the junks sent round to the western coast. The Koreans picked up courage to show fight with their vessels, which seemed to have been of a superior construction to those of their enemies. They allured the Japanese boats out to sea and then turned upon them suddenly and treated them so roughly that they were glad to get back to the protection of the harbor and to give up the purpose of cruising along the western coast. The result of this little success encouraged the Koreans so much that it may be said to have been a turning point in the invasion.

In the meantime the piteous appeals of the Koreans to China had produced some effect. A small army of five thousand men, which was raised in the adjoining province of Laotung, was sent to their aid. This insufficient force rashly undertook to attack the Japanese in Pingshang. But they led the invaders into the town, and then so thoroughly routed them that the escaped remnants made their way back to Laotung. This experience led the Chinese officials to see that if they wished to help the Koreans at all they must despatch a stronger force. This they set to work at once to do. They endeavored to gain some time by pretending to enter upon negotiations for an armistice. During the autumn months of A.D. 1592 the Japanese troops were almost idle. And they were very much taken by surprise when near the end of the year the Chinese army, forty thousand strong, besides Koreans, made its appearance on the scene. The Japanese commander had no time to call for help, and before he realized the imminency of the danger Pingshang was attacked. Being far outnumbered Konishi deemed it prudent to make his escape from the beleaguered town, and to save his army by a retreat, which was a painful and inglorious one.

The other division of the Japanese army under Katō, who had occupied the west coast, found its position untenable with a superior Chinese army threatening it. It also was compelled to retreat towards the south. But the veteran army of Katō was not content to yield all that it had gained without a struggle. A bloody engagement followed near Pachiung, in which the Chinese and Korean army suffered a significant defeat. The Chinese army then retired to Pingshang, and Katō was not in a condition to follow it over the impassable winter roads and with deficient supplies. The Japanese troops had suffered an experience such as never befell

;hem under the redoubtable leadership of Hideyoshi.
And the Chinese had had enough of the terrible
two-handed swords which the Japanese soldier
could wield so effectively.[1]

The chief obstacle to peace was the mutual distrust with which each of the three parties regarded
the others. Korea hated the Japanese with a perfect and justifiable hatred; she also feared and
despised the pompous and pretentious pride of
China. But in the negotiations which ensued the
country which had suffered most had least to say.
It remained for the two greater powers to come to
some agreement which should be satisfactory to
them; and whether Korea were satisfied or not was
of secondary moment.

The Japanese envoy proceeded to Peking and is
said to have negotiated peace on these conditions:
That the emperor of China should grant to Hideyoshi the honor of investiture, that the Japanese
troops should all leave Korea, and that Japan should
engage never to invade Korea again. There was
some jangling about the withdrawal of the Japanese
soldiers but at last this matter was arranged.

An embassy was sent by the Chinese government
to Japan to carry out the ceremony of investiture.
They arrived in the autumn of the year A.D. 1596.
Taikō Sama made elaborate preparations for their
reception. Some fears were felt as to how Taikō
Sama would regard this proposition of investiture
when he came to understand it. The Buddhist
priest, who was to translate the Chinese document

[1] See Mr. Aston's paper, *Asiatic Society Transactions*, vol. ix., p. 90.

into Japanese [1] for the benefit of Taikō Sama, was urged to make some modification in the wording to conciliate his ambition. But he was too honest to depart from the true rendering. He read to Taikō Sama and the assembled court a letter from the Chinese emperor granting him investiture as king of Japan, and announced having sent by the ambassadors the robe and the golden seal pertaining to the office.

Taikō Sama listened with amazement,[2] as he for the first time realized that the Emperor of China by this document had undertaken to invest him as king of Japan instead of (" Ming emperor "). He was in an uncontrollable rage. He tore off the robe which he had put on. He snatched the document from the reader and tore it into shreds, exclaiming: " Since I have the whole of this country in my grasp, did I wish to become its emperor I could do so without the consent of the barbarians." He was with difficulty restrained from taking the life of the Japanese ambassador who had negotiated the treaty. He sent word to the Chinese envoys who had brought the robe and seal to begone back to their country and to tell their emperor that he would send troops to slaughter them like cattle. Both Korea and China knew that a new invasion would

---

[1] A Japanese scholar could read such a document in the ideographic Chinese characters without translation ; but Taikō Sama was not a scholar and therefore was not aware of the purport of the document until it was translated to him.

[2] See Mr. Aston's description of this humiliating scene as given in *Asiatic Society Transactions*, vol. ix., p. 217 ; also Dening's *Life of Toyotomi Hideyoshi*, p. 360.

surely result from this disappointment. Katō and Konishi the Japanese generals in the previous campaign and who had gone home during the interval were ordered back to take command of the old troops and of fresh recruits which were to be sent. They busied themselves with repairing the fortifications which had been left in possession of the Japanese garrisons.

The disgraced and frightened Chinese ambassadors made their way back to Peking. They were ashamed to present themselves without showing something in return for the gifts they had carried to Taikō Sama. They purchased some velvets and scarlet cloth, which they represented as the presents which had been sent. They pretended that Taikō Sama was much pleased with the investiture, and that his invasion of Korea was due to the fact that the Korean government had interfered to prevent the free and kindly intercourse between China and Japan. The cloth and velvet, however, were at once recognized as European productions and not derived from Japan. So the ambassadors were charged with deceit and at last confessed.

The Japanese army was reinforced, it is said, with 130,000 fresh troops. Supplies, however, were difficult to obtain, and the movements were much hindered. A small Chinese army of 5,000 men arrived at the end of the year A.D. 1597 to aid the Koreans. An attack on the Japanese ships at Fusan was made by the Korean navy, but it was without difficulty repelled and most of the attacking ships destroyed. After some material advantages, which, however,

were not decisive, the Japanese troops were forced
to return to Fusan for the winter. The principal
engagement was at Yöl-san, a strong position, accessible both by sea and land. It was garrisoned by
troops of Katō's division, who were brave and determined. The army composed of Chinese and
Koreans, under the Chinese commander-in-chief
Hsing-chieh, laid siege to this fortress, and succeeded in cutting off all its communications. But
Kuroda and Hachisuka came to Katō's assistance,
and compelled the Chinese general to raise the siege
and retreat to Söul, the Korean capital. It was in
one of the battles fought during the summer of
A.D. 1598, that 38,700 heads of Chinese and Korean
soldiers are said to have been taken. The heads
were buried in a mound after the ears and noses
had been cut off. These grewsome relics of savage
warfare were pickled in tubs and sent home to
Kyōto, where they were deposited in a mound in
the grounds of the temple of Daibutsu, and over
them a monument erected which is marked *mimi-
zuka* or ear-mound. There the mound and monument can be seen to this day.[1]

The death of Taikō Sama occurred on the day
equivalent to the 18th of September, A.D. 1598, and
on his death-bed he seems to have been troubled
with the thought of the veteran warriors who were
uselessly wearing out their lives in Korea. In his
last moments he opened his eyes and exclaimed
earnestly : " Let not the spirits of the hundred
thousand troops I have sent to Korea become dis-

[1] See Satow and Hawes' *Handbook*, p. 369.

embodied in a foreign land."[1] Ieyasu, on whom devolved the military responsibility after the Taikō's death, and who had never sympathized with his wishes and aims regarding Korea, did not delay the complete withdrawal of the troops which still remained in Korea.

Thus ended a chapter in the history of Japan, on which her best friends can look back with neither pride nor satisfaction. This war was begun without any sufficient provocation, and its results did nothing to advance the glory of Japan or its soldiers. The great soldier who planned it and pushed it on with relentless energy gained nothing from it except vexation. Much of the time during which the war lasted he sat in his temporary palace at Nagoya in Hizen, waiting eagerly for news from his armies. Instead of tidings of victories and triumphs and rich conquests, he was obliged too often to hear of the dissensions of his generals, the starving and miseries of his soldiers, and the curses and hatred of a ruined and unhappy country. All that he had to show for his expenditure of men and money were several *saké* tubs of pickled ears and noses with which to form a mound in the temple of Daibutsu, and the recollection of an investiture by the emperor of China, which could only bring to him pain and humiliation.

The only beneficial results to Japan that can be traced to all this was the introduction into different provinces of some of the skilled artisans of Korea. The prince of Satsuma, Shimazu Yoshihiro, in

[1] See Dening's *Life of Toyotomi Hideyoshi*, p. 380.

A.D. 1598, brought home with him when he returned from the Korean war seventeen families of Korean potters,[1] who were settled in his province. They have lived there ever since, and in many ways still retain the marks of their nationality. It is to them that Satsuma *faïence* owes its exquisite beauty and its world-wide reputation.

When the Taikō realized that his recovery was impossible he tried to arrange the affairs of the empire in such a way as to secure a continuation of the power in his son Hideyori, who was at that time only five years old. For this purpose he appointed a council consisting of Tokugawa Ieyasu, Maeda Toshi-ie, Mōri Terumoto, Ukita Hide-ei and Uesugi Kagekatsu, of which Ieyasu was the president and chief. These were to constitute a regency during his son's minority. He also appointed a board of associates, who were called middle councillors, and a board of military officers called *bugyo*. He called all these councillors and military officers into his presence before he died, and made them swear allegiance to his successor Hideyori. There seems to have been among them a suspicion of the fidelity of Ieyasu, for the Taikō is represented as saying to two of his friends: "You need not be anxious about Ieyasu. He will not rebel against my house.[2] Cultivate friendship with him." Thus in his sixty-second year died (September, 1598) the greatest

---

[1] See Mr. Satow's paper entitled "The Korean Potters in Satsuma," *Asiatic Society Transactions*, vol. vi., p. 193 ; also as referred to in Mr. Satow's paper, Mr. Ninagawa's *Notice Historique et Descriptive sur les Arts et Industries Japonais*, part v., Tōkyō, 1877.

[2] "In point of fact, however, making Ongoschio (Ieyasu) regent was placing a goat in charge of a kitchen garden."—*Warenius*, p. 20.

soldier, if not the greatest man, whom Japan has produced. That he rose from obscurity solely by his own talents, is a more conspicuous merit in

HIDEYOSHI.

Japan than in most other countries. Family and heredity have always counted for so much in this land of the gods, that few instances have occurred in which men of humble birth have risen to eminence. That one such in spite of his low birth, in spite of personal infirmities, in spite of the opposition and envy of contemporaries, had risen to so high a position in the empire, has been a source of

pride and encouragement to thousands of his countrymen.

The Taikō was buried close to the Daibutsu
temple, which he himself had built to shelter the
colossal figure of Buddha, constructed in imitation
of the Daibutsu which Yoritomo had built at Kamakura. The figure was to be one hundred and
sixty feet in height, and the workmen had it nearly
finished when a terrible earthquake in A.D. 1596
shook down the building. In the following year the
temple was rebuilt, and the image was completed
up to the neck. The workmen were preparing to
cast the head, when a fire broke out in the scaffold-
ing and again destroyed the temple, and also the
image. It was one of the schemes of Ieyasu, so it
is said, to induce the young Hideyori to exhaust his
resources upon such expensive projects, and thus
render him incapable of resisting any serious movement against himself. He therefore suggested to
the boy and his mother that this temple and image,
which Hideyoshi had begun, should not fail of erec-
tion. They therefore resumed the construction,
and carried it on with great lavishness. It took
until A.D. 1614 to complete the work, and when it
was about to be consecrated with imposing ceremonies, Ieyasu, who by this time was supreme in the
empire, suddenly forbade the progress of the ceremony. He affected to be offended by the inscription which had been put on the bell,[1] but the real
reason was probably his desire to find some pretext
by which he could put a quarrel upon the adherents
of Hideyori.

[1] See Satow and Hawes' *Handbook*, p. 368.

CHAPTER X.

THE FOUNDING OF THE TOKUGAWA SHŌGUNATE.

AMONG all the friends and retainers of Hideyoshi the most prominent and able was Tokugawa Ieyasu. He was six years younger than Hideyoshi, and therefore in A.D. 1598, when the Taikō died, he was fifty-six years old. He was born at the village of Matsudaira in the province of Mikawa A.D. 1542. His family counted its descent from Minamoto Yoshi-ie, who in the eleventh century had by his military prowess in the wars against the Ainos earned the heroic name of Hachiman-Tarō. Therefore he was, as custom and tradition now for a long time had required for those holding the office of shōgun, a descendant from the Minamoto family.[1] The name Tokugawa, which Ieyasu rendered famous, was derived from a village in the province of Shimotsuke, where his ancestors had lived. His first experiences in war were under Nobunaga, side by side with Hideyoshi. He proved himself not only a capable soldier, prudent and painstaking, but also a good administrator in times of peace. Hideyoshi

---

[1] See the pedigree of Ieyasu as given in *Mittheilungen der Deutschen Gesellschaft*, etc., Heft i., p. 19.

had such confidence in him, and so much doubt
about the wisdom of requiring the guardians to wait
until his son, a mere child five years old, had grown
up to years of responsibility, that he is represented
as having said to Ieyasu: " I foresee that there will
be great wars after my decease; I know too that
there is no one but you who can keep the country
quiet. I therefore bequeath the whole country to
you, and trust you will expend all your strength in
governing it. My son Hideyori is still young. I
beg you will look after him. When he is grown up,
I leave it to you to decide whether he will be my
successor or not." [1]

As soon as the Taikō was dead, and the attempt
was made to set in motion the machinery he had
designed for governing the country, troubles began
to manifest themselves. The princes whom he had
appointed as members of his governing boards, began immediately to quarrel among themselves. On
Ieyasu devolved the duty of regulating the affairs of
the government. For this purpose he resided at
Fushimi, which is a suburb of Kyōto. His most
active opponent was Ishida Mitsunari, who had been
appointed one of the five *bugyō*, or governors, under
the Taikō's arrangement. They grew jealous of
Ieyasu, because, under the existing order of things,
the governors were of very minor importance.
Mitsunari had acquired his influence with the Taikō,
not through military achievements, but by intrigue
and flattery. He was cordially detested by such
disinterested friends as Katō Kiyomasa and others.

[1] See Dening's *Life of Toyotomi Hideyoshi*, p. 377.

The ground on which the opposition to Ieyasu was based was that he was not faithfully performing his duty, as he had promised to the dying Taikō, towards his child and heir. It is not improbable that even at this early day it was seen that Ieyasu proposed to disregard the pretensions of the youthful son of Hideyoshi, in the same way that he in his day had disregarded the claims of the heir of Nobunaga. The rough and warlike times, and the restless and ambitious manners of the feudal lords of these times, made it impossible to entrust the country to the hands of a child.

Under this strained relation, the members of the regency divided into two parties. Speaking broadly, it was again a contest between the north and the south of Japan. Ieyasu's association had been from the beginning with the Kwantō, and now more than ever his power was centred about Yedo. Mitsunari on the contrary had leagued himself with the princes of Chōsū and Satsuma, and with others of minor importance, all more or less representative of the southern half of the empire. The Christians chiefly sided with Hideyori and his adherents. Mitsunari himself was a Christian convert, and the Jesuit fathers explain that his position and that of the other Christian leaders were due to their conscientious desire to fulfil their oath of fidelity to Hideyori. That Ieyasu should have been derelict in such a solemn duty was a sufficient cause for their opposition to him.

Events now rushed rapidly to a culmination. One of the most powerful of the princes allied against

Ieyasu was Uesugi Kagekatsu, the lord of Echigo and Aizu. He had retired to Aizu after having solemnly made a covenant [1] with the others engaged in the plot to take measures against Ieyasu. He was summoned to Kyōto to pay his respects to the emperor, but on some trivial excuse he declined to come. Ieyasu now saw that nothing but war would settle the disputes which had arisen. He repaired to Yedo and to Shimotsuké, and made preparations for the conflict which he saw impending.

In the meantime the members of the league were busy. Mitsunari sent an urgent circular to all the feudal princes, charging Ieyasu with certain misdeeds and crimes, the chief of which was that instead of guarding the inheritance of the Taikō for his son, he was with the blackest guilt endeavoring to seize it for himself. A formidable army was gathered at Ōsaka consisting of 128,000 men. [2] Made up as it was from different provinces and officered by its provincial leaders, it lacked that element of unity and accord which is so essential to an army. The first movement was against the castle of Fushimi, which was the centre from which Ieyasu governed the country. After a short siege it fell and then, it is said, was accidentally burned to the ground.

The news of the attack upon Fushimi was brought to Ieyasu in Shimotsuké, and a council of his friends and retainers was held to determine what steps must

[1] This covenant is said to have been signed with blood in accordance with a custom still occasionally prevalent, in which a drop of blood is drawn from the middle finger and sealed by pressing it with the thumb nail. Rein's *Japan*, p. 297, note.

[2] See Dening's *Life of Toyotomi Hideyoshi*, p. 397.

be taken to meet the emergency. It was urged that the time had come when Ieyasu should meet his enemies, and settle by battle the questions which had risen between them. It was determined that all the scattered troops should be gathered together, and that they should march to Fushimi prepared to encounter the enemy in battle at whatever point they should meet them. The eldest son of Ieyasu, Hideyasu, was put in charge of Yedo and entrusted with the care of the surrounding provinces. This was an important trust, because the powerful prince Uesugi lay to the north of him and would seize the first opportunity to attack him. To Fukushima was given the command of the vanguard. The principal army was divided into two parts, one of which was to march along the Tōkaidō under the command of Ieyasu himself, the other was placed under the charge of Ieyasu's second son Hidetada, and was to take the route along the Nakasendō. The whole army consisted of 75,000 men, a number much smaller than the army of the league, but which had the advantage of being controlled by one mastering and experienced commander.

The armies met at Sekigahara,[1] a little village on the Nakasendō, October, A.D. 1600. One place on the neighboring hill is still pointed out whence Ieyasu witnessed the battle and issued his orders. Both sides fought with determined bravery, and the battle lasted the whole day. Cannon and other

---

[1] This place receives its name from a barrier that was erected in the ninth century to control the travel towards the capital. Its meaning is, "Plain of the Barrier." See Chamberlain's *Handbook*, p. 268.

firearms were to some extent made use of, but the old-fashioned weapons, the sword and the spear, were the terrible means by which the victory was decided. For a long time the battle raged without either party obtaining a decisive advantage. Notwithstanding his inferiority in numbers Ieyasu was completely victorious. The carnage was dreadful. The number of the confederate army said to have been killed was 40,000.[1] This seems like an impossible exaggeration, and the Japanese annalists are, like those of other nations, given to heightened statements. But that the loss of life on both sides was very great there can be no doubt.

Two ghastly mounds called Kubi-zuka, or head piles, are still shown where the heads of the decapitated confederates were buried. This battle must always stand with that at Dan-no-ura between the Minamoto and Taira families, as one of the decisive battles in the history of Japan. By it was settled the fate of the country for two hundred and fifty years.

It was fortunate that the victor in this battle was a man who knew how to secure the advantages to be derived from a victory. It is said that at the close of this battle when he saw success perching on his banners, he repeated to those around him the old Japanese proverb: " After victory tighten the strings of your helmet."[2]   The division of Hidetada joined

---

[1] See Dening's *Life of Toyotomi Hideyoshi*, p. 399.

[2] This proverb is quoted as having been used by Hideyoshi when remonstrating with Nobunaga about following up his victory over Imagawa Yoshimoto. See Dening's *Life of Toyotomi Hideyoshi*, p. 156.

him after the battle, and he promptly followed up
his victory by seizing the castles on his way and taking possession of Kyōto and Ōsaka. The feudal
princes who had stood aloof or opposed him nearly
all came forward and submitted themselves to his
authority. Uesugi and Satake in the north, who
had been among his most active opponents, at once
presented themselves to Hideyasu at Yedo and
made their submission. Mōri, the powerful lord of
the western provinces, who had been most active in
the confederation against him, sent congratulations
on his victory, but they were coldly received. Finally he was pardoned, being however deprived of
six out of his eight provinces. He was suffered to
retain of all his rich inheritance only Suō and
Nagato. Several of the leaders were captured,
among whom were Mitsunari, Konishi, and Ōtani,
who being Christians deemed it unworthy their faith
to commit *hara-kiri*. They were carried to Kyōto
where they were beheaded and their heads exposed
in the dry bed of the Kamo-gawa.

The work of reducing to order the island of
Kyūshū was entrusted to the veteran generals Katō
Kiyomasa and Kuroda Yoshitaka. The former
undertook the reduction of Hizen, and the latter
that of Bungo, Buzen, and Chikuzen. The house of
Shimazu, although it had taken sides against Ieyasu
in the great contest, duly made its submission and
was treated with great consideration. The whole of
the territory assigned to it by Hideyoshi after the
war of A.D. 1586 was restored to it, namely, the
whole of the provinces of Satsuma and Ōsumi, and

one half of the province of Hyūga. To Katō Kiyomasa[1] was given the province of Higo, which had, after the Korean war, been assigned to Konishi in recognition of his services, but which was now taken from his family because he had been one of Ieyasu's active opponents. The Kuroda family received as its inheritance a portion of the province of Chikuzen with its capital at Fukuoka, which it held until the abolition of feudal tenures in 1871.

Ieyasu was a peaceful and moderate character, and in the settlement of the disturbances which had marked his advent to power, he is notable for having pursued a course of great kindness and consideration. With the exception of the cases already mentioned there were no executions for political offences. It was his desire and ambition to establish a system of government which should be continuous and not liable, like those of Nobunaga and Taikō Sama, to be overturned at the death of him who had founded it. By the gift of Taikō Sama he had

[1] Kiyomasa was a bitter enemy of the Christians, owing no doubt to the rivalry and antagonism which had sprung up with Konishi, who was a Christian, in the Korean war. He is termed Toronosqui by the Jesuit fathers from a personal name Toronosuke which he bore in his youth, and he is characterized as "*vir ter execrandus*," on account of his persecution of the Christians in his province. Perhaps on account of this fierce opposition he was greatly admired by the Buddhists, and is worshipped under the name of Seishōkō by the Nichiren sect at a shrine in the temple of Hommonji at Ikegami. Another monument to his memory is the Castle of Kumamoto, which he built and which still stands as one of the best existing specimens of the feudal castles of Japan. As an evidence of its substantial character, in A.D. 1877, under the command of General Tani, it withstood the siege of the Satsuma rebels and gave the government time to bring troops to crush the rebellion.

already in his possession a large part of the Kwantō. And by the result of the war which had ended at Sekigahara, he had come into possession of a great number of other fiefs, with which he could reward those who had been faithful to him. It was the difficult and delicate part of his work to distribute judiciously among his supporters and retainers the confiscated estates. To realize how completely the feudal system as reformed by Ieyasu was bound to him and constituted to support and perpetuate his family, it is only necessary to examine such a list of the daimyōs[1] as is given in Appert's *Ancien Japon.*[2] Out of the two hundred and sixty-three daimyōs there enumerated, one hundred and fifty-eight are either vassals or branches of the Tokugawa family. But while he thus carefully provided the supports for his own family, he spared many of the old and well-rooted houses, which had incorporated themselves into the history of the country. He built his structure on the old and tried foundation stones. With far-sighted statesmanship he recognized that every new form of government, to be permanent, must be a development from that which precedes it, and must include within itself whatever is lasting in the nature of its forerunner.

The dual form of government had for many centuries existed in Japan, and the customs and habits of thinking, and the modes of administering justice and of controlling the conduct of men had become adapted to this system. It was therefore natural

---

[1] The plural of this word is here and elsewhere used in its English form, although no such plural is found in Japanese.

[2] *Ancien Japon,* par G. Appert, Tōkyō, 1888, vol. ii.

that Ieyasu should turn his attention to reforming and perfecting such a form of government. A scheme of this kind seemed best adapted to a country in which there existed on the one hand an emperor of divine origin, honored of all men, but who by long neglect had become unfit to govern, and in whom was lodged only the source of honor; and on the other hand an executive department on which devolved the practical duty of governing, organizing, maintaining, and defending. Though he was compelled to look back through centuries of misrule, and through long periods of war and usurpation, he could see straight to Yoritomo, the first of the shōguns, and could trace from him a clear descent in the Minamoto family. To this task, therefore, he set himself: to maintain the empire in all its heaven-descended purity and to create a line of hereditary shōguns who should constitute its executive department.

In pursuance of this plan, he sent his son Hidetada to the emperor to make a full report of everything that had been done in the settlement of the affairs of the country. The emperor was graciously pleased to approve his acts and to bestow upon him, A.D. 1603, the hereditary title of Sei-i-tai-shōgun. This was the title borne by Yoritomo when he was the real ruler of the country. Since that time there had been a long line of shōguns, the last of whom was Ashikaga Yoshiaki, whom Nobunaga deposed in 1573, and who had died 1597. With this new appointment began a line of Tokugawa shōguns that ended only with the restoration in 1868.

Ieyasu's most radical change in the system of
government consisted in the establishment of the
seat of his executive department at Yedo. Since
A.D. 794 Kyōto had been the capital where successive
emperors had reigned, and where Nobunaga and
Hideyoshi exercised executive control. Kamakura
had been the seat of Yoritomo and his successors.
But Ieyasu saw advantages in establishing himself
in a new field, to which the traditions of idleness
and effeminacy had not attached themselves, and
where the associations of his own warlike career
would act as a stimulus to his contemporaries and
successors. He remained at Fushimi until necessary
repairs could be made to the Castle of Yedo [1] and
the roads between it and the capital put in order.
The place which henceforth was to be the principal
capital of the country first comes into notice, as we
have before mentioned, as a castle built by Ōta Dōkwan in A.D. 1456. He had been placed here by the
authorities of Kamakura to watch the movements of
the restless princes of the north. Recognizing the
strength and convenience of the high grounds on
the border of Yedo bay, he built a castle which,
through many transformations and enlargements,
finally developed into the great feudal capital of the
Tokugawa shōguns. It was here that Ieyasu, after
the fall of Odawara, by the advice of Hideyoshi,[2]
established himself for the government of the provinces of the Kwantō which had been given to him.

[1] A full account of the Castle of Yedo will be found in a paper by
Mr. J. R. H. McClatchie in the *Asiatic Society Transactions*, vol.
vi., part 1, p.119.

[2] See p. 207.

And it was without doubt this earlier experience which led him to select Yedo as the centre of his feudal government. The reputation which this eastern region bore for roughness and want of culture, as compared with the capital of the emperor at Kyōto, seemed to him an advantage rather than an objection. He could here build up a system of government free from the faults and weaknesses which had become inseparable from the old seats of power. After the repairs and enlargements had been completed he took up his residence there. Besides this castle, Ieyasu had for his private residence, especially after his retirement from the shōgunate, an establishment at Sumpu, now called Shizuoka. Here he was visited by English and Dutch envoys in reference to the terms of allowing trade, and here, after the manner of his country, he maintained his hold upon the administration of affairs, notwithstanding his formal retirement.

A continued source of disquietude and danger to the empire, or at least to the plans of Ieyasu for a dynasty of Tokugawa shōguns, lay in Hideyori, the son and heir of Taikō Sama. He was born in 1592, and was therefore at this time, 1614, in his twenty-third year. As long as he lived he would be naturally and inevitably the centre to which all the disaffected elements of the country would gravitate. The failure of Ieyasu to support the cause of his old master's son would always prove a source of weakness to him, especially in a country where fidelity to parents and superiors was held in such high esteem. He determined, therefore, to bring to a conclusion these threatening troubles which had so long been hanging over him. Accordingly, on the ground that Hideyori was plotting with his enemies against the peace of the state, he set out from Sumpu, where he was then residing as retired shōgun, with an army of seventy thousand men. Hideyori and his mother had for a long time resided at the castle of Ōsaka, and against this Ieyasu directed his large army. It was bravely and skilfully defended, and without the help of artillery, which at this early day was rarely used in sieges, a long time elapsed before any decided advantage was gained. At last the defenders were tempted beyond the protection of their fortifications, and a battle was fought June 3, 1615. It is described by the Jesuit fathers, two of whom witnessed it, as being sanguinary beyond the example of the bloody battles of the Japanese civil wars. It resulted in the complete overthrow of Hideyori's adherents, and the destruction of the castle by fire. Both Hideyori and his mother were said to have perished in the conflagration. Reports were current that they had, however, escaped and taken refuge in some friendly locality. But no trace of them was ever found, and it was taken for granted that this was the end of Hideyori and his party.

Before ending this chapter, which is designed to record the establishment of the Tokugawa shōguns, reference should be made to the settlement of the questions left in dispute by Taikō Sama respecting Korea. There remained after the war, with all its attendant atrocities and sufferings, a feeling of intense bitterness towards the Japanese on the part both of the Koreans and Chinese. The absence of any sufficient cause for the invasion, and the avowed purpose of Taikō Sama to extend his conquests to China had awakened against him and his armies a hatred which generations could not wipe out. Soon after the recall of the Japanese troops which followed the death of Taikō Sama, Ieyasu opened negotiations with Korea through the daimyō of Tsushima. He caused the government to be informed that any friendly overtures on its part would be received in a like spirit. The king of Korea accordingly despatched an embassy with an autograph letter, addressed to the "king of Japan." A translation of this letter will be found in Mr. Aston's last paper [1] on Hideyoshi's invasion of Korea. Among other things it says: "The sovereign and subjects of this country were profoundly grieved, and felt that they could not live under the same heaven with your country. . . . However your country has now reformed the errors of the past dynasty and practises the former friendly relations. If this be so, is it not a blessing to the people of both countries? We have therefore sent you the present embassy in token of friendship. The enclosed paper contains a list of some poor productions of our country. Be pleased to understand this." This letter was dated in the year 1607. A friendly answer was returned to it, and from this time it may be understood that the relations between the two countries were placed on a satisfac-

[1] *Asiatic Society Transactions*, vol. xi., p. 124.

tory basis. These steps were taken on the part of Korea with the knowledge and approval of China, which now claimed to hold a protectorate over the peninsula of Korea. The same negotiations therefore which resulted in peaceful relations with Korea brought about a condition of amity with China which was not disturbed until very recent times.

The ruinous effects of this invasion, however, were never overcome in Korea itself. Her cities had been destroyed, her industries blotted out, and her fertile fields rendered desolate. Once she had been the fruitful tree from which Japan was glad to gather her arts and civilization, but now she was only a branchless trunk which the fires of war had charred and left standing.

TOKUGAWA CREST.

CHAPTER XI.

CHRISTIANITY IN THE SEVENTEENTH CENTURY.

To the readers of the story of Japan the most interesting episode is that of the introduction and subsequent extirpation of Christianity. We have therefore given an account of the first arrival of the Jesuit missionaries with the sainted Xavier at their head, and we have seen their labors crowned with a very wide success. During the times of Nobunaga and Hideyoshi the question had assumed something of a political aspect. In several of the provinces of Kyūshū the princes had become converts and had freely used their influence, and sometimes their authority, to extend Christianity among their subjects. In Kyōto and Yamaguchi, in Ōsaka and Sakai, as well as in Kyūshū, the Jesuit fathers had founded flourishing churches and exerted a wide influence. They had established colleges where the candidates for the church could be educated and trained. They had organized hospitals and asylums at Nagasaki and elsewhere, where those needing aid could be received and treated.

It is true that the progress of the work had met

with a severe setback in A.D. 1587, when Taikō Sama issued an edict expelling all foreign religious teachers from Japan. In pursuance of this edict nine foreigners who had evaded expulsion were burnt at Nagasaki. The reason for this decisive action on the part of Taikō Sama is usually attributed to the suspicion which had been awakened in him by the loose and unguarded talk of a Portuguese sea captain.[1] But other causes undoubtedly contributed to produce in him this intolerant frame of mind. Indeed, the idea of toleration as applied to religious belief had not yet been admitted even in Europe. At this very time Philip II., who had united in his own person the kingdoms of Spain and Portugal, was endeavoring to compel, by force of arms, the Netherlands to accept his religious belief, and was engaged throughout all his immense dominions in the task of reducing men's minds to a hideous uniformity.

Even in several of the provinces of Japan where the Jesuits had attained the ascendancy, the most forcible measures had been taken by the Christian princes to compel all their subjects to follow their own example and adopt the Christian faith. Takeyama, whom the Jesuit fathers designate as Justo Ucondono, carried out in his territory at Akashi a system of bitter persecution. He gave his subjects the option of becoming Christians or leaving his teritory. Konishi Yukinaga, who received part of the province of Higo as his fief after the Korean war, enforced with great persistency the acceptance

[1] See p. 204.

16

of the Christian faith, and robbed the Buddhist priests of their temples and their lands. The princes of Ōmura and Arima, and to a certain extent the princes of Bungo, followed the advice of the Jesuit fathers in using their authority to advance the cause of Christianity. The fathers could scarcely complain of having the system of intolerance practised upon them, which, when circumstances were favorable, they had advised to be applied to their opponents. It was this impossibility of securing peace and harmony, and the suspicion of the territorial ambition of Spain and Portugal, which drove Taikō Sama to the conclusion that the foreign religious teachers and the faith which they had so successfully propagated, were a source of imminent danger to his country. To him it was purely a political question. He had no deep religious impressions which had led him to prefer the precepts of the old Japanese faith to those of Christianity. These systems could not apparently live together, and it seemed to him the safest and most sensible way to extinguish the weaker and most dangerous before it became too strong. Hence he began that policy of repression and expulsion which his successor reluctantly took up.

During the first years of Ieyasu's supremacy the Christians were not disturbed. He was too much occupied with the establishment of the new executive department which he had planned. In 1606 the Portuguese resident bishop, Father Louis Cerqueria, was received by Ieyasu at Kyōto. The fathers speak of this audience with great hopefulness, and did not seem to be aware that the court which most of the Christian princes were at that time paying to Hideyori was likely to prejudice Ieyasu against them. Again in 1607 Ieyasu, who was then at Kofu in the province of Kai awaiting the completion of his castle at Yedo, expressed a desire to see the Provincial. Accordingly when he waited on Ieyasu he was received very cordially. The Christian fathers were much encouraged by these indications of the favor of Ieyasu. But whatever they may have been, they cannot be interpreted as showing any intention on his part to promote their religious proselytism. Even in the very midst of these assumed favors he issued in 1606 what may be called a warning proclamation,[1] announcing that he had learned with pain that, contrary to Taikō Sama's edict, many had embraced the Christian religion. He warned all officers of his court to see that the edict was strictly enforced. He declared that it was for the good of the state that none should embrace the new doctrine ; and that such as had already done so must change immediately.

This proclamation of Ieyasu did not, however, prevent the Catholics at Nagasaki from celebrating in a gorgeous manner the beatification[2] of Ignatius Loyola, the founder and first General of the Society of Jesus. The bishop officiated in pontifical robes, and the members of the society, together with the Franciscans, Dominicans, and Augustinians, made a

---

[1] See Dickson's *Japan*, p 227.

[2] His beatification was decreed by the pope in 1609, and his canonization in 1622.

solemn procession through the city. This celebration was in distinct contravention of the orders which had been issued against such public displays. It was made more emphatic by being also held on the same day in the province of Arima, whose daimyō was an ardent advocate of the Christian doctrine. These open and determined infractions of the directions of the government provoked Ieyasu to take severe measures. He began by punishing some of the native Christians connected with his own court, who were charged with bribery and intrigue in behalf of the daimyō of Arima. A number of these accused Christians were banished and their estates confiscated.

In the meantime both the English and Dutch had appeared on the scene, as will be more fully detailed in the next chapter. Their object was solely trade, and as the Portuguese monopoly hitherto had been mainly secured by the Jesuit fathers, it was natural for the new-comers to represent the motive of these fathers in an unfavorable and suspicious light. "Indeed," as Hildreth [1] says, "they had only to confirm the truth of what the Portuguese and Spanish said of each other to excite in the minds of the Japanese rulers the gravest distrust as to the designs of the priests of both nations." [2]

[1] Hildreth's *Japan*, etc., p. 176.

[2] The Jesuit historians relate with malicious satisfaction how one of the Spanish friars, in a dispute with one of Adams' shipwrecked company, to sustain the authority of the church appealed to the miraculous power which its priests still possessed. And when the Hollander challenged an exhibition of such power, the missionary undertook to walk on the surface of the sea. A day was appointed.

Whether it is true as charged that the minds of the Japanese rulers had been poisoned against the Jesuit fathers by misrepresentation and falsehood, it may be impossible to determine definitely; but it is fair to infer that the cruel and intolerant policy of the Spanish and Portuguese would be fully set forth and the danger to the Japanese empire from the machinations of the foreign religious teachers held up in the worst light.

During the latter years of Ieyasu's life, after he had settled the affairs of the empire and put the shōgunate upon a permanent basis, we see growing evidence of his prejudice against Christianity. That he had such prejudice in a very pronounced form is clear from his reference to the "false and corrupt school" in chapter xxxi. of the *Legacy*. And he had inherited from Taikō Sama the conviction that the spread of this foreign faith was a menace to the peace of the empire. The instructions [1] which were issued

The Spaniard prepared himself by confession, prayer, and fasting. A great crowd of the Japanese assembled to see the miracle, and the friar, after a confident exhortation to the multitude, stepped, crucifix in hand, into the water. But he was soon floundering over his head, and was only saved from drowning by some boats sent to his assistance.—Hildreth's *Japan*, etc., p. 140.

[1] "This will seem to you less strange, if you consider how the Apostle St. Paul commands us to obey even secular superiors and gentiles as Christ himself, from whom all well-ordered authority is derived: for thus he writes to the Ephesians (vii. 5): 'be obedient to them that are your temporal lords according to the flesh, with fear and trembling in the simplicity of your heart, as to Christ; not seeming to the eye, as it were pleasing men, but as the servants of Christ doing the will of God from the heart, with a good will seeming as to the Lord and not to men.'"

The above is an extract from an Epistle of St. Ignatius, the 26th to the members of the Society of Jesus, however, forbade any father to meddle in secular affairs or to interfere in any way with the political concerns of the government in which they were laboring. That there were occasional instances of the disregard of this regulation by the enthusiastic members of the order may be supposed, but it will be unjust and unfounded to attribute to this society a settled policy of interference in the affairs of the nations where they were employed as missionaries.

Ieyasu, evidently having made up his mind that for the safety of the empire Christianity must be extirpated, in 1614 issued an edict[1] that the members of all religious orders, whether European or Japanese, should be sent out of the country; that the churches which had been erected in various localities should be pulled down, and that the native adherents of the faith should be compelled to renounce it. In part execution of this edict all the members of the Society of Jesus, native and foreign,

of March, 1553, which is still regarded as authoritative and is read every month to each of the houses. It was supplied to me by Dr. Carl Meyer and verified by Rev. D. H. Buel, S. J. of St. Francis Xavier's College, New York City. Dr. Meyer has also pointed out that the Second General Congregation, 1565, severely forbids any Jesuit to act as confessor or theologian to a prince longer than one or two years, and gives the minutest instructions to prevent a priest from interfering in any way with political and secular affairs in such a position.

[1] This edict of Ieyasu is given by Mr. Satow in his contributions to the debate on Mr. Gubbins' *Review of the Introduction of Christianity into China and Japan.* Fifteen rules to guide the Buddhist priests in guaranteeing the orthodoxy of their parishioners are also given.—*Asiatic Society Transactions,* vol. vi., part i., p. 46.

were ordered to be sent to Nagasaki. Native Christians were sent to Tsugaru, the northern extremity of the Main island. Takeyama, who had already been banished by Taikō Sama to the province of Kaga, was ordered to leave the country. He was sent in a Chinese ship to Manila, where he soon after died. In order to repress any disturbance that might arise from the execution of this edict, ten thousand troops were sent to Kyūshū, where the converts were much the most numerous, and where the daimyōs in many cases either openly protected or indirectly favored the new faith.

In accordance with this edict, as many as three hundred persons are said to have been shipped from Japan October 25, 1614. All the resident Jesuits were included in this number, excepting eighteen fathers and nine brothers, who concealed themselves and thus escaped the search. Following this deportation of converts the most persistent efforts continued to be made to force the native Christians to renounce their faith. The accounts given, both by the foreign and by the Japanese writers, of the persecutions which now broke upon the heads of the Christians are beyond description horrible. A special service was established by the government which was called the Christian Enquiry,[1] the object of which was to search out Christians in every quarter and drive them to a renunciation of their faith. Both the foreign priests who had remained in the country in spite of the edict and the native converts

[1] See Gubbins' paper, *Asiatic Society Transactions*, vol. vi., part i., p. 35.

were hunted down and punished with the most appalling tortures. Rewards were offered for information involving Christians of every position and rank, even of parents against their children and of children against their parents. At what time this practice began it is difficult to say, but that rewards were used at an early period is evident from the re-issue of an edict in 1655, in which it is stated [1] that formerly a reward of 200 pieces of silver was paid for denouncing a father (*bateren*) and 100 for denouncing a brother (*iruman*); but from this time the rewards should be: for denouncing a father, 300 pieces; a brother, 200 pieces; and a catechist, 50 pieces. In 1711 this tariff was raised, for denouncing a father to 500 pieces, a brother to 300 pieces, and a catechist to 100 pieces; also for denouncing a person who, having recanted, returned to the faith, 300 pieces. These edicts against Christianity were displayed on the edict-boards as late as the year 1868.

The persecution began in its worst form about 1616. This was the year in which Ieyasu died, but his son and successor carried out the terrible programme with heartless thoroughness. It has never been surpassed for cruelty and brutality on the part of the persecutors, or for courage and constancy on the part of those who suffered. The letters of the Jesuit fathers are full of descriptions of the shocking trials to which the Christians were subjected. The tortures inflicted are almost beyond belief. Mr.

---

[1] See Mr. Satow's contributions to the debate on Mr. Gubbins' paper, *Asiatic Society Transactions*, vol. vi., part i., p. 51.

Gubbins, in the paper [1] to which reference has already been made, says: "We read of Christians being executed in a barbarous manner in sight of each other, of their being hurled from the tops of precipices, of their being buried alive, of their being torn asunder by oxen, of their being tied up in rice-bags, which were heaped up together, and of the pile thus formed being set on fire. Others were tortured before death by the insertion of sharp spikes under the nails of their hands and feet, while some poor wretches by a refinement of horrid cruelty were shut up in cages and there left to starve with food before their eyes. Let it not be supposed that we have drawn on the Jesuit accounts solely for this information. An examination of the Japanese records will show that the case is not overstated." [2]

The region around Nagasaki was most fully impregnated with the new doctrine, and it was here that the persecution was by far the most severe. This was now an imperial city, governed directly by officers from the government of Yedo. The gov-

---

[1] *Asiatic Society Transactions*, vol. vi., part 1, p. 35.

[2] See chapter xi. of a *Description of the Kingdom of Japan and Siam*, by Bernhard Warenius, M.D., Cambridge, Printing-House of John Hayes, Printer to the University, A.D. 1673. The volume is in Latin, which, as well as a translation of the same in manuscript, has been furnished to me by Mr. Benjamin Smith Lyman, of Philadelphia. Warenius was a Lutheran, and need not be suspected of being prejudiced in favor of the Jesuits. See also *History of the Martyrs of Japan*, *Prague*, 1675, by Mathia Tanner, containing many engravings of the horrible scenes, such as burnings, crucifixions, and suspensions in the pit, etc.; also *Histoire des Vingt-six Martyrs du Japon, Crucifié à Nagasaqui le 5 Février, 1597*, par D. Bouix, Paris, 1862.

ernor is called Kanwaytsdo by Warenius, relying on
Caron and Guysbert, but I have been unable to
identify him by his true Japanese name. Beginning
from 1616 there was a continuous succession of persecutions. In 1622 one hundred and thirty men,
women, and children were put to death, among
whom were two Spanish priests, and Spinola an
Italian. The next year one hundred more were put
to death. The heroism of these martyrs awakened
the greatest enthusiasm among the Christians. In
the darkness of the night following the execution
many of them crept to the place where their friends
had been burnt and tenderly plucked some charred
fragments of their bodies, which they carried away
and cherished as precious relics. To prevent the
recurrence of such practices the officers directed
that the bodies of those burnt should be completely
consumed and the ashes thrown into the sea. Guysbert in his account mentions that among those executed at Hirado was a man who had been in the
employ of the Dutch factory and his wife. They
had two little boys whom the factor offered to take
and have brought up by the Dutch. But the parents
declined, saying that they preferred to have the boys
die with them. A plan was devised by which the
heads of households were required to certify that
none of their families were Christians, and that no
priests or converts were harbored by them.

All this terrible exercise of power and the constantly recurring scenes of suffering were more than
the governor could endure, and so we find him at
last complaining that he could not sleep and that his

health was impaired. At his earnest petition he was relieved and a new governor appointed in 1626. He signalized his entrance upon his duties by condemning thirteen Christians to be burnt, viz.: Bishop Franciscus Parquerus, a Portuguese, seventy years old; Balthazar de Tores, a Dominican, fifty-seven years old, together with five Portuguese and five Japanese laymen. When it came to the crisis the five Portuguese renounced their faith and escaped death. On the twelfth of July nine more were executed, five by burning and four by beheading. On the twenty-ninth of July a priest was caught and executed who had concealed himself in a camp of lepers, and who had hoped in that way to escape detection.

The governor exerted himself to bring about recantations on the part of those who had professed themselves Christians. He promised special favors to such as would renounce their faith, and in many cases went far beyond promises to secure the result. He set a day when all the apostates dressed in their best clothes should present themselves at his office. Fifteen hundred appeared on this occasion, and were treated with the greatest kindness and consideration. But the officers began to see that putting Christians to death would not prevent others from embracing the same doctrine. There grew up such an enthusiasm among the faithful that they sought rather than avoided the crown of martyrdom. As Guysbert points out, the knowledge of the Christian religion possessed by these converts must have been exceedingly small; they knew the Lord's prayer and the *Ave Maria*, and a few other prayers of the Church, but they had not the Scriptures to read, and many of them could not have read them even if they had been translated into their own language. And yet these humble and ignorant people withstood death, and tortures far worse than death, with a heroism worthy of all praise.

On the eighth of February, 1627, twelve persons were captured in a hiding-place about a mile from Nagasaki; they were first branded with a hot iron on the forehead, and then on each cheek; then because they would not recant they were burnt to death. Subsequently forty more were captured, among whom were a father and mother with their three young children. The children were frightened at the dreadful preparations, and would have recanted, but their parents refused to permit them to take advantage of the offers of clemency. After the branding and beating, those who were not yet driven to recant were sent off to the boiling springs of Onsen in Arima. Here they were tortured by having the boiling water of the springs poured upon them, and by being compelled to breathe the suffocating sulphurous air which these springs emitted.

On the fourteenth of the following May, nine martyrs suffered all the torments which could be contrived and finally were drowned. August seventeenth five Christians were burnt and eighteen otherwise put to death, of whom one was a Franciscan monk and the rest were natives. October twenty-sixth three Japanese magnates who had joined Hideyori against Ieyasu were discovered to be Christians, and were shipped off to Macao. In the following year, 1628, it is said that three hundred and forty-eight persons were tortured for their faith, including torture by the boiling springs, beating with clubs, and burning. It had been reduced to such a science that when they saw a subject becoming weak and likely to die, they suspended their torments until he revived. Whenever a priest was captured in any household the whole family by whom he had been concealed were put to death.

Another new governor was sent to Nagasaki on the 27th of July, 1629. He came with the high purpose of rooting out every vestige of Christianity. He set about his work in the most systematic manner. Nagasaki, it must be understood, is laid out in streets which can be closed up by gates. Each street had its head man, and every five houses in each street were under the special charge of a separate overseer. These overseers were responsible as to what occurred and who were concealed in each of the houses under his charge. The gates were all closed at night and opened again in the morning.

The governor went through these streets house by house, and examined every person in every house. If the occupants were not Christians, or if they renounced their Christianity, they were allowed to go undisturbed; but if any one persisted in the new doctrine he was sent off to be tortured by hot water at the boiling springs. This torture was now improved by requiring the victim to have his back slit open and the boiling water poured directly on the raw flesh. He used the most monstrous means to force the people to renounce their faith. He compelled naked women to go through the streets on their hands and knees, and many recanted rather than suffer such an ordeal. Other cases are recorded too horrible to be related, and which only the ingenuity of hell could have devised. That any should have persisted after such inhuman persecutions seems to be almost beyond belief. Guysbert says that in 1626 Nagasaki had forty thousand Christians, and in 1629 not one was left who acknowledged himself a believer. The governor was proud that he had virtually exterminated Christianity.

But the extermination had not yet been attained. The severity of the measures adopted in Nagasaki had indeed driven many into the surrounding provinces, so that every place of shelter was full. They awaited in terror the time when they too should be summoned to torture and death. Usually they had not long to wait, for the service of the Christian Enquiry was active and diligent. New refinements of cruelty were constantly invented and applied. The last and one of the most effectual is denominated by the foreign historians of these scenes the *Torment of the Fosse.* Mathia Tanner, S. J., in his *History of the Martyrs of Japan,* published in Prague, 1675, gives minute accounts of many martyrdoms. His descriptions are illustrated by sickening engravings of the tortures inflicted. Among these he gives one illustrating the suspension of a martyr in a pit on the 16th of August, 1633. The victim is swathed in a covering which confines all parts of the body except one hand with which he can make the signal of recantation. A post is planted by the side of the pit, with an arm projecting out over it. The martyr is then drawn up by a rope fastened to the feet and run over the arm of the post. He is then lowered into the pit to a depth of five or six feet and there suffered to hang. The suffering was excruciating. Blood exuded from the mouth and nose, and the sense of pressure on the brain was fearful. Yet with all this suffering the victim usually lived eight or nine days. Few could endure this torture, and it proved a most effectual method of bringing about recantations. Guysbert says that he had many friendly conversations with those who had experienced the torture of the *Fosse*. They solemnly assured him "that neither the pain caused by burning with fire, nor that caused by any other kind of torture, deserves to be compared with the agony produced in this way." Not being able longer to endure the suffering, they had recanted and been set free. Yet it is told as a miraculous triumph of faith that a young girl was submitted to this torture, and lived fifteen days without recanting and at last died.

It is surely not unnatural that human nature should succumb to such torments. Even the well seasoned nerves of the Jesuit fathers were not always able to endure to the end. The enemies of the Jesuits delight in narrating the apostasy of Father Christopher Ferreyra, seventy years old, a Portuguese missionary and the provincial of the order. He was captured in Nagasaki, 1633, and was tortured by suspension in the *Fosse*. After five hours he gave the signal of recantation and was released. He was kept for some time in prison and compelled to give information concerning the members of his order in Japan. He was set at liberty and forced to marry, assuming the Japanese dress and a Japanese name. There was a report set on foot by the Jesuits that in his old age when on his death-bed he recovered his courage and declared himself a Christian, whereupon he was immediately carried off by the Japanese officers to the torture of the *Fosse*, where he perished a penitent martyr.

It was at this time that the method of trial called *E-fumi,*[1] or trampling on the cross, was instituted. At first pictures on paper were used, then slabs of wood were substituted as more durable, and finally in the year 1660 an engraver of Nagasaki, named Yusa, cast bronze plates from the metal obtained by despoiling the altars of the churches. These plates were about five inches long and four inches wide and one inch thick, and had on them a figure of Christ on the cross. We take from the French edition of Kæmpfer's *History of Japan*[2] an account of what he calls "this detestable solemnity." It was conducted by an officer called the *kirishitan bugyō,* or Christian inquisitor, and began on the second day of the first month. In Nagasaki it was commenced

---

[1] See Woolley's "Historical Notes on Nagasaki," *Asiatic Society Transactions*, vol. ix., part 2, p. 134; also Mr. Satow's contributions to the discussion of Mr. Gubbins' paper, *Asiatic Society Transactions*, vol. vi., part 2., p. 52. Specimens of the metal plates are in the Uyeno Museum of Tōkyō.

[2] See Kæmpfer's *Histoire de l' Empire de Japon*, tome i., p. 287

at two different places at once, and was carried on from house to house until the whole city was finished. The officers of each street were required to be present. The metal plate on which was a figure of the Saviour upon the cross was laid upon the floor. Then the head of the house, his family, and servants of both sexes, old and young, and any lodgers that might be in the house, were called into the room. The secretary of the inquisitor thereupon made a list of the household and called upon them one by one to set their feet on the plate. Even young children not able to walk were carried by their mothers and made to step on the images with their feet. Then the head of the family put his seal to the list as a certificate to be laid before the governor that the inquisition had been performed in his house. If any refused thus to trample on the cross they were at once turned over to the proper officers to be tortured as the cases required.

This same method of trial was used in the provinces about Nagasaki, the governor lending to the officers the plate which they might use.

Without following the entire series of events which resulted in the extirpation of Christianity, it will be sufficient to give a brief narrative of the closing act in this fearful tragedy. It is just, however, to explain that the Shimabara rebellion was not due to the Christians alone, but that other causes contributed to and perhaps originated it. In view, however, of the cruel persecutions to which the Christians were subjected, it is not surprising that they should have been driven to engage in such a

17

rebellion as that in Arima.[1] The wonder rather is
that they were not often and in many places impelled
to take up arms against the inhumanities of their
rulers. The explanation of this absence of resistance will be found in the scattered condition of the
Christian communities. Nowhere, unless it might
be in Nagasaki, was the number of converts collected in one place at all considerable. They were
everywhere overawed by the organized power of the
government, and the experience of those who joined
in this Arima insurrection did not encourage a repetition of its horrors.

The beginning of the revolt is traced to the misgovernment of the daimyō of Arima. The original
daimyō had been transferred by the shōgun to
another province, and when he removed from Arima
he left nearly all his old retainers behind him. The
newly instituted daimyō, on the contrary, who came
to occupy the vacated province brought with him a
full complement of his own followers. To make
room for these new retainers the old ones were dis-

---

[1] In the narrative which we give of this insurrection we have relied chiefly upon the accounts of Mr. Gubbins in his "Review of the
Introduction of Christianity," *Asiatic Society Transactions*, vol. vi.,
part 1, p. 36 ; of Mr. Woolley in his "Historical Notes on Nagasaki,"
do., vol. ix., part 2, p. 140 ; and on Dr. Geerts' paper on the "Arima
Rebellion and the Conduct of Koeckebacker, *do.*, vol. xi., p. 51. Mr.
Gubbins and Mr. Woolley had access to Japanese authorities, and we
have in their papers been enabled to see this bloody episode for the
first time from a Japanese standpoint. Dr. Geerts has rendered
an invaluable service in giving us translations of letters written by
Koeckebacker, the head of the Dutch factory during the events,
which show us how this insurrection was regarded by the Dutch East
India Company.

placed from their dwellings and holdings, and compelled to become farmers or to take up any other occupation which they could find. Like the *samurai* of other parts of Japan who had been unaccustomed to any calling except that of arms, these displaced retainers proved very unsuccessful farmers, and were of course very much dissatisfied with the new course of things. The daimyō was a cruel and inconsiderate man, who made small account of the hardships and complaints of the *samurai* farmers. The taxes were made heavier than they could pay, and when they failed to bring in the required amount of rice, he ordered them to be dressed in straw rain-coats which were tied around their neck and arms. Their hands were fastened behind their backs, and in this helpless condition the rain-coats were set on fire. Many were fatally burned, and some to escape the burning threw themselves into the water and were drowned.

This senseless cruelty awakened an intense feeling of hatred against the daimyō. And when his son who succeeded him was disposed to continue the same tyrannical policy, the farmers rose in insurrection against their lord. The peasants of the island of Amakusa, which lies directly opposite to the province of Arima, also joined in this rising, owing to their discontent against the daimyō of Karatsu.

The Christians, who had so long groaned under the persecutions of their rulers, seized this opportunity to rise, and joined the farmers. They declared that the time had now come for them to avenge the innocent blood of Christians and priests who had perished throughout the empire. The rising of the

Christians began at the village of Oyei in Amakusa, October, 1637. The excitement was intense, and in a few days it is said that eight thousand three hundred men and one thousand women were assembled at this village. They chose as their chief Shirō Tokisada the son of the head man of the village of Hara, who proposed to march immediately upon Nagasaki and open negotiations with foreign nations, and if possible obtain from them the help of troops. He was an enthusiast and without experience in war. The leading spirit in the insurrection seems to have been a *rônin* [1] named Ashizuka, who recommended that the insurgents should cross over to Shimabara. But Shirō and his enthusiastic followers resolved to attack the castle of Tomioka situated on the northwest coast of Amakusa. They were, however, unable to make any impression upon it, and were obliged to withdraw. Ashizuka and a few followers succeeded in breaking into the castle of Shimabara and seizing the arms and ammunition and provisions which were stored there. The government rice stores were seized both on the mainland and on the island of Amakusa. All the insurgents, including men, women, and children, then gathered into a deserted castle at Hara, which was capable of holding 40,000 to 50,000 persons. It was supposed to be impregnable, and was put in order and provisioned for a long siege. The number gathered here is estimated by the Japanese writers at 40,200, but this number without doubt is an exaggeration.

---

[1] A *rônin* was a retainer who had given up the service of his feudal master, and for the time being was his own master.

The local rulers finding themselves unable to cope with the rebellion, and seeing its proportions swelling every day, appealed to Yedo for help. The shōgun at this time was Iemitsu, the son of the preceding shōgun, and grandson of Ieyasu. He possessed many of the good qualities of his grandfather, and is looked upon, with the exception of Ieyasu, as the greatest of the Tokugawa line. He had imbibed all the prejudices of his predecessors against foreigners and against the religion of the foreigners. He feared that this rebellion was begun at their instigation, and would be carried on with their encouragement and help. He prepared therefore for a sharp and desperate struggle, which he was determined should be carried out to the bitter end.

Itakura Naizen was sent down as commander-in-chief, and given full powers. Under his direction the siege of the castle, in which the rebels were gathered, was commenced on the 31st of December, 1637. The daimyōs of Kyūshū, on the demand of the government, sent additional troops, so that the besieging army amounted to 160,000 men. Yet with all this force, urged on by an ambition to end this rebellion, no serious effect had yet been produced on the castle. The attacks which had been made had produced no breach in its walls. We have no information concerning the progress of affairs among the inmates. It must be remembered that a part of the rebels were *samurai* farmers, who were inured to arms, and who knew perfectly that neither consideration nor mercy would be shown them or their families in case the castle were taken.

The remainder of the besieged force were the Christian insurgents, who had been driven to this rebellion
by their cruel persecution.   Nothing could be worse
than what they had already endured, and they had
no expectation that if they were beaten in this con
test any pity would be shown to them.   Despair
made the attitude of both divisions of the rebels
one of determined resistance, and their obstinacy
led the besiegers to put forth every effort.

One step which they took in this matter led to
much discussion and to the widening of the breach
between the Dutch and the Portuguese.   On the
11th of January, 1638, the besiegers applied to
the Dutch at Hirado for a supply of gunpowder,
which request was complied with, and at the same
time an apology was tendered that no larger quantity could be sent.   Again, on the 15th of February a request for cannon to be used in the
siege was received, and the guns were sent.   Mr.
Koeckebacker says: "We gave the largest and most
uniform guns in our possession." [1]   Finally, on the
19th of February, Mr. Koeckebacker was asked to
send one of the Dutch ships [2] then at Hirado to
the assistance of the besiegers.   The *de Ryp* was
accordingly sent, and Mr. Koeckebacker himself accompanied her.   The guns which had been first sent
were mounted as a land battery, and the guns of the

[1] See Dr. Geerts' paper, *Asiatic Society Transactions*, vol. xi., p.
75.

[2] The ships in use at this time among the Japanese were far less
seaworthy than those of European nations.   The accompanying
figures given by Charlevoix, although probably somewhat fanciful,
show the impractical character of the vessels of that time.

PLEASURE YACHTS AND MERCHANT VESSEL.
(Redrawn from Charlevoix, *Histoire et Description de Japon.*)

de Ryp from her anchorage in the bay were trained on the castle. It was a new experience for the Japanese to see cannon used in the siege of a castle, but the effect was much less than had been expected. No practicable breach was made, and the final result seemed as far off as ever. " During the fifteen days from the 24th of February to the 12th of March, there were thrown into the camp of the enemy four hundred and twenty-six cannon balls from the twenty guns of the ship *de Ryp*." [1]

In the meantime the Japanese officers began to feel that it was not a dignified proceeding to call upon a foreign nation to help them to put down a local rebellion. Even the insurgents had shot an arrow into the imperial camp to which a letter was attached, deriding them for calling for assistance when there were so many courageous soldiers in Japan. Whatever may have been the cause, the Dutch received notice on the 12th of March that their ship was no longer required, and accordingly they returned to Hirado. The castle was taken by assault on the 12th of April, 1638, after a siege which had lasted one hundred and two days, and about seven months from the breaking out of the rebellion. By special orders from Yedo the insurgents captured in the castle were to the last man, woman, and child put to death.[2] The father of

---

[1] See Dr. Geerts' paper, *Asiatic Society Transactions*, vol. xi., p. III.

[2] Mr. Koeckebacker says: " The rebels counted in all, young and old, as it was said, about forty thousand. They were all killed except one of the four principal leaders being an artist who formerly used to gain his livelihood by making idols. This man was kept alive and

Shirō, the young leader, was crucified, and Shirō himself was decapitated, and his head exposed for seven days on the great pier at Nagasaki. The daimyō, whose misgovernment had brought on this rebellion in Amakusa, was stripped of most of his territories, and he was so intensely hated in what remained to him that he committed *hara-kiri*. The daimyō of Arima, whose misconduct and neglect had driven the *samurai* farmers into their fatal rising, was also permitted to take his own life.

The help, which the Dutch rendered in this siege, exposed them to much vituperation. Naturally, the Jesuit historians have taken a very unfavorable view of the Dutch share in this sad transaction. Dr. Geerts in his defence of the Dutch argues: " Koecke-backer did no more than any one else of any nationality would probably have done in the same difficult position. . . . His endeavor was to preserve from decline or destruction the interests intrusted to him, and this was done at the smallest possible price. . . . Moreover, the letters of Koecke-backer clearly show that the Japanese government

sent to Yedo."—Dr. Geerts' paper, *Asiatic Society Transactions*, vol. xi., part I, p. 107.

There is a tradition that a number of the prisoners who were captured at this castle were hurled down from the rocks of the island now called Papenberg in Nagasaki harbor. But Dr. Geerts ridicules this notion and says : " A little local knowledge would show it to be impossible to throw people from the rocks on Papenberg into the sea, as the rocks are by no means steep bluffs, but possess an inclined shape and a shore. A little knowledge of the Dutch language would further show that the name Papenberg means ' mountain of the priest,' in allusion to the shape of a Roman Catholic priest's cap or bonnet."
- *Asiatic Society Transactions*, vol. xi., part I, p. 115.

did not ask the aid of the Dutch in the persecution of Christians, as has often been asserted by foreign authors, who have not taken the trouble to inform themselves thoroughly on the subject, but they requested the guns and the aid of the Dutch vessel for the purpose of subduing rebellious subjects. . . . There could be no valid reason for Koeckebacker to refuse the pressing request for aid, and consequently he agreed to give assistance, as every wise man would have done in his place. . . . Koeckebacker did not take part in the general massacre which followed on the 11th of April, when the fortress of the rebels was taken by the imperial troops, as he left with his ship for Hirado on the 12th of March, leaving the guns behind in Arima. Had it been in his power to prevent such a general massacre after the fortress had been taken, and the rebels were prisoners, he would no doubt have done so." [1]

This frightful termination to the rebellion, followed as it was by severe and persistent measures against Christians everywhere, was apparently the death-blow to the church in the empire. No further efforts were made, either by the daimyōs of provinces or by the heads of the church, to make open headway against the determined efforts of the government. Whatever was done was in secret, and every means was tried on the part of those who still clung to the Christian belief, and especially of those who were still daring enough to try to minister to them, to conceal their locality and their identity. [2]

[1] See Dr. Geerts' paper, *Asiatic Society Transactions*, vol. xi., part 1, pp. 110 and 111.

[2] A Japanese writer thus sums up the result of the effort to introduce Christianity into his country : " After nearly a hundred years of

The history of Christianity in Japan from this time downward was that of a scattered and dismembered remnant struggling for existence. A long line of edicts reaching to modern times was directed against "the corrupt sect," repeating again and again the directions for its suppression. The *kiri-shitan bugyō*, or Christian inquisitor, had his office in Yedo, and under him was a numerous and active corps of assistants. Inouye Chikugo-no-Kami for a long time held this position. A place is still pointed out called *Karishitan Zaka*, or Christian Valley, where once stood the house in which were confined a number of the foreign priests. Here may be seen the grave of Father Chiara, who had under torture abjured his faith, and remained a prisoner for forty years, dying 1685.[1] Professor Dixon says that "there are two bamboo tubes inserted in sockets in front of the tomb, which I have never found empty, but always full of flowers in bloom. No one knows who

Christianity and foreign intercourse, the only apparent results of this contact with another religion and civilization were the adoption of gunpowder and firearms as weapons, the use of tobacco and the habit of smoking, the making of sponge-cake, the naturalization into the language of a few foreign words, and the introduction of new and strange forms of disease."—Shigetaka Shiga's *History of Nations*, Tōkyō, 1888. The words introduced into the language from the Portuguese, except several derived from Christianity, are as follows : *tabako*, tobacco ; *pan (pāo)*, bread ; *kasutera* (from Castilla), sponge-cake ; *tanto*, much ; *kappa (capa)*, a waterproof ; *kappu (copa)*, a cup or wine glass ; *birōdo (vellendo)*, velvet ; *biidoro (vidro)*, glass.—Rein's *Japan*, p. 312.

[1] See Mr. Satow's contributions to the discussion of Mr. Gubbins' paper, *Asiatic Society Transactions*, vol. vi., part 1, p. 61; also Satow and Hawes' *Handbook*, p. 22 ; also Griffis' *Mikado's Empire*, p. 262 ; and Professor Dixon's paper on the Christian Valley, *Asiatic Society Transactions*, vol. xvi., p. 207.

offer these flowers, but they must be descendants of the Doshin Christians, or believers in Christianity, or worshippers of Koshin." Here also was confined Father Baptiste Sidotti, a Sicilian Jesuit who ventured to enter Japan in 1707 with the purpose of resuming the work of the Jesuits which the persecution had interrupted.

And yet with all this vigilance and severity on the part of the government, what was the amazement of the Christian world to learn that the old faith still survived! In the villages around Nagasaki there were discovered in 1865,[1] not only words and symbols which had been preserved in the language, but even communities where had been kept alive for more than two centuries the worship bequeathed to them by their ancestors. We shall have occasion hereafter to refer to this interesting memento of the Christianity of the seventeenth century.

[1] See Chamberlain's *Things Japanese*, 1892, p. 300.

CHAPTER XII.

FEUDALISM IN JAPAN.

IEYASU was not only a general of eminent abilities, who had from his youth been accustomed to the responsibility and management of great campaigns, but he was a statesman who knew how to secure the advantage to be obtained from victories and conquests. After the decisive battle of Sekigahara, when the control of the empire became fixed in his hands, we hear little more of him as a general, excepting in the battle at Ōsaka, when the fortunes of Hideyori were finally and definitely settled. The common conception of Ieyasu is not that of a great commander like Hideyoshi, but rather of an organizer and law-maker, who out of confused and dismembered provinces and principalities of the empire constructed a firm and abiding state.[1] After his settlement of the dissensions at home, and his admirable adjustment of the outstanding difficulties with Korea and China, which we have already traced, we shall find Ieyasu principally engaged in framing a government which should be suited to the peculiar

[1] See *Legacy of Ieyasu*, cap. xv.

wants and founded on the historical antecedents of
the country.

There was one characteristic of Ieyasu which has
not received sufficient attention. Although not a
great scholar in any sense, even in the age in which
he lived, he was more familiar than most men of
affairs of his day with the Chinese classical writings,

IEYASU.

and was in the more leisurely periods of his life a
noted patron of learned men. The Chinese classics
were said to have been brought to Japan at an early
period, even before the first introduction of Buddhism. But the period was too early and the condition of the country too rude to make the reading
and study of the philosophical and political writings
of Confucius and Mencius an essential part of the

education of the people. The culture which Buddhism brought with it, accompanied with a knowledge
of the writing and reading of the Chinese letters,
was all that obtained any currency during the disturbed and warlike ages of Japanese history. But
when peace was at last established by the supremacy
of Ieyasu, and the active Japanese intellect had
some other employment than fighting, then learning took a great start. And as the only idea which
the Japanese possessed of learning was that which
prevailed in China and was imbedded in the Chinese
writings, they naturally turned to them for thought
and systematic training.

Fortunately Ieyasu was a man who appreciated
at its full value the effect of learning on the character of his people. He caused the Confucian classics [1]
to be printed at a press which he patronized in
Fushimi, and this was said to be the first time these
works had ever been printed in Japan. He gathered
scholars about him at Fushimi, at Yedo, and after
his retirement at Shizuoka (Sumpu). He favored
education and encouraged the daimyōs to establish
schools where the children of their retainers could
be taught not only military accomplishments but
the elements of a good education. The Chinese
classics were made the essentials of such an education, and the chief duty of a school was to teach the

[1] The *Confucian* classics consist of the Four Books, viz.: *The Great
Learning, The Doctrine of the Mean, The Confucian Analects,* and
The Sayings of Mencius ; and the Five Canons, viz.: *The Book of
Changes, The Book of Poetry, The Book of History, The Canon of
Rites,* and *Spring and Autumn* (*Annals of the State of Lu,* by Con-
fucius). Chamberlain's *Things Japanese,* 1892, p. 92.

pupils to read and write and understand the works
which their venerable and learned neighbor had
furnished them.

MIXING INK FOR WRITING.

(From Régamey's *Art and Industry.*)

Unfortunately this movement in behalf of learning was hampered by the impracticable nature of
the Chinese written language. Instead of a few
characters representing sounds, like European alpha-
bets, it consists of thousands of symbols, each representing an idea. The pupil must therefore spend
years in learning to make, and know and read the
mere signs of language. And in the modern neces-

STYLES OF LETTERS.

[Chinese Proverb: Hiroku koriwo aisuruwo jintoyu. To love universally is true humility.]
1. Kaisho (book letters). 2. Ditto. 3. Gyōsho (script letters). 4. Ditto. 5. Hirakaua (Japanese script).

sities of printing,[1] the compositor must handle not
less than 4,000 or 5,000 Chinese characters, besides
the Japanese *kana* and other needful marks. The
kana here mentioned were the result of a promising effort which was made to simplify the Chinese

ワ wa	ラ ra	ヤ yâ	マ ma	ハ ha	ナ na	タ ta	サ sa	カ ka	ア a
ヰ wi	リ ri	イ yi	三 mi	ヒ hi	ニ ni	チ chi	シ shi	キ ki	イ i
ウ wu	ル ru	ユ yu	ム mu	フ hu	ヌ nu	ツ tsu	ス su	ク ku	ウ u
エ we	レ re	エ ye	メ me	ヘ he	子 ne	テ te	セ se	ケ ke	エ e
ヲ wo	ロ ro	ヨ yo	モ mo	ホ ho	ノ no	ト to	ソ so	コ ko	オ o

JAPANESE SYLLABARY.

written language by expressing it in symbols representing sounds. Forty-seven *kana* letters—by repetition extended to fifty—each representing a syllable,
are used to express Japanese words.

The castle of Yedo was reconstructed and enlarged
after the battle of Sekigahara, while Ieyasu con-

[1] An accurate and amusing account of the printing of a modern
newspaper in Japan is given in Mr. Henry Norman's *Real Japan*, p.
43 *et seq.*

tinued to reside at Fushimi. The Jesuit fathers, who accompanied the Father Provincial on his visit to Ieyasu, assert that 300,000 men were employed in this work. Very much of the ground where the present city of Tōkyō now stands, was then, according to old maps, covered with water. In excavating the moat which surrounds the castle, and the canals connecting this moat with the Sumida-gawa, immense quantities of earth were obtained, which were used to fill up lagoons and to reclaim from the shallow bay portions which have now become solid land. This work of building the castle and fitting the city for the residence of a great population, was carried on by many of the successors of Ieyasu. The third shōgun, Iemitsu, the grandson of Ieyasu, made great improvements both to the castle and the city, so that the population and position of Yedo in no long time placed it as the chief city of the empire.[1]

The task to which Ieyasu devoted himself during the years of his residence at Yedo was that of consolidating and settling the feudal system of the empire. The daimyōs had for centuries been so accustomed to conduct themselves independently, and to govern each his own province in his own way, that they might be expected to resent any efforts to restrict their action. Fortunately Ieyasu was a mild and temperate man, who, while he could act

[1] For a history of the city of Yedo, and reference to the disasters to which it has been subject from fires, earthquakes, and pestilences, see Satow and Hawes' *Handbook*, p. 6. See also "The Castle of Yedo," by T. R. H. McClatchie, *Asiatic Society Transactions*, vol. vi., part 1, and "The Feudal Mansions of Yedo," *Asiatic Society Transactions*, vol. vii., part 3.

with firmness, was most considerate of the feelings and motives of others. After the decisive victory of Sekigahara he readily and cordially made terms with his enemies, and did not show himself rapacious in exacting from them undue penalties for their hostility. To the daimyō of Satsuma, as we have already seen, he restored the entire territory which Taikō Sama had given him. The daimyō of Chōshū was allowed to keep two of the provinces out of the ten which he had acquired by conquest, yet these two made him still one of the richest and most powerful princes in the empire. With others he dealt in the same liberal spirit, so that out of the old proud daimyōs whom he spared and permitted to continue in their holdings, he created for himself a body of fast friends.

But it must be remembered that the end Ieyasu had in view was to establish a system which should continue loyal to his successors, and to a line of successors who should be of his own family. Hence out of the confiscated territories, and out of those which were in part vacated as a fine on the former holders, and out of those which had become vacant by natural causes, he carved many fiefs with which he endowed members of his own family and those retainers who were closely affiliated with him. He had twelve children,[1] nine sons and three daughters. The daughters were married to three daimyōs. The oldest of his sons, Nobuyasu, had died at an early age. His second son, Hideyasu, had been adopted by Taikō Sama, and to him Ieyasu gave the province

[1] See Dickson's *Japan*, p. 294.

of Echizen as his fief. The third son, Hidetada,
who shared with his father the command of the
forces at the battle Sekigahara, had married a
daughter of Taikō Sama, and succeeded his father
as shōgun. On his youngest three sons he bestowed
the rich provinces of Owari, Kii, and Mito, and constituted the families to which they gave rise as the
Go-san-ké, or the three honorable families. In case
of a failure in the direct line, the heir to the shōgunate was to be chosen from one of these families.

Without undertaking to give a detailed account of
the feudal system as modified and established by
Ieyasu, it will be sufficient to give the classes of
daimyōs as they continued to exist under the Tokugawa shōgunate.[1] It must be understood that
feudalism existed in Japan before the time of
Ieyasu. It can be traced to the period when Yoritomo obtained from the emperor permission to send
into each province a *shiugo* who should be a military
man, and should act as protector of the *kokushū* or
governor, who was always a civilian appointed by
the emperor. These military protectors were provided with troops, for the pay of whom Yoritomo
got permission from the emperor to levy a tax.
Being active men, and having troops under their
command, they gradually absorbed the entire authority, and probably in most cases displaced the

[1] Those who desire a fuller explanation of this complicated and
difficult matter are referred to Dr. Yoshida's *Staatsverfassung und
Lehnwesen von Japan*, Hague, 1890, and to the paper on "The Feudal
System in Japan," by J. H. Gubbins, Esq., *Asiatic Society Transactions*, vol. xv., part 2 ; also to the introduction by Professor Wigmore, *do.*, vol. xx., Supplement, p. 25.

kokushū, who only represented the powerless government at Kyōto. Under the disturbed times
which followed the fall of the house of Yoritomo
these *shiugo* became the hereditary military governors of the provinces, and usurped not only the
functions but the name of *kokushū*. They became
a class of feudal barons who, during the interval
when no central authority controlled them, governed
each one his own province on his own responsibility.
Even after the establishment of a central authority,
and continuously down to the abolition of feudalism,
the government of the people was in the hands of
the daimyō of each province. The assessment of
taxes, the construction of roads and bridges, the
maintenance of education, the punishment of crime,
the collection of debts, the enforcement of contracts,
and indeed the whole circle of what was denominated law were in the hands of the local government.
In truth, in Japan as in other feudal countries there
was scarely such a thing as law in existence. The
customs that prevailed, the common-sense decisions
of a magistrate, the final determinations of the daimyō, were authoritative in every community. And
in all these each province was in a great degree a
law unto itself.

The classes of daimyōs as arranged and established
by Ieyasu were not altered by his successors, although the number included under each class was
liable to minor changes. Before Ieyasu's time there
were three classes of daimyōs, viz.: eighteen *kokushū*, who may be termed lords of provinces, thirty-
two *ryōshu* or lords of smaller districts, and two

hundred and twelve *jōshu* or lords of castles, that is two hundred and sixty-two in all. The distinction between the first two was one of rank, but the third differed from the others in the fact that the assessment in each case was less than 100,000 *kōku* of rice. The number of *kokushū* daimiates was increased by the addition of Kii and Owari, to which Ieyasu appointed two of his sons as daimyōs. A third son he appointed daimyō of Mito, which was already of the *kokushū* rank. He vacated this place by compelling the previous holder to accept in place of it another daimiate of equivalent value.

Ieyasu divided all daimyōs into two distinct classes, the *fudai* and the *tozama*. The term *fudai* was used to designate those who were considered the vassals of the Tokugawa family. The *tozama* daimyōs were those who were considered as equal to the vassals of the Tokugawa family, but who were not in fact vassals. Of the former there were originally one hundred and seventy-seven, and of the latter eighty-six.[1] Twenty-one of the *fudai* daimyōs were relatives of the shōgun's family, of whom three, as has been stated, were the " honorable families." All the others, numbering eighteen, bore the name of Matsudaira, one of the family names of Ieyasu, derived from a small village in the province of

---

[1] In the *Legacy of Ieyasu* will be found the following statement: "The *fudai* are those *samurai* who followed me and proffered me their fealty before the overthrow of the castle of Ōsaka in the province of Sesshū. The *tozama* are those *samurai* who returned and submitted to me after its downfall, of whom there were eighty-six."— See *Legacy of Ieyasu*, cap. vii.

Mikawa, where Ieyasu was born. This was allowed
to them as a special honor.

We give here the classification of the daimyōs as
enumerated by M. Appert[1] in his list for the epoch
about 1850:

1. Go-san-ké (three honorable families) . 3
2. Fudai daimyōs (vassals of Tokugawa
   family) 137
3. Tozama daimyos (equal to vassals) . 99
4. Kamon (all the other branches of Tokugawa family) 18
5. Daimyōs, not classified . . . 6

Total . . . 263

The five leading *tozama* daimyōs were Kaga,
Sendai, Aizu, Chōshū, and Satsuma, and although
they ranked after the *go-san-ké*, they had some
superior advantages. They were classed as *kyakubun*,
or guests, and whenever they paid a visit to the
capital of the shōgun, they were met by envoys and
conducted to their residences.

Besides these daimyōs of different classes, Ieyasu
established an inferior kind of feudal nobility, which
was termed *hatamoto*. This means literally *under
the flag*. They had small holdings assigned to them,
and their income varied very greatly. Mr. Gubbins,
in his paper, puts the number at about 2,000. It
was the custom to employ the members of this
minor class of aristocracy very largely in filling the
official positions in the shōgun's government. In-

[1] *Ancien Japon*, vol. ii.

deed, it was held as a common maxim, that the offices should be filled by poor men rather than by rich.[1] The *gokenin*, numbering about 5,000, were still another class who were inferior to the *hatamoto*. They had small incomes, and were mostly employed in subordinate positions. Beneath these again stood the ordinary fighting men, or common *samurai*, who were the retainers of the daimyōs and of the shōgun. They were the descendants of the soldiers of the time of Yoritomo, who appointed *shiugo* to reside with a company of troops in each province, for the purpose of keeping the peace. They had already grown to claim a great superiority over the common people, and Ieyasu encouraged them in this feeling of superciliousness. The people were divided into four classes, arranged in the following order: *samurai*, farmers, artisans, and merchants. And in his *Legacy* Ieyasu thus expresses himself[2]: "The *samurai* are masters of the four classes. Farmers, artisans, and merchants may not behave in a rude manner towards *samurai* . . . and a *samurai* is not to be interfered with in cutting down a fellow who has behaved to him in a manner other than is expected." Again he says[3]: "A girded sword is the living soul of a *samurai*."

The authority coming from so high and so revered a source did not grow less during the centuries of feudalism which followed. The *samurai* did not fail to use all the privileges which were allowed them

[1] Dickson's *Japan*, p. 303.
[2] See *Legacy of Ieyasu*, cap. xiv.
[3] See *Legacy of Ieyasu*, cap. xxxvii.

by Ieyasu's testamentary law. Especially in the large cities where great numbers of them were gathered, and where idleness led them into endless evil practices, the arrogance and overbearing pride of the *samurai* made them an intolerable nuisance. Nevertheless it must be allowed that nearly all that was good, and high-minded, and scholarly in Japan was to be found among the ranks of the feudal retainers. It is to them that the credit must be given of the great changes and improvements which have been initiated since Japan was opened up to foreigners. They were the students who went out into the world to learn what western science had to teach them. They have been pioneers in a return to a central authority and to the experiment of a representative government, and to the principles of freedom and toleration to which the country is committed. To them Japan owes its ancient as well as its modern system of education. Its old stores of literature, it is true, are not due to them, but surely all its modern development in newspapers, magazines, history, political science, and legal and commercial codes, is to be traced to the adaptability and energy of the old *samurai* class.

The *samurai* had the privilege of carrying two swords ; the principal one (*katana*) was about four feet long, nearly straight, but slightly curved toward the point, the blade thick and ground to a keen though blunt edge. It was carried in a scabbard thrust through the *obi* or belt on the left side, with the edge uppermost. Besides the *katana* the *samurai* carried also a short sword about nine and a half

SWORD-MAKER.

283

inches long, called *wakizashi*. The blade of the sword was fastened to the hilt by a pin of wood and could be readily detached. On the part of the blade inserted in the hilt, the maker's name was always inscribed, and it was a special matter of pride when he was one of the famous sword-smiths of Japan. The most noted makers were Munechika, Masamune, Yoshimitsu, and Muramasa, who ranged from the tenth down through the fourteenth century. The quality of the Japanese sword has been a matter of national pride, and the feats which have been accomplished by it seem almost beyond belief. To cleave at one blow three human bodies laid one upon another; to cut through a pile of copper coins without nicking the edge, were common tests which were often tried.[1]

It was an essential part of the education of a young *samurai* that he should be trained thoroughly in martial exercises. The latter part of every school day was given up to this kind of physical training. He was taught to ride a horse, to shoot with the bow, to handle the spear, and especially to be skilled in the etiquette and use of the sword.[2] They went

[1] For the general history of the sword, see Mitford's *Tales of Old Japan*, vol. i., p. 70; T. R. H. McClatchie's, The sword of Japan, *Asiatic Society Transactions*, vol. vi., p. 55 ; Chamberlain's *Things Japanese*, 1892, p. 396. For the mode of manufacture, see Rein's *Industries of Japan*, p. 430 ; and especially for the artistic decoration of swords, see Satow and Hawes' *Hand-book*, p. 114.

[2] I have been told by a young Satsuma *samurai* that when he was a boy it was a test of skill with the sword, to set a chop-stick (which was about six inches long) on its end and before it could fall over to draw a sword from its scabbard and cut it in two.

SWORD, SPEARS, AND MATCHLOCK.

through again and again the tragic details of the commission of *hara-kiri*, and had it impressed on their youthful imaginations with such force and vividness, that when the time for its actual enact-ment came they were able to meet the bloody reality without a tremor and with perfect composure.[1]

LANTERN.

The foundation of the re-lations between the feudal chiefs and their retainers lay in the doctrine of Confucius. The principles which he lays down fitted in admirably to the ideas which the histori-cal system of Japanese feu-dalism had made familiar. They inculcated absolute submission of the son to the father, of the wife to her husband, and of the servant to his master, and in these respects Japanese feudalism was a willing and zealous disciple. On these lines Ieyasu constructed his plans of government, and his successors enthusiastically followed in his footsteps.

In religious belief the nation by the time of Ieyasu was largely Buddhistic. Through ten centuries and

[1] For an account of *hara-kiri* see the "Story of the Forty-Seven Ronins" in Mitford's *Tales of Old Japan*, vol. i., p. I.

DAIBUTSU AT KAMAKURA
(From a photograph.)

a half the active propagation of this faith had been going on, until now by far the greater number of the population were Buddhists. In his *Legacy* Ieyasu expresses a desire to tolerate all religious sects except the Christian. He says: "High and low alike may follow their own inclinations with respect to religious tenets which have obtained down to the present time, except as regards the false and corrupt school (Christianity). Religious disputes have ever proved the bane and misfortune of the empire, and should determinedly be put a stop to." [1]

While he was therefore tolerant towards all the different sects of Buddhism and towards the old Shintō faith of the country, he particularly patronized the Jōdo sect to which his ancestors had been attached, and to which he charges his posterity to remain faithful.[2] In the archives of the Buddhist temple Zōjōji at Shiba in Tōkyō was preserved an account written by the head priest of the time, how Ieyasu, in 1590, visited the temple and took it under his patronage, saying,[3] "For a general to be without an ancestral temple of his own is as though he were forgetful of the fact that he must die. . . . I have now come to beg of you to let me make this my ancestral temple here." So that from the time of Ieyasu the Jōdo was the authorized sect to which the court of the shōguns was especially attached, and to this is to be attributed the fact that its

[1] See *Legacy of Ieyasu*, cap. xxxi.

[2] See *Legacy of Ieyasu*, cap. xxviii.

[3] T. R. H. McClatchie, "The Castle of Yedo," *Asiatic Society Transactions*, vol. vi., part 1, p. 131.

BELL AT KYŌTO.

temples and monasteries in Tōkyō have always been of the most majestic and gorgeous character.[1]

Ieyasu did not long hold the office of shōgun, which the emperor had conferred upon him in 1603. It is not easy to understand why a man, who was only sixty-three years of age and who was still in vigorous health, should wish to throw off the responsibilities of office and retire to private life. We must remember, however, that it was the custom of his country, consecrated by the usage of the imperial house and of the shōguns and regents who had preceded him. Morever, though he surrendered to his son the title of shōgun, he retained in his own hands a large part of the power which he had hitherto exercised.

It may be supposed that he was anxious to establish the succession of the shōgunate unquestionably in his own family. For this purpose he deemed it wise to initiate a successor while he still had the influence and the power to compel the acquiescence of the feudal lords of the empire. Acting upon these

[1] As illustrative of Buddhism at its greatest splendor we give here the figures of the great bronze image of Buddha at Kamakura, and of the great bell at the temple of Daibutsu in Kyōto. The former was erected about A.D. 1252 after plans initiated by Yoritomo before his death. The statue in its sitting posture is nearly fifty feet in height. It is constructed of separate plates of bronze brazed together. Formerly it was enclosed in a temple, but this was twice destroyed by tidal waves, and since its last destruction in 1494 it has not been rebuilt.

The bell given in the illustration is that at the temple of Daibutsu, the inscription on which is said to have offended Ieyasu. It is nearly fourteen feet in height and nine feet in diameter. Its weight is more than sixty-three tons.—See Satow and Hawes' *Handbook*, p. 368.

considerations Ieyasu, in 1605, retired in favor of his third son Hidetada. He received from the emperor the title of *sei-i-tai-shōgun,* which his father had held. Ieyasu took up his residence at Sumpu[1] (now Shizuoka), which was situated on Suruga bay, one hundred and fourteen miles from the shōgun's capital. Here he maintained a court and practically in all important matters governed the country. He was free, however, from the petty details of the administration, and devoted himself as an amateur to a literary life, to the collection and printing of books, and to the encouragement and patronage of literary men, in which he delighted.

In the meantime important events had been taking place which had great influence on the history of Japan. The contest between the Spanish on the one hand, and the Dutch and English on the other, was not confined to the Atlantic, but broke out in the Pacific, where the Portuguese and Spaniards had so long been predominant. A preliminary to the opening of trade with the Dutch were the arrival of William Adams and his extraordinary experiences in Japan. As we learn from his own letters,[2] he was

[1] In the account given by Don Rodrigo de Vivero, the late governor of Manila, of a visit made in 1608 by him in behalf of Spanish trade, Yedo is described as a city of seven hundred thousand inhabitants, and Sumpu, which he calls Suruga, where the emperor (as he denominates Ieyasu) lived, is estimated to contain from five to six hundred thousand inhabitants. He was so pleased with the country through which he travelled that he declares, "if he could have prevailed upon himself to renounce his God and his king he should have preferred that country to his own."—See Hildreth's *Japan,* etc., pp. 145, 147.

[2] These letters were written from Japan between 1611 and 1617. They were printed in part in Purchas' *Pilgrimes,* and are included in

born near Rochester in England, 1574, and when twelve years old was apprenticed to Nicholas Diggins as a pilot. With him he served for twelve years, then took service as pilot major of a fleet of five sail, which was about to be despatched by the " Indish Companie " to take part in the trade of the East Indies. This fleet had a rough time, and with fevers and scurvy and want of food a great part of the crews of the five vessels died. They sailed by the way of the straits of Magellan, then northward past Chili, and westward across the broad Pacific. Two of the ships turned back at the straits and returned to Holland. A third vessel was captured by the Spaniards, and the pinnace of a fourth was seized by eight men, and run into some island on their way, supposed to be one of the Sandwich Islands, and there wrecked, and the eight men probably eaten. The two vessels still remaining were the *Hope* and the *Charity*. The former of these was never more heard of. The sole remaining vessel was the *Charity*, of which Jaques Maihore was the master, and William Adams was the pilot. Sickness, especially the scurvy, which was the frightful scourge on board the vessels of that day, had reduced the crew, so that only four were able to walk, of whom Adams was one, and four more could creep on their knees.

In this condition they reached, on the eleventh of April, 1600, the northeastern coast of the island of Kyūshū, landing in the province of Bungo, whose

the publications of the Hackluyt Society. From the latter source they were printed in pamphlet form by the *Japan Gazette* at Yokohama, 1879. It is from this last source these references are taken.

prince in earlier days had been the friend and patron of the Portuguese Jesuits. They were kindly received, the governor of the district furnishing a guard to protect their property—too late however for the preservation of much of it—and a house in which the sick could be cared for. In a few days a Portuguese Jesuit and other Portuguese arrived from Nagasaki, through whom the Dutch could communicate with the natives. The national and religious animosity between the strangers and their interpreters could not fail, however, to manifest itself. The Portuguese tried to create the impression that the refugees were pirates and unworthy of protection and help.

In accordance with the usual custom, word was immediately sent to Ieyasu (whom Adams calls the emperor), who at this time was at the castle of Ōsaka. He sent boats to Bungo, by which Adams and one of the crew were conveyed to his castle. Adams gives an interesting account of his reception, of the questions asked concerning his country, and its relations to the Spanish and Portuguese. He took occasion to explain, that the object of the Dutch in entering the East was purely that of trade, that they had in their own country many commodities which they would be glad to exchange for the products of the eastern nations.

After this interview Adams was kept thirty-nine days in prison, expecting to suffer the punishment of crucifixion, which he understood was the common mode of disposing of such characters. He found afterwards that the Portuguese had been using means to poison the mind of Ieyasu by representing them as dangerous characters, and recommending that all the refugees should be put to death as a warning to others. But he tells us [1] that Ieyasu answered them, that "we as yet had done to him nor to none of his lands any harm or dammage [and it was] against Reason and Justice to put us to death. If our countreys had warres the one with the other, that was no cause that he should put us to death."

While Adams was thus kept in prison, the *Charity* had been brought to Sakai, near to Ōsaka. Finally he was set at liberty, and suffered to revisit his ship, where he found the captain and remnant of the crew. The goods and clothing on board had been stolen by the natives, which Ieyasu tried to recover for them. But everything had been so scattered that it was impossible to regain it, "savinge 50,000 Rs in reddy money was commanded to be geven us" [as compensation]. After this settlement they were ordered to sail with their ship to the "land of Quanto and neere to the citie Eddo," whither Ieyasu was about to proceed by land. Here they had a mutiny among their men, which ended in the entire disbanding of the crew, and the dividing up among them the money which they had received for their goods. Each man was left to shift for himself. The captain got permission to sail in a Japanese junk to Patan, where he hoped to meet Dutch vessels.

Adams himself was kept about the shōgun's court,

---

[1] First letter of Adams in pamphlet edition. Yokohama, 1878 p. 8.

and was made useful in various ways. His first achievement was to build a vessel of about eighteen tons burthen, which gained him great favor, in which he made several short voyages. Then in 1609, by command of the shōgun, he built another ship of one hundred and twenty tons burthen, which also was a successful venture. For it so happened that the governor of Manila was on his way to Nova Spania [1] in a large ship of one thousand tons burthen, and was wrecked on the east coast of Japan, in the province of Shimosa. The governor and those of his comrades who were saved from the shipwreck were sent on to Acapulco in the ship which Adams had just built. In the year following, the governor, in recognition of their kindness to him, sent back to the Japanese government a much larger vessel as a present, the original being sent to and retained at Manila.

Adams was a straightforward, honest fellow, and commended himself to Ieyasu by usefulness not only in such matters as building ships, but in furnishing information concerning foreign affairs, which at this time were pressing on the government. In order to render him more content, Ieyasu gave him a small holding at Hemi, near the present town of Yokosuka, a few hours' sail from Yedo. He himself speaks of this property as " a living like unto a lord-

---

[1] This name, Nova Spania or New Spain, was first given to the peninsula of Yucatan, and was afterward extended to the territory of Mexico conquered by Cortez. Finally it was given to all the Spanish provinces extending on the Pacific coast from Panama to Van Couver's island. Acapulco was the principal harbor on the Pacific coast.—See Prescott's *Conquest of Mexico*.

ship in England, with eighty or ninety husbandmen, that be as my slaves or servants."[1] He probably also had a residence in Yedo, for there is to this day a street called *An-jin-chō*, or Pilot Street, near Nihon-bashi, which is popularly believed to have been the street in which Adams lived. He himself says that he was known among the Japanese as "An-gin Sama," or Mr. Pilot. To console himself for the loss of his wife and children left in England, he married a Japanese wife, who, with several children, is mentioned by Captain Cocks in the visit above referred to. Notwithstanding his frequent endeavors to get back to England, he was never able to return, but after much important service both to the Dutch and English, to which we shall refer below, he died May 6, 1620.[2]

The first appearance of the Dutch after Adams' shipwreck, as above described, was in 1609, when the *Red Lion* and the yacht *Griffon* arrived at Hirado. They were well received by the daimyō, and

[1] Captain Cocks in his "Diary," contained in Purchas' *Pilgrimes*, part 1, book iv., gives an account of a visit he made to Yedo in 1616, on the business of the English trade, at which time he visited Adams' seat, which he calls "Phebe," doubtless mistaking the sound of the real name "Meni."—See Chamberlain's *Things Japanese*, 1892, p. 15.

[2] His place of burial was identified in 1872 by Mr. James Walter of Yokohama on a beautiful hill near Yokosuka, where both he and his Japanese wife lie buried. His will, which was deposited in the archives of the East India Company in London, divided his estate equally between his Japanese and English families. His Japanese landed estate was probably inherited by his Japanese son. His personal estate is stated at about five hundred pounds sterling.—See *Letters of William Adams*, p. 39.

a deputation was sent to Yedo to visit the shōgun. Adams, in his second letter, speaks of their being "received in great friendship, making conditions with the emperor (shōgun) yearly to send a ship or two." They were given a letter addressed to the "King of Holland," with which they went back, arriving home July, 1610. This letter, among other things, promises, "that they (your subjects), in all places, countries, and islands under mine obedience, may traffic and build homes serviceable and needful for their trade and merchandises, where they may trade without any hindrance at their pleasure, as well in time to come as for the present, so that no man shall do them any wrong. And I will maintain and defend them as mine own subjects." [1]

In accordance with this agreement the first vessel to arrive was a small yacht in July, 1611. A deputation from this vessel also went to visit the shōgun and the retired shōgun. It so chanced that a Portuguese party had preceded them by a few days. These deputations met at the court of Ieyasu. By the assistance of Adams, who was ready to do a favor to his old friends, the Dutch were kindly welcomed by the ex-shōgun's court, and in spite of the hostility, or perhaps aided by the hostility, of the Portuguese, they received from him a patent for continued trade. As given in Kaempfer in translation it is as follows:

"All Dutch ships that come into my empire of Japan, whatever place or port they may put into,

[1] Hildreth's *Japan*, etc., p. 142, quoted from Purchas, vol. i., p. 406.

we do hereby expressly command all and every one
of our subjects not to molest the same in any way,
nor to be a hindrance to them ; but, on the contrary,
to show them all manner of help, favor and assistance.   Every one shall beware to maintain the friendship, in assurance of which we have been pleased to
give our imperial word to these people ; and every
one shall take care that our commands and promises
be inviolably kept.

"Dated (in Japanese equivalent to) August 30,
1611." [1]

This was the authority on which the Dutch trade
in Japan began, and under which, with many changes
and vicissitudes, it continued to the time when the
country was opened by treaty to foreign nations.

The effort made by English merchants to open a
trade with the Japanese was made only a little after
this time.   Indeed, it is said that the report brought
back by the Dutch in the *Red Lion* concerning
Adams' presence and influence in Japan, gave the
impulse which started an expedition under Captain
John Saris in January, 1611.   Saris was an old
adventurer in the East, and therefore fitted to
encounter the varied experiences of his proposed
trip.   He carried a letter from James I., then king
of England, to Ieyasu the retired shōgun.   At Ban-
tam on his way he found that Adams' first letter, [2]
contained in the collection of his letters, and dated
October 22, 1611, had just been received by the

---

[1] Hildreth's *Japan*, etc., p. 157.
[2] See *Letters of William Adams*, No. 1.

English merchants. It encouraged Saris to push on in his expedition. He arrived at Hirado, June, 1613, where the daimyō welcomed him and immediately sent off a special messenger to the shōgun's court to summon Adams to their aid. He came at once, and by his advice Captain Saris with a party set out to pay his respects to the retired shōgun. He gives an interesting account [1] of this journey and visit, which resulted in a charter of privileges [2] for the London East India Company to trade in any port of the empire. Having arranged to his great satisfaction this important matter he returned to Hirado, where he established a factory to serve as the basis for future English trade. In this, however, he encountered no little opposition from the Dutch traders, who had a factory in the same place. For while these enterprising nations, who had been allies in the days of the Armada, could combine very readily in opposition to the Spanish and Portuguese, it was not easy for either of them to look on complacently while the other secured for itself superior advantages in the matter of trade. Captain Saris tried to come to some agreement with his rivals, so that the prices of commodities might be kept up, but he was compelled to see the Dutch factory, in order to crowd him out of the field, putting the goods which they had for sale at prices which were ruinous to both. Having established matters, however, on as satisfactory a footing as he could arrange, and having left

[1] See Purchas' *Pilgrimes*, part 1, book iv.

[2] These privileges are given in full by Hildreth, p. 169, taken from Purchas.

his comrade, Captain Cocks, in charge of the English factory, he sailed for home.

The subsequent events in the history of English trade with Japan may as well be traced here. The relations of the English and Dutch in the East grew steadily more inimical. Perhaps this was due to the increasing rivalry in trade and navigation which prevailed between them at home. In 1617 the London East India Company fitted out an expedition of five large vessels. This fleet arrived in the East in the summer of the following year. After much hostile skirmishing in which the Dutch obtained the permanent advantage, and the English commander was about to retire, word was brought to them from Europe that a peace had been arranged between the two countries. The English and Dutch vessels accordingly sailed to Japan, where they took a hand at trade; because in those days ships always were sent to the East prepared either to fight or trade as the case required. But this amicable arrangement did not last many years. The massacre at the Spice Islands in 1623, for which Cromwell afterward exacted an indemnity, ended all attempts at co-operation in the East. Soon after this the English company withdrew entirely from the Japanese trade, having lost in the effort forty thousand pounds. The Dutch were thus left without a rival, and we shall see on what conditions and at what sacrifices they continued to maintain their monopoly.

During the period of Ieyasu's retirement, which lasted from 1605 until his death in 1616, he devoted

himself, as we have seen, to the consolidation of his
family dynasty and to such literary occupations as
his leisure allowed.   He was a patron of the art derived from Korea, which then was popular in Japan,
of printing with movable types.[1]   This art fell into
disuse afterwards, but during Ieyasu's retirement in
Sumpu he interested himself in printing with blocks
as well as by the new method.   When he died he
was engaged in seeing through the press an edition
of an important Chinese work.

He left behind him a document, called the *Legacy
of Ieyasu*, which to those desirous of studying the
character and motives of the founder of the Tokugawa dynasty possesses a supreme interest.   Some
doubt has been thrown by Japanese critics on the
authenticity of this composition.   It has been asserted that it was not the work of Ieyasu and therefore not worthy of the reverence in which it has been
held.   But whether the *Legacy*[2] was originally composed by him or approved and sanctioned by him,
matters little for our purpose.   It dates from the
time of the founding of the Tokugawa shōgunate,

[1] Mr. Satow has collected many facts concerning the history of
printing in Japan, and among others has shown that printing with
movable type in Korea was used as early as 1317, that is one hundred
and twenty-six years before the date of the first printed book in
Europe.—*Asiatic Society Transactions*, vol. x., p. 63.

[2] A translation of this document was made by Mr. J. F. Lowder
and published in Yokohama in 1874.   We are indebted to W. E.
Grigsby, Esq., formerly professor of law in the University of Tōkyō,
for a valuable paper on the *Legacy of Ieyasu* in which a careful analysis is given and a comparison of its details is made with the provisions
for the regulation of early communities elsewhere.—See *Asiatic
Society Transactions*, vol. iii., part 2, p. 131.

and has been an unimpeachable authority during all its history. One of the singular features in the disposition of the *Legacy*, to which Professor Grigsby directs attention, was the secrecy in which it was kept. The original was preserved in Kyōto and was never seen, while an authenticated copy was kept at the shōgun's court in Yedo, and once a year was open to the inspection of all above a certain rank. To us it seems unaccountable that a body of so-called laws, by which the conduct of men was to be guided, should be kept secret from them. But it must be remembered that in those days there were no such things as laws in the sense we now understand the term. There were magistrates who heard causes and complaints, but their decisions were based not on laws which had been enacted by the government, but upon prevailing custom and upon the innate sense of justice which was assumed to be present in the mind of every man. Whatever laws or rules therefore were in existence were not for the information of the people, but for the guidance of the magistrates.

The *Legacy of Ieyasu* consists of one hundred chapters, arranged without any attempt at logical order. Each chapter treats of a single, separate subject, and is usually of a very moderate length. As Professor Grigsby has pointed out: " Sixteen chapters consist of moral maxims and reflections ; fifty-five are connected with politics and administrations ; twenty-two refer to legal matters, and in seven Ieyasu relates episodes of his own personal history." The moral maxims are quoted chiefly from the works of the Chinese sages, Confucius and Mencius. While the collection on the whole has a military aspect, and plainly encourages and promotes the well-being of a military class, yet we see in it the mild and peaceful nature of Ieyasu. The fifteenth chapter says: " In my youth my sole aim was to conquer and subjugate inimical provinces and to take revenge on the enemies of my ancestors. Yuyō teaches, however, that ' to assist the people is to give peace to the empire,' and since I have come to understand that the precept is founded on sound principle, I have undeviatingly followed it. Let my posterity hold fast this principle. Any one turning his back upon it is no descendant of mine. The people are the foundation of the empire."

His estimate of the social relations is given in the forty-sixth chapter, in which he says : " The married state is the great relation of mankind. One should not live alone after sixteen years of age, but should procure a mediator and perform the ceremony of matrimonial alliance. The same kindred, however, may not intermarry. A family of good descent should be chosen to marry into ; for when a line of descendants is prolonged, the foreheads of ancestors expand. All mankind recognize marriage as the first law of nature."

The old custom of servants and retainers following their masters to death, and committing suicide in order to accompany them, is referred to in the seventy-fifth chapter.[1] It is not improbable that

[1] Ieyasu may have had in mind a shocking example of *junshi* (dying with the master) which occurred in his own family. Tadayoshi,

some exhibition of this custom occasionally was
seen in the days of Ieyasu, for he very sternly con-
demns it thus : " Although it is undoubtedly an ancient custom for a vassal to follow his lord to death,
there is not the slightest reason in the practice. . . .
These practices are strictly forbidden, more especially to primary retainers, and also to secondary
retainers even to the lowest. He is the opposite of
a faithful servant who disregards this prohibition ;
his posterity shall be impoverished by the confiscation of his property, as a warning to those who disobey the laws." [1]

It is not necessary to follow in detail the line of
Tokugawa shōguns. Few of them impressed themselves in any marked manner on the history of their
country. Iemitsu, the third shōgun, who was a
grandson of Ieyasu, was a man of great ability, and
left many marks of his talents upon the empire.
Under his administration the capital made great
advances. He bound the daimyōs to his house by

his fifth son, to whom had been assigned an estate in Owari, died
young, and five of his retainers, in order to follow their master, committed *hara-kiri* in accordance with the old feudal custom. This is
believed to have been almost the last instance of the kind, and must
have touched Ieyasu very closely.—*Mikado's Empire*, by W. E.
Griffis, D.D., p. 272.

[1] Notwithstanding this positive prohibition left by Ieyasu, occasionally the strength of the old feudal habit was too great for the more
merciful spirit. It is said when the third shōgun of the Tokugawa
family (Iemitsu) died, two of the daimyōs, Hotta of Sakura and
Abe of Bingo, committed *hara-kiri*. Hotta's sword, still stained
with blood, is retained in the *kura* of the daimiate at *Tōkyō*, and on
the anniversary of the event is shown to the *samurai*, who appear on
the occasion in full dress.

requiring them to maintain residences in Yedo under the surveillance of the government. His mausoleum is placed with that of his grandfather amid the august glories of Nikkō. Tsunayoshi (1681–1709) during his incumbency was more than usually interested in the peaceful prosperity of his country, and is gratefully remembered for his patronage of education and letters. But on the whole they were content to fill the office of shōgun in a perfunctory manner, and to leave to subordinates the duty of governing.

Japan reached the acme of her ancient greatness during the Tokugawa dynasty. The arts which have given her such a deservedly high rank attained their greatest perfection. Keramics and lacquer, which are her most exquisite arts, achieved a degree of excellence to which we can now only look back with hopeless admiration. Metal-work, as shown in the manufacture of bronze and in the forging and mounting of swords, was scarcely less notable. The still higher art of painting, which came to Japan from China, rose during the Tokugawa period to the rank which it still holds in the estimation of the artistic world.

The best evidence, however, of the civilization of a people is found in their social condition. To learn the true culture of a nation it is necessary to study their education and literature, their laws and system of government, and their morals and religion. In some of these particulars it is still difficult to obtain an adequate knowledge of Japan. But gradually they are being revealed to us. The laws and legal

20

precedents [1] which prevailed during the Tokugawa period have been unearthed from the archives of the Department of Justice and are being published in the *Transactions of the Asiatic Society*.

The medical and scientific advancement of Japan in the seventeenth and eighteenth centuries was not co-ordinate with her progress in the arts. They were hampered with the old Chinese notions about a male principle and a female principle which were conceived to prevail in nature, and with the five elements to which the human organs were supposed to correspond. Fortunately nature has ways of healing diseases in spite of theories and drugs. To this benign principle must be assigned the fact that the human race has survived the surgery and medicaments of mediæval Europe as well as mediæval China and Japan. In one particular the medical art of Japan seems to have been differently, perhaps better, conducted than in Europe. It is narrated by the Japanese annalists,[2] that if a physican made a mistake in his prescription or in his directions for taking the medicine he was punished by three years' imprisonment and a heavy fine ; and if there should be any impurity in the medicine prescribed or any mistake in the preparation, sixty lashes were inflicted besides a heavy fine.

Three peculiar modes of medical practice deserve

[1] See *Asiatic Society Transactions*, vol. xx., Supplement, in which Prof. J. H. Wigmore has undertaken to publish the material discovered by him, with a valuable introduction on the " Administrative and Commercial Institutions of Old Japan."

[2] See Whitney's " Notes on Medical Progress in Japan," *Asiatic Society Transactions*, vol. xii., part 4, p. 276.

ŌBAN.

GOLD COIN, 1727, FULL SIZE.
Present value about one hundred Mexican dollars.

notice. The first was acupuncture, which consisted in inserting a thin needle through the skin into the muscles beneath. A second was the cauterization by *moxa*[1] (Japanese *mogusa*). This was effected by placing over the spot a small conical wad of the fibrous blossoms of mugwort (*Artemisia vulgaris latifolia*). The cone was kindled at the top and slowly burned till it was consumed. A painful blister was produced on the spot, which was believed to have a wholesome effect in the case of

CAUTERIZING WITH MOXA.

many complaints. A third mode of treatment is the practice of *massage* (*amma*), which western nations have borrowed, and which in Japan it has long been the exclusive privilege of the blind to apply.

Many of the improved notions of western medicine were introduced by the Dutch, and this accounts for the unprecedentedly rapid advance which this science has made since the opening of the country.

[1] See a description of this process in Kaempfer's *History of Japan*, and also in Whitney's " Medical Progress," *Asiatic Society Transactions*, vol. xii., part 4, p. 289.

CHAPTER XIII.

COMMODORE PERRY AND WHAT FOLLOWED.

THE most potent cause which led to the breaking down of the Tokugawa Shōgunate, was the attitude which the empire had assumed toward foreign nations. There were other causes which co-operated with this, but none which were capable of such far-reaching and revolutionary effects. We have seen that this attitude was due to the fears entertained concerning the designs of the Portuguese and the Spanish. These fears may have been unfounded, but they were none the less real and operative. Such fears may have been stimulated by the Dutch, who had no reason to deal tenderly with the fanatical enemies of the independence and religion of their country. The spirit of trade with large profits was at the bottom of the great enterprises which were sent out from Europe to the East and West Indies during the seventeenth century.

The rivalry between the Dutch and Portuguese resulted in the banishment of the latter, and the establishment of the Dutch at Nagasaki in 1640. They occupied the little artificial island of Deshima, about three acres in extent, where were erected their houses, their offices and stores, and where for more than two hundred years their trade was conducted. And this, together with a like limited arrangement with the Chinese, was the sole foreign intercourse allowed with Japan.

It is plain now that this seclusion was a great mistake. It would have been of inestimable value to this enterprising and progressive people, to have kept in the race for improvement with the other nations of the world. They would not at this late day be compelled, under a dreadful strain of resources, to provide themselves with the modern appliances of civilization. Long since they would have tried the experiments with which they are now engaged, and would have found a way through the intricacies of politics to a free and stable government. To Ieyasu and his successors the way of safety seemed to be, to shut themselves up and sternly deny admittance to the outside world, while they continued to work out their destiny in their own way.

With whatever shortcomings the Dutch are to be charged in their intercourse with Japan, the world owes a great debt of gratitude to them for what they accomplished. Whatever was known concerning Japanese history and civilization down to the times of Commodore Perry, came chiefly from the Dutch. And not less than the debt of the rest of the world is that of Japan herself. Although the influence of the government was always exerted against the admission of foreign ideas, not a few of the seeds of western civilization were by them planted in a fertile soil and bore abundant fruit. To Kaempfer and Baron von Siebold particularly we must always look for our knowledge of the Japan of the days of its seclusion. Many efforts were made at successive times to open intercourse by the representatives of different nations. The Russians were the most persistent, and their attempts did not cease until the imprisonment of Captain Galowin in 1811. In comparatively recent times numerous essays were made resulting in disappointment. The American brig *Morrison* in 1837, the British surveying ship *Saramang* in 1845, Captain Cooper in 1845, Commodore Biddle in 1848, Admiral Cecille in 1848, Commander Glynn in 1849, and Commander Matheson in the same year, all made efforts to communicate with the government, but were rebuffed. It is plain that affairs were rapidly verging towards a point when the isolation of Japan must be given up.

Several causes contributed to the creation of a special interest in the United States of America, concerning the opening of negotiations with Japan. One of these was the magnitude to which the whale fishery had attained, and the large financial investments[1] held in this industry by American citizens. A second cause was the opening of China to foreign trade as a result of the opium war. But the most active cause was the discovery of gold in California in 1848, and the consequent development of that state as a centre of trade. It was an early scheme to run a line of steamers from San Francisco to the newly opened ports of China. To Hongkong the

[1] See Griffis' *Life of Matthew Calbraith Perry*, p. 296.

distance is about 6,149 nautical miles, and if a steamer is to traverse the whole distance without a break, she must carry an enormous load of coal. The only remedy lay in establishing a coaling station on the Japanese islands, and this could only be effected when Japan abandoned her policy of seclusion and entered with a free heart into the comity of nations.

The interest of the government and people of the United States at last eventuated in the expedition under Commodore Matthew C. Perry. He had for a long time been convinced of the importance and feasibility of such an undertaking, and when he was summoned to take charge of it he made the most thorough preparation for his task.

At his suggestion the government procured all available books, maps, and charts, and he made himself master of every conceivable detail. From manufacturing establishments he secured models of railways, telegraphic lines, and other interesting industrial equipments. He realized the necessity of taking with him such a naval force that its appearance in Japanese waters would produce a profound impression upon the government. And knowing that all his predecessors, who had sought access by way of Nagasaki, had been repelled, he resolved to avoid it and its Portuguese and Dutch traditions and venture boldly into the bay of Yedo.

As soon as it was known that a diplomatic expedition was to be despatched to Japan under the command of Commodore Perry he was deluged with applications, both from England and America, to be permitted to join it.

But Perry resolutely declined all these enterprising offers. In his long career as a naval officer he had seen the danger of admitting on board men-of-war persons who were not under the authority of the commander. From such dangers he meant to be free. He therefore refused to take on board the ships of his squadron any but regularly accredited officers and men over whom he exercised legitimate control. He even made it a rule that if any of the officers kept diaries during the progress of the expedition, they should be the property of the Navy Department and could not be published without its permission and authority.

Commodore Perry carried with him a friendly letter from the President of the United States to the Emperor of Japan,[1] who is therein addressed as "Great and Good Friend." The letter pointed out the contiguity of the two countries and the importance of their friendship and commercial intercourse; it announced that Commodore Perry had been sent to give assurance of the friendly sentiment of the President, and to arrange for privileges of trade, for the care of shipwrecked sailors, and for the appointment of a convenient port where coal and other supplies might be obtained by the vessels of the United States.

After some provoking delays and disappointments the expedition sailed from Norfolk on the 24th of

---

[1] The term emperor was employed in this letter in accordance with the usage of the Jesuit Fathers, the Dutch writers, and William Adams, all of whom designated the shōgun as emperor, although this term could be properly applied only to the Tennō at Kyōto.

November, 1852,[1] proceeding by the way of the
cape of Good Hope to the China sea. There taking
on board Dr. S. Wells Williams as interpreter, and
visiting several ports in China, the Bonin islands,
and the Ryūkyū islands, they sailed to Japan. The
squadron, led by the *Susquehanna* and followed by
the *Mississippi*, the *Plymouth*, and the *Saratoga*,
entered Yedo bay, July 8, 1853.[2]

The Japanese government had been warned of the
preparation and coming of this expedition by the
Dutch. Eager to maintain their position with the
government the King of the Netherlands addressed
to the Shōgun a letter in 1844 suggesting the relax-
ation of the laws excluding foreign nations from
trade. But in the following year he received an
answer declining to make any changes.

With all the warning, however, which the government had received and the preparations which had
been made for the momentous occasion, the appearance of the squadron at the entrance of Yedo bay
was an intense surprise. Two large steam frigates
—the *Susquehanna* and the *Mississippi*—and two
sloops-of-war—the *Plymouth* and the *Saratoga*,—
although much inferior to the squadron promised,
composed such an array as had never before made
its appearance in Yedo bay. As they plowed through
the peaceful waters, in full view of the white-capped
peak of Fuji-yama, every height and vantage ground
along the shore seemed alive with troops and with

COMMODORE M. C. PERRY.

wondering and alarmed inhabitants. The vessels came to anchor off the village of Uraga, which is not far from the present site of the dockyards at Yoko-suka.

The account[1] of the preliminary negotiations conducted by Commodore Perry with the officers of the government is interesting, as showing the efforts made by them to send him to Nagasaki, and his absolute refusal to go thither or conduct his business through the Dutch or Chinese. When there seemed no other way, consent was given to receive, through an officer of adequate rank, the letter from the President of the United States to the Emperor of Japan. When he had formally delivered this letter, he took his departure with an intimation that he would return at a future day and receive the answer.[2]

There can be no doubt that the display of force which Commodore Perry took care to make in all his transactions with the Japanese officials at the same time that he was careful to convey assurances of his friendly purposes and objects, produced a deep impression on the government with which he had to deal. It is useless to deny that it was on this display of force that Commodore Perry largely relied for the success of his expedition. That he was prepared to use force had it been necessary we

---

[1] See the *Official Narrative of the Japan Expedition*, vol i., p. 233 *et seq;* also Griffis' *Life of M. C. Perry*, p. 314 *et seq;* also Bayard Taylor's *India, China, and Japan*, 1855, p. 411 *et seq*.

[2] I have received from Mr. F. S. Conover, who was a member of the Japan expedition as lieutenant of the navy, many interesting details of experiences in Yedo which I have incorporated in my account.

may feel sure.¹ But the instructions of his government and his own sense of international justice bound him to exhaust every peaceful resource before resorting to measures of coercion.

The government of the shōgun was greatly troubled by this responsibility so suddenly laid upon it. They knew not what would be the result of their refusal to enter upon negotiations when Perry returned. The seclusion in which they had kept themselves so long had cut them off from a knowledge of the relations in which the nations of the world stood to each other. Notwithstanding Commodore Perry's protestations of friendliness, they were afraid of his great ships and their powerful armaments. Should they, as they might easily do, make their way up the bay till they were within gunshot of the capital, what resistance could the government show, or how could it prevent them from battering down the castle and all the daimyōs' residences.

The sentiment of loyalty to the emperor and opposition to the shōgun, which had been growing up so insidiously and had now become really formidable, was a source of the greatest perplexity to the Yedo government. Should they proceed with their negotiations and make a treaty with the Americans, this anti-shōgun sentiment was ready to manifest itself

---

¹ " The question of landing by force was left to be decided by the development of succeeding events ; it was of course the very last measure to be resorted to, and the last that was to be desired ; but in order to be prepared for the worst, the Commodore caused the ships constantly to be kept in perfect readiness, and the crews to be drilled as thoroughly as they are in the time of active war."—*Japan Expedition*, vol. i., p. 235.

against them with terrible effect. If they refused to
negotiate, then they must be ready to meet the invaders of their soil with their miserable obsolete
armor and with hearts that two hundred years of
peace had rendered more obsolete than their armor.

The first thing to be done was to consult the daimyōs and learn to what extent they could rely on
their co-operation. The daimyō of Mito,[1] a descendant of the famous Mitsukuni, seemed to have inherited one at least of the opinions of his ancestor.
He advocated the observance of a greater reverence
for the emperor at Kyōto, and criticised the assump-
tion of imperial powers by the shōgun. At the
same time he was an ardent foreign-hater, and in
1841 had been placed in confinement because he had
melted down the bells of the Buddhist temples of
his domains, and cast cannon for their protection.
But now he was pardoned and appointed to take
measures for the defence of the country. On the
15th of July—the American squadron was still in
the bay, for it left on the 17th—the daimyō of Mito
sent in to the government a memorial[2] setting forth
his decisive views on the subject. He gave ten
reasons against a treaty and in favor of war. We
give them here in Mr. Nitobe's translation:

"1. The annals of our history speak of the ex-
ploits of the great, who planted our banners on alien
soil; but never was the clash of foreign arms heard

---

[1] See the *Kinsé Shiriaku*, a history of Japan from 1853 to 1869,
translated by E. M. Satow, Yokohama, 1876.

[2] See Nitobe's *Intercourse between the United States and Japan*,
p. 39.

within the precincts of our holy ground. Let not our generation be the first to see the disgrace of a barbarian army treading on the land where our fathers rest.

" 2. Notwithstanding the strict interdiction of Christianity, there are those guilty of the heinous crime of professing the doctrines of this evil sect. If now America be once admitted into our favor, the rise of this faith is a matter of certainty.

" 3. What! Trade our gold, silver, copper, iron, and sundry useful materials for wool, glass, and similar trashy little articles! Even the limited barter of the Dutch factory ought to have been stopped.

" 4. Many a time recently have Russia and other countries solicited trade with us; but they were refused. If once America is permitted the privilege, what excuse is there for not extending the same to other nations?

" 5. The policy of the barbarians is first to enter a country for trade, then to introduce their religion, and afterward to stir up strife and contention. Be guided by the experience of our forefathers two centuries back; despise not the teachings of the Chinese Opium War.

" 6. The Dutch scholars say that our people should cross the ocean, go to other countries and engage in active trade. This is all very desirable, provided they be as brave and strong as were their ancestors in olden time; but at present the long-continued peace has incapacitated them for any such activity.

" 7. The necessity of caution against the ships now lying in the harbor (*i. e.*, Perry's squadron) has brought the valiant *samurai* to the capital from distant quarters.   Is it wise to disappoint them?

" 8. Not only the naval defence of Nagasaki but all things relating to foreign affairs have been entrusted to the two clans of Kuroda and Nabeshima. To hold any conference with a foreign power outside of the port of Nagasaki—as has been done this time at Uraga—is to encroach upon their rights and trust. These powerful families will not thankfully accept an intrusion into their vested authority.

" 9. The haughty demeanor of the barbarians now at anchorage has provoked even the illiterate populace. Should nothing be done to show that the government shares the indignation of the people, they will lose all fear and respect for it.

" 10. Peace and prosperity of long duration have enervated the spirit, rusted the armor, and blunted the swords of our men. Dulled to ease, when shall they be aroused?   Is not the present the most auspicious moment to quicken their sinews of war?"

The government sent to all the daimyōs copies of the American letter to the shōgun, and asked for their opinions concerning the course to be pursued. Many answers were immediately received. They almost unanimously declared against the opening of the country. Some advocated the alternative suggested in the letter itself, to open the country temporarily and try the experiment for three years, or five years, or ten years. In the meantime the defences of the country and new and improved arms and armaments could be perfected. The government did indeed busy itself during Perry's absence in hurrying forward defensive preparations. The line of forts which still are visible in the shallow water of the bay opposite Shinagawa, the southern suburb of the capital, were hastily constructed. Bells from monasteries and metal articles of luxury were melted down and cast into cannon. Lessons were given and became quickly fashionable in the use of European small-arms and artillery. The military class from the various clans flocked to Yedo and Kyōto in large numbers, expecting to be called upon to defend their country against the impudent intrusion of the barbarians.

During this busy time of perplexity and preparation the Shōgun Ieyoshi,—the twelfth of the Tokugawa dynasty—died August 25, 1853. His son Iesada succeeded him as the thirteenth shōgun. The death of the reigning shōgun did not produce any marked effect upon the policy of the government. Long before this time the custom of abdication, and the habits of luxury and effeminacy in which the family of the shōgun was reared, had dragged the house down to the usual impotent level. The government was conducted by a system of bureaucracy which relieved the titular shōguns from all responsibility and allowed them to live in profitless voluptuousness. So that one died and another reigned in his stead without causing more than a ripple upon the surface of current events.

Shortly after the departure of the American squadron from Yedo bay, the Russian Admiral Pontiatine appeared in the harbor of Nagasaki, and made application for a national agreement to open ports for trade, to adjust the boundary line between the two nations across the island of Saghalien, and to live in neighborly intimacy. English vessels were also in Chinese waters watching the Russians, and the war, usually called the Crimean war, actually broke out in the spring of 1854. A visit from these vessels might therefore be expected at any time.

Commodore Perry during the interval between his two visits to Japan sailed to the ports of China where the Taiping rebellion was then in action. The confusion and insecurity occasioned by this uprising rendered the presence of the squadron most acceptable to the American merchants.

On the 13th of February, 1854, he made his appearance a second time in Yedo bay with a fleet of seven ships, viz., three steam frigates and four sloops-of-war. Three additional vessels were to join, and did join, the fleet in Yedo bay. So that when the fleet was all mustered there were ten fully armed vessels, comprising such an array as had never before appeared in Japanese waters.

After some haggling about the place where the negotiations should be conducted, it was finally settled that the place of meeting should be at Kanagawa, near the village (now the city) of Yokohama. Here after much deliberation and discussion, proposals and amendments, banquets and presents, a treaty was agreed upon. The signing and exchange took place on the 31st of March, 1854. It was immediately sent to Washington for ratification.

As this was the first formal treaty [1] made with

---

[1] See *Treaties and Conventions between Japan and Other Powers*, p. 735.

any western country we give a synopsis of its provisions.

Art. I. Peace and amity to exist between the two countries.

Art. II. The port of Shimoda to be opened immediately and the port of Hakodate to be opened in one year, and American ships to be supplied with necessary provisions in them.

Art. III. Shipwrecked persons of either nation to be cared for, and expenses to be refunded.

Art. IV. Shipwrecked and other persons not to be imprisoned but to be amenable to just laws.

Art. V. Americans at Shimoda and Hakodate not to be subject to confinement; free to go about within defined limits.

Art. VI. Further deliberation to be held between the parties to settle concerning trade and matters requiring to be arranged.

Art. VII. Trade in open ports to be subject to such regulations as the Japanese government shall establish.

Art. VIII. Wood, water, provisions, coal, etc., to be procured only through appointed Japanese officers.

Art. IX. If at any future day privileges in addition to those here enumerated are granted to any other nation, the same to be allowed to Americans.

Art. X. Ships of the United States not to resort to other ports than Shimoda and Hakodate except in stress of weather.

Art. XI. Consuls or agents of the United States to reside at Shimoda.

Art. XII. The ratification of this treaty to be exchanged within eighteen months.

As might have been expected, as soon as this treaty with the United States had been signed there was a rush of other nations to obtain similar terms. Admiral Sir John Sterling, acting in behalf of the government of Great Britain, negotiated a treaty which was signed at Nagasaki on the 15th of October, 1854. Admiral Pontiatine negotiated a similar treaty for Russia, which was signed at Shimoda on the 7th of February, 1855. A treaty with the Netherlands was signed on the 30th of January, 1856.

None of these were in any general sense commercial treaties, providing for trade and making regulations by which it might be conducted. They were rather preliminary conventions, making arrangements for vessels to obtain necessary provisions, and stipulating for the protection of those suffering shipwreck, and for vessels driven under stress of weather to take shelter in the harbors of Japan. They each provided for admission to two ports: The American treaty to Shimoda and Hakodate; the English treaty to Nagasaki and Hakodate; the Russian treaty to Shimoda and Hakodate.

All these treaties contained what is called "the most favored nation clause," so that where the privileges granted to any one nation were in excess of those granted previously to others, these privileges were also without further negotiation extended to the nations that had already made treaties.

These dealings with foreign nations produced the most intense excitement throughout the empire. The old sentiment of hostility to foreign intercourse showed itself in unmistakable intensity. The song of the Black Ship, by which term the vessels of foreign nations were designated, was heard everywhere. Two distinct parties came into existence called the *Jo-i* party, who wished to expel the barbarians ; and the *Kai-koku* party, who were in favor of opening the country.[1] The members of the latter party were principally connected with the shōgun's government, and had become impressed with the folly of trying to resist the pressure of the outside world. The *Jo-i* party was made up of the conservative elements in the country, who clung to the old traditions of Japan that had matured during the two centuries of the Tokugawa rule. Besides these conservatives there was also a party who nourished a traditional dislike to the Tokugawa family, and was glad to see it involved in difficulties which were sure to bring down upon it the vengeance of the nation. These were chiefly found among the southwestern daimiates such as Satsuma, Chōshū, Hizen, and Tosa. The daimyō of Mito[2] although connected with the shōgun's family was bitterly hostile to the policy of holding any friendly relations with foreigners. He was therefore regarded as the head of the *Jo-i* party, and many of the disaffected *samurai* rallied about him as their champion and leader.

[1] See the *Constitutional Development of Japan*, by Toyokichi Iyenaga, Ph.D., Johns Hopkins Press, 1891, p. 12.

[2] See p. 279.

It was charged against the shōgun that in making treaties with foreign nations he had transcended the powers[1] that rightly belonged to him. He was not the sovereign of Japan and never had been. He was only the chief executive under the emperor, and was not even next in rank to the emperor. It was impossible, therefore, that treaties made by the shōgun and not ratified by his sovereign should be regarded by the Japanese as legitimate and binding.

The question of the legality of the treaties which the shōgun had made was an important one, and interested not only the Japanese themselves but the foreigners whose privileges under these treaties were at stake. There is no doubt that Commodore Perry as well as all the subsequent negotiators, believed that in making treaties with the shōgun they were dealing with a competent authority. The precedents occurring in the history of Japan seemed all to bear in this direction. The Portuguese and the Spanish had dealt with the shōgun and never with the emperor. The Dutch had received from Ieyasu the privileges of trade and had ever since continued under the shōgun's protection. Captain Saris in his negotiations in 1614 received written assurances of protection and privileges of trade from the shōgun.

---

[1] See selections from a pamphlet by a German resident at Yokohama given in Mossman's *New Japan*, pp. 142, 143, and quoted in Nitobe's *Intercourse between the United States and Japan*. "The reason the Tycoon breaks his promise is because he cannot keep it, and the reason he cannot keep it, is because he had no right to give it."

It was because the shōgun's power had become weakened, and there had grown up an active sentiment against him, that the question in reference to his legitimate authority arose. " Had the treaty " (with Perry) " been concluded when the power of Yedo was at its former height, it is probable that no questions would have been asked." [1]

According to the terms of the treaty made with the United States it was provided that a consul should be appointed " to reside at Shimoda at any time after the expiration of eighteen months from the signing the treaty." In execution of this provision the United States government sent out Townsend Harris, who arrived in August, 1856. After some hesitation he was allowed to take up his residence at Shimoda. He was a man of great patience and tact, and gradually urged his way into the confidence of the government. He became the counsellor and educator of the officials in everything pertaining to foreign affairs. He was received December 7, 1857, by the shōgun with the ceremony due to his new rank of plenipotentiary which he had then received.[2] In a despatch, dated July 8, 1858, he tells of a severe illness which he had suf-

---

[1] See Nitobe's *Intercourse between the United States and Japan*, p. 59.

[2] Prince Hotta was at this time president of the Council of State (*Gorōjiu*) and had charge of this first audience. I have seen in the possession of his descendant, the present occupant of the beautiful family *yashiki* in Tōkyō, the original of the memorandum showing the arrangement of the rooms through which Mr. Harris was to pass, and the position where he was to stand during the delivery of his congratulatory remarks.

fered ; how the shōgun sent two physicians to attend him, and when a bulletin was sent to Yedo that his case was hopeless, the physicians " received peremptory orders to cure me, and if I died they would themselves be in peril."

The principal effort of Mr. Harris was the negotiation of a commercial treaty which should make provision for the maintenance of trade in specified ports of Japan. The treaties already made by Japan with foreign nations only provided for furnishing vessels with needed supplies, and for the protection of vessels driven by stress of weather and of persons shipwrecked on the Japanese islands. It remained to agree upon terms, which should be mutually advantageous, for the regular opening of the ports for trade and for the residence at these ports of the merchants engaged in trade.

The excitement occasioned by the steps already taken rendered the shōgun's government exceedingly reluctant to proceed further in this direction. It was only after much persuasion, and with a desire to avoid appearing to yield to the appearance of force [1] with which the English were about to urge the negotiation of a commercial treaty, that at last,

[1] In a despatch to the Secretary of State, dated November 25, 1856, Mr. Harris explains the condition of the negotiations in reference to a commercial treaty. He narrates his interview at Hongkong with Sir John Bowring, who told him that he was empowered to negotiate a commercial treaty. Mr. Harris shrewdly observes : "I shall call their (the Japanese government's) attention to the fact that by making a treaty with me they would save the point of honor that must arise from their apparently yielding to the force that backs the plenipotentiary and not to the justice of their demands."

on the 17th of June, 1857, a treaty " for the purpose of further regulating the intercourse of American citizens within the empire of Japan " was duly concluded. The port of Nagasaki was to be opened in addition to those already stipulated. American citizens were to be permitted to reside at Shimoda and Hakodate for the purpose of supplying the wants of the vessels which visited there.

This does not seem to have been adequate, for only about a year later a further treaty, revoking that of June, 1857, was arranged. It was signed at Yedo on the 29th of July, 1858. Equivalent treaties were negotiated by other nations, and it was under the terms of these that intercourse between Japan and the nations of Europe and America was conducted until 1894. They provided for the opening of the ports of Ni-igata and Hyōgo, and for the closing of Shimoda, which had been found unsuitable, and the opening in its place of Kanagawa.[1] They fixed dates for the opening of the cities of Yedo and Ōsaka, and provided for the setting apart of suitable concessions in each of them for residence and trade. They provided that all cases of litigation in which foreigners were defendants should be tried in the consular court of the nation to which the defendant belonged, and all cases in which Japanese citizens were defendants

---

[1] Although Kanagawa was made an open port for trade by these treaties, the adjoining village of Yokohama was found practically better suited for the purpose. The very proximity of Kanagawa to the *Tōkaidō,* which led foreigners to prefer it when the treaties were made, proved to be an objection in the disordered times that followed. On this account Yokohama rapidly rose to the importance which it still holds.

should be tried in Japanese courts. They fixed the limits within which foreigners at any of the treaty ports could travel, but permitted the diplomatic agent of any nation to travel without limitation. They prohibited the importation of opium. Commercial regulations were attached to the treaties and made a part of them, which directed that a duty of five *per centum* should be paid on all goods imported into Japan for sale, except that on intoxicating liquors a duty of thirty-five *per centum* should be exacted. All articles of Japanese production exported were to pay a duty of five *per centum*, except gold and silver coin and copper in bars. These trade regulations stipulated that five years after the opening of Kanagawa the export and import duties should be subject to revision at the desire of either party. The treaties themselves provide that on and after 1872 either of the contracting parties may demand a revision of the same upon giving one year's notice of its desire.

These stipulations in reference to a revision of the treaties, and especially of the tariff of duties to be paid on imported goods, were a source of great anxiety and concern to the Japanese government. The small duty of five *per centum*, which it was permitted to collect on the goods imported, was scarcely more than enough to maintain the machinery of collection. And while the initiative is given to it to ask for a revision of the treaties, it was not able for many years to obtain the consent of the principal nations concerned to any change in the original hard terms.

Another provision in the treaties which was the occasion of endless debate was that which required all foreigners to remain under the jurisdiction of the consuls of their respective countries. It was claimed on the part of the Japanese that this provision, which had been reasonable when the treaties were first made, had ceased to be just or necessary. The laws were so far perfected, their judges and officers had been so educated, and the machinery of their courts had been so far conformed to European practice that it was no longer reasonable that foreigners residing in Japan should be under other than Japanese jurisdiction. From 1872 until 1894 Japanese statesmen patiently presented to the Powers evidence that Japan was prepared to assure civilized jurisdiction over foreigners, but not until after her victory over China had demonstrated her military force did the majority of the nations acknowledge her capability in civilized government.

Any one who reads the diplomatic correspondence covering this period will see how serious were the troubles with which the country was called upon to deal. He will realize also how almost impossible it was for the diplomatic representatives of the western powers to comprehend the difficulties of the situation or know how to conduct the affairs of their legations with justice and consideration.

A succession of murders and outrages occurred, which awakened the fears of the foreign residents. It is plain enough now that this state of things was not so much due to the want of effort on the part of the government to carry out its agreements with foreign nations, as to the bitter and irreconcilable party hatred which had sprung up in consequence of these efforts. The feudal organization of the government, by which the first allegiance was due to the daimyō, rendered the condition of things more demoralized. It was an old feudal custom, whenever the retainers of a daimyō wished to avenge any act without committing their lord, they withdrew from his service and became *ronins*. Most of the outrages which occurred during the years intervening between the formation of the treaties and the restoration were committed by these masterless men. Responsibility for them was disclaimed by the daimyōs, and the government of Yedo was unable to extend its control over these wandering swash-bucklers. There was no course for the foreign ministers to pursue but to hold the shōgun's government responsible for the protection of foreigners and foreign trade. This government, which was called the *bakufu*,[1] had made the treaties with the foreign powers, as many claimed, without having adequate authority, and had thus assumed to be supreme in matters of foreign intercourse. It was natural therefore that the representatives of the treaty powers should look to the *bakufu* for the security of those who had come hither under the sanction of these treaties.

It was in consequence a bloody time through

---

[1] The word means Curtain Government, in reference to the curtain with which the camp of a general was surrounded. The term is equivalent to Military Government, and is used to designate the shōgun's as distinguished from the emperor's court.

which the country was called to pass. The prime minister and the head of the *bakufu* party was Ii Kamon-no-kami,[1] the daimyō of Hikoné in the province of Mino. On account of the youth of the shōgun he was created regent. He was a man of great resolution and unscrupulous in the measures by which he attempted to carry out the policy to which he was committed. By his enemies he was called the " swaggering prime minister (*bakko genro*)." Assured that the foreign treaties could not be abrogated without dangerous collisions with foreign nations, he sought to crush the opposition which assailed them. The daimyō of Mito, who had been the head of the anti-foreign party at Yedo, he compelled to resign and confined him to his private palace in his province. Numerous other persons who had busied themselves with interfering with his schemes and in promoting opposition in Kyōto, he also imprisoned.

Suddenly on the 23d of March, 1860, Ii Kamon-no-kami was assassinated as he was being carried in his *norimono* from his *yashiki* outside the Sakurada gate to the palace of the shōgun.

The assassins were eighteen *ronins* of the province of Mito, who wished to avenge the imprisonment of their prince. They carried the head of the murdered regent to the Mito castle, and after exhibiting it to the gloating eyes of the prince, exposed it upon a pike at the principal gate.

[1] See *The Life of Ii Naosuke*, by Shimada Saburo, Tōkyō, 1888 ; also the *Constitutional Development of Japan*, by Toyokichi Iyenaga, Ph.D., Johns Hopkins University, 1891, p. 15.

The death of the regent was an irreparable blow to the government. There was no one who could take his place and assume his *rôle*. His loss must be reckoned as one of the principal events which marked the decadence of the shōgun's power.

WRESTLERS.
(From Régamey's *Art and Industry*)

CHAPTER XIV.

REVOLUTIONARY PRELUDES.

THE outrages which now succeeded each other with terrible frequency were not confined to the native members of the opposing parties. Foreigners, who were so essentially the cause of the political disturbances in Japan, were particularly exposed to attacks. On the 14th of January, 1861, Mr. Heusken, the secretary and interpreter of the American legation, when riding home at night from the Prussian legation in Yedo, was attacked by armed assassins and mortally wounded. The object of this murder is supposed to have been the desire of one of the ministers of foreign affairs to take revenge on Mr. Heusken,[1] for his activity in promoting foreign intercourse.

The weakness and the fears of the government

[1] Mr. Heusken who had gone to Japan with Mr. Townsend Harris in 1858 was a Hollander by birth. The Dutch language at that time was almost the only medium through which communication could be had with the Japanese. A native interpreter turned the sentiment into Dutch, and then a person who understood both Dutch and English translated it into the latter tongue. This circuitous system of interpretation was, however, soon remedied by native scholars learning English, and by English and American scholars learning Japanese.

were shown by the warning, which they sent to the foreign ministers to avoid attending the funeral of Mr. Heusken, lest further outrages might be committed. They did attend, however, and no disturbances occurred. It only remains to mention that Mr. Harris subsequently made an arrangement with the government for the payment of an indemnity [1] of $10,000 to the mother of Mr. Heusken, who was then living at Amsterdam in Holland.

The next circumstance which awakened universal attention was an attack made on the British legation, on the night of the 5th of July, 1861. At this time the British minister occupied as a legation the buildings of the temple Tozenji, situated at Takanawa in the city of Yedo. It was guarded by a company of Japanese troops, to whom the government had entrusted its protection. Mr. Alcock had just returned by an overland journey from Nagasaki, and with a number of other Englishmen was domiciled in the legation. The attacking party consisted of fourteen *ronins* belonging to the Mito clan, who had banded themselves together to take vengeance on the " accursed foreigners." Several of the guards were killed, and Mr. Oliphant,[2] the secretary of legation, and Mr. Morrison, H. B. M's consul at Nagasaki, were severely wounded. On one of the party who was captured was found a paper,[3] which set forth

---

[1] See *American Diplomatic Correspondence*, November 27, 1861.

[2] A full account of this affair may be found in Alcock's *Capital of the Tycoon*, and in the *Life of Laurence Oliphant*.

[3] A translation of this paper cited from the correspondence presented to Parliament is given in Adams' *History of Japan*, vol. i., p. 138.

the object of the attack and the names of the four-teen *ronins* who had conspired for its accomplishment.

That the government regarded such outrages with alarm is certain. They took the earliest opportunity to express their distress that the legation under their protection had thus been invaded. They assured Mr. Alcock with the most pitiable sincerity that "they had no power of preventing such attacks upon the legation, nor of providing against a renewal of the same with a greater certainty of success." "They could not," they said, "guarantee any of the representatives against these attempts at assassination, to which all foreigners in Japan were liable, whether in their houses or in the public thoroughfares." [1] They pretended to punish, and yet were afraid openly to punish the persons engaged in this attack. [2] They promised to do what they could for the protection of the foreign representatives ; but their measures necessarily consisted in making the legations a kind of prison where the occupants were confined and protected.

And yet, with all these assurances of danger, the foreign representatives seem to have been singularly ignorant of the real difficulties with which the government had to deal. This was due, no doubt, to the want of candor on the part of the Japanese officials in not explaining frankly and fully to them the

[1] See Adams' *History of Japan*, vol. i., p. 139.

[2] In Mr. Satow's translation of *Kinsé Shiriaku* (p. 18) it is said that the *bakufu* ordered the house of Mito to arrest the men who had broken into the English temple residence, but they made their escape into Ōshiu and Dewa.

political complications which existed between the governments of Yedo and Kyōto. They represented a widespread discontent to have grown up since the negotiation of the treaties, owing to the increased price of provisions, the derangement of the currency, and the danger of famine. In view of these pressing difficulties they asked for the postponement of the time fixed by the treaties for opening a port on the western coast and Hyōgo on the Inland sea, and for the establishment of definite concessions in the cities of Yedo and Ōsaka. These modifications of the treaties were finally accepted, and it was arranged that the opening of the ports named above should be postponed for a period of five years from the first of January, 1863.

This postponement of the opening of the ports was the chief reason for sending to foreign countries their first embassy. This set out from Yokohama in January, 1862, and visited the United States, then England, and the other treaty powers. They were everywhere received with the utmost kindness and distinction. The immediate object of their mission was, as we have seen, accomplished. The opening of additional ports was deferred on condition that in those already opened the obstacles which had been put in the way of trade should be removed.

But, besides the attainment of this end, the visit of the embassy to foreign capitals and countries produced a salutary influence both on the foreigners whom they met and on the influential personages of which it consisted. The former learned to their surprise that they had a cultivated, intelligent, and clever race to deal with, whose diplomatists,[1] although inexperienced in European politics, were not unqualified to enter the courts of western capitals. But the revelation to the Japanese envoys was still greater and more surprising. For the first time they saw the terrible armaments of western powers, and realized the futility of attempting to make armed resistance to their measures. But they encountered on every hand not hatred and aversion, but the warmest interest and kindness,[2] and a desire to render them every courtesy. Instead of barbarians, as they had been taught to regard all foreigners, they found everywhere warm-hearted and intelligent friends who were anxious to see their country treated with justice and consideration.

On the 26th of June, 1862, a year after the first, a second attack was made upon the British legation. Lieutenant-Colonel Neale was at this time *chargé d'affaires*, and had just removed from Yokohama and resumed the occupancy of the temple of Tozenji. The government took the precaution to establish guards, who daily and nightly made their rounds to protect the buildings. Besides this there was a guard detailed from the British fleet to render the legation more secure. The officials persisted in claiming that only one person, Itō Gumpei, was engaged in the attack, and that it was a matter of

[1] See the account of the negotiations of this embassy with Earl Russell in Adams' *History of Japan*, vol. i., p. 177 *et seq.*

[2] One of the officials naïvely told the American minister when speaking of the reception of the embassy in the United States: "We did not believe you when you told us of the friendly feeling of your country for us; but we now see that all you said was true."

private revenge for an insult which one of the English guards had put upon him. Two of these guards were killed in the attack, and Itō Gumpei the assassin escaped to his own house, where he was permitted to commit *hara-kiri.* There was probably no plot on the part of those whose duty it was to protect the legation. But the uncertainty which hung over the affair, and the repetition of the violence of the preceding year led Colonel Neale to abandon his residence at Yedo and return to Yokohama. An indemnity of £10,000 was demanded and finally paid for the families of the two members of the guard who had been murdered.

In the meantime the relations between the courts at Kyōto and Yedo had become more and more strained. The efforts at reconciliation, such as the marriage between the young shōgun and the sister of the emperor in 1861, produced no permanent effect. The disease was too deep-seated and serious to be affected by such palliations. Shimazu Saburō, the uncle [1] and guardian of the young daimyō of Satsuma, came in 1862 to Kyōto with the avowed purpose of advising the emperor in this emergency. He was accompanied by a formidable body of Satsuma troops, and on these he relied to have his advice followed.

On his way thither he had been joined by a body of *ronins* who were contemplating the accomplishment of some enterprise which should be notable in

---

[1] The daimyō was really his own son who had been adopted by his brother, the former daimyō, and who on the death of his brother had succeeded him as daimyō. Shimazu Saburō was therefore legally the uncle of his own son.

the expulsion of foreigners. They imagined that the powerful head of the Satsuma clan would be a suitable leader for such an enterprise. They approached him therefore and humbly petitioned to be received under his standard. Not quite satisfied to have such a band of reckless ruffians under his command, he, however, scarcely dared to refuse their petition. He therefore permitted them to join his escort and march with him to Kyōto.

The emperor's court, although bitterly hostile to the liberal policy which prevailed at Yedo, were alarmed by the desperate allies which Shimazu was bringing with him. He presented their memorial to the emperor, and favored their wishes to use all the force of the country to dislodge the hated foreigner from its soil. Other powerful daimyōs were collected at the same time at the imperial capital, and its peaceful suburbs resounded with the clank of warlike preparations. The most notable of these was the daimyō of Chōshū, who at this time was joined with the Satsuma chief in the measures against the shōgun's government.

Shimazu continued his journey to Yedo in the summer of 1862, where he endeavored to impress on the *bakufu* the necessity of taking measures to pacify the country. It is safe to say that his suggestions were coldly received, and he was made to feel that he was in an enemy's camp. It is said that the shōgun refused to receive him personally, but referred him, for any business which he had to present, to the council. It is certain, therefore, when he left Yedo in September, 1862, with his train and escort, he was in no amiable frame of mind. And it was in this condition of irritation that he became the chief actor in an event which was the saddest of all the collisions between the Japanese and the foreigners.

The Satsuma train left Yedo **on the** morning of the 14th of September by way of the *Tōkaidō*, which runs through Kawasaki and skirts the village of Kanagawa. It consisted of a semi-military procession of guards on foot and on horseback, of *norimonos*, in which the prince and his high military and civil attendants were carried, of led-horses for them to ride when they desired, and of a long straggling continuation of pack-horses and men carrying the luggage of the train. It was said to contain not less than eight hundred *samurai* in attendance on their master.

The etiquette of the road for such trains was well settled in feudal Japan. The right of way was always accorded to the daimyō, and all unmilitary persons or parties were required to stand at the side of the road while the train was passing, to dismount if on horseback, and to bow to the daimyō's *norimono* as it was carried past. It may be supposed that the *samurai* in attendance upon the incensed Shimazu were in no humor to have these rules trifled with, and especially would not deal very tenderly with any foreigners who might fall in their way.

On the afternoon of the day on which the Satsuma train left Yedo, a small riding party left Yokohama for the village of Kawasaki, on a visit to the temple at that place. It consisted of one lady and three gentlemen, one of whom was Mr. Charles L. Richardson, who had for many years been a merchant at Shanghai, but who was visiting Japan previous to his return to England. A few miles north of the village of Kanagawa they encountered the head of the train, and for some distance passed successive parts of it. They were either ignorant of the etiquette which required them to withdraw during the passage of such a cavalcade, or underrated the danger of disregarding it.

Presently they came upon the troop which had special charge of the *norimono* in which the prince was carried. It was surrounded by a formidable body of retainers, armed with swords and spears. The reckless riders paid little heed to their scowling looks, and rode carelessly on, sometimes even threading their way through the interstices of the straggling train. When they were nearly opposite to the prince's *norimono*, which they were about to pass without dismounting or saluting, they were so alarmed by the evidences of danger that one of the gentlemen called out to Mr. Richardson who was riding ahead, " Don't go on, we can turn into a side road." The other also exclaimed, " For God's sake let us have no row." Richardson, who was foolhardy and ignorant of those with whom he had to deal, answered, " Let me alone, I have lived fourteen years in China and know how to manage these people." Suddenly a soldier from the centre of the procession rushed upon them with a heavy two-handed sword and struck Richardson a fatal blow on his side under the left arm. Both the other gentlemen were also

severely wounded, and the lady had her bonnet
knocked off by a blow aimed at her, but escaped unhurt. They all started at full speed towards home,
riding over the Japanese guards who undertook to
interfere. All except Richardson reached Kanagawa
without further hurt; he after riding a few rods fell
from his horse and died from the effect of his
terrible wound.¹

The excitement in the town was intense. There
was a proposition to organize immediately a force
and pursue after the train, in order to capture the
murderer and the Satsuma chief. It was with no
small effort and with the almost unanimous sentiment of the foreign community against him, that
Colonel Neale, the British *chargé d'affaires*, restrained them from an act which would have brought
quick vengeance upon the town and involved Great
Britain in a war with Japan. A demand was made
upon the government for the capture and punishment of the assassin of Mr. Richardson, and for the
payment of an indemnity of £100,000, by the
shōgun's government and an additional sum by
the daimyō of Satsuma.

Neither the surrender of the assassin nor the payment of this indemnity was willingly undertaken by
Satsuma. It ended therefore in Admiral Kuper
being despatched with a squadron of seven vessels to

¹ Dr. J. C. Hepburn, a resident in Kanagawa at this time, attended
to the wounded men at the U. S. Consulate. In a letter to me after
reading the above account, he says that, "it was the common report
at the time that Richardson did ride into Satsuma's train and that he
(Satsuma) said, 'Kill him.' It was the general belief that Richardson brought the whole catastrophe on himself."

Kagoshima in order to enforce on the recalcitrant daimyō the terms agreed upon with the government at Yedo. He arrived on the 11th of August, 1863, and was received with frowning batteries and a terrible typhoon of wind and rain. Negotiation failed to effect a settlement and the naval force was called upon to play its part. Three valuable new steamers, which the daimyō had recently purchased, were captured and burned. The batteries which lined the shore were dismantled by the guns of the ships. The city of Kagoshima, said to have had at this time a population of 180,000 and to have been one of the most prosperous towns in Japan, was almost completely destroyed by fire. After this drastic lesson the money demanded was paid, but the murderer of Richardson was not and probably could not be surrendered, and never has been publicly known.

The most important result which followed this severe experience was its moral effect on the Satsuma leaders. They had become convinced that western skill and western equipments of war were not to be encountered by the antiquated methods of Japan. To contend with the foreigner on anything like equal terms it would be necessary to acquire his culture and dexterity, and avail themselves of his ships and armaments. It was not long after this therefore, that the first company of Japanese students[1]

[1] In addition to Terashima there were in the company Mori Arinori, Yoshida Kiyonari, Hatakeyama Yoshinari, and others. They became deeply imbued with the spirit of western institutions and with the principles of constitutional liberty and toleration. Their influence

were sent to London under the late Count Terashima by the daimyō of Satsuma, and the purchase of cannon and ships of war was authorized.

In the meantime another collision still more serious had occurred with the treaty powers. The daimyō of Chōshū had, as we have seen, taken sides with the court of Kyōto against the more liberal policy of the shōgun's government. He had placed men-of-war as guards and had erected batteries within his territory on the shores of the Shimonoseki straits through which ships usually passed on their way to and from the western ports. It is claimed, and is not improbable, that he was encouraged by the Kyōto statesmen to attack foreign ships on their way through these narrow straits, in order to embroil the Yedo government with the treaty powers.

Accordingly on the 25th of June, 1863 the *Pembroke*, a small American merchant steamer on her way from Yokohama to Nagasaki was fired upon by two men-of-war belonging to the daimyō of Chōshū. She was not hit or hurt and escaped through the Bungo channel without injury. Shortly afterwards, on the 8th of July, the French gunboat *Kienchang* while at anchor in the straits, was also fired upon and severely injured. And lastly the Dutch

upon the new career of their country was marked and salutary. Through the agency of Mr. Laurence Oliphant a part of them became misled with the delusions of Thomas Lake Harris, and with him removed to Brocton on the shores of Lake Erie, U. S. where they resided for a time as members of the Brotherhood of the New Life. They had as associates in this singular community Lady Oliphant and her distinguished son, and like them were called upon to perform the ordinary menial employments connected with the community.

ship-of-war *Medusa*, in spite of a warning from the *Kienchang*, undertook to pass the straits and was fired upon by the ships and batteries of the daimyō of Chōshū, to which she responded with decisive effect.

News of these hostile acts was brought immediately to Yokohama. The U. S. Steamship *Wyoming* was lying there, and was at once despatched to avenge the insult to the American flag. She arrived at Shimonoseki on July 16th, and in a conflict with ships and batteries sunk a brig and exploded the boiler of a steamer. On the 20th inst. the French frigate *Semiramis* and the gunboat *Tancrede* under the command of Admiral Juares arrived to exact vengeance for the attack on the *Kienchang*. One of the batteries was silenced, and a force of two hundred and fifty men were landed who destroyed what remained.

These acts of signal vengeance were followed by negotiations for damages. The shōgun's government disavowed the actions of their rebellious subordinate ; but this did not free them from responsibility for the injuries which he had inflicted. The American minister secured the payment of twelve thousand dollars for alleged losses by the *Pembroke*, although as we have seen the vessel got off without any damage. Negotiations in regard to freeing the Inland sea from obstructions dragged along for almost a year. The *bakufu* promised to take measures to reduce to a peaceful attitude the daimyō of Chōshū whose territories bordered on the narrow straits of Shimonoseki. But the growing

political disturbances of the nation and the impover-
ishment of the shōgun's treasury made it impossible
to carry out its pacific designs.

Finally an expedition was organized by the treaty
powers to visit Shimonoseki, in order to destroy
whatever might be in existence there. It consisted
of nine British[1] ships-of-war, four Dutch, three
French, and one steamer, chartered for the occasion
to represent the United States.[2] It sailed from
Yokohama on the 28th and 29th of August, 1864.
The attack was made from the 5th to the 8th of
September. The daimyō, finding it useless to contend against such overwhelming odds, gave in his
absolute submission.

After the return of the expedition the representatives of the allied powers held a conference with the
Japanese ministers of foreign affairs with reference
to the final settlement of this unfortunate business.
A convention[3] was entered into between the interested parties, dated the 22d of October, 1864, by

[1] It should be stated here that a despatch to the British envoy from
Earl Russell arrived just after the sailing of the expedition in which
he says: "That Her Majesty's government positively enjoin you
not to undertake any military operation whatever in the interior of
Japan; and they would indeed regret the adoption of any measures
of hostility against the Japanese government or princes, even though
limited to naval operations, unless absolutely required by self-
defence." Had this order arrived in time, it is probable that the expedition would not have sailed.—*Correspondence Respecting Affairs in
Japan*, 1875, No. 1, p. 45.

[2] It will be remembered that the United States at this time had
occasion to use all her ships-of-war at home in the civil war that was
raging.

[3] See *Treaties and Conventions between the Empire of Japan and
Other Powers*, p. 318.

which an indemnity of three million dollars was to be paid by Japan to the four powers for damages and for expenses entailed by the operations against the daimyō of Chōshū. This sum was to be paid in instalments of half a million dollars each. The four powers agreed among themselves as to the division of this indemnity: That France, the Netherlands, and the United States, in consideration of the actual attacks made on their shipping, were to receive each one hundred and forty thousand dollars, and that the remaining sum should be divided equally between the four powers.

It has always been felt that the exaction of this large indemnity was a harsh if not an unwarrantable proceeding. The government of Yedo had disavowed and apologized for the conduct of the rebellious daimyō, and promised, if time were allowed, to reduce him to subjection. Of the powers which were allied in the expedition, Great Britain had suffered no damage, and the United States had already received an indemnity for the injuries and expenses of the vessel fired upon. To insist, therefore, upon the government not only paying for the damage inflicted, but for the expense of an unnecessarily large and costly expedition to suppress the rebellious subordinate, which was sent contrary to the express protest of the responsible government, seems too much like that overbearing diplomacy with which western nations have conducted their intercourse in the East.[1] The promised sum, how-

[1] The only additional circumstance that deserves mention in this connection is that in response to a widely expressed public sentiment

ever, was at last, after much financial distress, all paid, and the painful episode was ended.

One undesigned benefit resulted from the Shimonoseki expedition. Just as the bombardment of Kagoshima had taught the daimyō of Satsuma the folly of resisting western armaments, so now the daimyō of Chōshū had learned by an expensive experience the same bitter lesson. For the future these two powerful clans might therefore be counted on, not only to oppose the moribund government of Yedo, but to withstand the folly of trying to expel the foreigners who by treaty with an unauthorized agent had been admitted into the country. The Chōshū leaders had also taken advantage of their experiences in this conflict with foreigners to put their troops on a better basis as regards arms and organization. For the first time the privilege of the *samurai* to do all the fighting, was disregarded, and a division[1] of troops was formed from the common people, which was armed with foreign muskets and drilled in the western tactics. They went by the name of " irregular troops " (*kiheitai*), and played no small part in rendering nugatory the efforts of the shōgun to " chastise " the daimyō of Chōshū in 1865 and 1866.

Another noteworthy military event deserves mention here. Colonel Neale had applied to his government for a military guard to protect British interests

the Congress of the United States in 1883 refunded to Japan $785,000.87, her share in this indemnity.—See *Treaties and Conventions between the Empire of Japan and Other Powers*, p. 320.

[1] See translation of *Kinsé Shiriaku*, Yokohama, 1876, p. 59.

at Yokohama. Two companies of the 20th regiment were sent from Hongkong, and with the consent of the Japanese government took up their residence in 1864 at barracks in the foreign settlement. They were afterwards joined by a French contingent, and for many years they were a familiar sight, and gave a sense of security to the nervous residents.

While these serious collisions were taking place between Japan and the foreign powers, there was an increasing and irreconcilable animosity developed between the Kyōto and Yedo governments. The ostensible reason, which was put forward on all occasions, was the difference of opinion upon the question of the foreign treaties and foreign intercourse. The Yedo government had by the force of circumstances become practically familiar with the views of the representatives of foreign nations, and had been convinced that the task of expelling foreigners and returning again to the ancient policy of seclusion was far beyond the power of Japan. On the contrary, the court of the emperor was a hot-bed of anti-foreign sentiment in which all the ancient prejudices of the empire naturally flourished, and where the feudal princes who were jealous of the shōgun found a ready element in which to foment difficulties.

Two important games were in progress. Yedo was the field on which one of these was to be decided, and the players were the representatives of the treaty powers on the one side, and the shōgun's government on the other. Victory had already been virtually declared in favor of an open country and foreign intercourse. The other game was being played at Kyōto between the shōgun's friends and his enemies. The stake was a momentous one, namely, to determine whether the present dual government was to continue and who was hereafter to wield the destinies of the empire.

The government of the shōgun had long been convinced that it was necessary to make the best of the presence of foreigners in the country and that it was vain to make further exertions for their expulsion. But a vast number of the feudal retainers of the daimyōs were still bitterly hostile, and took frequent occasion to commit outrages, for which the government was held responsible. Besides the cases which have been already mentioned, a new legation which the British government had built in Gotenyama, a site which the Japanese government had set apart in Yedo for foreign legations, was burned to the ground in 1863. In the same year the temple buildings in Yedo which the United States had leased for a legation were burned. Twice the shōgun's castle in Yedo had been destroyed by fire. A murderous attack was made upon British subjects in Nagasaki; Lieutenant de Cannes of the French troops was assassinated in 1864; and in the same year Major Baldwin and Lieutenant Bird, two British officers were murdered at Kamakura.

These repeated outrages seriously disturbed the Yedo government, and led to several attempts to curtail the privileges which by the treaties were secured to foreigners. The last proposition of the kind which was made was one conveyed to the French government by an embassy sent out in 1864. They presented a request to have the port of Kanagawa closed up and trade to be confined to Hakodate and Nagasaki. They received no encouragement, however, and returned with their eyes " opened by the high state of material and moral prosperity which surrounded them," and reported the complete failure of their attempts at persuasion. "The *bakufu* reprimanded them for having disgraced their functions, and, reducing their incomes, forced them to retire into private life." [1]

It is necessary now to trace the course of events at Kyōto. According to the theory of the government of Japan the emperor was the supreme and unlimited ruler and the shōgun was his executive. The maintenance of the emperor and his court was a function of the shōgun, and hence it was almost always possible for him to compel the emperor to pursue any policy which he might desire.

At the time now under review Kōmei, the father of the present emperor, occupied the imperial throne. He had succeeded to this dignity in 1847 at the age of eighteen, and he died in 1866 at the age of thirty-seven. The shōgun was Iemochi, who in 1858 had been chosen from the family of Kii, because of the failure of an heir in the regular line. At the time of his election he was a boy of twelve years of age, and was placed under the guardianship of the prime minister Ii Kamon-no-kami. After the assassina-

---

[1] See translation of *Kinsé Shiriaku*, Yokohama, p. 50.

23

tion of the prime minister in 1861, Hitotsubashi Gyōbukyō, a son of the daimyō of Mito, was appointed guardian, and served in this capacity until the shōgun's death.

Around the court of the emperor were gathered many discordant elements. The party of the shōgun was always represented, and the daimyō of Aizu, its ardent friend and champion, had the honorable distinction of guarding the imperial palace. By invitation many other daimyōs were at Kyōto with retinues of officers and attendants, and with guards of troops. The southern and western daimyōs were present in imposing numbers, and although they did not always agree among themselves, they were in harmony in the general purpose to discredit the government at Yedo and to promote the imperial authority.

The expulsion of foreigners was the common subject of discussion and agitation. Although again and again it had been assured that it was impossible to dislodge the treaty powers from their position in the country, the court still continued to direct its efforts to this object. For the first time in two hundred and thirty years,[1] when Iemitsu went up to the imperial court, the Shōgun Iemochi visited Kyōto in 1863 in order to consult about the affairs of the country. In accordance with the precedent set by Iemitsu, the shōgun distributed on this occasion rich presents to the emperor and the officers of his court. He also scattered among the townspeople his largesses, until "the whole populace, moistened in

[1] See translation of *Kinsé Shiraku*, Yokohama, p. 24.

the bath of his mercy and goodness, were greatly pleased and gratified." [1]

Conferences [2] were held between the daimyōs who were present in Kyōto and the officials of the court, and in spite of the objections and remonstrances of the Yedo official, an imperial edict was issued and entrusted to the shōgun for execution, to expel from the country the hated foreigners. This edict was notified to the representatives of the treaty powers by the Yedo officials. They seemed, however, to regard their duty fully done when this notice was given. No serious steps were ever taken to carry out these expulsive measures, unless the obstruction of navigation of the Shimonoseki straits by the dai-myō of Chōshū be regarded of this character.

In 1863 a plot was alleged to have been formed by the Chōshū men to seize the emperor and carry him off to their own territory. The object aimed at by this plot was of course to get the court out of the hands of the shōgun's friends, and surround it by influences favorable to the plans of the southern daimyōs. The court, however, became alarmed by the reports in circulation, and steps were taken to forbid the Chōshū troops, who guarded Sakaimachi gate, access to the grounds of the imperial palace. Offended by this action they retired to their own territory. Seven of the most prominent court

---

[1] See citation in Adams' *History of Japan*, vol. i., p. 260.

[2] Toyokichi Iyenaga, Ph.D., in his pamphlet on the *Constitutional Development of Japan*, p. 17, traces the evolution of the present parliamentary institutions to the conferences which were held at this and subsequent times.

nobles (*kuges*) [1] who sympathized with Chōshū in his aims and purposes accompanied them, and were thereupon deprived of their rank and revenue.

The departure of the Chōshū clansmen and the triumph of the shōgun's party seemed to have put an end to the anti-foreign policy. The emperor and his court had been forced to the conclusion that the effort to expel the treaty powers was far beyond the powers of Japan, even if it were united and its exertions directed from one centre. From this time may be estimated to begin a new phase in the contest which was to end in the restoration of the original form of government.

The territory of Chōshū had become the rendezvous for all the disaffected elements of the empire. The daimyō was looked upon as the patriotic leader of the country, and *ronins* from all parts hastened to enroll themselves under his banner. In the summer of 1864 the Chōshū forces, to the number of several thousand, composed not only of the *samurai* of the province, but also of the disaffected *ronins* who had gathered there, and of the "irregular troops," *kiheitai*, which had been organized, started to re-enter Kyōto in order to regain the position they had previously occupied. The contest which followed has been described with lurid distinctness by native annalists. They were encountered by Hitotsubashi in command of the troops of Aizu, Echizen, Hikoné, and other loyal clans. After a battle which lasted several days, and which raged

---

[1] Among these was Sanjō Saneyoshi, who afterwards for many years was the prime minister of the restored government.

chiefly about the imperial palace, the Chōshū troops were completely defeated and forced to retire. It gives us an idea of the terrible earnestness of these Japanese warriors to read how a little remnant of

KIDO TAKEYOSHI.
(From a photograph.)

the Chōshū troops took refuge on Tennōzan; and when they heard their pursuers approaching, how seventeen of them committed *hara-kiri*[1]; and lest

[1] See Adams' *History of Japan*, vol. i., p. 431.

their heads should be recognized and their names
disgraced, how they had thrown themselves into the
flames of a temple which they had set on fire.
Three of the company who had performed the
friendly act of decapitation for their comrades had
escaped by mountain roads and made their way
back to Chōshū.

The usual concomitant of fighting in a town had
followed, and a great part of Kyōto had been destroyed by fire.[1] The Satsuma troops had taken an
important part in this repulse of Chōshū. They had
intervened at a very critical moment, and had captured a considerable number of Chōshū prisoners.
But they had treated them with great consideration,
and subsequently had even sent them home with
presents, so that the Chōshū men felt they really
had friends instead of enemies in the warlike southern clan. It is in this battle we catch the first
glimpse of the Chōshū leader, Kido Takeyoshi, then
known as Katsura Kogorō.[2] He must have been
about thirty-four years of age, and already gave
promise of the talents which made him one of the
most conspicuous and influential statesmen of the
restoration.

In 1865 Sir Harry Parkes arrived in Japan as the
envoy plenipotentiary of the British government.
He had resided in China from boyhood, and had
been especially conspicuous in the war between

---

[1] The annalist from whom Adams quotes gives the number of
houses burned as 27,000. Adams' *History of Japan*, vol. i., p. 434.

[2] See the Genji Yumé Monogatari and Satow's note in Adams'
History of Japan, vol. i., p. 407.

China and Great Britain in 1860. His career in Japan continued until 1883, when he was promoted to the court of Peking. He had the good fortune to be the representative of his country during the most

UDAIJIN IWAKURA TOMOMI.
(From a photograph.)

momentous years of modern Japanese history, and in many of the most important events he exerted an influence which was decisive.

The troubles in Chōshū were finally brought to a close. The efforts of the shōgun, although conducted at great expense, were unavailing. Satsuma, when summoned to render aid in crushing the rebellious prince, declined to join in the campaign. Through the efforts of Saigō Kichinoske,[1] a treaty of amity was effected between the two clans. The kind treatment of the Chōshū prisoners in the attack on Kyōto was remembered, and the help and alliance of the powerful Kyūshū clan were eagerly accepted. Peace was negotiated between the shōgun and the rebels. Thus the Chōshū episode was ended, with no credit to the shōgun's party, but with a distinct gain to the cause of the imperial restoration.[2]

It had long been recognized that the treaties which had been made by the foreign powers would possess a greatly increased influence on the Japanese people if they could have the sanction of the emperor. The shōgun Iemochi had been summoned to Kyōto by the emperor to consult upon the concerns of the nation, and was occupying his castle at Ōsaka. The representatives of the foreign powers thereupon concluded that it would be a timely movement to proceed with their naval armaments to Hyōgo, and

[1] This distinguished soldier is better known under the name of Saigō Takamori. He was originally an ardent anti-foreign partisan, and through this sentiment became an advocate of a restoration of the emperor. His services in this revolutionary movement were rewarded by a pension granted and accepted by the emperor's express command.—See Mounsey's *Satsuma Rebellion*, London, p. 22.

[2] In this reconciliation of the Satsuma and Chōshū clans the court noble, Iwakura Tomomi, took a prominent part, and after the restoration was complete he became one of the principal officers in the new government, holding the office of *Udaijin* until his death. He is best known to foreigners as the head of an embassy which visited western countries in 1872-3.

wait upon the shōgun at Ōsaka, with the purpose of urging him to obtain the imperial approval of the treaties. This was accordingly done, and an impressive display of the allied fleets was made at the town, which has since been opened to foreign trade.

The shōgun was both young and irresolute, and personally had neither weight nor influence. But his guardian, Hitotsubashi, was a man of mature years and judgment. He recognized the importance of obtaining the approval of the emperor to the foreign treaties, and of thus ending the long and ruinous agitation which prevailed in the country.

A memorial [1] was presented to the emperor in the name of the shōgun, setting forth the embarrassment under which the administration of the country had been conducted on account of the supposed opposition of the emperor to the treaties, and begging him to relieve them by signifying his sanction ; and assuring him that if this is not given, the foreign representatives who are at Hyōgo will proceed to the capital and demand it at his hands.

It ended in the sanction of the treaties being signified October 23, 1865, by the following laconic decree [2] addressed to the shōgun : " The imperial consent is given to the treaties, and you will therefore undertake the necessary arrangements therewith."

During this critical time the Shōgun Iemochi died September 19, 1866, at his castle in Ōsaka at the

[1] See this memorial as given in Adams' *History of Japan*, vol. ii., p. 24.

[2] See Adams' *History of Japan*, vol. ii., p. 24.

age of eighteen. He had been chosen in 1858, in the absence of a regular heir, by the determined influence of Ii Kamon-no-kami, who was then all-powerful at Yedo. He was too young to have any predominating influence upon affairs. Until the assassination of the prime minister Ii Kamon-no-kami in 1861 the boy shōgun had been under his guardianship. Since then that duty had been devolved upon Hitotsubashi, a son of the diamyō of Mito, who had been himself strongly pressed for the office of shōgun, but who was alleged to be too mature and resolute a character for the prime minister's purposes. As guardian, Hitotsubashi had taken an active part in the effort to obtain the sanction of the treaties, and the final success of this important step must in a great measure be attributed to him.

After the death of Iemochi without direct heirs, the office of shōgun was offered to Hitotsubashi as a representative of Mito, one of the " honorable families " from whom a shōgun was to be chosen in case of a failure of direct heirs. It is said that he accepted the office with great reluctance, knowing the troubles which would surely await him who assumed it. He assented only on the command of the emperor and the assurance of support from many of the diamyōs. He has thus the distinction of becoming the last of the long line of Tokugawa shōguns, under the name of Tokugawa Yoshinobu.[1]

A few months after the death of Iemochi, on the 3d of February, 1867, Emperor Kōmei also died

[1] See Adams' *History of Japan*, vol. ii., p. 37.

from an attack of small-pox. He is said to have
been strongly prejudiced against foreigners and
foreign intercourse, and it was claimed at the time
of his death, that when he sanctioned the foreign

THE REIGNING EMPEROR.

treaties the divine nature left him to fall a prey to
the ravages of ordinary disease. His son Mutsuhito,
then in his fifteenth year, succeeded him and is now
the reigning emperor, the one hundred and twenty-
first of his line.

It was thought that the death of an emperor of strong prejudices and of a mature age would naturally favor a more complete control by the new shōgun. It was not to be anticipated that an emperor, still only a youth, would pursue the same policy as his father, and undertake to assume a real and active part in the government of his country. But the shōgun and his friends underrated the influences which were gathered at Kyōto, and which now went far beyond an anti-foreign sentiment and were chiefly concerned with schemes for restoring the imperial power and unifying the form of government.

The daimyō of Tosa, who was a man of liberal sentiments and of great penetration, addressed a letter to the shōgun in October, 1867, in which he frankly says: "The cause [of our trouble] lies in the fact that the administration proceeds from two centres, causing the empire's eyes and ears to be turned in two different directions. The march of events has brought about a revolution, and the old system can no longer be persevered in. You should restore the governing power into the hands of the sovereign and so lay a foundation on which Japan may take its stand as the equal of other countries." [1]

The shōgun being deeply impressed with the wisdom of this advice drew up a document addressed to his vassals, asking their opinion of the advisability of his resignation. Among other things he says: "It appears to me that the laws cannot be maintained in face of the daily extension of our foreign

[1] Translation of *Kinsé Shiriaku*, Yokohama, p. 30.

relations, unless the government be conducted by
one head, and I propose therefore to surrender the
whole governing power into the hands of the im-

IMPERIAL CRESTS.

perial court. This is the best I can do for the
interests of the empire."[1] According to this an-

[1] Translation of *Kinsé Shiraku*, Yokohama, p. 80.

nounced resolution, on the 19th of November, 1867, the shōgun resigned into the hands of the emperor his authority. This surrender was accepted, and thus a dynasty which had lasted from 1603 came to an end. That this surrender might be declined and the power still continue to be held by the Tokugawa, was perhaps the hope and wish of the last shōgun. But it was not to be. The powerful clans who for years had labored for the destruction of the Tokugawa primacy were ready to undertake the responsibility of a new government. And although the change was not to be effected without a struggle, yet from this point may be counted to begin the new period of the restoration.

GATHERING LACQUER.

CHAPTER XV.

THE RESTORED EMPIRE.

THE resignation of the shōgun was accepted by the emperor, on the understanding that a conference of the daimyōs was to be called and its opinion taken in reference to the subsequent conduct of affairs. In the meantime the ex-shōgun, under the command of the emperor, was to continue the administration, particularly of those interests which concerned the foreign powers. But the allied western daimyōs feared the effect of leaving the administration in the hands of their enemies. The possession of the person of the emperor was always reckoned an important advantage. Especially was this the case when the emperor was only a boy, whose influence in the affairs of the government could have little weight. They resolved, therefore, to take measures which would definitely ensure the termination of the shōgun's power, and secure for themselves the result for which they had been so long laboring.

On January 3, 1868, by a so-called order of the emperor,[1] but really by the agreement of the allied

[1] See translation of *Kinsé Shiriaku*, Yokohama, p. 82.

daimyōs, the troops of the Aizu clan, who were in charge of the palace gates, were dismissed from their duty, and their place assumed by troops of the clans of Satsuma, Tosa, Aki, Owari, and Echizen. The *kugés* who surrounded the court and who were favorable to the Tokugawa party were discharged and forbidden to enter its precincts. The vacant places were filled by adherents of the new order of things. The offices of *kwambaku* and *shōgun* were by imperial edict abolished. A provisional plan of administration was adopted and persons of adequate rank appointed to conduct the several departments. "A decree was issued announcing that the government of the country was henceforth solely in the hands of the imperial court." [1]

One of the first acts of the new government was to recall the daimyō of Chōshū, who had been expelled from Kyōto, in 1863, and to invite back the *kugés* who had been exiled and deprived of their revenues and honors. The sentence of confiscation which had been pronounced upon them was abrogated and they were restored to their former privileges. One of them, Sanjo Saneyoshi, as prime minister spent the remainder of his life in reviving the ancient and original form of government. The Chōshū troops who had been driven out of the capital in 1863, were recalled and given a share with the loyal clans in guarding the palace of the emperor. This powerful clan, [2] which had suffered such a

---

[1] See translation of *Kinsé Shiriaku*, Yokohama, p. 82.

[2] With that talent for nicknaming which the Japanese exhibit, the leading party in the new government was called *Sat-chō-to ;* derived from the first syllables of the clans, Satsuma, Chōshū, and Tosa.

varied experience, was destined to take and maintain a leading position in the future development of the restored empire.

The Aizu and other clans which had been devoted friends of the Tokugawa shōguns were especially outraged by this conciliatory spirit shown to the Chōshū troops. They claimed that this clan by resisting the imperial commands had merited the opprobrious title of rebels (*chōtoki*), and were no longer fit for the association of loyal clans. But the Chōshū daimyō had been restored to the favor of his emperor, and moreover was allied with the clans whose power was paramount at Kyōto, so that the disapprobation of the Tokugawa adherents had little terror for him.

At the suggestion of his friends the shōgun retired to his castle at Ōsaka, and the troops attached to his cause also retreated and gathered under his standard. The situation of affairs was for a time uncertain. The shōgun had resigned, and his resignation had been accepted, but he had been asked by the emperor to continue his administration. Subsequently, under the pressure of the allied clans, the emperor had abolished the shōgunate and entrusted the administration to a provisional government. This last action the friends of the ex-shōgun resented as the doings of revolutionists. It is believed that he himself was averse to further conflict. Any step which he might take in the vindication of his rights must involve war with the allied clans, and he was not a man of war.

While these critical events were taking place, the

24

representatives of foreign powers came down from
Yedo to Hyōgo with an impressive array of men-of-
war. By invitation of the ex-shōgun they visited
him at Ōsaka. In reply to the representatives he
made an address,[1] complaining of the arbitrary conduct of those who now had possession of the imperial person, and notifying them that he was willing
and able to protect their rights under the treaties,
and asking them to await the action of a conference
to be summoned. In consequence of the conflict
which was now imminent, the representatives of the
treaty powers issued a notice to their citizens that
neutrality must be maintained under all circumstances, and arms and ammunition must not be sold
to either party.

The first armed conflict between the two parties
took place during the closing days of January, 1868.
Two of the allied daimyōs, Owari and Echizen, were
sent to Ōsaka to confer with the ex-shōgun, in the
hope that some terms might be agreed upon, by
which further difficulty could be avoided. They were
both Tokugawa daimyōs, Owari belonging to one of
the *go-sanké* families, and Echizen being a descendant of Ieyasu's son. They offered to the ex-shōgun
an honorable appointment, and if he would come to
Kyōto they assured him a ready audience before the
emperor. He promised to obey the emperor's command and visit the capital.

After the envoys had gone his friends raised sus-
picions in his mind concerning his personal safety.
The daimyōs of Aizu and Kuwana offered to accom-

---

[1] See Adams' *History of Japan*, vol. ii., p. 84.

pany him in case he determined to go. They organized, therefore, a force of about 10,000 men with which they proposed to escort him. He must have known that a formidable military escort like this would precipitate a conflict. However, he set out. The news of the preparations of the ex-shōgun was brought to Kyōto, and aroused a determination to resist his invasion of the capital. He had been invited to the palace by the emperor, but he was to come as a peaceful visitor. If he had determined to come with a guard composed of the enemies of the empire he must be resisted.

Troops of the Satsuma and Chōshū clans were, therefore, posted to intercept the march of the ex-shōgun's escort. It is believed that they numbered about 1,500 [1] men. The fighting took place on the roads leading from Ōsaka to Kyōto, and lasted during the 28th, 29th, and 30th of January. It ended in the complete defeat of the rebel army, although it so far outnumbered its adversaries.

The ex-shōgun being thus disappointed in his plan to enter the capital with a commanding force retired to his castle at Ōsaka, from which he proceeded on a steam corvette to Yedo. [2] The castle at

[1] The numbers here given, of 10,000 troops in the rebel army and 1,500 in the imperial army, are much less than those claimed by the Japanese authorities, but Mr. Satow who had means of ascertaining the truth gives the numbers as stated in the text. See Adams' *History of Japan*, vol. ii., p. 99, note.

[2] An incident connected with this return illustrates both the times and customs of the country. Hori Kura-no-kami, a prominent retainer of the ex-shōgun, besought his master to commit *hara-kiri* as the only way in which his own honor and the dignity of the Tokugawa clan could be preserved. He offered to join him in this tragic ceremony,

Ōsaka was burnt, and the defeated troops made their way by land to the same rendezvous. The antipathy existing between the Satsuma clan and the Tokugawa adherents showed itself in a very pronounced manner in Yedo. The Satsuma *yashiki*, which was occupied by troops of that clan and by *ronins* favorable to them was surrounded by Tokugawa troops and burnt. Collisions between the two parties were of constant occurrence, which continued until the arrival of the imperial troops restored order. In Hyōgo too, which with Ōsaka was opened to foreign trade on the first of January, 1868, there were difficulties between the foreigners and anti-foreign element in the population. But these troubles rapidly disappeared, because the new government took pains at once to make it plain that the treaties with foreign powers were to be kept, and outrages committed against those who were in the country under these treaties were not to be tolerated.

On February 8, 1868, the emperor sent to the foreign representatives a request that they communicate to their governments the fact that hereafter the administration of both internal and external affairs would be conducted by him, and that officers would be appointed to conduct the business which may arise under the foreign treaties.

In token of the sincerity of this communication an invitation was conveyed to the representatives of

but the ex-shōgun declined to end his life in this way. Thereupon the devoted retainer retired and in the presence of his own friends himself committed *hara-kiri*.

the powers then at Hyōgo to present themselves before the emperor on March 23d. The significance of this event can scarcely now be conceived. Never before in the history of the empire had its divine head deigned to admit to his presence the despised foreigner, or put himself on an equality with the sovereign of the foreigner. The event created in the ancient capital the utmost excitement. The French and Dutch ministers had each in turn been conducted to the palace and had been received in audience. No serious incident had occurred. But during the progress of Sir Harry Parkes,[1] the British representative, from his lodgings to the palace, two fanatical *samurai* rushed upon his escort, and before they could be overpowered wounded nine of them. One of the would-be assassins was killed and the other was captured after being desperately wounded. The party returned at once to the lodgings of the envoy who fortunately was uninjured.

The court, by whose invitation the ministers had undertaken to present themselves before the emperor, was overwhelmed with mortification. High officers at once waited upon Sir Harry and tendered their sympathy and profound regret. After making every reparation in their power, arrangements were made to hold the audience on the day following that originally appointed. It was held accordingly without further incident. Warned by this alarming occurrence, the government issued an edict, that as the treaties had now been sanctioned by the emperor, the protection of foreigners was henceforth

[1] *American Diplomatic Correspondence*, April 3, 1868.

his particular care ; that if therefore any *samurai* were to be guilty of an outrage against them, he should be degraded from his rank, and denied the honorable privilege of committing *hara-kiri ;* he should suffer the punishment of a common criminal and have his head exposed in token of dishonor. Miyeda Shigeru, the surviving culprit, was thus punished.

The scene of the brief contest was now shifted to the east. The ex-shōgun seemed to vacillate between a complete surrender of his power and a provisional retention of it until the will of the nation could be taken by a conference of the daimyōs. On the arrival of the imperial forces in Yedo the final terms of his future treatment were announced to the ex-shōgun : That he retire to Mito, and there live in seclusion ; that the castle in Yedo be evacuated ; and that the vessels and armaments now in the possession of the ex-shōgun be surrendered. These terms were accepted, and he took up his residence in his ancestral province of Mito. Subsequently he was permitted to remove to the castle of Sumpu at Shizuoka. With him the dynasty of Tokugawa shōguns vanishes from history.

His adherents, however, still continued to resist the imperial forces. For months the Aizu troops hovered about Yedo, and at last came to blows with the imperial troops at the grounds of the Uyeno temple on July 4, 1868. It was a hard-fought battle, and was at last decided by an Armstrong gun in the hands of the Hizen troops. The fine old temple was destroyed, and the rebel forces withdrew to the north.

Further complications arose—fighting at Utsuno-
miya, etc.,—but at last they were ended by the surrender of the castle of Wakamatsu, where the daimyō
of Aizu had made a stand. With generous fortitude
he took the blame upon himself and submitted to
the clemency of his sovereign.

It is only necessary now in order to bring to a
close the account of this short military contest, to
refer to the movements of the fleet lying at Shinagawa. It will be remembered that by the terms
accepted by the ex-shōgun these vessels were to be
surrendered to the imperial forces. There were
seven of them, mounting in all eighty-three guns.
They were under the command of Enomoto Izumi-
no-kami, who had learned in Holland the science of
naval war. He did not approve of his master sur-
rendering these muniments of war. On the morning
of the day when the vessels were to be delivered
over to the imperial commander, they had disappeared from their anchorage. In the night
Enomoto had got up steam, crept out through Yedo
bay, and sailed northward to more friendly climes.
The imperial fleet followed, and after some manœu-
vring at Sendai proceeded to Hakodate. Here the
warlike operations between the rebels and the
imperial troops lasted till July, 1869. Finally, the
leaders, Enomoto and Matsudaira Tarō, seeing that
it was hopeless to contend longer against a constantly increasing enemy, offered to commit *hara-kiri*,
in order that their followers might be saved by a
surrender. Their unselfish purpose was not, however, permitted. Then it was determined that the

two leaders should give themselves up to the besiegers, to save the rest. This was done. The prisoners were sent to Yedo, and their gallant conduct and heroic devotion to the cause of their prince were so keenly appreciated that they were all pardoned.

While these events were transpiring in the east and north, the work of establishing a system of administration was proceeded with at Kyōto.

A constitution was drawn up, detailing the various departments of the government, and the duties of the officers in each. These departments were: 1. Of supreme administration; 2. of the Shintō religion; 3. of home affairs; 4. of foreign affairs; 5. of war; 6. of finance; 7. of judicial affairs; 8. of legislative affairs. This scheme underwent several changes, and for a long time was regarded as only tentative.

The ablest men in the movements which were now in progress were afraid of the traditions of indulgence and effeminacy which attached to the court at Kyōto. In order to restore the government to a true and self-respecting basis, it seemed necessary to cut loose from the centuries of seclusion in which the emperor had remained, and enter upon the work of governing the empire as a serious and solemn task. It was in this spirit that Ōkubo Toshimichi of Satsuma, one of the ablest of the statesmen of the new era, made in 1868 a novel and startling proposition. It was in a memorial[1] ad-

[1] An English translation of this memorial will be found in Black's *New Japan*, vol. ii., p. 84. It shows what prejudices the statesmen of that day had to overcome. See also *American Diplomatic Correspondence*, 1868, p. 727.

dressed by him to the emperor. He proposed that the emperor should abandon the traditions which had grown up respecting his person and his court, and rule his empire with personal supervision. To do this successfully, he recommended that the capital be transferred from the place of its degrading superstitions to a new home. He suggested that Ōsaka be the place selected.

If the emperor's court had been under the same influences as had governed it in past years, such a proposition would have been received with horror. Perhaps even the bold proposer would have been deemed fit for the ceremony of *hara-kiri*. But the men who surrounded the emperor belonged to a different school, and the emperor himself, although he was still an inexperienced youth, had already begun to breathe the freer air of a new life. The proposition was welcomed, and led to the great change which followed. After discussion and consideration it was determined that the emperor should make his residence not in Ōsaka, which would have been a great and impressive change, but in Yedo, where for two hundred and fifty years the family of Ieyasu had wielded the destinies of the empire. By this change more than any other was emphasized the fact that hereafter the executive as well as the ultimate power was to be found in the same imperial hands.

Acting on these principles the emperor followed his victorious army and, November 26, 1869, arrived at Yedo and took up his residence in the castle. Reports were made to him of the complete settlement of all difficulties in the north and the establishment of peace. In token of his arrival the name of Yedo had been changed to Tōkyō[1] (eastern capital), by which name it has since been known. As a compensation to the disappointed and disheartened citizens of Kyōto, their city received the corresponding designation of Saikyō (western capital). The year-period, which from January, 1865, had borne the name of Keiō, had been changed to *Meiji*[2] (Enlightened Peace), and was fixed to begin from January, 1868. Heretofore the year-periods had been changed whenever it seemed desirable to mark a fortunate epoch. But by the edict establishing the *Meiji* year-period, it was settled that hereafter an emperor was to make but one change in the year-period during his reign.

The emperor returned to the western capital during the spring of 1869 for a brief visit. The usual etiquette of mourning for his father required his presence at the imperial tomb. He also availed himself of this visit to wed the present empress, who was a princess of the house of Ichijō,[3] one of the ancient families descended from the Fujiwara. He came back again in April, but there was so much opposition on the part of the inhabitants of the ancient

[1] See *Kinsé Shiriaku*, Yokohama, p. 116.

[2] See *Kinsé Shiriaku*, Yokohama, p. 125. Also *American Diplomatic Correspondence*, March 14, 1871.

[3] This house was one of the five regent families (*go-sekké*) all of the Fujiwara clan, from whom the *kwambaku*, *daijō-daijin*, or *sesshō*, the highest officers under the emperor, were always filled and from which the emperors selected their wives.—Dickson's *Japan* 2. 52.

capital to the complete loss of their emperor, that it was deemed most prudent for the newly married empress to remain behind. She did not set out for Tōkyō to join her husband until the November following, where she arrived without incident.

A surprising reminiscence of the Christianity which was supposed to have been extinguished in the seventeenth century came to light in 1865. Several Christian communities in the neighborhood of Nagasaki [1] were discovered, who had preserved their faith for more than two hundred years. Without priests, without teachers, almost without any printed instruction, they had kept alive by tradition through successive generations a knowledge of the religion which their ancestors had professed. These communities had no doubt maintained a discreet quiet as to the tenets of their belief. They had a traditional fear of the persecution to which their fathers had been subjected and sought by silence to remain undisturbed. It was the rejoicing at their discovery which directed the attention of the government to the fire which had been so long smouldering.

A new edict of the imperial government, displayed upon the public edict-boards in 1868, first called the notice of the foreign representatives to the measures which were being taken. [2] It was as follows: " The evil sect called Christian is strictly prohibited. Suspicious persons should be reported to the proper officers, and rewards will be given." Nearly all the

[1] See Chamberlain's *Things Japanese*, 1892, p. 300.
[2] Adams' *History of Japan*, vol. ii., p. 126. *American Diplomatic Correspondence*, May 30, 1868.

ministers of foreign powers remonstrated against this proclamation, as throwing discredit on the religions of their countries. The Japanese officials defended the punishment of Christians by alleging the national prejudice against them, which had come from the preceding centuries. They argued that the question was one of purely domestic concern, of which foreign nations could have no adequate knowledge, and in which they had no right to interfere.

The Christians chiefly lived in Urakami, a village near Nagasaki. They were said to number about four thousand. Orders were sent by the government from Tōkyō in June, 1868, that all the families who would not recant should be deported and put in the charge of daimyōs in different provinces. Only a small part of the Christians were thus exiled. The government probably dealt with greater leniency because they found the treaty powers so deeply interested. Subsequently the measures taken against the native Christians were withdrawn. In March, 1872, those who had been dispersed among the daimyōs were granted permission to return to their homes, and persecution for religious belief was ended forever.

On April 17, 1869, before his court and an assembly of daimyōs, the emperor took what has been called the charter oath [1] in five articles, in substance, as follows:

1. A deliberative assembly shall be formed, and all measures decided by public opinion.

[1] Iyenaga's *Constitutional Development of Japan*, p. 33.

2. The principles of social and political economics should be diligently studied by both the superior and inferior classes of our people.

3. Every one in the community shall be assisted to persevere in carrying out his will for all good purposes.

4. All the absurd usages of former times should be disregarded, and the impartiality and justice displayed in the workings of nature be adopted as the basis of action.

5. Wisdom and ability should be sought after in all quarters of the world for the purpose of firmly establishing the foundations of the empire.

The promise in the first article to establish a deliberative assembly was watched with the greatest solicitude. And when during the same year the *kogisho*[1] (parliament) was called together, great hopes were entertained of its usefulness. It was composed of persons representing each of the daimiates, who were chosen for the position by the daimyōs. It was a quiet peaceful debating society,[2] whose function was to give advice to the imperial government.

That it was a thoroughly conservative body is apparent from the result of its discussion upon several of the traditional customs of Japan. On the proposition to recommend the abolition of the privilege of *hara-kiri* the vote stood : Ayes 3, noes 200, and not voting 6. On the proposition to abolish the wearing of swords, which was introduced and

[1] See the despatch of Sir Harry Parkes, *British State Papers*, Japan, 1870.

[2] See Iyenaga's *Constitutional Development of Japan*, p. 35.

advocated by Mori Arinori, the final vote was unanimously against it in a house of 213.[1] After a short and uneventful career the *kogisho* was dissolved in the autumn of the same year in which it was summoned. It had been a step, but not a very important step, in the direction of parliamentary government.

We must now give an account of the most remarkable event in the modern history of Japan. We refer to the termination of feudalism by the voluntary surrender of their feudal rights on the part of the daimyōs. This action was a logical consequence of the restoration of the executive power into the hands of the emperor. It was felt by the statesmen of this period that in order to secure a government which could grapple successfully with the many questions which would press upon it, there must be a centralization of the powers which were now distributed among the powerful daimyōs of the empire. To bring this about by force was impossible. To discover among the princes a willingness to give up their hereditary privileges and come down to the position of a powerless aristocracy was something for which we have hitherto looked in vain.

Doubtless the *fainéant* condition of nearly all the daimyōs at this time made the accomplishment of this event more easy. With only a few exceptions, the hereditary princes of the provinces had come to be merely the formal chiefs of their daimiates. The real power was in the hands of the energetic and

---

[1] See *British State Papers*, 1870, Japan.

capable *samurai*, who were employed to manage the affairs. They saw that any scheme for transferring the political authority of the daimyôs to the central

MORI ARINORI.
(From a Photograph.)

government would render more important their services. They would become not merely the formal administrative functionaries, but the real officers to whom responsible duties and trusts would be confided. Some of this class of subordinates had already in the new imperial government tasted the savoriness of this kind of service, and they were ready to carry out a plan which seemed to have patriotism and practicability in its favor.

The most notable circumstance in this series of events was the presentation to the emperor of an elaborate memorial signed by the daimyōs of Chōshū, Satsuma, Tosa, Hizen, Kaga, and others, offering him the lists of their possessions and men. This memorial [1] appeared in the official gazette March 5, 1869. Its preparation is attributed to Kido Taka-yoshi, and bears supreme evidence to his learning and statesmanship. With lofty eloquence the memorial exclaims: "The place where we live is the emperor's land, and the food which we eat is grown by the emperor's men. How can we make it our own? We now reverently offer up the lists of our possessions and men, with the prayer that the emperor will take good measures for rewarding those to whom reward is due and taking from those to whom punishment is due. Let the imperial orders be issued for altering and remodelling the territories of the various classes. . . . This is now the most urgent duty of the emperor, as it is that of his servants and children.'

The example thus set by the most powerful and influential daimyōs was followed rapidly by others. Two hundred and forty-one [2] of the daimyōs united

[1] A translation of this memorial will be found in the *British State Papers*, 1870, Japan; also cited in Adams' *History of Japan*, vol. ii., p. 181.

[2] See an analysis of the daimyōs who joined in this memorial in *British State Papers*, 1870, Japan.

in asking the emperor to take back their hereditary territories. And in the end only a small number remained who had not so petitioned. Prince Azuki in his memorial says: 1. "Let them restore the territories which they have received from the emperor and return to a constitutional and undivided country. 2. Let them abandon their titles and under the name of *kwazoku* (persons of honor) receive such properties as may serve for their wants. 3. Let the officers of the clans abandoning that title, call themselves officers of the emperor, receiving property equal to that which they have hitherto held."

In response to these memorials a decree[1] was issued by the emperor August 7, 1869, announcing the abolition of the daimiates, and the restoration of their revenues to the imperial treasury. It was also decreed that the ranks of court nobles (*kugés*) and of daimyōs be abolished and the single rank of *kwazoku* be substituted.

Thus at one stroke the whole institution of feudalism which had flourished from the time of Yoritomo was cut away. The government made provision for the administration by creating prefectures (*ken*) to take the place of daimiates. This was done in 1871. At first the daimyōs were appointed governors of the prefectures. But it was soon found that these hereditary princes were as a class utterly unfit for the chief executive offices of their old provinces. Hence, one by one other competent persons were appointed to vacancies, until it came to be under-

---

[1] See *British State Papers*, 1870, Japan.

stood that competence and fitness were to be the requisite qualifications for such appointments.

The financial questions involved in the suppression of the feudal system were serious and difficult. When the daimyōs surrendered their fiefs, they did so with the understanding that they themselves should "receive such properties as may serve their wants,"[1] and that the emperor should take "measures for rewarding those to whom reward is due."[2] It was decided that each ex-daimyō, and each of the suzerains that were dependent on him, should receive one tenth of the amount of their income from their fiefs. The ex-daimyōs received this amount free of any claims upon them for the support of the non-productive *samurai*, who formed the standing armies of each clan. The central government assumed all the payments to the *samurai* for services of whatever kind. This heavy charge of the government was met by borrowing $165,000,000,[3] which was added to the national debt. With this sum they undertook to capitalize the pensions, which was finally accomplished by a compulsory enactment. Each claimant received from the government interest-bearing bonds for the amount of his income reckoned at from five to fourteen years' purchase according to its sum. Thus to the great relief of the country the matter of pensions was disposed of.

To many of the *samurai* this summary settlement had unfortunate results. The lump sums which

---

[1] See Prince Azuki's *Memorial.*

[2] See Kido's Original *Memorial.*

[3] See Mounsey's *Satsuma Rebellion*, pp. 247, 248.

they received were often soon consumed, and they were left penniless and helpless. The traditions under which they had been trained led them to look down upon labor and trade with disdain, and rendered them unfit to enter successfully on the careers of modern life. In many cases worry and disappointment, and in others poverty and want, have been the sequels which have closely followed the poor and obsolete *samurai.*

Several minor but noteworthy steps in reform were taken. The ancient disqualifications of the *eta* and *heimin* were removed in 1871, and these pariahs placed on the same legal footing as the rest of the population. The first railway in Japan was opened between Yokohama and Tōkyō in 1872. The European calendar, so far as it regarded the beginning of the year and the beginning of the months, was adopted in 1873. The year was still counted from Jimmu Tennō, 1873 of the Christian era corresponding to 2533 of the Japanese era, and also by the *Meiji* year-period, the commencement of which was from 1868.

Several international events deserve notice here. A number of Ryūkyū islanders (vassals of Japan) had been shipwrecked on Formosa and some killed by the semi-savage inhabitants. To punish this cruelty, and to insure a more humane treatment in the future, the Japanese government sent an expedition under General Saigō Tsugumichi. They made short work of the inhuman tribes and enforced upon them the lesson of civility. China, who claimed a sovereignty over this island, acknowledged the ser-

vice Japan had rendered, and agreed to pay an indemnity for the expenses of the expedition.

The long-pending dispute between Russia and
Japan concerning the boundary in Saghalien was
settled in 1875 by a treaty [1] which exchanged the
Japanese claims in Saghalien for the Kurile islands
(Chishima).

An unexpected attack by the Koreans upon a Japanese steamer asking coal and provisions awakened
an intense excitement in Japan.   An expedition
after the pattern of Commodore Perry's, under the
command of General Kuroda Kiyotaka, was despatched in January, 1876, to come to an understanding with the Koreans.   The negotiations were
entirely successful, and a treaty [2] of amity and commerce was concluded, and thus another of the
secluded kingdoms of the East had been brought
into the comity of nations.   Then outbreaks of this
kind in Saga, in Higo, in Akizuki, and in Chōshū
occurred, but they were all put down without difficulty or delay.   The promptness with which the
government dealt with these factions boded no good
to the reactionary movements that were ready to
break out in other places.

Although the Satsuma clan had taken the most
prominent part in the destruction of the shōgunate
and in the restoration of an imperial government,
there was in it a greater amount of conservatism and
opposition to modern innovations than was to be

[1] *Treaties and Conventions between Japan and Other Powers*,
Tōkyō, 1864, p. 646.
[2] *Treaties and Conventions between Japan and Other Powers*,
Tōkyō, 1884, p. 171.

found elsewhere. Indeed, the clan had split into two distinct parties, the one aiding in all the reforms and changes which the government was attempting to carry out, the other holding resolutely to the old feudal traditions which they saw endangered by the present attitude of the emperor's counsellors. The latter party had for its leaders Shimazu Saburō and Saigō Takamori, both of whom had played conspicuous parts in the recent history of their country. The government had tried to conciliate these two influential men and to secure their co-operation in the administration. But both had retired from Tōkyō, and declined longer to share the responsibility of a course which they could not approve.

Saigō, who was the idol of the *samurai*, after his retirement established near Kagoshima a military school, where the young men of that class were drilled in the duties of the army. Branch schools on the same model were also carried on in several other places in the province. In all it was said that not less than 20,000 young *samurai* were receiving a training in these dangerous schools. They were filled with the most violent antipathy to the government and were with difficulty restrained, even by their leaders, from outbreaks in sympathy with the uprisings which elsewhere were taking place.

The government was naturally solicitous concerning these collections of inflammable material. A collision with the students over the removal of some stores of arms and ammunition, revealed their readiness to break into rebellion. It is not improbable that designing conspirators took advantage of the open and chivalric character of Saigō tu push him into the initiation of hostilities. Admiral Kawamura, himself a Satsuma man and a connection of Saigō, was sent down to hold an interview with him and if possible to make a peaceful settlement. But the interview was declined. The rebellious elements were at once gathered together, and Saigō, at the head of a force of 14,000 men, started about the middle of February, 1877, on his march up the west coast of Kyūshū, on his way to Tōkyō. The conspirators estimated that a force of 30,000 troops could be counted on to take part in the expedition.

The first impediment in their march was the castle of Kumamoto,[1] where the government had a garrison of 2,000 to 3,000 men under General Tani. Saigō determined to reduce it before making further progress. He spent several weeks in this vain attempt. This was a precious delay for the government, which it spent in organizing and sending forward troops for opposing the advance of the rebels. All available forces were collected and put in motion to the seat of war. Prince Arisugawa-no-miya was appointed commander-in-chief and established his headquarters at Fukuoka.

The equipment of troops at the seat of government was under the supervision of General Saigō Tsugumichi, a younger brother of the rebel leader. Loyal as he was to his emperor, it was a painful task for him to organize war against his brother.

---

[1] This castle was built by Katō Kiyomasa after his return from the Korean war. It still stands, being one of the most notable castles of Japan.

With native delicacy he left to others the duty of fighting on the field, and confined himself to the less conspicuous part of gathering and sending troops as they were needed.

The rebels had besieged Kumamoto and had already reduced it to great straits. But the imperial forces came in time to its relief. There was desperate fighting, but at last the besiegers were compelled to withdraw.

They retreated toward the east coast with the apparent purpose of seeking a way to the north by Hyūga and Bungo. Promptly they were followed and confined to a defensive attitude. The most desperate battles were fought in this part of the campaign. Though disappointed and outnumbered, the rebels fought with consummate bravery. They were almost in the shadow of the mountains where their celestial ancestor was fabled to have descended upon the Japanese islands.[1] Their last stand was at Nobeoka in the northeast corner of Hyūga. Their leaders realized that to continue the contest would only cause unnecessary and hopeless slaughter.

Under these circumstances Saigō saw that to end the fighting and save his followers he must leave them. Accordingly with about two hundred of those who were personally devoted to him, he broke through the imperial line and escaped to Kagoshima. The army, finding they were forsaken, surrendered, August 19, 1877. Saigō, with his little band, entrenched himself on the summit of the hill Shiroyama overlooking Kagoshima. Here he was surrounded

[1] See p. 47.

by the imperial forces and bombarded night and day. The veteran leader was at last wounded in the thigh, and seeing that all hope of escape was gone, he requested one of his lieutenants to perform for him the friendly office of severing his head from his body. After the capture of the stronghold, the bodies of Saigō and his comrades were discovered. Admiral Kawamura himself with tender hands washed the bloody head of his dead friend, and saw that the bodies of all were decently buried. Thus, on September 24, 1877, the last and most serious of the attempts which have been made to disturb the empire in its new career came to an end.

There was, however, one mournful sequel to this rebellion. Ōkubo Toshimichi, a statesman and patriot of the purest type, had from the beginning resisted the reactionary movements of his clan. At the time of the rebellion he was minister of Home Affairs and put forth all his exertions to suppress it. A baseless slander that he had sent to Satsuma hired assassins to take Saigō's life, had been used by the reckless conspirators to force the rebel leader to an outbreak. This was believed by many of the *samurai*, not only in Satsuma but in other provinces. On May 14, 1878, Tōkyō was startled by the news that Ōkubo, while driving through a secluded spot in the old castle grounds, on his way to the emperor's palace, had been murdered. The assassins were from the province of Kaga, and gave as the reason for their crime their desire to avenge the death of Saigō. Japan could ill afford to spare at this time her most clear-headed statesman and her noblest and most unflinching patriot.

What followed these important events must be told in a summary manner. There was a powerful and growing party in the empire, who looked forward to a modification of the absolute form of

ŌKUBO TOSHIMICHI.
(From a Photograph.)

government to which they had returned in 1868. This party was particularly aggressive in the province of Tosa. They recalled to themselves and others the solemn pledge which the emperor had given to his people in his charter oath,[1] when he announced that "a deliberative assembly shall be formed, and all measures decided by public opinion."

The ruling minds in the government feared that the people were too inexperienced and too unaccustomed to deciding and acting for themselves to be entrusted with the grave duty of constitutional government. As a preparation for so important a step local assemblies were authorized and established in 1878. Matters referring to the government of each *fu* and *ken* were to be discussed, and to a certain extent decided in these assemblies. It was believed that the experience gained in such bodies would go far towards preparing men for service in an imperial legislative body. The expectations founded on these local assemblies were realized and in a fair degree they continued to fulfil their purpose.

In further pursuance of the plan of constitutional government, the emperor, on February 11, 1889, at his palace, promulgated a constitution[2] for his people. In the presence of his cabinet and court he took a solemn oath to govern under its limitations and powers. This constitution contains seven chapters consisting of one hundred and eleven articles: Chapter I. The Emperor; II. Rights and Duties of Subjects; III. The Imperial Diet; IV. The Ministers of State and Privy Council; V. The Judicature; VI. Finance; VII. Supplementary Rules. The emperor also announced that the imperial diet

---

[1] See p. 380.

[2] This able document was prepared by Count Itō Hirobumi. An official translation was published at Yokohama in 1889.

CHAPTER XVI.

THE CONSTITUTION AND THE WAR WITH CHINA.

THE Constitution had been drafted by Count Ito Hirobumi—now the Marquis Ito—a nobleman who had committed the capital offence of leaving his country, in the days of seclusion, and not only had been forgiven, on his timely return, with knowledge of London and a view of the world, but also, by virtue of that knowledge, had taken a leading part in the new enlivenment of the nation. He was sent abroad again to study methods of constitutional government, met Bismarck, and in talk with him conceived the plan of administration which should be suited to Japanese habits of thought as he understood them. He has had the main influence in the interpretation of the Constitution for seventeen years, and his opinion of it is aptly summarized in words of his own: "The Constitution will . . . open a wider field of activity for serving the Emperor." It does not provide for a government of the people by the people. The Emperor, "heaven-descended, divine and sacred," rules his subjects, always for their good. He is to have respect for law but the law cannot hold him to account. He does not, to be sure, except in emergencies, while the Diet is not sitting, originate laws, and the ordinances which he proclaims in these emergencies cease to be laws if they are not ratified by the next Diet; but the sanction, promulgation, and execution of laws are all with him. He alone declares war, makes peace, concludes treaties, confers distinctions.

He is advised by a Privy Council, who deliberate only when called upon by him, and whose advice he may reject. He is advised also by his Ministers of State, who are, moreover, heads of administrative departments, and are responsible to the Emperor only, not to the Diet.

The Diet is made up of two houses: the House of Peers and the House of Representatives. The House of Peers comprises (1) the members of the Imperial family, at majority, (2) princes and marquises, at the age of twenty-five, (3) counts, viscounts, and barons, twenty-five years old, who are elected by their orders for terms of seven years, (4) citizens, thirty or more years old, nominated by the Emperor, for life, and (5) citizens, thirty or more years old, elected from each prefecture (*Fu* or *Ken*) among the fifteen highest tax-payers in the district, subject to nomination by the Emperor. Their term is seven years. But the numbers of the lower orders must not exceed the numbers of the nobility.

The House of Representatives is elective. The election laws were announced eleven days after the

Constitution. They have been modified several times; there has been a redistribution of districts, and in 1902 the secret ballot was substituted for the signed ballot. Every citizen at the age of twenty-five who pays 10 yen in direct taxes is a potential voter. Every city containing not less than 30,000 inhabitants and every prefecture (except urban electoral districts) is an electoral district. While smaller urban electoral districts (cities) are entitled to return one member and larger cities containing more than 100,000 inhabitants are entitled to return one member for every 130,000 people, the rural districts in each prefecture send one member at the rate of every 130,000 people approximately. There is no restriction as to residence in regard to candidates. The term is four years.

This plan elects about 381 representatives, chosen by about seven per cent. of the adult males of Japan. The Diet is convened by the Emperor once a year; the President and Vice-President of the Lower House are nominated by him from candidates elected by the House, and he may send the members to their homes whenever he thinks best. Bills (except the budget, which is introduced by the Government in the House of Representatives first) are introduced by either House, or by the Government. The ministers may appear before the Diet to push their measures, but are not required to do so.

Thus, the intention of the makers of the Constitution was to retain in the Emperor the main force of administration, and this intention, based as it is upon the feudal habit of thought as well as the religious habit of thought which dominates the Japanese, has prevailed to the present day. The Emperor and his advisers have controlled and do control Japan. But they have not controlled it without struggles. In the intermediate time, between the Restoration and the proclamation of the Constitution, while the government was experimenting with local adminis- tration, in order to school the people in popular government, there had developed parties, with platforms. The Liberal party was formed in 1880. It insisted mainly on the equal rights of man and a constitutional government, with a single chamber. Its leader was Itagaki, called the "Rousseau of Ja- pan." In 1881 the Progressive party, made up of the intelligent middle class, led by Okuma, the "Peel of Japan," announced that it would support the throne, but also the people, and pronounced in favor of an Upper House. In the same year was organized the Constitutional Imperial party, led by Ito, with a platform which postulated the supereminence of the Emperor as the basis of order.

Obviously, there was nothing reactionary in the principles of any of these parties; no question of return to the days of seclusion. The country was long past that. Every one desired to try West- ern civilization, and the main questions among the parties were, (1) how fast could civilization be tried, (2) what manifestations of it should be tried, and (3) who should try them. In other words, so far as government was concerned, three questions presented themselves: (1) Were the people ready for representative government? (2) Were the people ready for party government according to English methods; that is to say, ought the ministers to be responsible to the Diet instead of to the Emperor? (3) Should the ancient advisers of the Emperor, the men who had assisted in the revolution, the "clansmen," continue to hold office, or be superseded by younger and more liberal men? Party spirit ran riot in the first years of the Constitution. The opposition was strong enough to nullify the power of any ministry that would not concede the demands of the Lower House, and the Emperor prorogued and dissolved one legislature after another until, in 1894, an event occurred which caused these struggles temporarily to cease. This event was the war between China and Japan.

The dissensions which gave rise to this war were mainly concerned with Korea. Korea had remained a closed country in spite of the somewhat desultory efforts of France and the United States to enforce the admission of foreigners. Early in the seventeenth century, in order to avoid invasions, the "Hermit Nation" had consented to send tributary missions to both China and Japan, and, after the Restoration, the Mikado's government sent a mission to the Korean regent, announcing the change of government. The mission was not received by the Regent, who abhorred the new-taught ideas of his neighbors. The military spirit

26

of the *samurai* was aroused at this slight to the envoys, and only by financial weakness were the Japanese withheld from waging immediate war. In 1874 the young Korean king assumed the throne and at first seemed inclined toward progressive measures; but the former Regent, the Tai-wen-kun, regained influence over him in 1875 and the reactionary spirit again prevailed. In September, 1875, a Korean fort fired on some sailors from a Japanese war-vessel which was surveying the coast. The Japanese bombarded the fort, and in 1876, as is noted in a preceding chapter, sent to Seoul a mission, supported by some thousands of soldiers, and arranged a treaty which assumed the independence of Korea as a state, and provided for commerce between the signatory nations. There was, however, China to be considered, and she had by no means recognized Korea's independence; moreover, the Korean Government still sent a yearly mission to Pekin. In 1872 China had acquired a previously neutral territory which extended to the borders of the Hermit Kingdom and therefore had a new interest in the peninsula. Thereafter there was perpetual friction in Korea. The Conservative party, which was in power, looked to China for advice; the Progressive party held for Japan. A mission was sent to Japan in 1882 to investigate the new civilization, and reported so favorably as to enrage the Conservatives. On two occasions in two years the Japanese legation was attacked by them, and each time the Japanese sent troops to Seoul and imposed an indemnity. China also, however, despatched troops to guard her interests. Believing that the Chinese had connived at the conspiracies against them, the Japanese sent Count Ito to China, and between him and Li-Hung-Chang was signed (April, 18 1885) the Tientsin convention, which provided that Chinese and Japanese troops should withdraw from Korea, and that before sending an armed force again to Seoul either country must inform the other.

In 1893 there arose a religious insurrection in Korea and the Conservative government faction sent to China for protecting troops. Exasperation in Japan against China had been waxing. The Chinese Resident in the Korean capital had persistently interfered in Korean affairs, and had—or at least the Japanese believed that he had—hampered commerce between Japan and Korea. Before sending soldiers and ships to support the Korean Government the Chinese despatched a note, according to the Tientsin convention, to inform Japan of their intention; but in that note Korea was called a "protectorate" and "dependency" of China, and the characterizations set Japan aflame. The Tientsin convention had provided that if either of the contracting countries should introduce troops into Korea the other might do likewise, and the force that Japan sent took possession of Seoul.

The Japanese Government in vain invited the co-operation of China in establishing order, and presented to the Korean Government a programme of reforms, suggesting that the presence of Chinese troops commanded by generals who had character-ized Korea as a "dependency" was incompatible with the independence of the country, which Japan, for her part, acknowledged. The Korean Govern-ment replied that the Chinese troops were present by its own request. Thereupon, July 22, 1894, the Japanese troops took possession of the royal palace and of the King, and caused the government to request Japanese aid in driving out the Chinese. With this, relations between China and Japan be-came so strained that, in spite of offers of pacification from foreign Powers, war was evidently at hand.

On paper, the military strength of the Chinese, including the "Eight Banners," the "Green Stand-ard," the "Volunteers," and the "Trained Army," was upwards of 1,000,000 men, whereas the Japa-nese army comprised about 70,000 men—well drilled, it is true, and armed with a breech-loading rifle. The equipment of the Chinese, on the other hand, was of the most primitive character. Indeed, cer-tain troops were armed with bows and arrows only, the one division furnished with modern weapons being the Trained Army, which had also been some-what exercised in European drill. It numbered less than 100,000. The navy was in somewhat more efficient condition, having been trained by English officers; but of its four squadrons only one, the Pei Yang, or northern division, was con-cerned with the war. It consisted, at the outset of the struggle, of twenty-seven vessels, including two battle-ships of 7400 tons. The Japanese fleet also comprised twenty-seven fighting craft of all kinds, but among them the heaviest were cruisers of 4200 tons.

Foreign nations followed the war with interest, partly because it seemed to be the contest of a pigmy with a giant; for although it was conceded among military authorities that the Japanese, with their superior alertness, might gain a few battles at first, still there was a general belief in an enormous latent power of the vast Chinese Empire, which would awake in time of need. A second cause of interest in the struggle was the illustrations which it promised to afford, particularly on the sea, of the efficiency of modern devices of war.

Fighting began before war was declared. There was a Chinese force at Asan on the bay of Chemulpo southwest of Seoul; and on the 21st of July the Chinese Government began to send transports with reinforcements to these troops and to others on the Yalu River, the boundary between China and Korea. To intercept these transports, the Japanese sent their three fastest cruisers, the *Akitsushima*, *Yoshino*, and *Naniwa*, and on the 25th they met the Chinese *Tsi-yuen* and *Kuan-yi* near the coast of Korea. The Chinese opened fire; in an hour the *Kuan-yi* was disabled and the *Tsi-yuen* fled. After the battle the *Naniwa* sighted the transport *Kowshing*, flying the British flag. This vessel, which had been chartered by China as a troop-ship, had on board 1000 soldiers, twelve guns, and Major von

Hannecken, a German military adviser to the Chinese, Captain (afterwards Admiral) Togo of the *Naniwa* ordered the *Kowshing* to surrender; the mandarins commanding the Chinese troops maintained that they would die first, and Togo sank the transport. Major von Hannecken and a few other Europeans sprang into the sea, under fire from the Chinese, and were rescued; but more than 1000 persons were drowned.

On the same day (July 25, 1894), General Oshima set forth from Seoul to confront the Chinese troops which had fortified a strong position near Asan. On the night of the 28th they stormed the redoubts and drove the Chinese, under General Yeh, out in confusion. The Japanese returned exultant to Seoul after this their first land engagement with foreign troops for three hundred years. On the first of August declarations of war were issued by both countries. Until the middle of September the combatants were occupied in bringing up troops for the serious work of the war. The Chinese concentrated forces at Ping-yang and the Yalu River, meaning to proceed southward and drive the Japanese into the sea. But the Japanese struck first. Ping-yang was a fortified city, defended by the Ti-dong River, and by five forts on uplands to the north. The Japanese advanced in three detachments. Their mixed brigade under Oshima created a diversion on the river front opposite the town. Under cover of this diversion the main army crossed the Ti-dong near its mouth and approached the city

from the west, and from the north two other detachments crossed the river and suddenly appeared
among the hills. On the morning of the 15th these
turned the Chinese rear at Ping-yang, captured the
city, and drove the defenders, with heavy loss, beyond the Yalu River.

On the 17th of September occurred the great
naval battle for which the world had been waiting.
The Chinese fleet, which had convoyed five troop-
ships to the Yalu, met on their return voyage, near
Hai-yang Island, the main squadron and the first
flying squadron of the Japanese fleet, which had
been sent out on a reconnoitring expedition. The
encounter was unexpected on both sides, but the
fleets cleared for action. The Chinese, under Admiral Ting, had ten vessels formed in a single line
abreast, with two battle-ships, the *Chen-yuen* and
the *Ting-yuen* in the centre. The Japanese fleet, under Admiral Ito, was very uneven in point of speed.
The four cruisers of the flying squadron could
steam from nineteen to twenty-three knots; but the
vessels of the main squadron ranged from nineteen
to thirteen knots, and besides there were to be
protected a little gunboat and an armed merchant
steamer. The flying squadron led the column, which
started across the Chinese front with the intention
of attacking the weaker vessels on the right flank,
and before this squadron had turned the line, the
(Chinese) *Yang Wei* was afire. At this moment two
other Chinese vessels and six torpedo-boats appeared
to the westward, and the flying squadron started

toward them, but they made off. In the meantime the main squadron passed the right wing of the Chinese and set on fire the *Chao-yung*, which presently sank. But the *Hiyei* could not keep up with the main Japanese squadron, and found herself in the midst of the Chinese fleet. The little gunboat *Akagi* went to her aid, but both vessels were in danger, and the flying squadron circled back to their aid and also to that of the *Saikio Maru*, the merchant steamer, which had escaped two torpedo attacks and was in imminent peril. The approach of the cruisers enabled the three weaker vessels to escape. Meanwhile the main squadron had passed entirely around the Chinese fleet, and the flying squadron had encircled it in the opposite direction. Having accomplished this, both divisions, approaching on opposite sides and from the rear, engaged their opponents, whose line of battle had been entirely lost. The *Chih-yuen* and the *King-yuen* were sunk, but the two battle-ships, the *Ting-yuen* and *Chen-yuen*, successfully resisted the attack of the entire Japanese fleet, though the flagship, the *Ting-yuen*, was afire and the upper works of both vessels were wrecked with shot from the Japanese quick-firing guns. Sunset put an end to the battle and during the night the Japanese lost sight of the enemy. This was the first naval battle between modern fleets with rapid-firing guns; and because of the long resistance of the two iron-clads to the devastating attack of the Japanese quick-firers, all navies increased the size of their new battle-ships.

The battle has been pronounced by some critics a victory for the Japanese, and by others a drawn battle, because the Japanese did not pursue their victory and annihilate the rest of the Chinese fleet. The Chinese lost four vessels, and afterwards a fifth ran aground and was blown up by her crew. The Japanese lost no vessels, though their flagship, the *Matsushima*, suffered severely, as also did the *Hiyei*. The Chinese lost about seven hundred killed and about two or three hundred wounded; the Japanese losses were about 115 killed and 41 wounded. Victory or not, the combat cleared the sea of Chinese war-vessels and gave the Japanese free course for their transports.

After the capture of Ping-yang the Japanese reorganized their forces, forming an army corps at the Yalu commanded by Marshal Yamagata, and meanwhile preparing a second army at home. On October 24th Yamagata crossed the river, surprised the Chinese under General Sung, by a flanking attack upon their left, and drove them back upon Feng-huang-cheng, where a large number of the Chinese soldiers deserted. General Sung burned the town and retreated with the remnant of his army to Mukden.

During November the first army occupied itself with the capture of minor places in the vicinity of Fong-wang, breaking up the force of the fugitives of Sung's army at Hsin-yen, and establishing a civil administration in the captured territory. The advance on Mukden was delayed pending the operations of a second army, which had set forth from Japan against Port Arthur. It was commanded by Marshal Oyama, and left the Fai-dong River October 23d. It landed on the 24th at Hua-yuan-kon, about forty miles northwest of Port Arthur, and after an expeditious march, diversified by a few skirmishes, arrived, November 5th, before the defences of Kinchow, the key of the isthmus called the Regent's Sword, that connects the peninsula upon which Port Arthur is situated with the mainland. On the 6th, with no men killed and but few wounded, General Yamaji had taken the town, and, as the Japanese entered, the Chinese fled to Port Arthur by the western gate. Next day, advancing upon the forts which defended the very narrowest part of the isthmus, along the coast of Ta-lien Bay, the victorious army frightened the defenders away, though the forts were of modern construction and heavily armed. The fleet had intended to assist the army in the reduction of these forts, and had entered Ta-lien Bay on the morning of the 7th of November, timidly, for fear of torpedoes. It even fired a few shots at the forts before it saw the Japanese flags waving above them. With the control of the bay and the isthmus the Japanese had the garrison of Port Arthur "enclosed in a bag."

After ten days of preparation they resumed their march toward the stronghold. During the four days of progress to the outermost line of the defences several skirmishes took place, and here the Chinese showed some spirit, even making a sortie with 3000 men upon a Japanese regiment—an attack which was, however, immediately repulsed.

Port Arthur is one of the strongest fortresses in the world. It is surrounded by successive ranges of hills crowned by forts. The most important of these forts were those on Itzu Shan, Antzu Shan, and Wang-tai at the west, that on Sungshu Shan, and further to the eastward, extending in a southerly direction, those of Ehrlung Shan. On the Tiger's Tail—a strip of land which forms the southern boundary of the harbor—were eight forts, but they had no part in the defence of the town. Each of these forts was heavily equipped with modern guns, and the garrison numbered more than 13,000.

With a garrison of more warlike troops, the capture of such a place must have been a matter of weeks, if not of months, as indeed subsequent events showed; but the Chinese yielded after one day of fighting. On the night of the 20th of November the field-guns of General Yamaji arrived, and at daybreak opened fire. Forty guns were assigned to the fortifications to the west, and in about an hour the return fire from the first fort ceased, and the Japanese infantry stormed the position. The defenders fled. General Yamaji at once brought up field-pieces to command Sungshu Shan, and that fort fell at eleven in the morning.

The assailing force at Ehrlung Shan had harder fighting, but at half-past twelve it drove out the defenders, and the way was opened to Port Arthur.

There remained only a fort on Huang-Chin-shan, and the forts on the Tiger's Tail. The former had heavy coast guns, which had been well served during the morning, but in a single charge, the Japanese were masters of the hill.

The Chinese fled from the city and during the night abandoned the works on the Tiger's Tail. They had put to death with torture many Japanese prisoners, whose limbs, impaled on stakes, confronted their comrades, and the victorious troops could not be restrained from retaliation. They looted the town, and put to death a considerable number of the inhabitants.

The fall of Port Arthur, which gave to the Japanese a fine naval base of operations, with admirably equipped docks, startled the Chinese Government, which sent, rather informally, an envoy to ascertain upon what terms the Japanese would treat for peace. He was not, however, received.

In the meantime, the first army, in Manchuria, repelled a Tartar force, under General Iko-ten-ga, from the northwest, and a descent on the part of the Chinese, from the Motien pass; and, resuming the offensive, pushed forward (December 13th) to Hai-cheng, on the road of communications between Peking and Mukden. There were Chinese forces at Liao-yang at the northeast, Nuchwang at the northwest, and Ying-kow at the southwest; and during the rest of the war the Japanese were occupied in preventing their junction. They defeated General Sung, who was advancing from

Ying-kow with about 10,000 men, in a battle in the snow at Kang-na-sai on the 19th of December. It was one of the most stubbornly fought contests of the war, and the losses were nearly equal. A Chinese army of 20,000 men approached Hai-cheng in January, but never made any serious attack.

The second army, at Port Arthur, had been preparing for a northward advance, and on the 10th of January, 1895, a mixed brigade under General Nogi, after sharp fighting, occupied Kaiping. The Chinese opposition was more steadfast in this than in previous battles and their marksmanship had improved. The occupation of Kaiping furnished a good support for Katsura, at Hai-cheng, and the armies rested for some weeks.

Meanwhile the Japanese turned their attention to Wei-hai-wei, which, with Port Arthur opposite, guarded the gulf of Pechili. The Chinese fleet had taken refuge in this harbor, and if it could be captured, troops could be transported freely to Taku. The road to Peking, which the Japanese ardently desired to capture, would thus be greatly shortened. The entrances of the bay, at the east and west of a large island, had been closed by double booms made of hawsers of steel wire and protected by torpedoes. The land defences on the south consisted of seven forts, and on the north of five. On Liu Kung Island there were two forts, and on a smaller island, Gih Island, one. The garrison of the stronghold was about 10,000 men. In the harbor were twenty-six vessels, including the two battle-ships the *Ting-yuen* and the *Chen-yuen*, seven other war-vessels, eleven torpedo-boats, and six gunboats.

On the 19th of January, fifty transports, convoyed by the greater part of the Japanese fleet, crossed to Yung Cheng, a town a few miles to the eastward of Wei-hai-wei. Upon the previous day three Japanese vessels had made a diversion at Teng Chou, about a hundred miles west of the objective point, and had drawn the attention of the Chinese in that direction, so that the landing of the Japanese was opposed by only one battery, which was presently silenced by the guns of the fleet. On the 26th of January the landing was completed, and the Japanese advanced toward the forts. From the land forces the opposition was unimportant; but as the Japanese occupied position after position the Chinese fleet in the harbor harassed them. Owing to the state of the roads, the assailants could carry no siege guns, and had to rely on the artillery captured in the forts to reply to the fire of the war-vessels. The guns in the western forts were destroyed by the Chinese sailors themselves. In the eastern forts, however, there were captured twelve powerful pieces, and with them the Chinese vessels were confined in the extremity of the harbor. By the 1st of February the land defences had been captured, and the Chinese ships were surrounded. Cut off by Admiral Ito's fleet from leaving the harbor, and opposed on shore by a strong Japanese force, they were nevertheless out of reach of gun-fire and were in no apparent peril, for the entrance to the harbor was defended by the forts on Liu Kung Island. On the night of the 3d of February the Japanese opened a passage between the boom and the shore. Before daybreak on the 5th, ten torpedo-boats attempted to enter the harbor. Five were injured, three were lost, and one was abandoned; but the Chinese flagship, the *Ting-yuen*, was torpedoed and sank to her decks in the morning. On the 6th of February, at four in the morning, five other torpedo-boats entered the harbor, and, firing seven torpedoes, destroyed the *Lai-yuen*, the *Wei-yuen*, and a gunboat, and withdrew without loss.

These disasters demoralized the Chinese, and on the 7th, after the Japanese had blown up the magazine on Gih Island, the Chinese torpedo-boats fled through the western entrance of the harbor, only to be captured by Japanese cruisers. Admiral Ting still resisted, hoping for reinforcements. On the 9th the *Ching-yuen*, which had advanced to shell the captured forts, was sunk. On the 11th the Chinese admiral received word from Li-Hung-Chang that no aid need be expected, and on the 12th he surrendered the remainder of his ships and committed suicide. The generals of the Chinese on Liu Kung Island also killed themselves. By the terms of surrender the Chinese garrison and the officers of the navy were set free.

In the course of the preparations for the expedition against Wei-hai-wei, China had prepared a second peace embassy, which arrived in Japan

January 31, 1895. It consisted of two envoys and a large staff, including an American adviser, Mr. Foster, but it did not have powers to accede to the full demands of the Japanese without further communication with the Tsung-li-Yamen, and negotiations failed.

The Chinese from Nuchwang and Liao-yang made several attacks upon the Japanese at Hai-cheng, but these were easily repulsed, and during the latter part of February, General Yamaji having joined General Nogi at Kaiping, and General Katsura at Hai-cheng having been reinforced, the Japanese in turn moved forward. The second army had pushed forward to Taiping Shan, had attacked the Chinese intrenchments at the point of the bayonet, and had driven General Sung back to Po-miao-tzu, thus preventing his co-operation with the Nuchwang and Liao-yang armies.

On the 28th of February Katsura began operations for the separation of the latter forces. In a series of encounters he pushed back the Liao-yang army and pursued it until the second of March. Then he turned, and, on the 4th, attacked Nuchwang on the northwest and east. Here the Chinese resisted vigorously with Gatling guns, and, even after the Japanese had entered the town, delivered a house-to-house combat until almost midnight, killing forty-two Japanese and wounding 174, but losing more than 1800, mainly in their retreat. The Japanese took 2000 prisoners, and captured a quantity of ammunition and several guns. On the

7th of March General Yamaji occupied Ying-kow, which had been evacuated by General Sung, who had retreated northwestward to Tien-chwang-tai; and here on the 9th of March the combined Japanese armies routed his forces, destroying, during the battle and the retreat, more than 2000 men.

This was the last important battle of the war. On the 19th of March a new embassy, headed by Li-Hung-Chang and accompanied by General Foster, Wu-Ting-Fang, and a suite of 132 persons, arrived at Shimonoseki provided with full powers to make a treaty. In the course of the negotiations, on the 24th of March, a fanatic shot the Chinese envoy in the cheek. The Japanese were excessively mortified at this breach of hospitality; the envoy received more than 10,000 letters of sympathy and the Mikado proclaimed an armistice in Manchuria, Pechili, and Shan-tung until the 20th of April. The wound was found not to be dangerous, negotiations were soon resumed, and on the 17th of April the treaty was signed. On the 8th of May it was ratified at Chefoo. It provided for an indemnity of 300,000,000 yen and the concession to Japan of Formosa, the Pescadores Islands, and the Liao-tung Peninsula, including Port Arthur.

But the Powers feared that the possession of Port Arthur would give Japan too much influence in China, Germany, France, and Russia jointly requested Japan to leave the peninsula to China, and to this the Mikado and his advisers consented, without condition

CHAPTER XVII.

THE STRUGGLE WITH RUSSIA.

THE efficiency of the Japanese arms had raised the country in the estimation of the Powers, and one of the first results of the war was a revision of the treaties between Japan and the other nations, including particularly the abolition of extra-territorial jurisdiction, which was especially galling to Japanese pride. The statesmen of the country had made every effort to show to the world that the Japanese differed in no essential way from European peoples, and deserved the treatment accorded to civilized nations. They had revised their entire legal code according to European models, had organised a police system, had joined the International Postal Union, had even encouraged the adoption of European clothes, and in short, had made every effort to demonstrate their equality in civilization with Occidental races.

After 1872, when, according to the treaties signed with the Tokugawa government, Japan might demand a modification of her agreements with the Powers, several attempts to gain such modifications were made; but for one reason or another none succeeded until the establishment of the courts of justice in 1894, and the exhibition of Japan's prowess in war. England, indeed, signed a treaty on equal terms before the war (July, 1894). During the war, the United States signed a similar agreement, and the other Powers followed. All of these treaties were to come in force in May, 1899, and to hold for twelve years. Extra-territoriality was abolished in all parts of Japan. Foreigners were to be judged by Japanese courts, according to Japanese law, and were permitted to live anywhere in Japan and to hold movable property. The customs tariff was arranged by separate treaty with each nation, and differed, of course, with regard to the character of the imports and exports of each country; but the most - favored - nation clause, which is reciprocal and unconditional in all treaties, produced a certain uniformity in the rates.

Controversies in the Diet began again immediately after the war, at first on the question, ostensibly at least, of the retrocession of the Liao-tung Peninsula. In 1898 Russia leased Port Arthur for twenty-five years, and England promptly leased Wei-hai-wei. These occupations were used as tools by the opposition, which desired to remove from power the "clansmen," who had not, it was alleged, properly upheld Japanese claims to the territory captured by Japanese armies. In 1898 the Liberal and Progressive parties joined forces under the name of the Constitutional party, which had a majority in the House of Representatives and was led by chiefs trained in parliamentary tactics. Marquis Ito, who was the Minister President of the Cabinet, resigned; and at his suggestion, for the first time, an opposition Cabinet was formed, including Okuma and Itagaki. Advocates of party government expected much from this Cabinet, but it could not, or at least did not, overcome dissensions, and fell in six months. There succeeded a Conservative government, with Yamagata as Minister President, which lasted until 1900, when Ito was again called to face the Boxer riots in China. In 1901 there was formed a combination of parties under the name of the Association of Friends of the Constitution (*Rikken-Seiyu-kai*). It made friends with Ito, who insisted, however, that the principle of parliamentary cabinets should be abandoned. Ito's ministry fell before the year was out, on the question of raising a foreign loan for military expansion; and Katsura took his place as Minister President, while Ito became President of the Privy Council, whose advice the Emperor usually follows. The Katsura ministry was chosen mainly from the Upper House, without regard to party sympathies, and remained in power until 1906, when it gave place to a government under Saionji, which continued the policy of its predecessor. There was no question of the responsibility of ministers to the Diet; that problem was obscured by the more vital considerations of war with Russia.

By this time, the effort of the Japanese to take

advantage of the ultimate manifestations of Western civilization had begun to produce its effect. Relay after relay of young men, and a few young women, had returned to their homes from universities in the United States and England and Germany, informed as to the laws, sciences, and industrial developments of the West. Under the guidance, and for many years under the instruction, of foreign teachers, a system of schools had been established. There were upwards of 27,000 public schools, with compulsory education up to the age of ten. There were about three hundred secondary schools, including seventy schools for girls. There were about sixty normal schools, and two State Universities, one at Tokyō, the other at Kyōto. Among the children of school age, more than ninety-three *per centum* were availing themselves of school privileges. In most of the schools, Japanese teachers had displaced the foreign instructors. The medical and engineering colleges had begun to produce the extraordinary results which were apparent in the war with Russia, in which the Japanese doctors proved themselves the equals of any in the world. Comparative freedom of the press was permitted, and an extraordinary number of newspapers sprung up, which presently began to exert a considerable political and educational influence, particularly the *Nichi Nichi*, the *Kokumin*, the *Hochi*, the *Jiji*, the *Nippon*, and the *Mainichi*.

No less eager were the Japanese to avail themselves of foreign knowledge in the development of industrial affairs; but here solid progress was less rapid than it had been in educational, military, and administrative matters, because the class affected was less accustomed to self-discipline than were the *samurai.* Baron Shibusawa, who developed the company system, describes the Japanese as impulsive, impatient, disinclined to union, and not trained in such business honesty as was demanded by other nations. These traits, he says, "make it hard for the people to achieve business success." That success has, besides, been hampered by lack of capital on the part of the Japanese. Nevertheless, progress in these matters was by no means slow. After the payment of the indemnity from China, indeed, which was spent mainly in developing the resources of the country, there ensued a period of exceedingly rapid expansion, which brought on a collapse and depression in 1900 and 1901. The banking system was developed and perfected. The gold standard was adopted. A special bank was established for the purpose of making loans on immovable property, thus furnishing capital for the development of agriculture and manufactures. The main industries of the country had always been agricultural; about sixty *per centum* of the population are farmers. After the restoration, however, and particularly after the promulgation of the Constitution which permitted every Japanese to change his residence as he pleased, the population began to drift toward the cities. Manufacturing increased rapidly. Foreign machinery was imported. Great industrial centres were developed. The main industries were the raising and manufacture of silk, the raising of rice and tea, and the manufacture of cotton. Ship-building was enlivened after the Chinese War, and several companies were organized, some of which had, before the Russian War, docks capable of receiving vessels of 8000 to 10,000 tons. Steamship companies also flourished, one of which, the Nippon-Yusen Kaisha, had developed services of commodious steamers to Bombay, London, Antwerp, Hong Kong, Seattle, and Melbourne. The government aided in the development of ship-building, organizing ship-yards and afterwards turning them over to private companies. One of these yards, the Kawasaki, at Kobe, ultimately built a plant capable of turning out ships of 20,000 tons. In the government yards, also, of which the largest is at Yokosuka, several war-ships have been built.

The government also took in hand the development of mining and organized a school of mines. Government experiments with mining, however, proved to be unprofitable; but concessions were made to private corporations, which flourished, producing gold, silver, copper, hematite, quicksilver, oil, and other mineral products in considerable quantities.

Railways were first built by the government in 1872, but within ten years a number of private corporations started up, and by the beginning of the Russian War there were more than four thousand miles of track in the Empire.

Every kind of foreign custom or device was made welcome. The bicycle and the telephone had a great popularity. Electric railroads were built in several cities, and even in parts of the country. Brick structures, lighted by electricity and equipped with the most modern improvements, were built for offices; the clerks wore coats and trousers during office hours and returned at night to their native houses, took off their shoes, assumed their native clothing, and sat down upon their white mats to their native rice and fish. To the eye the experiments of this ancient people with modern devices present a spectacle of incongruities. But, as those who have guided the nation point out, it is merely a season of trial; those things which are not suitable for Japanese civilization are to be discarded; those that survive to be retained—with improvements.

As soon as the Chinese War was over, foreseeing possible complications with Russia, Ito and Yamagata set about a reorganization of the army and navy, with the plan of doubling the force of soldiers by 1905, and the sea power by 1904. The army was to consist of three divisions—the active army, liable for foreign service, in which every able-bodied man twenty years of age should serve three years; the first reserve, with a service of four years and four months; the second reserve, with a service of five years more. At the expiration of service, the men mustered out were to join the second division, the National Army for home defence. The navy at the beginning of the war with Russia consisted of six battle-ships, six armored cruisers, fourteen protected cruisers, forty torpedo-boats, and twenty-four destroyers, besides more than fifty transports and other auxiliary vessels.

The first trial of the efficiency of the new troops came in 1900, when the Chinese association called the "Boxers," attempting to drive foreigners from China, mastered Peking, killed the Japanese Secretary of Legation and the German Minister, besieged the other Ministers of foreign Powers in the legations, and overran a considerable part of the Pechili province, including the city of Tientsin. The Powers hastily sent troops to the relief of the legations. England desired to intrust the Japanese with the entire responsibility of rescuing the besieged ministers, and Japan was ready to take the responsibility, provided that she should have the moral support of the other Powers. But this was not granted, and a mixed force of Japanese, Americans, English, Germans, French, and Russians, in a short campaign, captured the Chinese forts at Taku, drove the Chinese from Tientsin, and finally entered Peking in time to save the larger number of the defenders of the legations. In every engagement the Japanese troops were to the fore: they were first to enter Taku and Tsin, and voluntarily undertook the assault upon the most difficult gates of the capital. Moreover, after the occupation of the city, when the soldiers of all the other nations looted the Chinese more or less freely, the Japanese refrained entirely from plunder.

The "Boxer" insurrection was by no means confined to Pechili. Disturbances occurred also in
Manchuria, endangering the Russian trans-Siberian
railroad; and Russia sent a force which occupied
Blagovestchenk, overran Manchuria, and at last
took possession of Neuchwang. When the Powers,
having established order in Peking, withdrew their
forces in 1901, Russia maintained her occupation
of Manchuria, promising, however, to abandon it
to China, in three evacuations, at intervals of six
months, beginning October 8, 1902, and ending
October 8, 1903. The first evacuation was accomplished on time; but the second was not, and, in the
face of the protest of the Powers, Russia began to
send troops into Manchuria, to protect, it was
alleged, concessions for wood-cutting, granted to
private corporations in Manchuria and Korea—corporations in which, it was rumored, the Grand
Dukes of Russia, and even the Tzar were interested.
At the same time Russian agents tried to wring a
promise from China that no other Power should be
allowed to occupy Manchuria, after the Russian
withdrawal, and even that no ports should be newly
opened to foreign consuls. The principle of the
open door in China had been insisted on by the
Powers, and in 1902, in a treaty of alliance between
England and Japan (which provided that when one
of the signatory nations should be at war with two
other nations, it should have armed support from
the ally) the maintenance of this principle in China
and Korea had been prescribed.

In August, 1903, Admiral Alexieff was nominated by imperial ukase Viceroy of the Amur and Kwang-tung territories, and on the appointed date, the Russian soldiers had made no movement toward evacuation. Under the advice of the Powers, China demanded their withdrawal. Russia refused to evacuate the province without a guarantee from China that her terms as to the "closed door" should be accepted, and moreover began negotiations with Korea for a lease of Yongampo, which was to have been an open port. There ensued a diplomatic correspondence between Russia and Japan, the latter Power believing its interests in Korea and Manchuria to be endangered by the Russian occupation.

The Japanese Minister of Foreign Affairs, Baron Komura, offered to come to an agreement with Russia to "respect the independence and territorial integrity of the Chinese and Korean empires," recognizing the special interests of Russia in Manchuria, and of Japan in Korea, but maintaining that Japan and other Powers must not be "impeded in the enjoyment of rights and privileges acquired by them under existing treaties with China." The replies of Count Lamsdorff to the Japanese proposition came slowly, and meantime Russia was hurrying troops into Manchuria. Popular feeling in Japan was somewhat at fever heat; indeed, as a writer describes it, for months the government had been sitting on the safety-valve. At last, on February 5th, the Japanese Minister to Russia,

Baron Kurino received instructions to leave St. Petersburg, and communicated them to Count Lamsdorff.[1]

Japan was quite ready for this struggle. For many years the War Department had been taking thought of little else. Its maps showed every elevation and depression of the ground in Korea and Manchuria. The equipment of its armies was perfect, so far as inspection could make it so. Its new powder invented by Dr. Shimose had been subjected to severe tests. Its soldiers had been drilled patiently to fight intelligently, as well as desperately. Particularly its system of communications had been organized; throughout the ensuing war, the soldiers never lacked cartridges nor food. Its hospital corps won the admiration of all nations. The weakness of the Japanese armies was perhaps in cavalry, which was not heavy enough to endure the charge of the tall Russians, but that was not due to lack of care on the part of the Japanese. They had made experiments in raising horses of all kinds, and had developed powerful chargers, but the backs of these proved too broad for the short men of Nippon, and so, perforce, lighter horses had to be used. At the outset of the war, fifty transports were waiting to carry the first army to Korea, and every item of cargo was waiting to be put aboard.

[1] A translation of the correspondence between Japan and Russia over the points of difference that resulted in the war will be found in Appendix V.

As in the Chinese War, so in this war between Russia and Japan it is said that the first shot was fired by the Russians, and fired before official declaration of war had been made. The gunboat *Korietz* was lying, with the cruiser *Variag*, in the harbor of Chemulpo, on the 8th of February, 1904. A shot from her was directed toward the Japanese convoy of a fleet of transports, carrying troops to Korea. The Japanese did not reply and the troops were landed; but on the next morning, Rear-Admiral Uriu, in command of the Japanese squadron, sent word to the Russians that war existed, and that they must leave neutral waters before noon or be sunk in the harbor. In the face of an overwhelming force the two vessels left the harbor, and were destroyed within an hour. Meanwhile at Port Arthur on the night of February 8th a Japanese torpedo flotilla had damaged the Russian battle-ships *Retvisan* and *Tsarewitch*, and the cruiser *Pallada*, and in the course of the next night seriously injured the cruisers *Diana*, *Askold*, and *Novik*. These misfortunes aroused Russian energy. A state of war was proclaimed on the 10th of February. General Kuropatkin was presently appointed to the military command of Manchuria, and Admiral Makaroff was sent to take over the Port Arthur squadron. In the meantime Admiral Togo was hammering at this fleet. On February 14th his torpedo-boats disabled the cruiser *Boyarin*. Several brave attempts on the part of the Japanese to close the entrance of Port Arthur by sinking vessels in it, however, failed.

ADMIRAL TOGO.
(From a Photograph.)

But on April 13th a new serious disaster befell the
Russians. Admiral Makaroff was enticed to sea in
chase of certain Japanese vessels, and his flagship,
the *Petropavlovsk*, struck a Japanese mine, which
had been laid in the probable Russian course, and
sank. The Admiral, the main hope of the Russian
navy, was drowned, with the greater part of his
crew, as was also the eminent painter Verestchagin.
Eighty persons were saved.

From Vladivostok a Russian squadron of four
cruisers ranged along the Korean coast, sank a Japanese vessel at Gensan, and a Japanese transport,
eluded for some time Admiral Kamimura, who had
been sent to oppose it, and threatened a descent
upon Japanese territory. But on June 27th the
Japanese Admiral met them, sank one of their vessels, the *Rurik*, and drove two others back to
Vladivostok. The fourth ran aground and sank
in April.

Admiral Togo, with the principal Japanese fleet,
had been watching the Russian vessels at Port
Arthur. His own fleet had not escaped catastrophe. On April 15th, in a fog, a Japanese cruiser,
the *Kasuga*, had rammed the *Yoshino* and sunk her,
and the battle-ships *Yashima* and *Hatsuse* had struck
Russian mines and had been lost. But Togo had
kept the Russian fleet shut up in Port Arthur, so
that the Japanese could, without danger, transport
their armies to the continent for the land campaign.
One of these armies had begun the siege of Port
Arthur, and as it pressed the stronghold closer, the

Russian vessels made several efforts to escape from the harbor and join the small squadron at Vladivostok. On June 23d Togo drove the entire fleet back into port, but on August 10th it made another attempt to escape. This time the Japanese scattered its units, and nullified its power. The *Pallada* and *Novik* sank, the *Sevastopol, Retvisan, Poltava,* and *Peresviet* returned to Port Arthur, and the other vessels fled to neutral ports, where they were disarmed.

The operations on land had been pushed no less successfully and systematically. Everything, down to the smallest details, was prepared for the concentration and transportation of the first army, and in the beginning of April it had landed in Korea, and had driven the Russians beyond the Yalu River. General Kuroki, in command of this force of 40,000 men, concentrated at Wiju. On the opposite bank of the river the Russians under General Sassulitch, with 10,000 men, had fortified the heights, meaning to delay the Japanese advance as long as possible, so that troops might be sent over the Siberian railroad to reinforce General Kuropatkin, and, when his position was no longer tenable, to retire. The rapidity of march of the Japanese, however, turned his retreat into disaster. Kuroki encompassed both the right and the left flanks of the Russians, and drove them back along the road to Liao-yang. The Japanese reserves, marching quickly, caught up with the rear-guard of the Russians on three sides, and captured twenty-

GENERAL KUROKI.
(From a Photograph.)

one guns, six Maxims, and 1000 prisoners. The
Japanese lost 1000, the Russians 4500. Kuroki
pursued to Feng-huang-cheng and occupied the
Motien-ling, the pass over the hills to the plains,
beyond Liao-yang. On July 4th and 17th the
Russians tried to retake this pass, without success.
The first army, now in a position to menace Kuropatkin's rear, in case he should advance with his
whole army toward Port Arthur, rested for several
weeks.

During this campaign the second Japanese army,
under General Oku, had been landing in the Liao-
tung Peninsula, at Yentao Bay. On May 5th the
commander despatched a column to take possession
of Port Adams, and the railroad to Port Arthur.
The other divisions, landing farther south, approached Kinchow. As in the Chinese War, Kinchow guarded the isthmus leading to the peninsula,
and it was more strongly fortified by far than it had
been under the Chinese. Ten forts, with seventy
heavy guns, eight machine guns, and two batteries
of quick-firing rifles defended Nan Shan, on an
eminence to the southward of the city, with a garrison of 15,000 men. The Japanese army of about
45,000, of whom, however, not all were in action,
extended across the land from Kinchow Bay to the
Korean Sea. On May 26th, supported by four
gunboats in Kinchow Bay, Oku hurled one attack
after another against the hill, only to lose his men
among the barbed wire entanglements at its foot.
In the late afternoon no important advantage had

been gained by the assailants. But, just before sundown, the fourth division, forming the right wing, under General Ogawa, waded through the shallows of Kinchow Bay to the Russian left, and suddenly appeared upon the heights. The first and third divisions, the centre and left, encouraged, charged once more, and by seven o'clock the Russians had abandoned their seventy-eight guns, and were retiring to Port Arthur. The Japanese lost 3500 men in their fight of sixteen hours; the Russians, about 2000.

The fall of Nan Shan uncovered the port of Dalny, with its fine dock, which was abandoned by the Russians and occupied by Oku on the 29th. With fresh troops from Japan, and a part of Oku's force, an army was formed under the command of General Nogi, to capture Port Arthur. Oku, with the greater part of his command, pushed northward, and defeated General Stackelberg, who had been sent to attack him, at Tilissu on June 14th and 15th, capturing sixteen guns. On July 25th he fought his way to Tashih-shiao where he defeated a Russian force under Kuropatkin himself; on July 27th he pushed on to Nuchwang, driving the Russians back to Hai-cheng.

A third Japanese army, under General Nodzu, which had been landed at Takushan, had made its way northward, by way of the Fenshon-ling, to Kaiping, had taken the town after three days of hard fighting, and now co-operated with Oku against Hai-cheng. After this had been accomplished,

Kuropatkin withdrew his forces to Liao-yang, leaving a rear-guard at An-shan-chau.

By August 24th, at the end of the rainy season, the three Japanese armies were ready to advance. On the right was Kuroki. In the centre and on the left Nodzu and Oku had forced the Russians from An-shan-chau, and Oku was closing in upon Kuropatkin's right. General Oyama was in command of the combined Japanese force, which pressed back the Russians upon their formidable defences at Liao-yang, and began to assault these, August 30th, on the south and southwest, while Kuroki moved northward, with the object of pushing to the Russian rear and cutting off his retreat. Thus he separated from the second army, and exposed himself to the attack of Kuropatkin's whole force. But the Russian was not prepared to throw himself between the armies. For the moment the attack of the centre and left armies occupied him.

This attack began with an artillery duel, involving more than 1000 guns on both sides, followed by persistent infantry charges from Oku and Nodzu against the outer redoubts, which were set upon hills and defended by barbed wire entanglements, pits containing stakes, and other devices for hampering the Japanese rushes. During this day these rushes made no important gain; but by the 31st Oku had brought up the five-inch rifles captured at Nan Shan, and his artillery fire was more effective. The Japanese guns were probably better served than the Russian, and the "Shimose" powder proved to be a manageable and powerful explosive. Nevertheless, the Russian guns were never quite silenced, and one rush after another was repelled. At seven in the evening Oku sent in vain, for the third time in twenty-four hours, his entire line against the entrenchments. A fourth attack was planned for three in the morning. But meanwhile Kuroki's movement to the north threatened to cut the Russian communications, and Kuropatkin, drawing off part of his force to confront the first army, ordered the abandonment of the first and second southern positions. Oku's men entered the works without opposition. On the 2d of September began another stubborn attack, without perceptible advantage to the Japanese. It was renewed during the night and during the next day, when the Japanese left began to shell the town and the railroad bridge. In the evening the central army rushed one after another of the Russian forts, and at 12.20 of September 4th took possession of the northern portion of the town. The Russians had fled, and Oku on the left seized the railroad bridge at 3.30.

Meanwhile, Kuroki had crossed the Tai-tse and threatened the Russian line of withdrawal. He occupied Hyentai, a low hill, the central point among several elevations, which lay between the Japanese front and the railroad. Among these hills, particularly at Hyentai, occurred desperate struggles. The hill was occupied and retaken by one party or another, mainly in night hand-to-hand attacks. It was in the hands of the Japanese on the night of the fourth. But by this time Kuropatkin's entire force, except a small rear-guard, had crossed the river. Kuroki could not hope to give it battle, unsupported as he was by the other armies, but, as it retreated, pursued to the Hun River, where both forces paused to take breath. About 180,000 men on each side had been engaged in the battle. Both armies were tired out. Neither had slept for six days. The Russians were too weary to divide Kuroki from the other armies and overwhelm him, even if they had not had the discouragement of defeat; the Japanese were too much exhausted to pursue.

A quiet month elapsed. Both sides were strengthening themselves for new efforts. According to the Japanese system the gaps in the line left by battles were filled up by relays from home, and at this time the term of active service was extended for five years, so that the available army comprised 600,000 men. At the same time Kuropatkin was receiving 3000 recruits daily over the railroad, and arrangements for the organization of a second army were begun in Russia.

Two divisions of the Russians were on the Hun; four at Mukden; the rest of Kuropatkin's army was at the Tie-ling. All the Japanese had crossed the Tai-tse, and were drawn up facing the Hun, with a front of about ninety-three miles. They had perhaps 150,000 men. On October 2d Kuropatkin either felt strong enough to, or was commanded to,

advance to the rescue of Port Arthur. He encountered the Japanese on October 9th, and there
followed eight days of desperate fighting. The
first attack of the Russians caused the Japanese to
withdraw their outposts, but the centre resisted
stoutly. On the 10th the left and centre were
attacked, and thenceforth counter-assaults upon
important situations occurred every day and night.
But the Japanese in the main held their positions,
and on the 11th began a general advance, which
developed more strongly on the 12th, and on the
13th broke the right and centre of the Russians,
and on the 14th had driven them across the Hun.
Desultory fighting still continued, and on the night
of the 17th the Japanese lost sixteen guns. But
the battle wore out with the Japanese lines advanced fifteen miles toward Mukden. In these
engagements the Russian losses are reckoned at
60,000 men, and the Japanese at 16,000. The winter was coming on and both armies entrenched
themselves for another period of preparation, and
meanwhile awaited the result of the long and closely-
pressed siege of Port Arthur.

General Nogi had assumed command of the third
Japanese army, destined to reduce this formidable
fortress. Advantage had been taken by the Rus-
sian engineers of every natural means of defence.
At the east were the Ehrlung Shan, Bandusan, and
Kikwan forts, in the first line, dominated by Pine
Tree Hill and Inner Kikwan; and to the west of
the railway there were Antzu Shan, Itzu Shan, and

203 Metre Hill; besides the Golden Hill fort on the seaboard, which was equipped with heavy guns from the fleet, and other forts. The number and strength of forts, redoubts, and trenches had been greatly augmented since the Chinese War. The approaches were defended by trenches on the sides of the hills, banked up so as to be invisible at artillery range, and were, moreover, guarded with mines and with entanglements of barbed wire, charged with a mortal current of electricity. General Stössel had a garrison of upwards of 30,000 men.

The capture of such a fortress seemed impossible. It was not reduced until January 1st, and the siege is said to have cost more than 50,000 in killed and wounded. Nogi, who had moved south from Kerr Bay, drove in the Russian outposts, with some difficulty, and by the beginning of August was within six miles of the town. August 16th, he sent to General Stössel a summons to surrender which was refused, and on the 19th he began a general bombardment and attack, which lasted until August 26th, and, it is said, cost the Japanese 15,000 men. The assaults were pushed day and night. The night attacks were illuminated by star-bombs, by the eight or nine searchlights of the Russians, and by the continuous flashes of exploding shells. On the 22d the Japanese carried the Banu Shan redoubts, and these, in spite of all the Russian attacks, they held.

174 Metre Hill, to the west of the railroad, fell

into the hands of the Japanese on August 19th, and, although this was not in itself very important, possession of it was the preliminary step to the assault of the western hills, particularly 203 Metre Hill, which commanded the harbor. In the harbor were the vessels which had escaped from the battle of August 10th. A powerful fleet was in preparation in Russia to sail to the aid of Port Arthur; and so long as the vessels in the harbor remained fit for service, ready to fall upon the Japanese communications, if not opposed, Admiral Togo could not safely make preparations to meet this new enemy. It was obviously necessary to destroy the vessels in the port as soon as might be.

From the works at Osaka had come a battery of eleven-inch howitzers, and their 500-pound shells had already made some impression on the Russian forts. After one or two general assaults on 203 Metre Hill, which were repulsed with great loss, the Japanese resorted to their sappers, and drove parallels within a hundred and fifty feet of the Russian works. On the 27th of November the entire Japanese artillery fire was concentrated upon the hill, and at night the Japanese rushed out of their trenches and carried the summit. The Russians, however, re-formed and recaptured it. The next morning the Japanese charged again, unsuccessfully, and once more at four in the afternoon, when they won the crest, which, however, shrapnel from the higher summits soon compelled them to abandon. Day and night, until December 5th, the assaults continued. In the afternoon of that day, at last, the Japanese drove the defenders from the ruins of their trenches, and this time created a diversion by feinting a movement upon the eastern forts. The Russians hurried to meet this new threat, and before they could return the Japanese had fortified themselves too strongly to be dislodged. This hill was not used for batteries, however, but as an observation point for directing the fire of the eleven-inch guns, which were brought to its rear. From here they could discharge a plunging fire upon the harbor, and had soon disabled all of the larger Russian vessels except the *Sevastopol*, which anchored out of range and was presently torpedoed. The eleven-inch shells ruined the town; it is said that every third house was struck.

Meanwhile, on the east the Japanese had dug their parallels up the hills often so close to the Russian works that the voices of each party were audible in the trenches of the other. During the entire autumn of 1904 fighting in these trenches was a daily event, and often, particularly at night, it was hand-to-hand fighting. Parties of Russians, armed with grenades, made nightly sorties upon the trenches, and sometimes drove the defenders out of their works. The Japanese, too, used grenades, and, in their assaults, gun-cotton, fired from hand-mortars made of bamboo. By December 18th they had tunnelled under the north fort of Ehrlung-shan, and had laid seven mines, with two tons of dynamite. The explosion, a complete surprise to the defenders, was terrific. A Japanese force which had pushed too close, in order to be ready to rush into the fort, was severely damaged by the débris; but a second force took its place, and finally entered the walls. On the 31st of December, by a similar mine, the Japanese blew up the parapet of the Sungshushan fort, and took possession of the works.

The life and soul of the defenders, General Kondrachenko, had been killed on December 16th by an exploding eleven-inch shell. General Stössel had long seen the futility of the defence. Ammunition for his heavy guns had run short, and the larger part of his garrison was in the hospital. On January 1st he proposed to surrender, and on January 4th delivered over the fortress. The officers were permitted to retain their sidearms, and, if they chose, to return to their own country on parole. Among the prisoners were four admirals, eight generals, and a large number of minor officers; the total number of officers and men surrendered was 32,286. Five hundred and forty-six guns, with a quantity of ammunition, and other military supplies, and thirty-nine vessels of various character, mainly damaged, fell into the hands of the victors.

On the 25th of January, Kuropatkin's right wing, commanded by General Gripenberg, crossed the Hun and in a flanking movement rolled up the left wing of the Japanese and took the villages of Chen chieh-pu and Hei-kan-tai. On the next day Oyama sent up reinforcements to make an assault on the latter town, but in the meantime the Russians had brought up thirty guns, and every attack of the Japanese failed. Both sides were heavily reinforced, and on the 28th, by a night attack, the Japanese possessed themselves of the place. General Kuropatkin ordered a retreat. The Russian losses in this fight are estimated at 10,000, and the Japanese, at 7000. General Gripenberg, believing that if he had been properly supported the Russians might have gained a victory, resigned his command and returned to Russia. After this battle the opposing forces again assembled themselves for what proved to be the final land battle of the war. It is estimated that the forces of the Russians had increased to 300,000 men, and the Japanese had brought over a new army under General Kawimura, which took its place on the extreme right wing beyond Kuroki. On the left wing the veterans of Port Arthur had joined the Manchurian army, and it was their appearance which finally turned the Russian advance into a rout. General Kuropatkin began the advance by a cavalry raid on the left flank, meaning to cut off the communications with Liao-yang, while General Linevitch was to engage the centre and General Rennenkampf was to turn their left. The struggle was severe in the centre and at one time there was a question whether General Linevitch would not break through, but General Nogi gradually pushed back the Russian attack, and by the second of March was in a flanking position on the enemy's right. On the Japanese right, also, Kawimura and Kuroki were beginning to drive back the Russian attack.

The Japanese centre had resisted the Russian assaults, and the entire Russian line was changed to confront Nogi, who was closing in upon it. Until March 8th the colossal struggle along a hundred miles of front was waged furiously. But on that day Kawimura succeeded in turning the Russian left, and Oku and Nodzu in driving back the centre, and on the 9th the Russian army was in confused retreat. Mukden was in Japanese hands on the 10th, and the entire Russian force, except the centre under General Linevitch, became a disorganized body of fugitives driven back upon Harbin. In this battle the losses of the Japanese are estimated at from 60,000 to 100,000; those of the Russians at 150,000, including 40,000 prisoners. The spoils of the victory were some 60 guns, 200,000 shells, 25,000,000 rounds of small-arms ammunition, 23 Chinese carts full of maps, and large amounts of rations and fuel. The Russian army, however, was defeated, not annihilated. General Kuropatkin was superseded in his command by General Linevitch, and volunteered to take a subordinate position. The two armies now paused again to prepare for a new conflict.

In the meantime a powerful fleet of twenty-nine fighting ships had left Russia, in October, 1904, to relieve Port Arthur and intercept Japanese communications. The commander was Admiral Rodjestvensky. On the Doggerbank in the North Sea a portion of this fleet came across an English fishing fleet and being in somewhat hysterical dread of

Japanese torpedo-boats, fired and sank two British vessels. This episode might have brought about war between England and Russia but for the coolness of the British Government, which referred the matter to a board of arbitration. The board exonerated the Admiral from any fault in the matter, but prescribed heavy damages which the Russians paid. The fleet voyaged to the East, partly through the Suez Canal, partly around the Cape of Good Hope. The two divisions joined at Annam. The Russian ships had taken provisions freely and had spent more than the legal time at several French ports, and the Japanese protested at what they asserted was a violation of the neutrality laws on the part of France. But these protests were not pressed in view of the result of the battle which took place in the Japan Sea.

On May 14th the Russian fleet left neutral waters, presumably directing its course toward Vladivostok. Admiral Togo had been watching the course of the enemy. In a secluded harbor, Chien-hai Bay in Korea, in telegraphic communication with Japan, he had been preparing his fleet, which was in numbers superior to the Russian fleet, and, although somewhat inferior in heavy guns, had a considerable advantage in the eight-inch and six-inch batteries. His scouts, by wireless telegraphy, kept him perfectly informed of the movements of the Russians, and in the morning of May 27th he knew that the Russian fleet was to pass through the Korean Straits in two columns, with the strength

of the fleet, four battle-ships, at the head of the right
column. He set forth with the plan of meeting the
enemy about two o'clock somewhat north of Okino
Shima, in the east channel, and, as was usual among
the Japanese throughout the war, he carried out
his plans on schedule time. He had organized a
battle-ship squadron, including his armored cruisers, to meet the Russian battle-ships; his other
cruisers he sent down the long line of Russian ships
which disappeared beyond the horizon. It was a
foggy day with a heavy sea, and the Japanese approached the Russians from the westward, somewhat
obscured by what sunlight there was. At first
Togo made as if to pass the head of the Russian
column to the westward, but about two o'clock he
turned to the eastward and took an oblique course
across the Russian front with his battle-ship squadron. The Russians began to fire at a distance of
about six miles; the Japanese reserved their fire
until within a distance of about two miles, and concentrated their entire force on the *Oslyabya*, which
led the left column and which presently caught fire.
The flagship *Kniaz Suvaroff*, which led the right
column, and the *Imperator Alexander III* soon fell
out of line in distress. The *Borodino* took the place
of the flagship at the head of the line, but by this
time the Russian course had been forced from the
northeast around to the southeast. The Russian
line, now formed in single file, tried to turn the
Japanese rear, and escape to the north; but this
manœuvre the Japanese met by facing square about,

so as to cross the Russian front, and thrust it southward and eastward in confusion. Meanwhile Admiral Uriu with the cruiser squadron had sailed
southward and had encompassed the rear of the
enemy, taking advantage of superior speed, and
passing to and fro, appearing now on the right and
now on the left of the Russian line. The Japanese
vessels were not entirely free from injury. The
Asama of Togo's squadron had been temporarily
disabled, and the *Naniwa* and *Kasagi* of Uriu's
fleet were not in fighting condition, but in the main
their formation held; whereas by five o'clock the
Russian fleet was scattered into small groups of
ships mainly striving to escape. There was no
organization. The Admiral had been wounded early
in the battle; his fleet was dispersed in groups and
each group was hunted down by the assailants.
The most powerful Russian battle-ships, the *Oslyabya*, the *Imperator Alexander III*, and the *Borodino*
had been sunk. At night, when the sea had become calmer, the Japanese torpedo-boats assailed
the scattered groups. The Russians fought bravely,
sinking three torpedo-boats, but the *Kniaz Potem-
kin*, the *Sissoi Veliky*, the *Navarini*, and three
armored cruisers were torpedoed. On the 28th
the battle-ship and armored cruiser squadron came
upon a section of the enemy under Admiral Nebo-
gatoff, including the *Orel* and the *Imperator Nicolas
I*, and the Admiral at once surrendered. In the
afternoon two Japanese destroyers captured two
Russian destroyers, one of which, the *Biedovi*,

bore Admiral Rodjestvensky, wounded. Of the Russian fleet, six battle-ships had been sunk and two captured. Four cruisers had been sunk, one escaped, only to be destroyed on the rocks beyond Vladivostok. One coast defence vessel had been sunk and two captured, and five destroyers had been sunk, and one captured. Three cruisers escaped to Manila, where they were disarmed; one reached Vladivostok. Another vessel, the *Lena*, crossed the Pacific, and put into San Francisco harbor, where she was detained. One destroyer reached Shanghai, and two others found refuge at Vladivostok. Of the 12,767 men in the Russian crews, almost 4000 had been killed or drowned, more than 7000 were prisoners. The Japanese loss was 115 killed and 450 wounded. The victory was gained partly by superior marksmanship on the part of the Japanese, partly by greater rapidity of fire, and partly by superior mobility.

This victory gave to the Japanese complete command of the sea, with ample opportunity not only to send supplies to the army in Manchuria, but also to begin operations against Vladivostok and to occupy the island of Sakhalin, in July, with little opposition. Preparations for new operations were pushed with energy; and on the Russian side, the Tsar proclaimed his determination to send a new army to General Linevitch.

But the uselessness of further struggle had been long apparent to the rest of the world, as well as to the Russian and Japanese statesmen. Russian armies had not shown the slightest promise of ability to turn back the Japanese, and on the other hand, evidently it would be difficult, perhaps impossible, for the bearers of the Sunrise Flag to carry their standard into Russia. In this situation, probably after consultation with the European Powers, President Roosevelt suggested to both governments the desirability of negotiations, between plenipotentiaries of the contesting nations, to ascertain whether a treaty of peace might not be mutually acceptable. The suggestion was accepted, and after some deliberation Washington was chosen as the meeting-place; but in summer Washington is hot, so the peace conference met near Portsmouth, New Hampshire, in the General Equipment Building of the Navy Yard. The Tsar sent Count Sergius Witte, and the Ambassador to Washington, Baron Roman Romanovitch Rosen; the Japanese, Baron Jutaro Komura and the Minister to Washington, Mr. Kogoro Takahira. The negotiations began August 5th, and were conducted in secret. But from day to day the large corps of newspaper correspondents ascertained the proceedings, and the accuracy of their information, in general, is confirmed by both parties. Baron Komura proposed a number of conditions, which were refused in bulk by the Russian commissioners, whereupon the Japanese proposed consideration of each condition in detail.

To the greater number of the demands of Japan the Russians acceded, with little debate. The contested paragraphs, as they came up for discussion, were deferred until the last. The main points of difference were the question of an indemnity of perhaps $600,000,000, to be paid by Russia, and the cession of the island of Sakhalin to Japan. Before these points had been decided, Mr. Sato, the first secretary of the commission, had announced to the correspondents that he expected a favorable issue of the conference. But during the discussion of them there ensued a period of gloom. Neither side seemed disposed to relinquish its standpoint. But after several conferences at Washington between the President and Baron Rosen and Baron Kaneko, a special envoy from Japan, the Russians agreed to cede half of Sakhalin, and the Japanese agreed to forego the cession of the other half, and the indemnity. This concession came to pass on August 26th, and a treaty was forthwith drawn up and sent to the Mikado and the Tsar for ratification. As published, October 16th, the agreement consists of fifteen articles. Russia acknowledged Japan's paramount interest in Korea; transferred the lease of Port Arthur, Ta-lien, and the adjacent territory, and the railway connecting Port Arthur with Chang-chung-fu and Kuan-chang-tsu, as well as the coal mines in the neighborhood, and the southern part of Sakhalin, below the 50th parallel, with the proviso that no military measures should be taken by the Japanese which might impede navigation in the straits of La Perouse and Tartary. The contracting Powers mutually agreed to evacuate Manchuria—excepting the Liao-tung Peninsula—within eighteen months, and to restore the control thereof to China; not to obstruct any commercial measures, common to all countries, which China might take in this region; and to develop their railways for commercial purposes only, except in the Liao-tung Peninsula. Russia was to arrange with Japan for the granting to Japanese fishermen of rights to pursue their trade in the Japan, Okhotsk, and Bering seas, and the Japanese agreed to respect the rights of Russian subjects in the ceded territory. Finally, both Powers were to make estimates of the cost of taking care of prisoners, and Russia agreed to pay to Japan the difference caused by the larger number of Russian prisoners who fell into Japanese hands.

In both Japan and Russia this treaty was badly received. A large party in Russia desired to continue the war, feeling that, with an available army of perhaps 600,000 men opposed to the Japanese, Russia was not yet defeated. The Japanese people had hoped for an indemnity and the whole of Sakhalin, and in Tōkyō there were serious riots. Martial law had to be proclaimed, and stones were thrown at Marquis Ito, who was held accountable for the concessions to Russian demands. But rebellion, which threatened to be revolution, in Russia at once threw the Japanese question into the shade. And in Japan the agitation calmed as the people saw how much more they had gained than they had demanded at the beginning of the war.

The result of the struggle put Japan in the position of a first-class Power—the dominant Power, indeed, in Eastern affairs. In 1906 she raised her important legations to embassies. Her position had been strengthened by a treaty of alliance concluded with England, August 12th, 1906, for the maintenance of peace in East Asia and in India, the preservation of the common rights of all nations in China, including free commercial rights, and the preservation of the territorial rights of the contracting Powers in East Asia and India. In the case of an unprovoked attack upon one of the contracting Powers in these regions, the other was to come to its assistance. The predominance of England in India was expressly recognized in this agreement, and also the predominance of Japan in Korea.

The war over, Japan at once began to establish a protectorate in Korea. The population of the Mikado's Empire has increased with great rapidity. In 1906 it was about 51,000,000, and was beginning to press hard upon the land. It needed an outlet. Korea is a region that promises rich rewards to those who shall develop its resources, and Japanese colonists have been sent thither in great numbers. The Marquis Ito concluded a treaty with the king, in November, 1905, whereby all diplomatic business was transferred to Japan. Ito himself was sent to Seoul as Resident General. The Min family protested to the Powers against this, asserting that the treaty was signed practically under compulsion; nevertheless, the Korean representatives at the capitals of Europe and America were withdrawn, and Korean foreign affairs were placed in the hands of the Japanese.

Resources and Ideals
of
Modern Japan
By
Baron Kentaro Kaneko, LL, D.

I

THE RUSSO-JAPANESE WAR AND THE RESOURCES OF JAPAN.

In the early years of the nineteenth century, England fought against Napoleonic militarism in defence of European civilization; and at the dawn of the twentieth century, it became necessary for the little island empire of Japan to take up arms in defence of Anglo-American civilization in the Far East. Just as truly as the great cause of civilization was at stake upon the battle-fields of Europe, so the future of this same civilization, in its Asiatic development, hung upon the destiny of Japan.

In order to enumerate the facts intelligibly enough for a legitimate inference as to the results of this last conflict, we must make a rapid survey of the history of the Russian occupation of Manchuria, for it was the Manchurian question which precipitated the Russo-Japanese War.

Prior to the time of the Chino-Japanese War of 1894–95, foreign Powers, becoming aware of the enormous resources and immense possibilities of central China, had vainly sought to gain for foreign trade a free access to that portion of the Celestial

Empire. But neither European diplomacy nor pluck of American commercialism could avail to open that close-barred door. The Chinese are too obstinate to be persuaded and not docile enough to be taught. But when Japan had China at her mercy, in 1895, one of her principal demands was that four ports, Sou-Chow, Kan-Chow, Sha-Shi, and Chang-King, should be thrown open for the trade of the world.

When the war ended, the Liao Tung Peninsula was given to Japan by the treaty of Shimonoseki. But no sooner had this cession been made than Russia, with the support of France and Germany, declared that any holding of Manchurian territory by Japan would constitute a menace to the peace of Asia. In order to avert this supposed menace, Japan consented to restore the peninsula to China, never for a moment thinking that Russia would ultimately come into possession of it.

But scarcely a year had passed when, in 1896, Russia made a secret agreement with China by which she obtained the right to construct a railway through the northern part of Manchuria, for the purpose of giving her a shorter access to the port of Vladivostok, and this railway was afterwards extended through the southern part of the peninsula.

Nor was this all. In the following year, 1897, Russia obtained permission from China to winter her fleet at Port Arthur, and in 1898, Port Arthur and also Dalny were formally leased to Russia. Then followed the rapid fortifying of these places and other important strategic positions in the province;

and finally Russia arrogated to herself the right to ignore completely Chinese sovereignty in Manchuria, and also existing treaty rights of Japan and other Powers in regard to that region of the Celestial Empire. Such occupation of Manchuria by Russia was not only destructive of the principle of equity in regard to commercial opportunities, and an impairment of the territorial integrity of China, but it was also a flat contradiction of the principle of the maintenance of permanent peace in Asia, for which principle alone Japan had given up her spoils of victory.

Moreover,—and this was of still greater moment to Japan,—Russia, thus situated on the flank of Korea, would be a constant menace to the separate existence of that empire, and in any event would exercise there a predominant influence. For years, Russia had been seeking to encroach upon Korea. After having obtained, some years ago, the concession of an enormous forest belt in the upper range of the Yalu River, she obtained, in 1902, from the Korean Government the right to use Yongampo, near the mouth of the river, as a lumber depot in which to receive her timber as it came down the stream.

Japan soon had reason to suspect that Russia had converted the place into a fortification, an idea not dispelled when a member of the Japanese Legation at Seoul, who had been sent to investigate the matter, was refused permission to land.

The situation of affairs in Manchuria was also a cause of great anxiety. The continued presence of a large Russian army in this province was in itself a

violation of the agreement made by all the Powers
after the Boxer outbreak in China. It had then
been agreed that all troops sent into the Chinese
Empire for the defence of the legations, and to aid
in restoring order, should be withdrawn at the earliest possible moment, Russia alone being allowed a
longer delay in consequence of her interests in
Manchuria, which might be endangered by ill-sub-
dued Boxers or general brigandage. A "railway
police" was allowed her for a time, but the 8th of
October, 1903, was fixed as the limit of her military
occupation of the province.

As early as April of that year it became perfectly
evident that, instead of fulfilling this engagement to
withdraw her troops, Russia was resolved to retain
her position there, and strengthen it in every way,
pouring troops into Manchuria until she occupied
the whole province, and finally announcing her intention to hold it.

In view, therefore, of the situation in Manchuria
and Korea, the Japanese Government on the 28th
of July opened negotiations with the Russian Government "in a spirit of conciliation and frankness,
with a view to the conclusion of an understanding
to compose questions which are the cause of interest
and natural anxiety."

The Japanese Government drew up proposals as
the basis of these negotiations, and these proposals
were submitted to Count Lamsdorff on August 12,
1903, it being clearly stated therein that the negotiations were to settle the matter relating to Manchuria
and Korea.

After full five months' delay, on December 11, 1903, the Russian counter-proposals were received by the Japanese Government, and it was a surprise to the Japanese to find from these that Russia had stricken out Manchuria from her consideration and had confined herself entirely to Korea. Japan thereupon offered counter-proposals, restoring the omitted clauses bearing on Manchuria. Another delay ensued, and repeated requests for an early answer were made by the Japanese Government, but without avail.

Meanwhile, what was Russia doing?

She was hurrying her warships to the Asiatic station, sending troops and military supplies into Manchuria, and, without any disguise whatever, preparing for war.

Let me cite from a report on "Russian Preparations."

"Her warlike preparations in the Far East have been going ahead since April, 1903, when she failed to carry out her treaty engagements. During that time the increase made in her naval strength in the Far East was as follows: Three battle-ships, tonnage 38,488; one armored cruiser, tonnage 7727; five cruisers, tonnage 26,417; seven destroyers, tonnage 2450; one gunboat, tonnage 1344; two vessels for laying mines, tonnage 6000. Total number of vessels nineteen, with a total tonnage of 82,426. In addition to these vessels, the Russian Government sent torpedo-boat destroyers in sections by rail to Port Arthur, where the work of putting them together has been hastened, and seven of them have already been completed. Furthermore, two vessels of the volunteer fleet were armed at Vladivostok and hoisted the Russian naval ensign.

"During the same period the increase of Russia's land forces in the Far East has been equally marked. Since the 29th of June, 1903, when under the pretext of trial transportation on the Siberian Railway the Russian Government sent to China two infantry brigades, two artillery battalions, and a large force of cavalry, troops have been constantly sent by military train from Russia to the Far East, until the Russian forces were over forty thousand. At the same time, plans were being made for sending, if necessary, over two hundred thousand more men.

"During the same period there has been the greatest activity possible at Port Arthur and Vladivostok, and the work has been carried on day and night to strengthen the fortifications of those naval ports, while forts have been built at Liao Yang, Nunchun, and other strategic points, and large quantities of arms and ammunition have been sent to the Far East by the Siberian Railway and the vessels of the volunteer fleet. In the middle of October, 1903, a train of fourteen cars was hurriedly sent from Russia laden with the equipment of a field hospital.

"During the latter part of January and up to the beginning of February, 1904, Russian military activity was still further intensified. On January 21st, a formal order to prepare for war was given by Admiral Alexieff to the forces that were stationed in the vicinity of the Yalu. On February 1st, the military commandant at Vladivostok, under orders of his government, requested the Japanese commercial agent at that port to notify his nation that a state of siege might be proclaimed at any moment, and to make immediate preparations to withdraw to Habrovsk. About the same date, all of the warships at Port Arthur, except a battle-ship under repairs, made a naval demonstration by leaving port, while troops were advanced in large numbers from Liao Yang toward the Yalu."

Being thus informed that all hope of peaceful result from their negotiations with Russia was gone, and that there was no other course to be taken, the Japanese Government, on February 5, 1904, sent the following telegram to the Russian Government:

"In the presence of delays which remain largely unexplained and naval and military activities which it is difficult to reconcile with entirely pacific aims, the Imperial Government have exercised in the depending negotiations a degree of forbearance which they believe affords abundant proof of their loyal desire to remove from their relations with the Imperial Russian Government every cause for future misunderstanding. But finding in their efforts no prospect of securing from the Imperial Russian Government an adhesion to either Japan's moderate and unselfish proposals, or to any other proposals likely to establish a firm and enduring peace in the extreme East, the Imperial Government have no other alternative than to terminate the present futile negotiations.

"In adopting that course the Imperial Government *reserve to themselves the right to take such independent action as they may deem best to consolidate and defend their menaced position, as well as to protect their established rights and legitimate interests.*

"The Imperial Government of Japan, having exhausted without effect every means of conciliation with a view to the removal from their relations with the Imperial Russian Government of every cause for future complications, and finding that their just representations and moderate and unselfish proposals in the interest of a firm and lasting peace in the extreme East are not receiving the consideration which is their due, *have resolved to sever their diplomatic relations with the Imperial Russian Government, which for the reason named have ceased to possess any value.*"

This brings us to the outbreak of hostilities. Suitably to the declaration made in Japan's final message to the Russian Government, she began to move troops to Korea, and Japanese transports, conveyed by Japanese torpedo-boats and war-vessels, reached the Bay of Chemulpo on February 8th.

On their arrival, this flotilla met the Russian war-vessel *Korietz*. She made hostile demonstrations, and *fired the first shot of the war* at one of the torpedo-boats, which thereupon returned the fire. On the following day, Rear-Admiral Uriu sent a letter to the captain of the *Variag*, challenging him to combat outside the harbor; at the same time he addressed individual communications to the commanders of war-vessels of the United States,

England, Italy and France, then in Chemulpo, requesting them, in case the *Variag* and *Korietz* did not leave the harbor before noon, to change their anchorage. About eleven o'clock the same morning, the two Russian war-vessels steamed from the harbor into the open sea and there began the first naval battle between Russia and Japan.

The world in general has grown so accustomed to hear it said that Russia's resources in men, money, and natural wealth are unlimited, and Japan's comparatively small, that it is doubly interesting to note the fact that throughout the war Japan has never at any time been brought into contact with an antagonist who has proved to be formidable or dangerous to her. The tactics pursued have won for the Japanese the admiration of expert military opinion everywhere; among Western critics especially, the quality and efficacy of Japanese strategy have become axiomatic.

War finances are of a different character from those dealt with by the ordinary budget, and therefore the financial statement of the Japanese Government in connection with the war expenditures may be the most illuminating manner of presenting information on the resources of Japan:

"When the negotiations between Japan and Russia took such a turn as almost to cut off every hope of peace being maintained, it became imperatively necessary to make such prompt military preparations as would put Japan in a state of readiness for all eventualities, as well as, with equal expedition, to provide the requisite financial means.

In accordance, therefore, with Article LXX. of the Japanese Constitution, the Imperial Urgency Ordinance was promulgated on December 28, 1903, as a special financial measure whereby authority was given for diverting the funds kept under special account, issuing exchequer bonds, and making temporary loans to meet expenditures incurred for military preparations. The total amount of expenditures which were sanctioned, in accordance with the above-mentioned imperial ordinance, was, up to the end of March, 1904, about $78,000,000. It is proposed to raise this sum by issuing exchequer bonds for $50,000,000, diverting $12,500,000 of the funds kept under special account, and making temporary loans for the balance. The loan of $50,000,-000 has already been floated with great success, the total amount subscribed by the Japanese people reaching four and one-half times the sum called for —that is, $225,000,000. As, moreover, the bonds were allotted chiefly among the lower and middle classes, it is evident that, in the event of another loan being raised at home, ample money will be forthcoming to provide for it. But the aforesaid urgency measure was no more than an expedient devised to meet an emergency. Peace having been broken in February, 1904, the Diet was convened in March and gave its consent to the urgency financial measure of December, 1903. It approved various measures relating to war finance; it passed the budget for extraordinary war expenditures, and for the expense involved in diplomatic and other State affairs connected with the war. These expenses are to be met by the imposition of extraordinary special taxes, the provision including increased rates of stamp duty, the replacing of the leaf tobacco monopoly (which was previously in force) by the monopoly on tobacco manufacture, which the government has long had in contemplation, the appropriation of funds under special accounts; public loans, exchequer bonds, and temporary loans. In order, at the same time, to prevent serious economic changes arising from the inflation of the currency by expediting the return of moneys paid for war purposes, and to encourage thrift among the people, regulations were made for the issue of saving-loan-bonds by the Hypothec Bank.''

In this extraordinary war budget both revenue and expenditure amount to $190,000,000. The sources of revenue are as follows:

1. Increased receipts expected from the imposition of extraordinary special taxes, and from the establishment of the tobacco-manufacture monopoly, $31,000,000.

2. The amount set apart out of the surplus of $24,000,000; obtained by further retrenchments of the budget to be actually carried out in the present fiscal year (1905); also through some funds having become unnecessary for ordinary naval and military expenditure, an additional $4,000,000.

3. Loans from funds under special accounts, $15,000,000.

4. Funds to be obtained by means of public loans, exchequer bonds, and temporary loans, $140,000,000.

Besides this, there are the expenditures needed for diplomatic and other matters connected with national affairs, as they may be defrayed from time to time according to the requirements of the developing situation. The total reserve fund for the purpose has, therefore, been put at $20,000,000, to which it has been decided to set apart the balance of the surplus of $24,000,000 remaining after deducting the $4,000,000 which is to be appropriated for war expenditures.

As to the total amount of war expenditure, that obviously depends on the number of soldiers and sailors engaged; on the area of the field of operations, as well as on its nearness or distance from the home country; on the number of battles, and on the length of the war in point of time. Yet, judging from experience since the Crimean War, in the Austro-Italian War, the war in which Denmark was engaged, the Franco-German War, the Russo-Turkish War, and the Transvaal War, an approximate estimate may be given.

The average monthly expenditure in those wars, for an army of 100,000 men, ranged from a minimum of $12,000,000, to a maximum of $25,000,000, excepting that of the Austro-Prussian War expenses. In the Japanese war against China, in the year 1894–95, the Japanese spent, every month, on the average, the sum of $5,500,000. Since then, the price of goods has risen both in Japan and in Manchuria. The armies employed in the present campaign are much larger than those sent against the Chinese. What is more, being unable to utilize for the present war the organization and plan of operations which suited well enough for the campaign of 1894–95, completely new arrangements had to be made for the operations against the Russians. Taking, then, experience in Europe since the Crimean War, and Japanese experience in the war against China, it may be said that were Japan to send 200,000 soldiers to Manchuria at the present time (May, 1905), their support for each month would cost $12,500,000. The naval operations of the war must also be kept in mind. Expenditure for this purpose will amount, per month, to $3,000,000.

It thus appears that the war expenditure for the year beginning in April and ending in March will amount to $186,000,000; and as the government's estimate of the war expenditure for the fiscal year is $190,000,000, we shall have—this estimate being correct—a surplus of $4,000,000.

But it is said that, owing to the government having issued a large amount in national loans, the people of Japan are now under heavy financial burdens. It is argued that if the Japanese Government continues to create national debts, either in the home or in the foreign market, she will ultimately find herself in a position where it will be impossible for her to pay even the interest on the amounts of her indebtedness. With no other resources at her disposal, and with no mortgages to pledge her security on foreign loans, Japan, it is held, will in a very short time find her credit gone, not only in the foreign but also in the home market.

Let us glance for a moment over the route which

Japan has already travelled. From the year 1870, the date of her first national loan, to the date of the loan of $150,000,000 for the war expenditure, the gross total of her loans has aggregated the sum of $432,459,459.50 outstanding in foreign and home markets, a sum which in amount is about three times the national revenue of Japan.

What of other countries? France, for example, has a national loan more than eight times the annual revenue of that country; Italy has a national loan equivalent to seven years of its revenue; in the case of England, the national loan represents about five years of the government's income; with the United States, nearly four times the total revenue equals the amount of the national loan. The loan of Japan, reaching only three times the national income, being only $8.64 per capita of its population, is then, not a large but a very small amount when considered in relation to the proportions and per capitas which obtain in other countries. It can therefore be safely asserted that the Japanese loan does not constitute for the people of Japan anything like the heavy financial burden which some have supposed it to be.

And now, to sum up this review of the economic and financial conditions of Japan:

Enough has been said to show that in a comparatively brief space of time there has been an enormous increase in her industrial and commercial prosperity; that the national revenues have advanced in amount literally by leaps and bounds; that her financial condition and prospects were never so good as at present; and that firmly guiding her ship of state through the problems of the moment, Japan has every reason to anticipate a smooth and prosperous voyage for the future of her national life. Already the faith of the Japanese people in that future is shown by the fact that when the government planned to issue exchequer bonds to the amount of $50,000,-000, they responded with the offer of four or five times that amount, and in place of the minimum rate of application, fixed by the government at $47.50, showed their willingness to contribute a much larger sum. This of itself shows how patriotic the Japanese really are, but it also indicates something more; for as patriotic feeling cannot be manifested in such a manner unless there is enough money forthcoming, the taking up of bonds on such liberal terms reveals the existence of a people on whose thrift—a priceless national possession— the government of Japan can always depend. If it were necessary to say anything more in illustration of the industrial energy and thrift of the people of Japan, I should only need to mention the fact that the issue of $50,000,000 exchequer bonds not only did not—as the government thought it might—disturb the money market, but simply paved the way, after the bonds had been eagerly taken up, for a second issue of exchequer bonds by the Japanese Government to the amount of another $50,000,000.

Observe, meanwhile, that in all this patriotism there is an element of voluntary retrenchment, not to say self-sacrifice. Not only have the people felt encouraged to engage more extensively in industrial enterprises, but they have freely given up what is known as "luxurious expenditure," and have resorted to not a few of the practical economies of life as a means of enabling them to contribute all the more to the expenses of the war.   It is therefore in the self-confidence born of economic strength that the Japanese people have encouraged their government to prosecute this war to its conclusion utterly regardless of financial considerations and of what the operations may cost.   They have determined, should it become necessary, to spend the whole of the national wealth in realizing the objects for which hostilities were begun.   They have self-reliance enough to feel that, should the war be prolonged for three, or even five years more, Japan will be strong enough to respond to its most exacting demands upon her economic and financial resources.

II

JAPAN'S POLICY AND IDEALS: DOMESTIC AND FOREIGN.

To the people of Europe and America generally the readiness of Japan to cope with an enemy so formidable as Russia, was and still is no less than a mystery. The ease with which this Eastern nation has inflicted severe defeats upon a great Western Power is likewise a thing that has astonished the whole modern world. Japan, every one is saying, scarcely existed as a factor in the world's history fifty years ago. It was only when Commodore Perry halted his squadron in the Bay of Yedo that Japan began to count in Western eyes as of any consequence at all. How comes it, then, that this baby among nations, born so late in the Christian era, properly commencing, so to speak, its career only after the Restoration of 1868—how comes it that this merely precocious child has shown itself able to accomplish within a few months what any of its elders would have been proud to achieve? The question seems difficult to answer, though to such of the Japanese as have thought the matter out, the answer is simple enough.

In the first place, the notion that Japan is "new" or "young" is radically false. She is neither newer nor younger than the German Empire, which appeared upon the scene in 1871, after Sedan. She is no more in the nursery than that nation whose first Parliament declared Victor Emmanuel King of Italy in 1861. Looking at the case even in this superficial aspect of recent events, glancing back no further than fifty years, it is plain that her "youth" is imaginary. As a matter of fact, Japan is old, very old indeed. So are her institutions. So are her traditions. So are her ideals. The authentic history of Japan dates six hundred and sixty years further back than the beginning of the Christian era. Her present Emperor is the direct descendant of Jimmu Tenno, her first sovereign—making the present dynasty the oldest imperial dynasty existing on the globe at the present time.

"Well, what of it?" might be asked. For one might object that Japan, far away under the rising sun, isolated during all the long ages from any contact whatsoever with the moving growth of the West, simply stood still, dragging out a permanently primitive existence until Commodore Perry came and opened the land to Western culture and Western progress. No idea, however, could be more mistaken than this. We grant, to be sure, that in a sense Perry woke her up. We admit that the Japanese were laggards and needed to be roused. But—and this is the point which frequently is overlooked—*something was there to wake up.*

In all truth, Japan possessed an ancient and complete civilization long before Europe ever took cognizance of her being. That state of civilization represented all the principal departments of human thought and activity. If Rome had her army of indomitable warriors, her profound law givers, her wise and just rulers, so had Japan. She, too, like the Romans, had a venerable, rational religion. Like the Greeks, she had her teachers and systems of philosophy; like them, her painters, sculptors, architects. Phœnicia and Carthage were eminent in trade and commerce, in maritime venture; Japan also has ever been the home of commerce, industry, and shipping. Agriculture, literature, and education would furnish examples for analogies no less striking. There were, in short, variously developing or progressing in the island empire the various branches of the civilization which Europe now boasts, independently of and concurrently with their unfolding and growth in Europe. The Japanese lived secluded from the rest of mankind, but within the limits of their own little island country they had a whole world of armies, law courts, books, workshops, churches, schools, theatres, studios, etc. They had their cycles, in those islands, of warfare, statesmanship, religious movement, social phenomena, philosophical teaching, commercial enterprise. In other words, her civilization had just as sound and substantial a foundation as that of any country on the map to-day. There is no good reason for the supposition, either, that they are intellectually an inferior race. Upon the premises just stated, how, indeed, should the Japanese be intellectually inferior?

To extend the comparison with Europe a little further, it must be observed that the present general condition of Japan (and especially her efficient military régime) is the fruit of a feudal system similar to that once prevailing in the monarchies of Europe that are now constitutionally governed—just as Japan is. Her strength, like the strength of the European Powers, lies in devotion to the military ideal. In no country has the training of soldiers ever been more thorough or more exacting than with the Japanese. Their *Samurai*, or Knights of Feudal Japan, composing a large portion of the entire nation, to this day maintain the same lofty spirit of honor and valor and patriotism as the Spartans of old.

Among Europeans and Americans the Japanese are frequently called "a nation of imitators." This proposition is true to a certain extent only, for its veracity diminishes upon a close study of her national history. To those who really believe that they are, and shall remain, nothing but mere imitators, it may be pointed out: Here was a nation flooded all of a sudden with an ocean of new and foreign ideas thirty-seven years ago, and this nation has been weighing and balancing these strange and novel things, and has been sifting them out and has been quite calmly discriminating between them, deciding to keep the good ideas and to throw out the bad ones. This, surely, is not a nation of imitators, but rather one of keen and sagacious adapters. At the beginning of the national era, the Japanese undoubtedly did imitate, but such imitation was only preliminary to adaptation. After adapting foreign institutions and systems to their own customs and needs, the Japanese now find themselves starting on the road of originality. This can be shown by their progress—social and political —during the last thirty-seven years. Witness, likewise, the achievements of Japan's fleet against the Russians, the strategy of her admirals, commanding squadrons where not a European or American face is to be seen. Has not Japan shown Europe and America how to conduct a modern naval campaign? Has she not taught them what can be done with torpedoes—if properly managed? Nor has she cause to blush for her land campaign, planned by a general staff of Japanese and carried out by Japanese generals without the assistance of a single foreign officer. Has she not driven the Russians from their stronghold on the Yalu? Did she not capture the castle of Feng-Wang-Chung without firing a single shot? The strategy, the bravery, the originality displayed all through perfectly express the spirit of the *Samurai*. Besides, Japan has been using her own Arisaka cannon, made in Japanese arsenals, and her own rifle, invented by General Murata, to say nothing of Dr. Shimose's smokeless powder—an explosive five times more potent than any other, not excepting the redoubtable lyddite.

After all, there is nothing mysterious or wonderful about her recent successes; for it is Japan and not the Russians who have the advantage of an ancient historic civilization, gray and mature in knowledge and experience and resource. So there is no further need to dwell on the much-neglected fact that when her very good friend Commodore Perry came to Japan he found a country where *there was something to wake up.* Before the advent of Commodore Perry, Japan was a sealed casket containing the compressed atoms of Oriental civilization—the golden shrine of the *Samurai* spirit, only waiting for some one to open it! And President Fillmore was the benefactor to give the renowned and ever-to-be revered Commodore the key of the "open-door" policy for Japan, honestly as well as earnestly urging upon Japan that, if she allowed the opportunity to pass, some other Power might compel her, at the point of the bayonet or at the cannon's mouth, to open her ports. Finally, by means of the gentle suasion and advice which the United States brought to bear, Japan was induced to adopt the "open door" policy, which was forever accepted and established for Japan by the Emperor on his accession to the throne in 1868.

The commonly received opinion among American and European jurists hitherto seems to have been that constitutional government was not compatible with the social and political status of Oriental nations. Therefore, when a constitution was tried in the Ottoman Empire, no surprise was expressed by Western observers that the experiment resulted in a fiasco. And when the Emperor of Japan announced by imperial edict in 1881 that at the end of ten years constitutional government would be established in Japan, Western scholars and statesmen naturally thought the attempt would prove as abortive in Japan as in Turkey.

Nevertheless, in 1890, the first Japanese Parliament was convened in accordance with the terms of the constitution, which had been promulgated the year before, and during the fifteen years that have intervened since that time twenty sessions have been held. In spite of boisterous meetings and stormy discussions—which are not, after all, so uncommon in European or American legislative bodies—constitutional restrictions have been respected and constitutional prerogatives upheld, until now it can be justly claimed that constitutional government has passed the experimental stage in Japan, and has become an integral part of the body politic.

After the Imperial Restoration, in 1868, his Majesty, the Emperor, in the solemn oath which he then took, proclaimed five liberal principles, one of them being to this effect:

"We shall henceforth seek knowledge and wisdom in the outside world and establish the National Assembly, where the important affairs of State shall be decided by public opinion."

This is the fundamental principle of Japan's national policy, in accordance with which all subsequent reorganization and changes, both social and political, have been undertaken and consummated. Under its guidance, in 1875, the judicial system was perfected by the establishment of the Court of Cassation to maintain a uniform interpretation and application of the law. Japan already had courts of first instance and courts of appeal, but there was no court superior to all others—a court of final appeal wherein all judicial matters could be decided and unified.

In the same year, also, an imperial edict was issued creating a senate, and clearly providing that in future all contemplated legislation should be submitted by the cabinet to this body for discussion. Thus, even at that early day a system was established in Japan resembling the organization adopted by some Western nations of co-ordinate governmental branches, the executive, legislative, and judicial. This may be termed the first step taken by the Imperial Government to pave the way for the adoption of the constitutional system.

In the way of educating the people in the conduct of public affairs, the Senate, in 1879, passed a law establishing an assembly in each of the provinces of the Empire, consisting of representatives elected by the taxpayers and empowered to discuss and vote upon the annual estimates of local revenue and expenditure submitted by the governors of the provinces. This was in effect a system similar in principle and in operation to local self-government as found in Western countries.

This exercise of the right to discuss and vote upon provincial taxation and expenditures led to vigorous demands for the creation of a parliament, it being urged that such action was the only means of establishing zealous public interest in the welfare of the country. It was pointed out also that a parliament would be in accord with the principle enunciated in the imperial oath of 1868. Public speeches and newspaper discussions intensified the popular demand, and as a result the famous imperial proclamation of 1881 was issued, announcing that a constitution would be promulgated and the Parliament opened in 1890. Discussion of the question showed that public education and capacity for this important change had reached a more advanced stage than some had thought would be possible; and, in consequence of a voluntary purpose, his Imperial Majesty decided that he might, with due regard for the national welfare, fix a definite time when the intention graciously announced at the time of the Restoration would be carried into effect.

As it was, nothing was done by haphazard or in haste. Ample time was given for the preparations that had to be made, and systematic steps were taken to make those preparations complete. The Emperor appointed Marquis Ito to go abroad for the purpose of studying the constitutions of European countries, thereby intrusting him with the important task of preparing the draft of the Constitution. In 1884, after four years devoted to close study of the constitutional systems of Europe, the Marquis returned to Japan, and soon thereafter a commission was appointed to prepare the draft under his guidance.

Until 1888, the work of the commission proceeded under the personal direction of Marquis Ito, when it was finally completed and submitted for the imperial sanction. Thereupon, in the spring of 1888, the

Emperor organized the Privy Council and opened meetings for the consideration of the draft, which began in May and continued until January. His Imperial Majesty presided at all these meetings. After this careful deliberation, the Constitution was promulgated by the Emperor in person on the 11th of February, 1889.

There is an important difference between the constitutions of Western nations and that of Japan. The former are the outcome of popular uprisings against the tyranny of rulers—in other words, of a demand, as of natural right, by the people; consequently, even in monarchical Europe, constitutions are drawn in such terms as to lay the greatest stress upon popular rights, while at the same time curtailing the power of the sovereign. The Japanese Constitution, on the other hand, emanated from the Emperor, the fountain-head of all power. Before the people dreamed of popular rights or of a parliament, the Emperor had already marked out the grand policy of establishing constitutional government in the future, because of his evident desire and purpose to elevate the country to an equal place among the civilized nations of the world, not only because he wished it, but also because that course was in strict accordance with the national policy bequeathed by his imperial ancestors. Following that policy, our Constitution was drawn up with close adherence to and careful preservation of the fundamental principle of the Imperial Government from time immemorial.

In form, however, it is similar to Western constitutions, with this difference: that the text of the Constitution contains only the fundamental principles of State, namely, the prerogatives of the Emperor; the rights and duties of the people; the powers of Parliament; the powers and duties of ministers of State and judiciary and finance. These are all embodied in seventy-six articles. Matters of detail, such, for example, as provisions relating to the rules and proceedings of Parliament, the laws for the election of members, the national budget, etc., are separate from articles enunciating fundamental principles and are embodied in laws supplementary to the Constitution and enacted at the same time. It may be asked, Why was such a separation necessary? Because, when the first Parliament was opened, the government, as well as the members, in deliberating on national affairs, might find it necessary to make changes in the laws relating to such subjects as those just enumerated. If such changes had to be made in the text of the Constitution, opportunity might be afforded for unscrupulous politicians to attempt to secure other changes affecting fundamental principles; and even if the attempt proved a failure, it would certainly lessen the authority of the Constitution. But when matters of detail are separated from the constitutional text, amendments, rendered necessary by changing conditions, can be easily made. This has been found to be the case especially with regard to the law relating to the election of members, in which the provisions concerning qualifications of members and other details have been modified from time to time in order to conform to the progress of the people and to changes in national conditions.

Summing up the work of the Japanese Parliament during the fifteen years of its existence, it can safely be said that the adoption of a constitutional form of government in Japan has elevated the country and educated the people to a higher and better sense of their power and responsibilities in the body politic and of their duties to the State.

From the beginning of Japan's international relations with the outside world, the Japanese have advocated arbitration, and have bound themselves to have international difficulties settled by this means. In the year 1875, a Chilean vessel brought five hundred Chinese slaves into the harbor of Yokohama, under the flag of a Christian nation, on board a ship of a Christian nation. Japan stopped that vessel and took every one of those Chinese slaves on shore and gave them freedom. The Chilean Government made the strongest protest against the action, but Japan moved not a bit. She stood on the ground of the protector of the peaceful subjects of the Chinese Empire, and upheld the principle of international law forbidding the slave trade in Christendom. But Japan had no support from the outside world; the Christian nations stood aloof. Consequently, the Chilean Government and the Japanese Government finally agreed to submit the matter to arbitration, and the arbitrator was the Czar of Russia. After the close of the investigation, the Czar gave the decision in

Japan's favor. This was the beginning of her national history with the outside world.

The meaning of Russia's Manchurian policy is now no longer a secret. Her aim was to dominate the province, to exclude from it all foreigners, and then to exploit it in her own interests. It is equally clear that if Russia should ever become supreme in Manchuria, no "open-door" policy would ever be allowed sway there. After Russia has been permitted to obtain undivided supremacy in Manchuria, it will be impossible for the free commercial intercourse contemplated by the United States and Japan to assert itself in the province from which Russia pledged herself to withdraw.

Nor is this all. According to Russian law, while a foreign corporation in Russian territory can be sued by the Russians in her courts, they cannot sue Russian subjects or Russian companies in the same way. Therefore, in case Manchuria ever becomes Russian territory, all rights to sue in the courts will be denied to such foreign corporations as happen to be carrying on business in the province.

Who will now undertake the responsibility of opening up the resources of China? This is a burning question of the time. To-day that vast country, with its splendid possibilities, is wedged in from several sides by territorial encroachments on the part of European Powers. The nations, however, which have the greatest interest in the development of Chinese commerce are either Anglo-Saxon or under the influence of Anglo-Saxon civilization.

The United States Government has, from the very

beginning, adopted the "open-door" policy in China —a policy diametrically opposed to that of Russia, which is aiming at the dismemberment of the Chinese Empire, as evidenced by the attempted annexation of Manchuria to her Siberian dominions. Two policies are therefore represented: the one being known as the "open-door," advocated by the United States, and the other being the dismemberment aimed at by Russia. Japan, because under the influence of Anglo-Saxon civilization, is now fighting for the maintenance of that "open-door" policy which the United States above all other countries is interested in upholding. On the other hand, the dismemberment of China is indorsed by those European Powers which are guided by the principle of militarism, that is, by Russia, France, and Germany.

Now the question is as to which of these two principles shall be adopted with regard to the future of Manchuria after the war. The Manchurian people—that is to say, the Chinese in Manchuria—have been treated badly by the Russians during the past years and they are ready to welcome any policy that is milder and more lenient than the one under which they have been ruled. Herein lies the great opportunity for England and the United States to introduce commercial freedom and equality, thereby carrying out the "open-door" principle of the United States in tangible form. Manchuria may thus become an opening wedge, as it were, for the introduction of liberal Anglo-Saxon ideas, which by this means would also find rapid extension in China, not only in a commercial but in a political sense, by serving as an object-lesson as to the difference between Russian rigor and Anglo-Saxon lenity and moderation.

Should European absolutism fix itself upon Asia, a little time will see the complete transformation of the map, and vast regions now lying beneath the legend "Chinese Empire" will be inscribed with the names of foreign governments. To-day there are three wedges started toward the heart of China and waiting only a stroke to split her territories asunder. The stroke will fall when Russia wins—if that time comes. The victory of Russia will fasten Russia's grasp permanently upon Manchuria; permit Germany, now occupying Kiau-Chow, to seize all the province of Shantung lying round about this concession; and open the way for France to extend the frontiers of Tonkin further into the Chinese domain. This dismemberment—the seizing by outside peoples of territories to which they have no right but the force that makes them stronger than the ancient holders—involves not merely violation of the ideals of honor and justice, but also violence to interests that are materially vital to the world—its commerce and peace.

Let us now consider what has been called "the yellow peril"—a phrase much used since the outbreak of the Russo-Japanese War. What do they mean when they talk of "yellow peril"? They mean that when Japan becomes supreme in the Orient she will unite under her banner all the peoples of Asia, and that through this combination Europe will be threatened by a peril which is called "yellow" because it will array the so-called "yellow" races against the races that are white. And they argue that, however just the cause of Japan may be in her struggle against Russia, Europe must not merely do nothing in the way of sympathizing with or helping her, but must side with Russia and aid her in so defeating and crushing Japan that she will never again be able to rise as an independent Power. Here is another cruel conclusion reached from no basis of actuality or fact. Look for a moment at the origin of the phrase "yellow peril." It was manufactured by a German treacherous diplomat in order to rouse feelings of fear as well as the passion of hatred among the peoples of the West at the expense of the Japanese. Let me therefore describe the true history of the only "yellow peril" the world has ever had. For there was once a "yellow peril," and the nations suffered from it. The first "yellow peril" in history was the invasion of Europe by the Mongolians in the year 1241 A.D. Penetrating to Moscow, they continued their march into Austria, and swarmed into other parts of Europe, devastating and plundering wherever they went. After thus terrorizing Europe and ravaging its eastern territories, the Mongols directed their course to Japan. They reached the Japanese islands in 1268, and the results of the "yellow peril" there were far more terrible than any which Europe had experienced. For thirteen years subsequent to that date, up to 1281, Japan had the "yellow peril" with her in its most menacing form. At one time the Mongolians were in actual occupation of her northern coast. During the period of their stay they burned the villages, killed women and children, and plundered the Japanese of their treasures, not leaving a single conceivable act of wickedness uncommitted. Such was the terror inspired by the "yellow peril" as Japan knew it, that even to-day in Japan it is customary to stop children crying by telling them that the "yellow man" or the Mongol will get them. All the while the Japanese people resisted the invaders, and the patriotic defence of their country enabled them to rout utterly and defeat the enemy, with the slaughter of one hundred thousand Mongolians.

When, therefore, we hear people talk of the "yellow peril" in the East, with obvious reference to Japan, we feel bound to reply by asking who it was that, by the gallantry of its people, crushed back the tide of Mongolian invasion, and saved Europe from the wickedness of the only "yellow peril" which the world has ever known? And if, ignoring the fact that Japan was once the savior of Europe when Europe did not even know who had saved her, both Europe and America agree in fearing a modern "yellow peril," then it may be asserted, without the slightest chance of being successfully contradicted, that Japan has far more reason to fear a "white peril" in the East than the world or any part of it has to anticipate danger from Japan. Observe the advance of the European nations into Asia. What are the extension of French Tonquin and the occupation of Kiau-Chow by Germany if not "white perils" for the Chinese Empire? There is another "white peril" for China on her northern border in Russia's occupation of Manchuria, but it is far more of a "white peril" for Japan. She regards it as a real and dangerous menace to her national existence, not for a moment imaginary in character like the "yellow peril" so much talked about in Europe and America. The phrase about the "yellow peril" is nothing more than a trick concocted by disingenuous and treacherous diplomats to disturb and bring to an end the cordial feelings which characterize the relations toward Japan of the United States and England.

Japan, and only Japan, stands in the Far East for the progressiveness of the West—for freedom, for higher civilization—and her success will mean the extension of modern ideas naturally and peaceably through vast Asiatic domains—the occidentalizing of the East.

KENTARO KANEKO.

New York,
    May, 1905.

APPENDIX I.

LIST OF EMPERORS.[1]

NAME.	Date of Access.	Date of Death.	Age at Death.
	B.C.	B.C.	
1. Jimmu...............	660	585	127
2. Suizei	581	549	84
3. Annei	548	511	57
4. Itoku................	510	477	77
5. Kōshō................	475	393	114
6. Kōan.................	392	291	137
7. Kōrei	290	215	128
8. Kōgen................	214	158	116
9. Kaikwa	157	98	111
10. Sūjin	97	30	119
		A.D.	
11. Suinin	29	70	141
	A.D.		
12. Keikō................	71	130	143
13. Seimu	131	190	108
14. Chūai................	192	200	52
Jingō (Empress Regent)[2]	201	269	100
15. Ōjin.................	270	310	110
16. Nintoku	313	399	110

[1] The list here printed is the official list issued by the government, and has been revised by Mr. Tateno, the Japanese Minister at Washington.

[2] In the official list Jingō is not reckoned, and the time of her reign is counted with that of her son and successor.

	Name.	Date of Access.	Date of Death.	Age at Death.
17.	Richū.	400	405	67
18.	Hanzei	406	411	60
19.	Inkyō	412	453	80
20.	Ankō	454	456	56
21.	Yūriyaku	457	479	—
22.	Seinei	480	484	41
23.	Kenzō	485	487	—
24.	Ninken	488	498	50
25.	Muretsu	499	506	18
26.	Keitai	507	531	82
27.	Ankan	534	535	70
28.	Senkwa	536	539	73
29.	Kimmei	540	571	63
30.	Bidatsu	572	585	48
31.	Yōmei	586	587	69
32.	Sujun	588	592	73
33.	Suiko (Empress)	593	628	75
34.	Jomei	629	641	49
35.	Kōkyoku (Empress)	642	—	—
36.	Kōtoku	645	654	59
37.	Saimei (re-accession of Kōkyoku	655	661	68
38.	Tenji	668	671	58
39.	Kōbun	672	672	25
40.	Temmu	673	686	65
41.	Jitō (Empress)	690	702	58
42.	Mommu	697	707	25
43.	Gemmyō (Empress	708	721	61
44.	Genshō (Empress)	715	748	69
45.	Shōmu	724	756	56
46.	Kōken (Empress)	749	—	—
47.	Junnin	759	765	33

	NAME.	Date of Access.	Date of Death.	Age at Death.
48.	Kōken (re-enthroned)...	765	770	53
49.	Kōnin	770	781	73
50.	Kwammu	782	806	70
51.	Heijō	806	824	51
52.	Saga	810	842	57
53.	Ninna	824	840	55
54.	Nimmyō	834	850	41
55.	Montoku	851	858	32
56.	Seiwa	859	880	31
57.	Yōzei	877	949	82
58.	Kōko	885	887	58
59.	Uda	888	931	65
60.	Daigo	898	930	46
61.	Shujaku	931	952	30
62.	Muragami	947	967	42
63.	Reizei	968	1011	62
64.	Enyū	970	991	33
65.	Kwazan	985	1008	41
66.	Ichiyō	987	1011	32
67.	Sanjō	1012	1017	42
68.	Go-Ichijō	1017	1028	29
69.	Go-Shujaku	1037	1045	37
70.	Go-Reizei	1047	1068	44
71.	Go-Sanjō	1069	1073	40
72.	Shirakawa	1073	1129	77
73.	Horikawa	1087	1107	29
74.	Toba	1108	1156	54
75.	Shutoku	1124	1164	46
76.	Konoye	1142	1155	17
77.	Go-Shirakawa	1156	1192	66
78.	Nijō	1159	1165	23
79.	Rokujō	1166	1176	13

	NAME.	Date of Access.	Date of Death.	Age at Death.
80.	Takakura	1169	1181	21
81.	Antoku	1181	1185	15
82.	Go-Toba	1186	1239	60
83.	Tsuchi-mikado	1199	1231	37
84.	Juntoku	1211	1242	46
85.	Chūkyō	1222	1234	17
86.	Go-Horikawa	1221	1234	23
87.	Yojō	1232	1242	12
88.	Go-Saga	1242	1272	53
89.	Go Fukakusa	1246	1304	62
90.	Kameyama	1259	1305	57
91.	Go-Uda	1274	1324	58
92.	Fushimi	1288	1317	53
93.	Go-Fushimi	1298	1336	49
94.	Go-Nijyō	1301	1308	24
95.	Hanazono	1308	1348	52
96.	Go-Daigo	1318	1339	52
97.	Go-Murakami	1339	1368	41
98.	Go-Kameyama	1373	1424	78
99.	Go-Komatsu	1382	1433	57
100.	Shōkō	1414	1428	28
101.	Go-Hanazono	1429	1470	52
102.	Go-Tsuchi-mikado	1465	1500	59
103.	Go-Kashiwabara	1521	1526	63
104.	Go-Nara	1536	1557	62
105.	Ōgimachi	1560	1593	77
106.	Go-Yojō	1586	1617	47
107.	Go-Mizuo	1611	1680	85
108.	Myōshō (Empress)	1630	1696	74
109.	Go-Kōmyō	1643	1654	22
110.	Go-Nishio	1656	1685	49
111.	Reigen	1663	1732	79

	NAME.	Date of Access.	Date of Death.	Age at Death.
112.	Higashiyama	1687	1709	35
113.	Naka-mikado	1710	1737	37
114.	Sakuramachi	1720	1750	31
115.	Momozono	1747	1762	22
116.	Go-Sakuramachi (Empress).	1763	1813	74
117.	Go-Momozono........	1771	1779	22
118.	Kōkaku..............	1780	1840	70
119.	Jinkō................	1817	1846	47
120.	Kōmei...............	1847	1867	37
121.	Mutsuhito (reigning emperor)	1868		

APPENDIX II.

LIST OF YEAR PERIODS.[1]

NAME.	Japanese Era.	Christian Era.
Taikwa	1305	645
Hakuchi	1310	650
Saimei	1315	655
Tenji	1322	662
Sujaku	1332	672
Hakuhō	1333	673
Suchō	1346	686
Jitō	1347	687
Momm	1357	697
Daihō	1361	701
Keiun	1364	704
Wadō	1368	708
Reiki	1375	715

[1] From *Japanese Chronological Tables*, by William Bramsen, 1880.

The system of counting from year-periods (*nengō*) was introduced from China. These periods of Japanese history do not correspond to the reigns of the emperors. A new one was chosen whenever it was deemed necessary to commemorate an auspicious or ward off a malign event. By a notification issued in 1872 it was announced that hereafter the year-period should be changed but once during the reign of an emperor. The current period, *Meiji* (Enlightened Peace), will therefore continue during the reign of the present emperor.

The numbers in the second column of this table indicate the years as counted from the founding of the empire by Jimmu Tennō. According to the official chronology this occurred B.C. 660.

Name.	Japanese Era.	Christian Era.
Yōrō	1377	717
Jinki	1384	724
Tembiō	1389	729
Tembiō shōhō	1409	749
Tembiō hōji	1417	757
Tembiō jingo	1425	765
Jingo keiun	1427	767
Hōki	1430	770
Tenō	1441	781
Enriaku	1442	782
Daidō	1466	806
Kōnin	1470	810
Tenchō	1484	824
Jōwa	1494	834
Kajō	1508	848
Ninju	1511	851
Saikō	1514	854
Tenan	1517	857
Jōgwan	1519	859
Gwangiō	1537	877
Ninna	1545	885
Kwampei	1549	889
Shōtai	1558	898
Engi	1561	901
Enchō	1583	923
Jōhei	1591	931
Tengiō	1598	938
Tenriaku	1607	947
Tentoku	1617	957
Ōwa	1621	961
Kōhō	1624	964
Anna	1628	968

Name.	Japanese Era.	Christian Era.
Tenroku	1630	970
Ten-en	1633	973
Jōgen	1636	976
Tengen	1638	978
Eikwan	1643	983
Kwanna	1645	985
Ei-en	1647	987
Eiso	1649	989
Shōriaku	1650	990
Chōtoku	1655	995
Chōhō	1659	999
Kwankō	1664	1004
Chōwa	1672	1012
Kwannin	1677	1017
Ji-an	1681	1021
Manju	1684	1024
Chōgen	1688	1028
Chōriaku	1697	1037
Chōkiū	1700	1040
Kwantoku	1704	1044
Eijō	1706	1046
Tengi	1713	1053
Kōhei	1718	1058
Jiriaku	1725	1065
Enkiū	1729	1069
Jōhō	1734	1074
Jōriaku	1737	1077
Eihō	1741	1081
Ōtoku	1744	1084
Kwanji	1747	1087
Kahō	1754	1094
Eichō	1756	1096

NAME.	Japanese Era.	Christian Era.
Jōtoku	1757	1097
Kowa	1759	1099
Chōji	1764	1104
Kajō	1766	1106
Tennin	1768	1108
Tenei	1770	1110
Eikiū	1773	1113
Genei	1778	1118
Hō-an	1780	1120
Tenji	1784	1124
Daiji	1786	1126
Tenjō	1791	1131
Chōjō	1792	1132
Hō-en	1795	1135
Eiji	1801	1141
Kōji	1802	1142
Tenyō	1804	1144
Kiū-an	1805	1145
Nimbiō	1811	1151
Kiūju	1814	1154
Hōgen	1816	1156
Heiji	1819	1159
Eiriaku	1820	1160
Ōhō	1821	1161
Chōkwan	1823	1163
Eiman	1825	1165
Ninan	1826	1166
Ka-ō	1829	1169
Jō-an	1831	1171
Angen	1835	1175
Jishō	1837	1177
Yōwa	1841	1181

NAME.	Japanese Era.	Christian Era.
Ju-ei	1842	1182
Genriaku	1844	1184
Bunji	1845	1185
Kenkiū	1850	1190
Shōji	1859	1199
Kennin	1861	1201
Genkiū	1864	1204
Kenei	1866	1206
Jōgen	1867	1207
Kenriaku	1871	1211
Kempō	1873	1213
Jōkiū	1879	1219
Jō-ō	1882	1222
Gennin	1884	1224
Karoku	1885	1225
Antei	1887	1227
Kwangi	1889	1229
Jō-ei	1892	1232
Tempuku	1893	1233
Bunriaku	1894	1234
Katei	1895	1235
Riakunin	1898	1238
En-ō	1899	1239
Ninji	1900	1240
Kwangen	1903	1243
Hōji	1907	1247
Kenchō	1909	1249
Kōgen	1916	1256
Shōka	1917	1257
Shōgen	1919	1259
Bunō	1920	1260
Kōchō	1921	1261

NAME.	Japanese Era.	Christian Era.
Bunei	1924	1264
Kenji	1935	1275
Kōan	1938	1278
Shō-ō	1948	1288
Einin	1953	1293
Shōan	1959	1299
Kengen	1962	1302
Kagen	1963	1303
Tokuji	1966	1306
Enkiō	1968	1308
Ōchō	1971	1311
Shōwa	1972	1312
Bumpō	1977	1317
Gen-ō	1979	1319
Genkō	1981	1321
Shōchū	1984	1324
Kariaku	1986	1326
Gentoku	1989	1329
Shōkiō	1992	1331
Kemmu	1994	1334
Engen	1996	1336
Kōkoku	1999	1339
Shōhei	2006	1346
Kentoku	2030	1370
Bunchū	2032	1372
Tenju	2035	1375
Kōwa	2041	1381
Genchū	2044	1384
Meitoku	2050	1390
Ō-ei	2054	1394
Shōchō	2088	1428
Eikiō	2089	1429

NAME.	Japanese Era.	Christian Era.
Kakitsu	2101	1441
Bunan	2104	1444
Hōtoku	2109	1449
Kōtoku	2112	1452
Kōshō	2115	1455
Chōroku	2117	1457
Kwanshō	2120	1460
Bunshō	2126	1466
Ōnin	2127	1467
Bummei	2129	1469
Chōkō	2147	1487
Entoku	2149	1489
Mei-ō	2152	1492
Bunki	2161	1501
Eishō	2164	1504
Dai-ei	2181	1521
Kōroku	2188	1528
Tembun	2192	1532
Kōji	2215	1555
Eiroku	2218	1558
Genki	2230	1570
Tenshō	2233	1573
Bunroku	2252	1592
Keichō	2256	1596
Genna	2275	1615
Kwanei	2284	1624
Shōhō	2304	1644
Kei-an	2308	1648
Jō-ō	2312	1652
Meireki	2315	1655
Manji	2318	1658
Kwambun	2321	1661

NAME.	Japanese Era.	Christian Era.
Empō	2333	1673
Tenna	2341	1681
Jōkiō	2344	1684
Genroku	2348	1688
Hō-ei	2364	1704
Shōtoku	2371	1711
Kiōhō	2376	1716
Gembun	2396	1736
Kwampō	2401	1741
Enkiō	2404	1744
Kwanen	2408	1748
Hōreki	2411	1751
Meiwa	2424	1764
Anei	2432	1772
Temmei	2441	1781
Kwansei	2449	1789
Kiōwa	2461	1801
Bunkwa	2464	1804
Bunsei	2478	1818
Tempō	2490	1830
Kōkwa	2504	1844
Ka-ei	2508	1848
Ansei	2514	1854
Manen	2520	1860
Bunkiū	2521	1861
Genji	2524	1864
Kei-ō	2525	1865
Meiji	2528	1868

APPENDIX III.

LIST OF SHŌGUNS.[1]

I.—*The Dynasty of Minamoto.*   1186–1219.

1. Minamoto Yoritomo, 1186–1199, died ; received his appointment as shōgun in 1192.

NOTE.—In this as in the later cases, the dates will be cited which correspond to the attainment of power and its general recognition, but which do not, in many cases, correspond to the grant of the title, which frequently was much later.

2. Minamoto Yori-iye, 1199–1203, son of the preceding, first deposed by his grandfather, Hōjō Tokimasa, and banished to Izu, there was murdered in 1204.

3. Minamoto Sanetomo, 1203–1219, eleven years old, brother of the preceding, murdered by his nephew Kokio, the son of Yori-iye.

The Time of the Shadow Shōguns.   1220–1338.

The shōguns of this period, taken partly from the Fujiwara family, partly from the princes of the imperial house, were mostly children, and in every instance the weak agents of the Hōjō family, whose chiefs, as regents (*shiken*), had the power in their hands, although the

---

[1] Translated from the chronology of the shōguns in *Mittheilungen der deutschen Gesellschaft fur Natur und Volkerkunde Ostasiens* Heft 3, 1873.

nominal bearers of the same were likewise principally only children.

4. Fujiwara Yoritsune, 1220–1243, nine years old, dethroned by Hōjō Tsunetoki, died 1256.

5. Fujiwara Yoritsugu, 1244–1251, son of the preceding, seven years old, deposed by H. Tokeyori, died 1256.

6. Munetaka Shino, 1252–1265, eleven, according to others thirteen, years old, deposed by H. Tokimune, died 1274.

7. Koreyasu Shino, 1266–1289, son of the preceding, three years old, deposed by H. Sadatoki, died 1325 (1326?).

8. Hisa-akira Shino, or, as he was called, Kumei Shino, 1289–1307, sixteen years old, deposed by H. Sadatoki, died 1328.

9. Morikuni Shino, 1308–1333, son of the preceding, seven years old, dethroned by Nitsuda Yoshisada, died in the same year.

10. Moriyoshi Shino, 1333–1334, son of the reigning Emperor Go-Daigo, dethroned by Taka-uji, murdered, in 1335, by Minamoto Nao-yoshi.

11. Nari-Yoshi Shino, 1334–1338, dethroned and murdered by Taka-uji.

II.— The Regents of the Hōjō Family.

Hōjō Tokimasa, died 1215, did not have the title of regent (*shiken*).

Hōjō Yoshitoki, 1205–1224, from 1205 regent (*shiken*), murdered.

Hōjō Yasutoki, 1225–1242, died.

Hōjō Tsunetoki, 1243–1246, grandson of the preceding, retired in favor of his younger brother, Tokiyori, and died thirty-three years old.

Hōjō Tokiyori, 1246–1256, retired in favor of his son, Tokimune, and died 1263, thirty-seven years old.

Hōjō Tokimune, 1257–1284, seven years old, under the guardianship of H. Nagatoki and H. Masamura, died.

Hōjō Sadatoki, 1284–1300, adopted son of the preceding, retired in favor of Morotoki, the grandson of Tokiyori, but continued to exercise a potent influence over the regency, died 1311.

Hōjō Morotoki, 1300–1311, died.

Hōjō Takatoki, 1312–1326, the son of Sadatoki, nine years old, under the guardianship of Hirotoki and Munenobu, retired in favor of his younger brother, Yasuye, who likewise soon withdrew.

Until the fall of the Hōjō family Takatoki really conducted the regency, although others held the title. After the taking of Kamakura by Nitta Yoshisada in 1333, he killed himself.

III.— *The Dynasty of Ashikaga.* 1334–1573.

12. Ashikaga Taka-uji, 1334–1358, died fifty-three years old.

13. Ashikaga Yoshimori, 1359–1367, retired in favor of his son Yoshimitsu, died 1408, fifty-one years old.

14. Ashikaga Yoshimitsu, 1368–1393, retired in favor of his son, Yoshimochi, at the age of thirty-seven years, died 1409.

15. Ashikaga Yoshimochi, 1394–1422, retired in favor of his son, Yoshikatsu.

16. Ashikaga Yoshikatsu, 1423–1425, died nineteen years old. Ashikaga Yoshimochi, 1425–1428, the fifteenth shōgun, took the power again, and died forty-three years old.

17 Ashikaga Yoshinobu, 1428–1441, murdered by Aka-

matsu Mitsusuke, forty-eight years old. From 1429 called Yoshinori.

18. Ashikaga Yoshikatsu, 1441–1443, son of the preceding, eight years old, died.

19. Ashikaga Yoshinari, called Yoshimasa, 1443–1473, brother of the preceding, eight years old, retired, and died in 1490.

20. Ashikaga Yoshinao, 1473–1489, died twenty-five years old; from 1488, called Yoshihiro.

21. Ashikaga Yoshimura, 1490–1493, nephew of Yoshimasa, twenty-five years old, taken prisoner and dethroned by Hosokawa Motomoto.

22. Ashikaga Yoshimitsi, 1493–1508, had to flee, died 1511; from 1449 called Yoshitaku, and from 1502 Yoshisumi; Yoshitada, 1508–1521, is Yoshimura, who from the year 1501 bore the name, and since that time was the shōgun of the enemy at war with Yoshisumi, had to flee, was deposed, and died, 1523.

23. Ashikaga Yoshinaru, 1521–1546, son of Yoshisumi, retired in favor of his son, Yoshifushi, died 1550, forty years old.

24. Ashikaga Yoshifushi, 1547–1565, eleven years old, killed himself in his palace, having been confined there by the rebels.

25. Ashikaga Yoshigi-ei or Yoshinaga, 1568 died, important as opposition shōgun.

26. Ashikaga Yoshi-aki, 1568–1573, deposed by Nobunaga, died 1597.

IV.—The Time of the Usurpation. 1573–1603.

27. Taira-no-Nobunaga, 1573–1582, killed himself, having been forced to do so by Akechi Mitsuhide.

Akechi Mitsuhide, who usurped the title of shōgun, ruled only twelve days, and fell conquered by Hideyoshi.

28. Samboshi, 1582–1586, grandson of Nobunaga.

29. Toyotomi Hideyoshi, 1586–1598, was never shōgun, but kwambaku ; (on his retirement called Taikō-sama).

30. Hidetsugu, 1591–1595, nephew of the preceding, killed himself, was also kwambaku.

31. Hideyori, 1600–1615, son of Hideyoshi, killed himself, conquered by Ieyasu. According to other accounts, he escaped and fled to Satsuma ; was Naifu (Minister of the Interior) from 1603.

V.—*The Dynasty of the Tokugawa.* 1603–1868.

32. Ieyasu, 1603–1605, died 1616 ; 1603 appointed shōgun (posthumous title Gongensama). The shōguns of this dynasty frequently retired, as soon as their successors grew up, but in spite of this fact they continued to lead the regency.

33. Hidetada, 1605–1623, died 1632, son of the preceding.

34. Iemitsu, 1623–1651, died 1652, son of the preceding.

35. Ietsuna, 1651–1680, died, son of the preceding.

36. Tsunayoshi, 1681–1709, son of Iemitsu, killed by his wife.

37. Ienobu, 1709–1712, grandson of Iemitsu, died.

38. Ietsugu (Ietsubo according to Klaproth), 1713–1715, died, son of the preceding.

39. Yoshimune, 1716–1745, retired, died 1751, formerly fifth Prince of Kii.

40. Ieshige, 1745–1760 (according to others 1761 or 1762), son of the preceding, died.

41. Ieharu, 1760–1786, son of the preceding, died.

42. Ienari, 1787–1836, died 1841, son of the preceding.

43. Ieyoshi, 1837–1852, son of the preceding.

44. Iesada, 1853–1857, son of the preceding.

45. Iemochi, 1858–1866, died, formerly thirteenth Prince of Kii.

46. Yoshihisa (Yoshinobu according to Adams, vol. ii. p. 37), 1867–1868, son of the Prince of Mito, Nari-akira, adopted by the Prince of Hitotsubashi, retired at the fall of shōgunate in 1867.

APPENDIX IV.

LAWS OF SHŌTOKU TAISHI.[1]

[From *Dai Nihonshi*, vol. xii., folio 28 to 31.]

I.—Harmony shall be esteemed and obedience shall be held in regard. Because dissensions prevail, therefore men are often unfaithful to their prince and disobedient to their fathers. Let adjoining districts be left in peace, thus harmony between superior and inferior shall be cultivated and co-operation in matters of state shall be promoted, and thus the right reason of all things may be reached and the right thing accomplished.

II.—Let bountiful honor be always paid to the three precious elements of Buddhism, that is, to its priests, its ritual, and its founder. It is the highest religion in the universe, and all people in all generations must pay becoming reverence to its doctrines. Do not harshly censure men's wickedness but teach them faithfully until they yield obedience. Unless men rely upon Buddhism there is no way to convert them from the wrong to the right.

III.—To the commands of the Emperor men must be duly obedient. The prince must be looked upon as the heaven and his subjects as the earth. The earth contains all things and the heaven stretches over it. The

---

[1] The translation of these laws of Shōtoku Taishi was furnished by Mr. Tsuji Shinji, late vice-minister of state for education, and by Mr. Matsumoto Kumpei.

four seasons pass orderly along and the spirit of the universe is harmonious. If the earth were to cover the heaven the effect would be distraction. Hence the prince must command and the subject obey; superiors must act and inferiors yield. Men ought therefore to pay due heed to the orders of the Emperor; if not they will bring ruin on themselves.

IV.—Politeness must be the chief rule of conduct for all officers and their colleagues in the court. The first principle governing subjects must be politeness. When superiors are not polite then inferiors will not keep in the right; when inferiors are not polite their conduct degenerates into crime. When both prince and subjects are polite, then social order is never disturbed and the state is kept in a condition of tranquillity.

V.—Covetousness and rapacity must be expelled from the hearts of officers, and they must adjudicate with just discrimination in all suits that come before them. Even in a single day there are thousands of such suits, and in the course of years how great must be the accumulation! If the suit is won through bribery, then the poor man can obtain no justice but only the rich. The poor man will have no sure place of dependence, and subjects will be driven to abandon their duty.

VI.—To punish vice and to encourage virtue is the rule in good ancient law. The virtuous man must therefore be promoted, and the vicious man must be surely punished. The man who is untruthful is a powerful instrument to endanger the state and a keen weapon to destroy the nation. The flatterer loves to tell the faults of the inferior to the superior, and also to disclose the errors of the superior to the inferior. Such men are alike unfaithful to the prince and unfriendly to fellow-citizens, and in the end fail not to stir up social disorder.

VII.—The duty of men in the government must be assigned according to their capacity. When intelligent men take service the applause of the people follows, but when bad men are in office calamities ensue. If wise officers are put on duty the matters of state are well managed, and the community is free from danger and prosperity prevails. Therefore in ancient times the wise king never selected the office for the man, but always selected the man to suit the office.

VIII.—Too often officers and their colleagues come early to their offices and retire soon ; so that the public work accomplished in a single day is small. It is incumbent on them to devote sufficient time to their tasks ; if not, then the work of the government cannot be done.

IX.—Everything must be faithfully done, because fidelity is the origin of justice. The distinction between good and bad, between success and failure, depends on fidelity. When both prince and subjects are faithful then there are no duties which cannot be accomplished, but when both are unfaithful nothing can be done.

X.—Give up all thoughts of indignation and be not angered with others on account of a disagreement of opinion. Each one may have a different point of view and may therefore come to a different conclusion. If the one side be right then the other must be wrong, or the cases may be just reversed. It would be unjust to set down one man as surely wise and another as positively stupid ; because men cannot attain perfection in their characters. It is impossible to decide either side to be perfectly right or perfectly wrong. While you are angry with another who has a different view from you, you cannot be sure lest you be in the wrong. Therefore though you may think yourself in the right, it is safer to follow the opinions of the many.

XI.—Let merit and demerit be carefully considered, and let rewards and punishments be meted out accordingly. In times past this has often failed to be justly done. It is incumbent on all who are entrusted with the direction of public affairs and on all officers of the government to look carefully after the distribution of rewards and punishments.

XII.—Governors of provinces and their deputies must be careful not to impose too heavy duties on their subjects. One state never has more than one prince, and in like manner the subjects cannot have more than one master. The prince is the head of all his dominions and of all his subjects. The officers of government are also the subjects of the prince; and there is no reason why they should dare to lay undue burdens upon others who are subjects of the same prince.

XIII.—Each officer of the government has his appointed duty. Sometimes officers complain of the stagnation of business, which, however, is caused by their own absence from their appointed duties. They must not make a pretence of the performance of their duties, and by their neglect interrupt public affairs.

XIV.—Subjects and officers must not be jealous of each other. If one person is envious of another, the second is sure to be envious of the first. Thus the evils of jealousy never end. If men shall envy each other on account of their talent and wisdom, no single wise man would ever be obtained for government service through a thousand years. What a noble method of governing a state would that be which expelled from its service all wise men!

XV.—To sacrifice private interests for the public good is the duty of the subject. When men are selfish there must be ill-will; when ill-will comes, then with it must come iniquity, which will disturb the public welfare. Ill-will is sure to bring about the breaking of wholesome rules and the violation of the laws of the state. It is for this reason that the harmony between superior and inferior spoken of in the first article is so important.

XVI.—To select a convenient season in which to employ men for public work is the rule of good ancient law. Winter is a time of leisure ; but during the season between spring and autumn, in which they are employed on their farms and in feeding silk-worms, it is not expedient to take men from their work, or interfere with them in their efforts to supply food and clothing.

XVII.—Important matters should only be settled after due conference with many men. Trifling matters may be decided without conference, because they are not so material in their effects ; but weighty matters, on account of their far-reaching consequences, must be discussed with many councillors. It is thus that the right way shall be found and pursued.

APPENDIX V.

THE NEGOTIATIONS BETWEEN JAPAN AND RUSSIA.

1903–1904

Official Correspondence

Presented to the Imperial Diet, March, 1904

No. 1.

BARON KOMURA TO MR. KURINO.

TOKIO, July 28th, 1903.

(Telegram.)

THE Japanese Government have observed with close attention the development of affairs in Manchuria, and they view with grave concern the present situation there. So long as there were grounds for hope that Russia would carry out her engagement to China and her assurances to other Powers on the subject of the evacuation of Manchuria, the Japanese Government maintained an attitude of watchful reserve. But the recent action of Russia in formulating new demands in Peking and in consolidating rather than relaxing her hold on Manchuria compels belief that she has abandoned the intention of retiring from Manchuria, while her increased activity along the Corean frontier is such as to raise doubts regarding the limits of her ambition. The unrestrained permanent occupation of Manchuria by Russia would create a condition of things prejudicial to the security and interest of Japan. Such occupation would be destructive of the principle of equal opportunity and in impairment of the territorial integrity of China. But, what is of still more serious moment to the Japanese Government, Russia stationed on the flank of Corea would be a constant menace to the separate existence of that Empire, and in any event it would make Russia the dominant power in Corea.

Corea is an important outpost in Japan's line of defence, and Japan consequently considers the independence of Corea absolutely essential to her own repose and safety. Japan possesses paramount political as well as commercial and industrial interests an influence in Corea, which, having regard to her own security, she cannot consent to surrender to, or share with, any other Power. The Japanese Government have given the matter their most serious consideration and have resolved to approach the Russian Government in a spirit of conciliation and frankness with a view to the conclusion of an understanding designed to compose questions which are at this time the cause of just and natural anxiety ; and in the estimation of the Japanese Government, the moment is opportune for making the attempt to bring about the desired adjustment.

The Japanese Government, reposing confidence in your judgment and discretion, have decided to place these delicate negotiations in your hands. It is the wish of the Japanese Government to place their present invitation to the Russian Government entirely on an official footing, and you are accordingly instructed to open the question by presenting to Count Lamsdorff a Note Verbale to the following effect :

"The Imperial Japanese Government, believing that the Imperial Russian Government share with them the desire to remove from the relations of the two Empires every cause of future misunderstanding, would be glad to enter with the Imperial Russian Government upon examination of the condition of affairs in the Extreme East where their interests meet, with a view to a definition of their respective special interests in those regions. If, as is confidently hoped, this suggestion meets approval in principle, the Imperial Japanese Government will be prepared to present to the Imperial Russian Government their views as to the nature and scope of the proposed understanding."

In presenting the foregoing note to Count Lamsdorff, you will be careful to make him understand that our purposes are entirely friendly, but that we attach great importance to the subject. You will present the note to Count Lamsdorff as soon as possible, and keep me fully informed regarding the steps taken by you under this instruction ; and immediately upon the receipt of an affirmative reply from the Russian Government, the substance of our proposals will be telegraphed to you.

No. 2.

MR. KURINO TO BARON KOMURA.

PETERSBURG, July 31st, 1903., Received, August 2d.,

(Telegram.)

YOUR Excellency's telegram of the 28th instant was duly received. In accordance with the instructions contained therein, I saw Count Lamsdorff to-day and, before handing to His Excellency the Note Verbale, I stated substantially as follows :

"The condition of affairs in the Far East is becoming more and more complicated, and unless something be done at present with the view of removing all causes of misunderstanding between Japan and Russia, the relations of the two countries will increase in difficulty, entailing nothing but disadvantages to both countries. Under the circumstances, the Imperial Government, fully animated by a spirit of frankness and conciliation, have decided to approach the Imperial Russian Government with a view to arrive at an understanding."

I then handed to him the Note Verbale, saying that I was so instructed. After he had seen it, I expressed my ardent hope that the Russian Government would share the above view in the same spirit. Count Lamsdorff said that he was perfectly satisfied with the decision of the Japanese Government, for, as he had said to me very often, an understanding between the two countries is not only desirable, but is the best policy ; should Russia and Japan enter into full understanding, no one would in future attempt to sow the seeds of discord between the two countries. So far as he was concerned, he was, he said, in perfect accord with the view of the Japanese Government ; but he wished to see the Emperor on the subject before a definite answer was given. He expects to see the Emperor next Tuesday, and promised to give me an answer on the following day. He added that the Emperor would surely approve the matter.

No. 3.

BARON KOMURA TO MR. KURINO.

TOKIO, August 3d, 1903.

(Telegram.)

IN reference to my telegram of the 28th July, the Japanese Government, after giving most serious consideratior to the condition of affairs in those centres where the interests of the two Powers meet, have decided to propose the following as the basis of an understanding between Japan and Russia :

"1.   Mutual engagement to respect the independence and territorial integrity of the Chinese and Corean Empires and to maintain the principle of equal opportunity for the commerce and industry of all nations in those countries.

"2.   Reciprocal recognition of Japan's preponderating interests in Corea and Russia's special interests in railway enterprises in Manchuria, and of the right of Japan to take in Corea and of Russia to take in Manchuria such measures as may be necessary for the protection of their respective interests as above defined, subject, however, to the provisions of Article I of this Agreement.

"3.   Reciprocal undertaking on the part of Russia and Japan not to impede development of those industrial and commercial activities respectively of Japan in Corea and of Russia in Manchuria, which are not inconsistent with the stipulations of Article I of this Agreement.

"Additional engagement on the part of Russia not to impede the eventual extension of the Corean railway into southern Manchuria so as to connect with the East China and Shan-hai-kwan-Newchwang lines.

"4.   Reciprocal engagement that in case it is found necessary to send troops by Japan to Corea, or by Russia to Manchuria, for the purpose either of protecting the interests mentioned in Article II of this Agreement, or of suppressing insurrection or disorder calculated to create international complications, the troops so sent are in no case to exceed the actual number required and are to be forthwith recalled as soon as their missions are accomplished.

"5.   Recognition on the part of Russia of the exclusive right of Japan to give advice and assistance in the interest of reform and good government in Corea, including necessary military assistance.

"6.   This Agreement to supplant all previous arrangements between Japan and Russia respecting Corea."

In handing the foregoing project to Count Lamsdorff, you will say that it is presented for the consideration of the Russian Government ir. the firm belief that it may be found to serve as a basis upon which to construct satisfactory arrangement between the two Governments, and you will assure Count Lamsdorff that any amendment or suggestion he may find it necessary to offer will receive the immediate and friendly consideration of the Japanese Government. It will not be necessary for you to say much in elucidation of the separate items of the project as they are very largely self-explanatory ; but you might point out that the project taken as a whole will be found to be but little more than the logical and essential development and extension of the principles already recognized by the two Governments, or of conditions embodied in the engagements which the project is designed to supplant.

The foregoing instruction is sent to you in anticipation that the answer to the Note Verbale presented by you will be favorable ; but you will not act on that instruction until you receive further instructions which will be given after you have communicated to me

---

No. 4.

MR. KURINO TO BARON KOMURA.

PETERSBURG, August 5th, 1903.
Received, August 6th,   "

(Telegram.

COUNT Lamsdorff says he is authorized by the Emperor to open negotiations with me on the subject of the Note Verbale.

No. 5.

BARON KOMURA TO MR. KURINO.

TOKIO, August 6th, 1903.

(Telegram.)

IN reference to your telegrams dated the 31st ultimo and 5th instant, you will state to Count Lamsdorff that the Imperial Government fully appreciate the friendly spirit with which the Russian Government received the proposal of the Japanese Government to enter upon negotiations with regard to an understanding between the two countries, and then present at once the project to the Russian Government in accordance with instructions contained in my telegram of the 3d instant.

No. 6.

MR. KURINO TO BARON KOMURA.

PETERSBURG, August 12th, 1903.
Received, August 14th, "

(Telegram.)

COUNT Lamsdorff, being now very much occupied, could not receive me until to-day, when I handed to His Excellency the proposed project in English in accordance with your instructions. I added that the longer the conclusion of an accord is postponed the more difficult will it become, as the condition of affairs in the Far East is now getting more and more complicated. I asked him to hasten the matter as much as possible. He said he would examine the project with care.

No. 7.

MR. KURINO TO BARON KOMURA.

PETERSBURG, August 24th, 1903.
Received, August 25th, "

(Telegram.)

COUNT Lamsdorff received me yesterday by special arrangement, and I asked his views *as well as* the attitude of the Russian Government regarding our proposals, adding that the Japanese Government are now impatiently waiting for a reply. He said that he had studied the project seriously, but that the Emperor having been absent over a week on account of the manœuvres, he had been unable to take any steps in the matter; but he asked my opinion about transferring the negotiations to Tokio as there were many details which would have to be referred to Admiral Alexieff. I said to him that the Japanese Government having confided the matter to me, I should prefer to proceed with it, but that I was willing to communicate his opinion to you.

He stated that he has already sent copy of our project to Port Arthur with the view of obtaining the opinion of Admiral Alexieff. After such conversation, he said the question of Japanese railway enterprise in Manchuria would be difficult, but upon all other points perhaps the Russian Government would be able to come to an understanding. I said that in order to arrive at a satisfactory understanding, mutual concessions as well as a spirit of conciliation are necessary, and that the Japanese Government would be prepared to give favorable consideration if any suggestions should be made by Count Lamsdorff.

No. 8.

BARON KOMURA TO MR. KURINO.

TOKIO, August 26th, 1903.

(Telegram.)

IN reference to your telegram of the 24th instant, you will say to Count Lamsdorff that the Japanese Government would prefer to continue negotiations in St. Petersburg, believing that by so doing the work will be greatly facilitated. You can add that there are no details to be considered in connection with pending negotiations which require local knowledge, and that the Japanese Government, having placed the negotiation in your hands, would dislike to make any change. You will say to Count Lamsdorff that the Japanese Government are anxiously awaiting a definite reply from his Government to their proposals, and you will continue to use every endeavor to obtain from him such a reply as soon as possible.

No. 9.

MR. KURINO TO BARON KOMURA.

PETERSBURG, August 27th, 1903.

Received August 28th, "

(Telegram.)

I saw Count Lamsdorff to-day on the subject of your telegram dated the 26th instant. He said he had audience of the Emperor last Tuesday, and was told that His Majesty desires very much the early conclusion of an *entente* satisfactory for both countries, and expressed his wish to conduct the negotiations at Tokio so as to expedite the matter. Then Count Lamsdorff added that the Emperor is to leave here for the country next Monday, and then for foreign countries for some time, and at the same time the Ministers concerned would be absent from St. Petersburg. Consequently, negotiations in Tokio would be much the easier and quicker way of concluding the matter. I said, referring to my conversation with Count Lamsdorff of the 23d instant, that the proposed understanding

involved mostly questions of principles and politics rather than details, and consequently that the continuation of negotiations at St.
Petersburg would be proper and at the same time the quickest way
to arrive at a satisfactory understanding. He repeated what he had
just said and insisted upon his proposition.

Under the circumstances, I think it hardly possible to change the
course now proposed by Count Lamsdorff under authority of the
Emperor. I also think that negotiations at Tioko would entail
many disadvantageous consequences; and definite instruction for
the further course is awaited.

No. 10.

BARON KOMURA TO MR. KURINO.

TOKIO, August 29th, 1903.

(Telegram.)

IN reference to your telegram of the 27th instant, you will say to
Count Lamsdorff that the Japanese Government still think that negotiations will be facilitated if continued in St. Petersburg since the
negotiations relate to principles and not to details ; and you will add
that he and you having been duly authorized in the matter, and the
proposals of Japan having been presented to him, the Japanese Government had supposed that the seat of negotiation had been agreed
to. You will accordingly urge upon Count Lamsdorff the desire of
the Japanese Government to continue the negotiations in St. Petersburg, and express a hope that his Government will reconsider the
question. You will also say that the Japanese Government presume
they are justified in assuming from the proposal to transfer negotiations to Tokio, that our proposals are in principle acceptable to the
Russian Government as the basis of negotiations.

No. 11.

MR. KURINO TO BARON KOMURA.

PETERSBURG, August 31st, 1903.
Received, September 2d, "

(Telegram.)

I saw Count Lamsdorff to-day and explained fully the purport of
your telegram of the 29th instant. The substance of his reply is as
follows :

He said that the negotiations relate to principles, but principles must be decided upon examination of local and practical questions. Accordingly the Russian Government desired to transfer the discussions to Tokio on account of the necessity of consultation with Admiral Alexieff, and also to manifest a sense of deference to Japan as the proposal had been made by her, and that the acceptance of the proposal at St. Petersburg does not signify that the seat of negotiations should be at the same place. He added that the proposal to transfer the negotiations to Tokio does not necessarily mean that our proposals are acceptable to the Russian Government, as bases for negotiations could not be determined without reference to practical questions concerning which Baron Rosen and Admiral Alexieff have much better knowledge than he himself.

I urged as my opinion that, this being the most important question of high politics between our two countries, perhaps the Emperor had much to decide, and consequently it would be very convenient if the negotiations were conducted at St. Petersburg, and wished his serious reconsideration of the question of transfer as such reconsideration is much desired by the Japanese Government. I objected also to the suggestion of transfer on the ground that the question relates to principles as well as to the direction of international political concerns which may not be within the powers conferred upon Admiral Alexieff. If I remember rightly, I said, I understand that his authority is limited to mere questions of local administration. He said that on this question Admiral Alexieff would only be consulted and decide nothing, and added that he, Count Lamsdorff, is also desirous to settle the question as quickly as possible, and that is the reason why he suggested the transfer. The Russian Counter-Proposals are being prepared by persons having local knowledge, consequently the transfer of negotiations to Tokio would expedite the matter. Should the negotiations be conducted at St. Petersburg, he would be obliged to attend to the matter personally with me ; but this autumn he has to be long absent from the city on account of his attendance upon the Emperor. In case of his journey to Vienna and Rome, he may also visit a certain foreign country and would be liable to be frequently interrupted in the negotiations. But in case of negotiations at Tokio, he could direct them by telegraph, and telegrams from Tokio could always follow him wherever he might happen to be ; besides, he said, as we know very well, the Russian way of conducting business here is not very expeditious. At the conclusion, he said he is to have audience of the Emperor to-day, and will explain to him the reasons why an early understanding between the two countries is desirable as mentioned by me; and he promised to repeat to His Majesty the special desire of the Japanese Government to conduct the negotiations at St. Petersburg; but he added that no change of view on the subject could be expected.

No 12.

BARON KOMURA TO MR. KURINO.

TOKIO, September 2d, 1903.

(Telegram.)

IN reference to your telegram of the 31st ultimo, you will say to Count Lamsdorff that it being the acknowledged desire of both Powers to arrive at an understanding as soon as possible, the Japanese Government fear that discussions would be greatly protracted if the negotiations were now to be transferred to Tokio without some accepted basis for negotiations; and you will add that the Japanese Government, having presented their proposals in concrete form to the Russian Government, believe that negotiations, wherever conducted, would be greatly facilitated if the Russian Government were primarily to announce whether such proposals can in principle be accepted as the basis for negotiations. The Japanese Government do not understand that the acceptance of those proposals as such basis would exclude amendments that might be regarded as necessary. On the contrary, such acceptance would merely fix a definite point of departure, which is desirable in all negotiations and very important in the present case. You will use every endeavor to secure the desired announcement from the Russian Government.

No. 13.

MR. KURINO TO BARON KOMURA.

ST. PETERSBURG, September 5th, 1903.

Received, September 6th, "

(Telegram.)

I SAW Count Lamsdorff yesterday. With the view of preventing any misunderstanding about the sense of the instruction contained in your telegram of the 2d instant, and also with the view of impressing upon the Russian Government the feeling of importance placed by the Japanese Government on the matter, I prepared a Note Verbale, which I handed to him. We then had a rather prolonged discussion on the question. The substance of his remarks is as follows :

According to his experience of 40 years in the Foreign Office, negotiations of an international character had always been conducted on the proposals of one Power together with the reply of the other, and it was not usual to accept the proposition of one Power as the sole basis of negotiations. Baron Rosen had already been commanded by the Emperor to study seriously the proposition of the Japanese Government, and at the same time to prepare and elaborate Counter-Proposals in consultation with Admiral Alexieff, and, if the Japanese Government were willing to enter into negotiations, to commence immediately the *pourparlers*, adopting the propositions of the Japanese Government and the Russian Counter-Proposals as the basis of negotiations. I said during the discussion that if the Russian Government were really animated by a desire to enter into a satisfactory arrangement with Japan, I should deem it highly necessary that the Russian Government should instruct their negotiators to adopt as the basis the Japanese proposals, or at least the essential principles thereof, so as to facilitate the attainment of the object of the negotiation, for I am inclined to doubt if Admiral Alexieff is disposed to enter into negotiations with Japan in a spirit of conciliation which is of prime necessity in order to arrive at a satisfactory understanding. He said that when he received our project there were only two courses open for Russia to take, either to reject our proposals or to enter into negotiations on them. The Russian Government have adopted the latter course ; this does not, however, signify acceptance of our project in its entirety or in principle ; but having agreed to the proposition to enter into an *entente* they have decided to examine the propositions and to prepare Counter-Proposals so that the two might be used as the basis of negotiations. Besides, he said that in our project there are certain clauses which could not be reconciled with Russian interests, and others which require modifications ; and he could not say that the Russian Government accepted our proposals even in principle as basis, but only in conjunction with their Counter-Proposals.

Having exhausted every effort for the attainment of the desire of the Japanese Government, I am now fully convinced that it will not be possible to change the course proposed by Count Lamsdorff ; and I think that there is no other way for Japan but to agree to his suggestion. Count Lamsdorff is to leave here on the 10th instant for Darmstadt to attend the Emperor of Russia.

No. 14.
BARON KOMURA TO MR. KURINO.

TOKIO, September 9th, 1903.

(Telegram.)

IN reference to your telegram of the 5th instant, you are hereby instructed to inform Count Lamsdorff that the Japanese Government consent to transfer negotiations to Tokio, and you will add that the Japanese Government trust that instructions to the Russian Minister at Tokio are of such a character as to enable him to present the Russian Counter-Proposals without delay and to proceed immediately with the negotiations.

No. 15.
MR. KURINO TO BARON KOMURA.

PETERSBURG, September 9th, 1903.
Received, September 10th, "

(Telegram.)

I SAW Count Lamsdorff to-day. He said Baron Rosen and Admiral Alexieff have already been instructed by telegraph, by order of the Emperor, to prepare the Counter-Proposals as quickly as possible and to commence negotiations at the earliest date, and he does not think it necessary to repeat the same instruction.

No. 16.
BARON KOMURA TO MR. KURINO.

TOKIO, September 24th, 1903.

(Telegram.)

BARON Rosen left Tokio on the 22d instant for Port Arthur. Previously to his departure, he called on me and told me that he had been instructed under Imperial order some time ago to hold himself ready to start at once for Port Arthur, whenever necessity might arise to do so, in order to expedite the preparation of the Russian Counter-Proposals between Admiral Alexieff and himself, and that he had just received from the Admiral a request to repair to Port Arthur for personal consultation on the subject. He added that he expected to come back within about eleven days.

No. 17.

BARON KOMURA TO MR. KURINO.

Tokio, October 5th, 1903.

(Telegram.)

Baron Rosen came back to Tokio on the 3d instant. He called on me on the same day and handed to me the following as the Russian Counter-Proposals, which, he said, was sanctioned by the Emperor of Russia, upon joint presentation by Admiral Alexieff and himself:

1. Mutual engagement to respect the independence and territorial integrity of the Corean Empire.

2. Recognition by Russia of Japan's preponderating interests in Corea and of the right of Japan to give advice and assistance to Corea tending to improve the civil administration of the Empire without infringing the stipulations of Article I.

3. Engagement on the part of Russia not to impede the commercial and industrial undertakings of Japan in Corea, nor to oppose any measures taken for the purpose of protecting them so long as such measures do not infringe the stipulations of Article I.

4. Recognition of the right of Japan to send for the same purpose troops to Corea, with the knowledge of Russia, but their number not to exceed that actually required, and with the engagement on the part of Japan to recall such troops as soon as their mission is accomplished.

5. Mutual engagement not to use any part of the territory of Corea for strategical purposes nor to undertake on the coasts of Corea any military works capable of menacing the freedom of navigation in the Straits of Corea.

6. Mutual engagement to consider that part of the territory of Corea lying to the north of the 39th parallel as a neutral zone into which neither of the Contracting Parties shall introduce troops.

7. Recognition by Japan of Manchuria and its littoral as in all respects outside her sphere of interest.

8. This Agreement to supplant all previous Agreements between Russia and Japan respecting Corea.

No. 18.

BARON KOMURA TO MR. KURINO.

TOKIO, October 8th, 1903.

(Telegram.)

IN reference to my telegram of the 5th instant, I have begun discussion with the Russian Minister to Japan taking our proposals and the Russian Counter-Proposals as the basis and with a view to secure, if possible, the recognition by Russia of the fundamental principles laid down in our proposals.

No. 19.

BARON KOMURA TO MR. KURINO.

TOKIO, October 16th, 1903.

(Telegram.)

IN reference to my telegram of the 8th instant, negotiations are now going on between Baron Rosen and myself regarding the following proposals, which I had presented as amendment to the Russian Counter-Proposals :

Article II. Insert the phrase "including military assistance" between "assistance" and "to Corea." Change the word "civil" into "internal."

Article III. Insert the phrase "the development of" between "impede" and "the commercial." "Undertakings" to be changed into "activities," and "taken" into "to be taken," and "them" into "those interests."

Article IV. Recognition of the right of Japan to send troops to Corea for the purpose mentioned in the preceding Article or for the purpose of suppressing insurrection or disorder calculated to create international complications.

Article VI. Mutual engagement to establish a neutral zone on the Corea-Manchuria frontier extending . . . . . . kilometres on each side into which neutral zone neither of the Contracting Parties shall introduce troops without the consent of the other.

Article VII. To be struck out and replaced by the following three Articles :

VII. Engagement on the part of Russia to respect China's sovereignty and territorial integrity in Manchuria and not to interfere with Japan's commercial freedom in Manchuria.

VIII. Recognition by Japan of Russia's special interests in Manchuria and of the right of Russia to take such measures as may be necessary for the protection of those interests so long as such measures do not infringe the stipulations of the preceding Article.

IX. Mutual engagement not to impede the connection of the Corean Railway and the East China railway when those railways shall have been eventually extended to the Yalu.

Article VIII. of the Russian Counter-Proposals to be numbered Article X.

No. 20.

BARON KOMURA TO MR. KURINO.

TOKIO, October 22d, 1903.

(Telegram.)

THE result of discussions between Baron Rosen and myself on our amendments to the Russian Counter-Proposals is as follows :

Amendments to Articles II. and VI. accepted *ad referendum*, Article III. accepted, and Article IV. reserved for further discussion. It is in Article VII. of our amendment to Article VII. of the Russian Counter-Proposals that no agreement could be reached, each insisting on the impossibility of accepting the other's proposition. The contention of the Russian Minister is :—1st, that the Russian Article VII. is the only compensation to Russia for the concessions to be made by her in respect of Corea ; and, 2d, that admission of the Japanese amendments on this point would be contrary to the principle always insisted on by Russia that the question concerning Manchuria is one exclusively for Russia and China, admitting of no interference on the part of any third Power.

Our contention is :—1st, that Japan does not ask for any concession from Russia with respect to Manchuria, her proposal being simply to have confirmed in the Agreement the principle which has been voluntarily and repeatedly declared by Russia; and 2d, that Japan possesses in Manchuria her treaty rights and commercial interests, and she must obtain from Russia a guarantee for the security of those rights and interests as well as of the independence of Corea, which would be constantly menaced by Russia's definitive occupation of Manchuria.

No. 21.

BARON KOMURA TO MR. KURINO.

TOKIO, October 29th, 1903.

(Telegram.)

IN reference to my telegram of the 22d instant, as the result of further discussions, the amendment on Article IV was finally accepted *ad referendum*. Regarding Article VI, my proposal of fixing the extent of the neutral zone at 50 kilometres on each side of the frontier was accepted *ad referendum*. As to Article VII, no agreement could yet be reached.

No. 22.

BARON KOMURA TO MR. KURINO.

TOKIO, October 30th, 1903.

(Telegram.)

I PRESENTED to Baron Rosen on the 30th instant the following as definite amendments of the Imperial Government to the Russian Counter-Proposals:

1. Mutual engagement to respect the independence and territorial integrity of the Chinese and Corean Empires.

2. Recognition by Russia of Japan's preponderating interests in Corea and of the right of Japan to give to Corea advice and assistance, including military assistance, tending to improve the administration of the Corean Empire.

3. Engagement on the part of Russia not to impede the development of the commercial and industrial activities of Japan in Corea, nor to oppose any measures taken for the purpose of protecting those interests.

4.   Recognition by Russia of the right of Japan to send troops to Corea for the purpose mentioned in the preceding Article or for the purpose of suppressing insurrection or disorder calculated to create international complications.

5.   Engagement on the part of Japan not to undertake on the coasts of Corea any military works capable of menacing the freedom of navigation in the Straits of Corea.

6.   Mutual engagement to establish a neutral zone on the Corea-Manchurian frontier extending 50 kilometres on each side, into which neutral zone neither of the Contracting Parties shall introduce troops without the consent of the other.

7.   Recognition by Japan that Manchuria is outside her sphere of special interest and recognition by Russia that Corea is outside her sphere of special interest.

8.   Recognition by Japan of Russia's special interests in Manchuria and of the right of Russia to take such measures as may be necessary for the protection of those interests.

9.   Engagement on the part of Japan not to interfere with the commercial and residential rights and immunities belonging to Russia in virtue of her treaty engagements with Corea, and engagement on the part of Russia not to interfere with the commercial and residential rights and immunities belonging to Japan in virtue of her treaty engagements with China.

10.   Mutual engagement not to impede the connection of the Corean railway and the East-China railway when those railways shall have been eventually extended to the Yalu.

11.   This Agreement to supplant all previous Agreements between Japan and Russia respecting Corea.

———

No. 23.

BARON KOMURA TO MR. KURINO.

TOKIO, November 1st, 1903.

(Telegram.)

BARON Rosen called on me October 31st and stated that the definite proposals which I presented to him as amendments to the Russian proposals as reported in my telegram of the 30th October were beyond his instructions and that he would, November 1st, telegraph the full text of the said proposals to his Government and ask for further instructions.   Accordingly you are instructed to see as soon as possible the Acting Minister for Foreign Affairs in the absence of Count Lamsdorff, and say to him that in preparing the proposals in question, the Japanese Government did no fail to take into full consideration the wishes of the Russian Government. You will inform him that in proposing a joint engagement to respect the independence and territorial integrity of China equally with Corea, the Japanese Government were merely asking a reaffirmation of declarations already spontaneously made by Russia, and when it is considered that Russia is prepared to make such an engagement respecting Corea, the reason for excluding China is not understood. The Japanese Government are prepared to admit that the Manchurian question, so far as it does not affect their rights and interests, is purely a Russo-Chinese question ; but Japan has extensive and important rights and interests in that region, and the Japanese Government think that in declaring that Manchuria is outside their sphere of special interest, they are at least entitled to ask for a correlative engagement on the part of Russia not to interfere with the commercial and residential rights and immunities belonging to Japan in virtue of her treaty engagements with China.   You will in addition point out that the invitation of the Japanese Government which originated the present negotiations, had in view a definition of the special interest of Japan and Russia in those regions of the Far East where the interests of the two Powers meet. The Japanese Government could not have anticipated that the Russian Government, in accepting that invitation, would wish—as might be inferred from Article VII of their Counter-Proposals—to restrict the proposed definition exclusively to the region in which Japan possesses special interests.

No. 24.

MR. KURINO TO BARON KOMURA.

PETERSBURG, November 3d, 1903.
Received,   November 3d,   "

(Telegram.)

I saw the Acting Minister for Foreign Affairs on the 2d November. He said, as his personal opinion, that Japan is making the same demands only in different form and that those demands are too great. I asked in what respects the Japanese Government are considered to be demanding too much, and I added that we do not ask anything more than the recognition of existing treaty rights and immunities of Japan in Manchuria. He then stated that Baron Rosen had said nothing on the subject. The only difficulty, he said, is the connection of the Corean and Manchurian railways. To my question whether there are no other difficulties, he answered that the railway question is the only difficulty, although it had been accepted *ad referendum ;* and in conclusion I asked him to use his best influence for the satisfactory solution of the question, as the Japanese Government are fully animated by the spirit of conciliation, and I urged him to advise Count Lamsdorff in the same sense and, if possible, to approach the Emperor of Russia on the question. He said that he is willing to do so, and added that Count Lamsdorff will return at the end of this week.

No. 25.

MR. KURINO TO BARON KOMURA.

PETERSBURG, November 13th, 1903.
Received,   "   "   "

(Telegram.)

I SAW Count Lamsdorff November 12th, and asked whether he had received a copy of the telegram which I had handed to Prince Obolensky and whether any action had been taken in the matter. He answered that he had submitted the telegram to the Emperor, and that before his departure from Darmstadt, he sent under an Imperial order instructions to Baron Rosen to continue negotiations with the Japanese Government. I asked him whether it is on the basis of our last proposal that Baron Rosen was instructed to go on negotiating. Count Lamsdorff said that Baron Rosen had been ordered by the Emperor to examine our last proposal with Admiral Alexieff and to make modification if necessary, and added that at this moment Baron Rosen and Admiral Alexieff must be engaged in the preparation of Counter-Proposals. I remarked to Count Lamsdorff that according to the view of Prince Obolensky, the connection of Corean and Manchurian railways is the question that divides the two Governments; but the Japanese Government having subsequently modified the article relating to the question, I cannot believe that it is the principal point on which an agreement cannot be established. Count Lamsdorff replied that he thinks for his part that it is the Manchurian question which divides the two parties, as he had said from the very beginning the Russian Government consider always that this question is a question exclusively between Russia and China, and it must be reserved to his Government to take all proper measures to safeguard their very considerable interests in Manchuria by means of an arrangement with China. I explained to him that Japan is ever ready to recognize the special and considerable interests which Russia has in Manchuria, and that she has no intention whatever of trespassing upon them, but that Japan has a perfect right to demand that the independence and territorial integrity of China shall be respected and the rights and the interests of Japan in that region shall be formally guaranteed. Count Lamsdorff answered that the objection relates to the form rather than the substance of the proposal. In Manchuria other Powers also have rights and interests, and Russia cannot enter into special arrangement with each of those Powers regarding Manchuria. I observed that should the Russian Government be in accord with Japan in principle, it is deeply to be regretted that an understanding cannot be reached, merely because of failure to find a suitable formula by which to bring the two Governments to an arrangement, and that I could not but ardently ask him to use his influence to bring about a satisfactory solution according to the principles already admitted by Russia.

No. 26.

BARON KOMURA TO MR. KURINO.

TOKIO, November 21st, 1903.

(Telegram.)

BARON Rosen informed me November 20th that he received a telegram November 14th from Admiral Alexieff to the effect that Admiral Alexieff had already forwarded the Counter-Proposals to St. Petersburg. Baron Rosen added that he had not yet received any instructions on the subject of the Counter-Proposals. Consequently you are instructed to see Count Lamsdorff as soon as possible, and after explaining to him Baron Rosen's statements as above, you will

say that the Japanese Government are anxious to proceed with the
negotiations with all possible expedition; and you will urge him to
exert his influence to secure the early dispatch of instructions to
Baron Rosen in order that the negotiations may be resumed and
concluded without delay.

No. 27.

MR. KURINO TO BARON KOMURA.

PETERSBURG, November 22d, 1903.
Received,   "   23d,   "

(Telegram.)

I SAW Count Lamsdorff on the 22d November. He said that the
modifications are already in the hands of the Emperor, but on
account of the illness of the Empress, the former does not attend to
any business affairs; hence the delay. I asked him to use his best
endeavors to obtain the earliest possible Imperial order on the question. He said in reply that it will be better for me to write him a
note giving the purport of instructions I have received from you:
then he will immediately send it to the Emperor. At the end of
the conversation I asked whether it is not possible for me to get
some information about the modifications proposed by Admiral
Alexieff. He seemed rather puzzled to give a direct answer; but he
said that the Russian Government are ready to en er into immediate
agreeme t with Japan regarding Corea, even making large concessions, but as to Manchuria, Russia once took possession of the country by right of conquest; nevertheless, she is willing to restore it to
China, but with certain guarantees assuring security to the enormous
interest which Russia has in Manchuria. While China is still insisting upon her refusal to give such guarantees, it is not possible for
Russia to come to any arrangement with a third Power respecting
Manchuria, as the question is exclusively between the two countries
concerned. Then I said that if I accurately judge the nature of our
proposition, it is not the intention of the Japanese Government to
interfere with direct negotiations between the two Governments concerned, as may be seen from the first part of Article VII of our last
proposition; but we only wish the independence and integrity of
China as repeatedly declared on the part of Russia and security for

our important interests in that province. This is not for the purpose of interfering with the affairs of the two Powers concerned, but only to prevent misunderstanding between Russia and Japan regarding the province where both Powers have some interest; and I added that if in principle such an *entente* could in some form or other be arrived at, perhaps even negotiations between Russia and China might be more easily carried out. He thereupon repeated his request for me to write him a note as above mentioned, and that I should add my own opinion in it, and that he would immediately send it to the Emperor. He told me that he expects to have audience on the 25th November at Skernevice and that the note could be sent to him towards this evening. I judge from the tone of Count Lamsdorff's conversation that the modifications proposed by Admiral Alexieff will not be favorable to our proposition regarding China and Manchuria.

No. 28.

BARON KOMURA TO MR. KURINO.

TOKIO, November 28th, 1903.

(Telegram.)

YOU report in your telegram of November 22nd that Count Lamsdorff expected to have audience of the Emperor on the 25th instant. Accordingly you are instructed to see Count Lamsdorff as soon as possible and ask him what action has been taken regarding further instructions to Baron Rosen.

No. 29.

MR. KURINO TO BARON KOMURA.

PETERSBURG November, 27th, 1903.
Received, " 28th, "

(Telegram.)

COUNT Lamsdorff told me he did not see the Emperor November 25th, on account of the sickness of the Empress. Interior inflammation of her right ear has necessitated an operation. He said that he immediately despatched to the Emperor my note mentioned in my telegram of November 22d.

No. 30.

BARON KOMURA TO MR. KURINO.

TOKIO, December 1st, 1903.

(Telegram.)

THE Japanese Government have from the first attached the highest importance to a speedy solution of the questions which form at this time the subject of negotiations between Japan and Russia. It seemed to them that in a matter of such vital moment as that which engages the attention of the Cabinets of Tokio and St. Petersburg, a quick conclusion was only second in importance to a satisfactory conclusion. Consistently with that view the Japanese Government have at all times during the progress of the negotiations made it a special point to give prompt answers to all propositions of the Russian Government. The negotiations have now been pending for no less than four months, and they have not yet reached a stage where the final issue can with certainty be predicted. In these circumstances the Japanese Government cannot but regard with grave concern the situation for which the delays in negotiations are largely responsible. You are instructed to see Count Lamsdorff as soon as possible and place the foregoing considerations before him in such form and manner as to make your representations as impressive as possible. You will add that the Japanese Government believe they are rendering service to the general interest in thus frankly explaining to the Russian Government the actual state of things.

No. 31.

MR. KURINO TO BARON KOMURA.

PETERSBURG, December 2nd 1903.
Received,   "   3d,   "

(Telegram.)

I HEARD that the Russian Government are still repeatedly communicating with Admiral Alexieff.

No. 32.

MR. KURINO TO BARON KOMURA.

PETERSBURG, December 4th, 1903.

Received,   "   "   "

(Telegram.)

COUNT Lamsdorff received me on the night of December 3d. I handed him a French translation of your telegram of December 1st, together with a letter which I addressed to him expressing fully the pressing situation under which the Japanese Government are now laboring. He said that the question requires consideration still, and he is in communication with Admiral Alexieff; but the Emperor is to return December 5th, and he said that he will fully explain the urgency of the matter on the occasion of his audience on the following Tuesday. He thinks he will then be able to send instructions to Baron Rosen. To my question whether it is not possible for him to have audience at an earlier date, he said that Saturday is the fête of Crown Prince, no business is transacted on Sunday, and he will be occupied with other affairs on Monday. He promised to let me know the result of his audience next Wednesday.

No. 33.

MR. KURINO TO BARON KOMURA.

PETERSBURG, December 9th, 1903.

Received,   " 10th, "

(Telegram.)

COUNT Lamsdorff told me December 9th that an Imperial order had been sent yesterday to Admiral Alexieff and Baron Rosen to continue the negotiations in accordance with the Counter-Proposals of Admiral Alexieff, but that the Japanese propositions have been fully considered. I asked whether he could inform me of the nature of the propositions on which Baron Rosen is authorized to continue the negotiations. He said that they will be officially communicated within two or three days through Baron Rosen to the Japanese Government.

No. 34.

BARON KOMURA TO MR. KURINO.

Tokio, December 12th, 1903.

(Telegram.)

BARON ROSEN called on me December 11th and, under instructions of his Government, officially presented to me the following Counter-Proposals of the Russian Government in reply to our definitive amendments as stated in my telegram of October 30th:

1.   Mutual engagement to respect the independence and territorial integrity of the Corean Empire.

2.   Recognition by Russia of Japan's preponderating interests in Corea and of the right of Japan to assist Corea with advice tending to improve the civil administration.

3.   Engagement on the part of Russia not to oppose the development of the industrial and commercial activities of Japan in Corea, nor the adoption of measures for the protection of those interests.

4.   Recognition by Russia of the right of Japan to send troops to Corea for the purpose mentioned in the preceding Article, or for the purpose of suppressing insurrections or disorders capable of creating international complications.

5.   Mutual engagement not to make use of any part of the Corean territory for strategical purposes and not to undertake on the Corean coast any military works capable of menacing the freedom of navigation in the Straits of Corea.

6.   Mutual engagement to consider the territory of Corea to the north of the 39th parallel as a neutral zone, within the limits of which neither of the Contracting Parties shall introduce troops.

7.   Mutual engagement not to impede the connection of the Corean and East China Railways, when those railways shall have been extended to the Yalu.

8.   Abrogation of all previous agreements between Russia and Japan respecting Corea.

———

No. 35.

BARON KOMURA TO MR. KURINO.

Tokio, December 21st, 1903.

(Telegram.)

IN an interview with the Russian Minister, December 21st, I

pointed out the fundamental difference in territorial compass between Japan's original proposals and Russia's new Counter-Proposals
and after fully explaining the reasons which induced the Japanese
Government to believe it to be desirable in the general interest to
include in the proposed understanding all regions in the Extreme
East where the interests of the two Empires meet, I expressed the
hope that the Russian Government would reconsider their position
regarding that branch of the question. I also informed him fully
respecting the amendments which the Japanese Government consider
it necessary to introduce into Russia's new Counter-Proposals. Accordingly, in order to remove every possibility of misunderstanding
on the part of Russia respecting the attitude of the Japanese Government, you are instructed to deliver to Count Lamsdorff a Note Verbale to the following effect:

The Imperial Government have examined with great care
and attention the new Russian Counter-Proposals of the 11th instant. They regret to find that the Imperial Russian Government
did not see their way in those proposals to give to the compass of
the suggested understanding the same territorial extension as was
deemed essential by Japan. The Imperial Government, in their
original invitation to the Imperial Russian Government in August
last, endeavored to make it entirely clear that they desired, with a
view to remove from their relations with the Imperial Russian
Government every cause for future misunderstanding, to bring
within the purview of the proposed arrangements all those regions
in the Extreme East where the interests of the two Empires meet,
and they cannot bring themselves to the conviction that a full
realization of that desire can be expected if a large and important
portion of those regions is wholly excluded from consideration.
Accordingly, the Imperial Government feel constrained to ask the
Imperial Russian Government to reconsider their position on the
subject, and they hope that the Russian Government will be able
to see their way to arrive at a satisfactory solution of the question.
The Imperial Government also find it necessary to ask for the
following amendments to the new Russian Counter-Proposals:

   a. Article II to read: "Recognition by Russia of Japan's
preponderating interests in Corea and of the right of Japan to
give Corea advice and assistance tending to improve the administration of the Corean Empire."

b. Article V to read: " Mutual engagement not to undertake on the Corean coast any military works capable of menacing the freedom of navigation in the Straits of Corea;" and

c. Article VI to be suppressed.

As the principal part of these amendments cannot be said to be in excess of the modifications which were agreed to *ad referendum* at Tokio, and as the Imperial Government consider those changes indispensable, it is hoped that they will receive the ready agreement of the Imperial Russian Government.

In presenting the foregoing note to Count Lamsdorff, you will say that I have spoken to Baron Rosen in a similar sense, and you will also express the desire for an early response.

No. 36.

MR. KURINO TO BARON KOMURA.

PETERSBURG, December 23rd, 1903.
Received, " 24th, "

(Telegram.)

UPON receipt of your telegraphic instructions, I saw Count Lamsdorff December 23rd at 2 P. M. He told me he had received a telegram from Baron Rosen, stating that the latter had had an interview with you, and that particulars would follow, but such particulars had not been received yet by him. When I handed him the Note Verbale, he said that he would study it together with report from Baron Rosen, and that he would do his best to send the Russian answer at the earliest possible date; but he added that he would have to communicate with Admiral Alexieff. In conclusion, I stated to him that under the present circumstances it might cause serious difficulties, even complications, if we failed to come to an *entente*, and I hoped he would exercise his best influence so as to enable us to reach the desired end.

No. 37.

MR. KURINO TO BARON KOMURA.

PETERSBURG, January 1st, 1904.
Received, " 2nd, "

(Telegram.)

I SAW Count Lamsdorff January 1st, and asked whether any action had been taken regarding our last propositions. He said they had been fully considered; and he asked me to assure you that Baron Rosen will soon be instructed to proceed with the negotiations in a friendly and conciliatory spirit, and he added that he saw no reason why we could not arrive at an *entente.*

No. 38.

BARON KOMURA TO MR. KURINO.

Tokio, January 7th, 1904.

(Telegram.)

Baron Rosen handed to me January 6th the following reply of the Russian Government to our last propositions of December 21st last:

" Having no objection to the amendments to Article II of the Russian Counter-Proposals as proposed by the Imperial Japanese Government, the Imperial Government considers it necessary:

" 1. To maintain the original wording of Article V which had already been agreed to by the Imperial Japanese Government, that is to say, ' mutual engagement not to use any part of the territory of Corea for strategical purposes, nor to undertake on the coasts of Corea any military works capable of menacing the freedom of navigation in the Straits of Corea.'

" 2. To maintain Article VI concerning a neutral zone (this for the very purpose which the Imperial Japanese Government has likewise in view, that is to say, to eliminate everything that might lead to misunderstandings in the future; a similar zone, for example, exists between the Russian and British possessions in Central Asia).

" In case the above conditions are agreed to, the Imperial Government would be prepared to include in the projected agreement an Article of the following tenor:

" ' Recognition by Japan of Manchuria and her littoral as being outside her sphere of interests, whilst Russia, within the limits of that province, will not impede Japan nor other Powers in the enjoyment of rights and privileges acquired by them under existing treaties with China, exclusive of the establishment of settlements.' "

No. 39.

BARON KOMURA TO MR. KURINO.

TOKIO, January 13th, 1904.

(Telegram.)

YOU are instructed to deliver to Count Lamsdorff a Note Verbale to the following effect, which, you will say, is intended to confirm to him the views of the Imperial Government communicated by me to Baron Rosen on the 13th January:

The Imperial Government, in order to arrive at a pacific solution of the pending questions and to firmly establish the basis of good relation between Japan and Russia, and in addition with a view to protect the rights and interests of Japan, have given most careful and serious consideration to the reply of the Imperial Russian Government which was delivered by His Excellency Baron Rosen on the 6th instant. They have finally come to the conclusion that the following modifications are necessary, *i. e.*:

1. Suppression of the first clause of Article V of the Russian Counter-Proposals (presented to the Japanese Government through Baron Rosen December 11th), that is to say, " not to use any part of Corean territory for strategical purposes."

2. Suppression of the whole Article (VI) concerning establishment of a neutral zone.

The Russian proposal concerning Manchuria to be agreed to with the following modifications:

a. Recognition by Japan of Manchuria and its littoral as being outside her sphere of interest and an engagement on the part of Russia to respect the territorial integrity of China in Manchuria.

b. Russia within the limits of Manchuria will not impede Japan nor other Powers in the enjoyment of rights and ɪ rivileges acquired by them under the existing treaties with China.

c. Recognition by Russia of Corea and its littoral as being outside her sphere of interest.

4. Addition of an article to the following effect:

Recognition by Japan of Russia's special interests in Manchuria and of the right of Russia to take measures necessary for the protection of those interests.

The grounds for these amendments having been frequently and fully explained on previous occasions, the Imperial Government do not think it necessary to repeat the explanations. It is sufficient here to express their earnest hope for reconsideration by the Imperial Russian Government.

It should be further remarked that the suppression of the clause excluding the establishment of settlements in Manchuria is desired because it conflicts with stipulations of the new Commercial Treaty between Japan and China. In this respect, however, Japan will be satisfied if she receives equal treatment with another Power which has already acquired similar rights in regard to settlement in Manchuria. The statement in the Russian reply that the Japanese Government have agreed to the original wording of Article V of the Russian Counter-Proposals is erroneous, no such agreement ever having been expressed by the Imperial Government.

The above-mentioned amendments being proposed by the Imperial Government entirely in a spirit of conciliation, it is expected that they will be received with the same spirit at the hands of the Imperial Russian Government ; and the Imperial Government further hope for an early reply from the Imperial Russian Government since further delay in the solution of the question will be extremely disadvantageous to the two countries.

No. 40.

BARON KOMURA TO MR. KURINO.

TOKIO, January 23rd, 1904.

(Telegram.)

YOU are instructed to sound Count Lamsdorff respecting the probable nature of Russia's reply to our last note and when the reply will be delivered.

No. 41.

MR. KURINO TO BARON KOMURA.

PETERSBURG, January 25th, 1904.
Received,   "   "   "

(Telegram.)

IN reference to your telegram of 23rd instant, I saw Count Lamsdorff January 24th and asked his views in regard to our last proposals and also how soon the Russian answer could be given. He was not inclined to enter into details, but said that there are certain points to which he could not agree. He expects to lay his views before the Emperor next Tuesday, January 26th, and he hopes to be able to send an answer before long.

M. de Hartwig, whom I saw this afternoon, told me that the Department of Foreign Affairs is yet in communication with Admiral Alexieff, and he cannot say how soon an answer can be sent to Japan.

No. 42.

BARON KOMURA TO MR. KURINO.

TOKIO, January 26th, 1904.

(Telegram.)

As the situation admits of no indefinite delay in the settlement of the questions involved, you will seek an interview with Count Lamsdorff at the earliest opportunity and state to him as an instruction from your Government that, in the opinion of the Imperial Government a further prolongation of the present state of things being calculated to accentuate the gravity of the situation, it is their earnest hope that they will be honored with an early reply, and that they wish to know at what time they may expect to receive the reply.

No. 43.

MR. KURINO TO BARON KOMURA.

PETERSBURG, January 26th, 1904.
Received, " 27th, "

(Telegram.)

IN reference to your telegram of the 26th instant, the Russian Minister for Foreign Affairs said that the Ministers of War, Marine, and other authorities concerned are to meet on the 28th January for the consideration of the question, and that their decision will be submitted to the Emperor for sanction, and he remarked that it had been the intention of Admiral Alexieff to come here ; but that idea was now abandoned, and his opinion will soon be received by telegraph.

Under these circumstances, he says, he is unable to give the exact date when the reply will be given; but he can say it will not be much delayed. He said that he had received reports from official sources to the effect that Japan had sent a considerable number of troops, munitions and war materials to Corea, and asked me whether I could give any explanation regarding it. I simply answered that I knew nothing of such facts, and regretted not being able to give him any explanation. He added that such action on the part of Japan causes a very bad impression, while the two Governments are engaged seriously in such important negotiations. Telegraph me for my information whether the reports are true, and if so, the details.

No. 44.

BARON KOMURA TO MR. KURINO.

TOKIO, January 26th, 1904.

(Telegram.)

IN reference to your telegram of 26th instant, you will see Count Lamsdorff at an early opportunity and say to him that you have been authorized to deny positively the statement that Japan has sent to Corea a considerable number of troops, munitions and war materials. As a matter of fact, no troops have recently been sent to Corea nor any ammunitions have been sent beyond the amount required for the ordinary use of the Japanese troops stationed in Corea. You will then ask him whether the report that Russian troops are being concentrated on the Corean frontier is true, and if so, that such military movement is to be highly deprecated. Finally, you will ask him whether he is not able to acquaint you, for your own information, with the nature of the decision taken at the proposed conference of the Ministers on the 28th January, and whether he can indicate the approximate date on which the Russian reply is to be given.

No. 45.

MR. KURINO TO BARON KOMURA.

PETERSBURG, January 28th, 1904.
Received, " 29th, "

(Telegram.)

COUNT Lamsdorff is satisfied with the explanation contained in your telegram of to-day. As to the question regarding the concentration of Russian troops near the Yalu, he does not believe it to be true, and he remarked that such newspaper reports are very regrettable. I tried to obtain information about the decision of to-day's meeting. He said that it is not possible for him to say anything concerning it, as it will not be sent to the Emperor, and that until the respective Ministers have been received by the Emperor respecting the question, nothing can be said definitely. He stated that the Grand Duke Alexis and the Minister of Marine are to be received in audience next Monday, and the Minister of War and himself on Tuesday; and he thinks an answer will be sent to Admiral Alexieff on the latter day. I pointed out the urgent necessity to accelerate the dispatch of an answer as much as possible, because further prolongation of the present condition is not only undesirable but rather dangerous. I added that all the while the world is loud with rumors and that I hoped he would take special steps so as to have an answer sent at an earlier date than mentioned. He replied that he knows the existing condition of things very well, but that the dates of audience being fixed as above-mentioned, it is not now possible to change them; and he repeated that he will do his best to send the reply next Tuesday.

No. 46.

BARON KOMURA TO MR. KURINO.

TOKIO, January 30th, 1904.

(Telegram)

IN reference to your telegram of January 28th, you are instructed to see Count Lamsdorff at the earliest opportunity and state to him substantially in the following sense:—

" Having reported to your Government that the Russian Government would probably give a reply on next Tuesday, you have been instructed to say to Count Lamsdorff that, being fully convinced of the serious disadvantage to the two Powers concerned of the further prolongation of the present situation, the Imperial Government hoped that they might be able to receive the reply of the Russian Government earlier than the date mentioned by Count Lamsdorff. As it, however, appears that the receipt of the reply at an earlier date is not possible, the Imperial Government wish to know whether they will be honored with the reply at the date mentioned by Count Lamsdorff, namely, next Tuesday, or, if it is not possible, what will be the exact date on which the reply is to be given."

If Count Lamsdorff specifies the day on which the reply is to be given, you will see him on that day and ask him to acquaint you with the exact nature of the reply.

————

No. 47.

MR. KURINO TO BARON KOMURA.

PETERSBURG, February 1st, 1904.

Received, " " "

(Telegram.)

REGARDING your telegram of the 30th January, I saw Count Lamsdorff in the evening January 31st. He says he appreciates fully the gravity of the present situation, and is certainly desirous to send an answer as quickly as possible; but the question is a very serious one and is not to be lightly dealt with. In addition, the opinions of the Ministers concerned and Admiral Alexieff had to be brought into harmony; hence the natural delay. As to the date of sending an answer, he says, it is not possible for him to give the exact date, as it entirely depends upon the decision of the Emperor, though he will not fail to use his efforts to hurry the matter.

————

No. 48.

BARON KOMURA TO MR. KURINO.

TOKIO, February 5th, 1904. 2.15 P.M.

(Telegram.)

FURTHER prolongation of the present situation being inadmissible the Imperial Government have decided to terminate the pending negotiations and to take such independent action as they may deem necessary to defend their menaced position and to protect their rights and interests. Accordingly you are instructed to address to Count Lamsdorff, immediately upon receipt of this telegram, a signed note to the following effect:—

" The undersigned, Envoy Extraordinary and Minister Plenipotentiary of His Majesty the Emperor of Japan, has the honor, in pursuance of instructions from his Government, to address to His Excellency the Minister for Foreign Affairs of His Majesty the Emperor of all the Russias the following communication:

" The Government of His Majesty the Emperor of Japan regard the independence and territorial integrity of the Empire of Corea as essential to their own repose and safety, and they are consequently unable to view with indifference any action tending to render the position of Corea insecure.

" The successive rejections by the Imperial Russian Government, by means of inadmissible amendments, of Japan's proposals respecting Corea, the adoption of which the Imperial Government regarded as indispensable to assure the independence and territorial integrity of the Corean Empire and to safeguard Japan's preponderating interests in the Peninsula, coupled with the successive refusals of the Imperial Russian Government to enter into engagements to respect China's territorial integrity in Manchuria, which is seriously menaced by their continued occupation of the province, notwithstanding their treaty engagements with China and their repeated assurances to other Powers possessing interests in those regions, have made it necessary for the Imperial Government seriously to consider what measures of self-defence they are called upon to take.

" In the presence of delays which remain largely unexplained, and naval and military activities which it is difficult to reconcile with entirely pacific aims, the Imperial Government have exercised in the depending negotiations a degree of forbearance which they believe affords abundant proof of their loyal desire to remove from their relations with the Imperial Russian Government every cause for future misunderstanding. But finding in their efforts no prospect of securing from the Imperial Russian Government an adhesion either to Japan's moderate and unselfish proposals or to any other proposals likely to establish a firm and enduring peace in the Extreme East, the Imperial Government have no other alternative than to terminate the present futile negotiations.

" In adopting that course the Imperial Government reserve to themselves the right to take such independent action as they may deem best to consolidate and defend their menaced position, as

well as to protect their established rights and legitimate interests
" The Undersigned, etc., etc."

No. 49.

BARON KOMURA TO MR. KURINO.

TOKIO, February 5th, 1904. 2. 15 P. M.

(Telegram.)

YOU are instructed to address to Count Lamsdorff a signed note to
the following effect simultaneously with the note mentioned in my
previous telegram:—

" The Undersigned, Envoy Extraordinary and Minister Plenipotentiary of His Majesty the Emperor of Japan, has the honor,
in pursuance of instructions from his Government, to acquaint
His Excellency the Minister for Foreign Affairs of His Majesty
the Emperor of all the Russias that the Imperial Government
of Japan, having exhausted without effect every means of
conciliation with a view to the removal from their relations with the
Imperial Russian Government of every cause for future complications, and finding that their just representations and moderate and
unselfish proposals in the interest of a firm and lasting peace in
the Extreme East are not receiving the consideration which is
their due, have resolved to sever their diplomatic relations with
the Imperial Russian Government, which for the reason named
have ceased to possess any value.

" In further fulfilment of the command of his Government, the
Undersigned has also the honor to announce to His Excellency
Count Lamsdorff that it is his intention to take his departure from
St. Petersburg with the staff of the Imperial Legation on....date.

" The Undersigned, etc., etc."

No. 50.

MR. KURINO TO BARON KOMURA.

PETERSBURG, February 5th, 1904. 5.5 A.M.
Received,   "   "   " 5.15 P.M.

(Telegram.)

IN compliance with the request of Count Lamsdorff, I went to see him at 8 P.M. February 4th. He told me that the substance of the Russian answer had been just sent to Admiral Alexieff to be transmitted to Baron Rosen. He added that Admiral Alexieff may happen to introduce some changes so as to meet local circumstances, but in all probability there will be no such changes. He then stated as his own opinion that Russia desires the principle of independence and integrity of Corea, and also of necessity the free passage of the Corean Straits. Though Russia is willing to make every possible concession, she does not desire to see Corea utilized for strategic purposes against Russia, and believes it useful for the consolidation of good relations with Japan to establish by common accord a buffer region between confines of direct influence and action of the two countries in the Far East. The above is expressed entirely as his personal opinion, and I cannot say whether the same is the substance of the above-mentioned answer, though it seems to be very probable.

No. 51.

MR. KURINO TO BARON KOMURA.

PETERSBURG, February 6th, 1904. 5.57 P.M.
Received,   "   7th, "   5.45 A.M.

(Telegram.)

IN reference to your two telegrams of yesterday's date, I presented to Count Lamsdorff to-day at 4 P.M. the notes as instructed. I shall withdraw from here with my staff and students on the 10th instant.

INDEX.

A

Abdication and adoption, 118

Abdication of emperors, object of, 126

Acupuncture, 308

Adams, William, his early life, 292; lands in Japan, 292; appears before the shōgun, 293; at the shōgun's court, 294; builds vessels, 295; will of, 296, note; his burial-place identified, 296, note

Adoption and abdication, 118

Ages of early emperors, 35

Ainos, the original race, 20; present characteristics of, 21; number of, 22; arts of, 23; and the bear feast, 24; measurement of, 31

Aizu troops, dismissed from guardianship of gates, 368; offended by recall of Chōshū, 369

Akechi's treason against Nobunaga, 192

Ama-terasu-ō-mi-kami, is produced, 41; retires, 43; is induced to reappear, 44

Animals, domestic, in Japan, 14; wild, in Japan, 15; domestic and wild, in prehistoric times, 93

An-jin-cho (Pilot Street), in Yedo, 296

Anjiro, meeting with Xavier, 172; baptism of, 172

Areas of Japanese islands, 18

Arisugawa - no - miya appointed commander-in-chief, 390

Arms in early times, 92

Arquebuse introduced by the Portuguese, 170

Arts in the Tokugawa period, 305

Ashikaga shōgunate, foundation of, 163

Ashikaga Taka-uji and Nitta, feud between, 160; secures the principal rewards, 160

Aston, W. G., on the invasion of Korea, 210, note

Audiences, first, of foreign representatives, 373

Azuma, origin of name, 71

B

Bear, the, among the Ainos, 24

Bell at Kyōto, 289

Benkei, legends concerning, 145

Black current (Kuro Shiwo), its origin and course, 6

Boats in prehistoric times, 93

Books on various subjects brought from China, 110

British envoy receives a despatch concerning Shimonoseki, 348, note

British legation attacked, 336; the second time attacked, 339

British troops quartered at Yokohama, 350

Buddhism, quarrel over its introduction, 104; triumphant in Japan, 106

INDEX TO SUPPLEMENTARY CHAPTERS.

THE STORY OF THE NATIONS

The Story of the Nations.

In the story form the current of each National life is distinctly indicated, and its picturesque and noteworthy periods and episodes are presented for the reader in their philosophical relation to each other as well as to universal history.

It is the plan of the writers of the different volumes to enter into the real life of the peoples, and to bring them before the reader as they actually lived, labored, and struggled—as they studied and wrote, and as they amused themselves. In carrying out this plan, the myths, with which the history of all lands begins, will not be overlooked, though these will be carefully distinguished from the actual history, so far as the labors of the accepted historical authorities have resulted in definite conclusions.

The subjects of the different volumes have been planned to cover connecting and, as far as possible, consecutive epochs or periods, so that the set when completed will present in a comprehensive narrative the chief events in the great STORY OF THE NATIONS; but it is, of course, not always practicable to issue the several volumes in their chronological order.

Nos. 1–61, each.......................... $1.50
Half leather..............................   1.75
Nos. 62 and following Nos., each (by mail,   1.50
                                       net   1.35
Half leather (by mail, $1.75)...........net 1.60

For list of volumes see next page.

THE STORY OF THE NATIONS

GREECE. Prof. Jas. A. Harrison.

ROME. Arthur Gilman.

THE JEWS. Prof. James K. Hosmer.

CHALDEA. Z. A. Ragozin.

GERMANY. S. Baring-Gould.

NORWAY. Hjalmar H. Boyesen.

SPAIN. Rev. E. E. and Susan Hale.

HUNGARY. Prof. A. Vámbéry.

CARTHAGE. Prof. Alfred J. Church.

THE SARACENS. Arthur Gilman.

THE MOORS IN SPAIN. Stanley Lane-Poole.

THE NORMANS. Sarah Orne Jewett.

PERSIA. S. G. W. Benjamin.

ANCIENT EGYPT. Prof. Geo. Rawlinson.

ALEXANDER'S EMPIRE. Prof. J. P. Mahaffy.

ASSYRIA. Z. A. Ragozin.

THE GOTHS. Henry Bradley.

IRELAND. Hon. Emily Lawless.

TURKEY. Stanley Lane-Poole.

MEDIA, BABYLON, AND PERSIA. Z. A. Ragozin.

MEDIÆVAL FRANCE. Prof. Gustave Masson.

HOLLAND. Prof. J. Thorold Rogers.

MEXICO. Susan Hale.

PHŒNICIA. George Rawlinson.

THE HANSA TOWNS. Helen Zimmern.

EARLY BRITAIN. Prof. Alfred J. Church.

THE BARBARY CORSAIRS. Stanley Lane-Poole.

RUSSIA. W. R. Morfill.

THE JEWS UNDER ROME. W. D. Morrison.

SCOTLAND. John Mackintosh.

SWITZERLAND. R. Stead and Mrs. A. Hug.

PORTUGAL. H. Morse-Stephens.

THE BYZANTINE EMPIRE. C. W. C. Oman.

SICILY. E. A. Freeman.

THE TUSCAN REPUBLICS. Bella Duffy.

POLAND. W. R. Morfill.

PARTHIA. Geo. Rawlinson.

JAPAN. David Murray.

THE CHRISTIAN RECOVERY OF SPAIN. H. E. Watts.

AUSTRALASIA. Greville Tregarthen.

SOUTHERN AFRICA. Geo. M Theal.

VENICE. Alethea Wiel.

THE CRUSADES. T. S. Archer and C. L. Kingsford.

VEDIC INDIA. Z. A. Ragozin

BOHEMIA. C. E. Maurice.

CANADA. J. G. Bourinot.

THE BALKAN STATES. William Miller.

THE STORY OF THE NATIONS

Heroes of the Nations.

A SERIES of biographical studies of the lives and work of a number of representative historical characters about whom have gathered the great traditions of the Nations to which they belonged, and who have been accepted, in many instances, as types of the several National ideals. With the life of each typical character will be presented a picture of the National conditions surrounding him during his career.

The narratives are the work of writers who are recognized authorities on their several subjects, and, while thoroughly trustworthy as history, will present picturesque and dramatic "stories" of the Men and of the events connected with them.

To the Life of each "Hero" will be given one duodecimo volume, handsomely printed in large type, provided with maps and adequately illustrated according to the special requirements of the several subjects.

Nos. 1–32, each.........................$1.50
Half leather.............................1.75
No. 33 and following Nos., each
               (by mail $1.50, net 1.35)
Half leather (by mail, $1.75).........net 1.60

For full list of volumes see next page.

HEROES OF THE NATIONS

NELSON. By W. Clark Russell.

GUSTAVUS ADOLPHUS. By C. R. L. Fletcher.

PERICLES. By Evelyn Abbott.

THEODORIC THE GOTH. By Thomas Hodgkin.

SIR PHILIP SIDNEY. By H. R. Fox-Bourne.

JULIUS CÆSAR. By W. Warde Fowler.

WYCLIF. By Lewis Sergeant.

NAPOLEON. By W. O'Connor Morris.

HENRY OF NAVARRE. By P. F. Willert.

CICERO. By J. L. Strachan-Davidson.

ABRAHAM LINCOLN. By Noah Brooks.

PRINCE HENRY (OF PORTUGAL) THE NAVIGATOR. By C. R. Beazley.

JULIAN THE PHILOSOPHER. By Alice Gardner.

LOUIS XIV. By Arthur Hassall.

CHARLES XII. By R. Nisbet Bain.

LORENZO DE' MEDICI. By Edward Armstrong.

JEANNE D'ARC. By Mrs. Oliphant.

CHRISTOPHER COLUMBUS. By Washington Irving.

ROBERT THE BRUCE. By Sir Herbert Maxwell.

HANNIBAL. By W. O'Connor Morris.

ULYSSES S. GRANT. By William Conant Church.

ROBERT E. LEE. By Henry Alexander White.

THE CID CAMPEADOR. By H. Butler Clarke.

SALADIN. By Stanley Lane-Poole.

BISMARCK. By J. W. Headlam.

ALEXANDER THE GREAT. By Benjamin I. Wheeler.

CHARLEMAGNE. By H. W. C. Davis.

OLIVER CROMWELL. By Charles Firth.

RICHELIEU. By James B. Perkins.

DANIEL O'CONNELL. By Robert Dunlop.

SAINT LOUIS (Louis IX. of France). By Frederick Perry.

LORD CHATHAM. By Walford Davis Green.

OWEN GLYNDWR. By Arthur G. Bradley. $1.35 net.

HENRY V. By Charles L. Kingsford. $1.35 net.

EDWARD I. By Edward Jenks. $1.35 net.

AUGUSTUS CÆSAR. By J. B. Firth. $1.35 net.

FREDERICK THE GREAT. By W. F. Reddaway.

WELLINGTON. By W. O'Connor Morris

CONSTANTINE THE GREAT. By J. B. Firth.

HEROES OF THE NATIONS

MOHAMMED.　　By D. S. Margoliouth.

WASHINGTON.　By J. A Harrison.

Other volumes in preparation are:

MOLTKE.　By Spencer Wilkinson.

JUDAS MACCABÆUS.　By Israel Abrahams.

SOBIESKI.　By F. A. Pollard.

ALFRED THE TRUTHTELLER. By Frederick Perry.

FREDERICK II.　By A. L. Smith.

MARLBOROUGH.　By C. W. C. Oman.

RICHARD THE LION-HEARTED By T. A. Archer.

WILLIAM THE SILENT.　By Ruth Putnam.

CHARLES THE BOLD.　By Ruth Putnam.

GREGORY VII.　By F. Urquhart.

MAHOMET.　By D. S. Margoliouth

New York—G. P. PUTNAM'S SONS, Publishers—London

Date Due